RANDOM
HOUSE
LARGE
PRINT

ALSO BY TOM BROKAW
AVAILABLE FROM
RANDOM HOUSE LARGE PRINT

The Greatest Generation
The Greatest Generation Speaks
A Long Way from Home

BOOM!

Personal Reflections
on the '60s and Today

R A N D O M H O U S E
L A R G E P R I N T

TOM BROKAW

BOOM!

VOICES OF THE SIXTIES

**The Library of Congress has established
a Cataloging-in-Publication record for this title.**

ISBN: 978–0-7393–2682–4

www.randomhouse.com/largeprint

FIRST LARGE PRINT EDITION

10 9 8 7 6 5 4 3 2 1

This Large Print edition published in accord with
the standards of the N.A.V.H.

Jacket design: Gene Mydlowski and Thomas Beck Stvan
Author photograph (back jacket, top): © NBCU Photo Bank.

Jacket photographs: (top row) Charlene Stimley Priester, courtesy
of Charlene Stimley Priester; Gloria Steinem, © AP Newsfeatures;
Kris Kristofferson, courtesy of Kris Kristofferson; Tom Brokaw,
NBCU Photo Bank; Jim Webb, courtesy of Jim Webb; (middle row)
Paul Simon, courtesy of Paul Simon; The Smothers Brothers,
AP Images; Anne Taylor Fleming, courtesy of Karl Fleming;
Sam Brown, courtesy of Sam Brown; Warren Beatty, © Burton
Berinsky/Landov; (bottom row) Judith Rodin, courtesy of Judith
Rodin; Ruth Simmons, courtesy of Ruth Simmons; Arlo Guthrie,
© Getty Images; Hillary Clinton, © Brooks Kraft/Corbis;
Andrew Young, © Bettmann/Corbis; (spine) Pat Buchanan,
© Corbis; Joan Didion, © Ted Streshinsky/Corbis;
Dick Cheney, © University of Wyoming/Associated Press

To the memory of
Robert F. Kennedy,
Dr. Martin Luther King Jr.,
and Captain Gene Kimmel, USMC

And, as always,
to Jean Brokaw, my mother,
and to Meredith,
the most important influences
in my life, whatever the times

CONTENTS

PART TWO: Aftershocks: Consequences, Intended and Otherwise 357

The Reagan Revolution and the Democrats' Identity Crisis 429

Second Thoughts and the Long View   514

The War Without End   543

I Am Woman   609

INTRODUCTION

What Was That All About?

The times they are a-changin'.

—BOB DYLAN

The thing the Sixties did was to show us the possibilities and the responsibility that we all had. It wasn't the answer. It just gave us a glimpse of the possibility.

—JOHN LENNON

When I began to tell members of that large, raucous generation born just after World War II, the baby boomers, that I was thinking of writing a book on the aftershocks of the Sixties, a number of them laughed a little nervously and said, "What are you going to call this one? **The Worst Generation?**"

Their references to my book about the generation that grew up in the Depression and fought in World War II were a little defensive and a little defiant. More than a few baby boomers had told me over the years that **they** represented the greatest generation. After all, they said, they were the largest, the best educated, and the wealthiest generation in American history. More important, many believed they had stopped a war, changed American politics, and liberated the country from the inhibited—and inhibiting—sensibilities of their parents.

I assured my boomer buddies that I don't think they represent the worst—far from it—but I also teased that I didn't think many of them were as great as they thought they were.

They did give us the Sixties. There's no doubt about that. But the bottom line has yet to be drawn under those turbulent times. Conclusions have yet to be established. Thumbs up or thumbs down?

Former president Bill Clinton, who was a bearded student and famously avoided the draft during the Sixties, says in these pages, "If you thought something good came out of the Sixties, you're probably a Democrat; if you thought the Sixties were bad, you're probably a Republican." The evidence is still coming in and the jury is still out—and forty years later we don't seem anywhere near being able to render a verdict.

In fact, here we are, nearing the end of the first decade of the twenty-first century, and as you will discover in this book, many of the debates about the political, cultural, and socioeconomic meaning of the Sixties are still as lively and passionate and unresolved as they ever were. Moreover, those debates and the issues involved are a critical and defining part of our contemporary dialogue about where this nation is headed now and how it gets there. The presidential election of 2008 in many respects may be an echo chamber of the election of 1968, with the lessons learned or ignored in Vietnam applied to the war in Iraq.

So I decided to organize a virtual reunion of a cross section of the Sixties crowd, in an effort to discover what we might learn from each other, forty years later. Just like your high school or college reunion, not everyone showed up for this one. Some who did will surprise you with what they have to say about then and now. You'll meet some famous names from the Sixties, but also those who went through life-changing experiences entirely comfortable in their anonymity.

Personally, as someone who lived through the Sixties—a time I count as beginning with the assassination of President John F. Kennedy in 1963 and ending with the resignation of President Richard M. Nixon in 1974—I have many personal memories of that turbulent, exhilarating, depressing, moving, maddening time that simply do not come together in a tidy package of conclusions.

Nineteen sixty-eight was the volcanic center of the Sixties, with landscape-altering eruptions every month: political shocks, setbacks in Vietnam, assassinations, urban riots, constant assaults on authority, trips on acid, and a trip around the moon.

Nineteen sixty-eight was the year when Kris Kristofferson says he did "a one-eighty turn" in his life;

it was also the year Pat Buchanan realized his dream of a conservative victory in the presidential election.

There are many voices and many different judgments in these pages, but there is at least one common conclusion. Everyone agrees that the Sixties blindsided us with mind-bending swiftness, challenging and changing almost everything that had gone before.

Boom! One minute it was Ike and the man in the gray flannel suit and the lonely crowd . . . and the next minute it was time to "Turn on, tune in, drop out," time for "We Shall Overcome" and "Burn, baby, burn." While Americans were walking on the moon, Americans were dying in Vietnam. There were assassinations and riots. Jackie Kennedy became Jackie O. There were tie-dye shirts and hard hats; Black Power and law and order; Martin Luther King Jr. and George Wallace; Ronald Reagan and Tom Hayden; Gloria Steinem and Anita Bryant; Mick Jagger and Wayne Newton. Well, you get the idea.

Boom!

Few institutions escaped some kind of assault or change. The very pillars of the Greatest Generation—family, community, university, corporation, Church, law—were challenged to one degree or another. Nothing was beyond question, and there were far fewer answers than before. A **Time** magazine cover story on a Southern theological philosopher stopped America in its tracks with the front-cover question "Is God Dead?"

Boom!

Authority lost its privileged place almost overnight. Authority figures—fathers, mothers, cops, judges, teachers, senators, and the president of the United

States—were suddenly spending as much time defending their conduct as they were exercising their power. University presidents and deans were physically thrown out of their offices. Flags were burned and cops were routinely called "pigs."

Boom!

Crew-cut veterans of World War II looked up at the dinner table and—**boom!**—they saw a daughter with no bra, talking about moving in with her boyfriend, and a son with hair down to his shoulders, wearing a T-shirt with a swastika superimposed over an American flag, discussing his latest plot to avoid the draft. In those same families, however, Mom came to realize her life did not have to be defined by the walls of the kitchen and laundry room.

Boom!

A good deal of the assault on authority was uneven. Citizen coalitions rallied around common interests and forced politicians to abandon smoke-filled rooms.

Lawyers banded together to represent the poor against the insensitivities of the establishment.

The public began to question the effects of pollution, overpopulation, and overconsumption, injecting energy into the nascent environmental movement.

Boom!

Ralph Nader took on the auto industry—the high church of American capitalism—and changed it, forcing it to become protective of the safety of the vehicles and their occupants. Dr. Martin Luther King Jr.'s words and personal courage, embodied in his philosophy of nonviolence, struck a mighty blow against racism.

Other challenges to authority were mindless and self-serving, exaggerated acts designed to replace one kind of authoritarian excess with another.

Dick Armey, the former North Texas State University economics professor who was part of the Newt Gingrich–led Republican takeover of Congress in 1994, said famously, "I think all the troubles in the country began in the Sixties." His ideological opposite, Michael Heyman, a former dean of the UC Berkeley law school and chancellor of the university, was sympathetic to the students' demands for more free speech in 1964. But as the movement expanded he became personally conflicted by what he calls "the anarchy—there was a lot of provocation . . . like the filthy speech . . . which infuriated me because it strengthened the hand of the right so much."

Boom!
Kids in ponytails and dressed in Army fatigues stood at barricades and demanded a revolution in which they would have a fully equal voice in determining university curricula and faculty appointments. At the same time they denied fellow students who simply wanted to attend class their right to exercise that choice.

Boom! The Sixties also brought us bean sprouts, brown rice, veggies, yogurt, whole-grain bread, holistic medicine, and drugs, lots of drugs—from homegrown marijuana to laboratory-produced speed and LSD, from heroin to glue sniffing. Drug use went from an exaggerated fear in the Fifties, when a little pot was considered a satanic doomsday, to a badge of honor in the Sixties. "If you remember the Sixties, you weren't there." Ha, ha.

Boom! The popular American music scene underwent a transformation that continues to this day. Singer-songwriters such as Bob Dylan, the Beatles, Mick and the Rolling Stones, Paul Simon, James Taylor, Judy Collins, Kris Kristofferson, Neil Young, and the great stable of Motown artists provided the sound track of that time and beyond, with their songs of rebellion and generational angst.

Boom! Sexuality, hetero and homo, came out of the bedroom and into the open. A combination of birth-control pills and a determination to defy the Fifties' strictures on premarital sex brought on a rush of freelance fornication and created new freedoms for women by liberating them from the consequences of unintended pregnancies.

It was all part of the Sixties mantra "If it feels good, do it."

Before the twentieth century, most of history's movers and shakers had been young (and almost exclusively young men) because the average life span was so short. In colonial America, if a man made it through the Revolution, he was living on borrowed time once he reached thirty-five. Survivors of the Civil War could expect the grim reaper to come calling before they were fifty. World War II vets could expect to blow out the candles on their sixty-fifth birthday.

This unprecedented longevity and the fecundity that accompanied it (the babies started booming), combined with the increasingly affluent lifestyle enjoyed on the home front during the Fifties, resulted in a demographic phenomenon.

Adolescence became for most young Americans a period of learning and leisure from youth to young adulthood. This extended adolescence accounted for a new market, as the young were eager for clothes and gadgets, sporting goods, sweets, and fast foods, and, most of all, entertainment that said, "We're here and we have our own ideas."

As Jann Wenner, an enterprising boomer as the founder of the **Rolling Stone** magazine empire, says, "It was a cheeky, fun time—with the Beatles and all that great music. We were making our own rules." There was also so much money around, he says, that "all you had to do was go to the post office and get a check from your parents."

That wasn't true for everyone, of course, but the rapidly expanding American middle and upper middle classes were cashing in on all that prosperity of post–World War II America.

Increases in the standard of living, complemented by advances in technology, were almost dizzying in the postwar period. The FCC started granting television licenses at the beginning of the 1950s, and by 1955 more than half of the homes in America had a black-and-white TV set. By 1960, almost 90 percent had more than one—and many of them were wired for "living color."

The development of the 45 rpm single record, at the end of the 1940s, just in time for the arrival of rock and roll, at once made popular records unbreakable and easily portable. Bill Haley and the Comets released "Rock Around the Clock" in the spring of 1954, and the modern pop culture was born. The kids now had their own artists and their own sound. That grown-ups thought it tasteless and vulgar and probably downright dangerous was icing on the cake. Two years later, on September 9, 1956, Elvis Presley suddenly appeared amid the usual boring acrobats and hand puppets on **The Ed Sullivan Show**—television's monument to middle-class mass entertainment.

Everyone knew that Sullivan wouldn't allow the cameras to show anything below Elvis's waist; but everyone knew what was going on down there. He sang his hit "Don't Be Cruel" to some sixty million viewers—the largest single audience in history to that date.

Hollywood quickly discovered the enthusiasms and the angst, not to mention the hormones, of this large new adolescent audience with time to waste and money to spend. **Rebel Without a Cause,** starring James Dean ("the first American teenager"), appeared in 1955 and signaled another new phenomenon.

Many of these youngsters were able to extend their adolescence past high school and into college. Their fathers had used the GI Bill to get an education, and they wanted their children to have every advantage they'd had and more.

In my age group, we were often the first in our families to attend college. We approached the opportunity with a sense of awe and obligation to get on with our lives in the workaday world. Five years later, boomers took college for granted and converted campuses into staging grounds for their campaigns against anything that smacked of the establishment.

So in the reunion I organized I asked, "What seemed so important at the time that seems a little foolish or wrongheaded now? Who were the winners and who were the losers? Can we tell yet?"

How do you sum up a time when change rolled across the country in hurricane proportions, when there were so many contradictions and so many paradoxes? A time when Elvis gave way to Dylan, when Richard Nixon arose from the political dead after two Kennedys were murdered, when Ozzie and Harriet were replaced by Archie and Edith Bunker? When men in military uniform went from being respected figures in society to targets of vilification?

At this reunion, you will hear from Arlo Guthrie but also from Karl Rove. You'll meet young women struggling with "the mommy track." You will hear from civil rights veterans who worry that their cause has lost its way, from Vietnam vets who came back and from their contemporaries who fought against the war, not in it.

For the most part, I am like the old class president at this reunion. I call on others and then let them have their say. I am here as a journalist but also as a citizen, a grandfather now and a young man then.

I began my marriage and my career as a journalist in 1962, a straight-arrow product of the Fifties. By the time the decade was over, I'd had my first taste of marijuana, I had long hair, and on weekends I wore bell-bottoms and peasant shirts when, as a family, we went to hippie arts festivals in the hills north of Los Angeles. But Meredith and I were raising our children essentially as we had been raised by our Great Depression and World War II parents back in the Midwest.

Weekdays I was covering the political fallout

of the counterculture for NBC News, dressed in the correspondent's uniform of suit and tie, looking more like a narc than one of the crowd, as I wandered through the neighborhood of Haight-Ashbury, holy ground of peace-and-love hippies and druggie runaways from across the country.

I often thought of myself as a generational straddler: one foot in the psychedelic waters of the Sixties and the other still firmly rooted to the familiar terrain of the Fifties.

Everyone who went through the Sixties sees it through his or her own distinct prism. The conventional view is that it was a time mainly of flower children and angry protestors, of black power and militant feminism. But it was also the beginning of the resurrection of the political right, which had been soundly defeated in 1964.

The Sixties were a time when the nerve endings of the body politic were constantly stimulated with new sensations, but it was also a time of mindless fantasy, groundless arrogance, spiritual awareness, callow youth, and misguided elders.

Reunions are funny things. Not everyone chooses to attend them. And you can never be sure that you'll like everyone who turns up. But for this virtual fortieth, I am confident that the people attending have something to say that is worth hearing, about then and now. I also believe that on many of the most important levels, the meaning of that amazing decade is still emerging, and that for the rest of my days, when my mind wonders back to the Sixties, I will probably think: **Boom!**—what was that all about?

PART ONE

Something's Happening Here

A Loss
of Innocence

I felt everyone else
wanted to be in our world.
We were the last generation
to be cooler than our kids.

—Tom McGuane

There's a big "what if" over the Sixties. . . .
Who knows what would have happened
if King and Kennedy were alive?

—Tom Hayden

In 1968 AMERICA was deeply divided by a war in Southeast Asia and it was preparing to vote in a presidential election in which the choices were starkly different. The country was in the midst of a cultural upheaval unlike anything experienced since the Roaring Twenties. Everyone wondered whether America could regain its balance.

Forty years later, another war, this one in the Middle East, is deeply dividing the United States. Republican and Democratic candidates for president are laying out starkly different scenarios for the country's future. The place of America in the world is hotly debated. The popular culture is again an issue.

The eve of 2008 is not exactly the Sixties all over again, but we still have a lot to learn from that memorable, stimulating, and dangerous time in American life forty years ago.

I arrived in Los Angeles to join NBC News in 1966, and by then, Charles Dickens's opening lines in **A Tale of Two Cities** had never seemed so prophetic. Were these the best or the worst of times? I wish I could say I felt the tremors of seismic change beginning and spreading out across the political and cultural landscape, but I was mostly trying to find my way. I was a twenty-six-year-old pilgrim from the prairie heartland, raised with the sensibilities of a Fifties working-class family. I was the father of a toddler with another child on the way.

I fit the prototype of the typical young white male of the time. I had been a crew-cut apostle of the Boy Scouts, reciting the Pledge of Allegiance to the flag, attending Sunday school and church, drinking too much beer in college but never smoking dope; marijuana in the Fifties and early Sixties was the stuff of jazz musicians and hoodlums in faraway places.

Before I married the love of my life, my high school classmate Meredith, we had never spent a night together. In those days, parked cars and curfews were the defining limits of courtship.

We were married in 1962, when Meredith was twenty-one and I was twenty-two, in a traditional Episcopal church wedding with a reception at our hometown country club. We left the next day with all our worldly possessions, including the five table cigarette lighters we had received as wedding presents, in the backseat of the no-frills Chevrolet compact car her father had given us as a wedding gift.

We were eager to see a wider world, but only one step at a time. California was still four years away. Our first stop was Omaha, Nebraska, which then was an unimaginative and conservative midsize city a half day's drive down the Missouri River from our hometown. We could barely afford ninety dollars a month to

During the time I was covering the political rise of Ronald Reagan

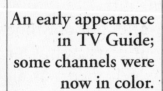 
An early appearance in TV Guide; some channels were now in color.

The happy beginning of a long journey;
our wedding day, August 17, 1962

rent a furnished apartment, but when we went looking, in the stifling heat of a Great Plains August, I was
dressed in a jacket and tie, and Meredith was wearing
part of her honeymoon trousseau, including a girdle
and hose. Five years later, I rarely wore a tie except on
television, and Meredith was freed not only of girdles
but also of hose and brassieres on California weekends.

In 1962, I had an entry-level reporter's job at an
Omaha television station. I had bargained to get a salary
of one hundred dollars a week, because I didn't feel I
could tell Meredith's doctor father I was making less.
Meredith, who had a superior college record, couldn't
find any work because, as one personnel director after
another told her, "You're a young bride. If we hire you,
you'll just get pregnant before long and want maternity
leave."

In retrospect, the political and cultural climate in
the early Sixties seems both a time of innocence and
also like a sultry, still summer day in the Midwest: an
unsettling calm before a ferocious storm over Vietnam,
which was not yet an American war. Dr. Martin Luther
King Jr. was confronting racism in the South and getting a good deal of exposure on **The Huntley-Brinkley
Report** on NBC and **The CBS Evening News with
Walter Cronkite,** the two primary network newscasts,
each just fifteen minutes long.

In the fall of 1963, first CBS and then, shortly
after, NBC expanded those signature news broadcasts
to a half hour. As a sign of the importance of the
expansion, Cronkite and Huntley and Brinkley were
granted lengthy exclusive interviews with President
Kennedy. ABC wouldn't be a player in the news major

leagues until the 1970s, when Roone Arledge brought to ABC News the energy and programming approach he had applied to ABC Sports. Kennedy, America's first truly telegenic president, was a master of the medium, fully appreciating its power to reach into the living rooms of America from sea to shining sea.

During our time in Omaha, John F. Kennedy was not a local favorite. The city's deeply conservative culture remained immune to Kennedy's charms and to his arguments for social changes, such as civil rights and the introduction of government-subsidized medical care for the elderly. I'm sure many of my conservative friends at the time thought I was a card short of being a member of the Communist Party because I regularly championed the need for enforced racial equality and Medicare.

One of the most popular speakers to come through Omaha in those days was a familiar figure from my childhood, when kids in small towns on the Great Plains spent Saturday afternoons in movie theaters watching westerns. Ronald Reagan looked just like he did on the big screen. He was kind of a local boy who had made good, starting out as a radio star next door in Iowa and moving on to Hollywood, before becoming a television fixture as host of **General Electric Theater.**

Reagan's Omaha appearances were part of his arrangement with GE, which allowed him to be an old-fashioned circuit-riding preacher, warning against the evils of big government and Communism, while praising the virtues of big business and the free market. He was every inch a star, impeccably dressed and groomed. But those of us who shared his Midwestern roots were a bit surprised to find that although he was completely cordial, he was not noticeably warm. That part of his personality remained an enigma even to his closest friends and advisers throughout his historically successful political career.

In Omaha the only time he lightened up in my presence was when I noticed he was wearing contact lenses and I asked him about them. He got genuinely excited as he described how they were a new soft model, not like the hard ones that could irritate the eyes. He even wrote down the name of his California optometrist so Meredith could order a pair for herself. (Later, when he became president, I often thought, "He's not only a great politician, he's a helluva contact lens salesman.")

President Kennedy also passed through Omaha, but only for a brief stop at the Strategic Air Command headquarters there. In those days, SAC was an instantly recognized acronym because the bombers it comprised—some of which we could see because they were always in the air ready to respond in case of an attack—were a central component of America's Cold War military strategy.

More memorable for me was a visit to SAC by the president's brother Attorney General Robert F. Kennedy. The younger Kennedy was a striking contrast to the president, who had been smiling and chatty with the local press and even more impressive in person than on television. Unlike the president, who was always meticulously and elegantly dressed, the attorney general was wearing a rumpled suit, and the collar on his blue button-down shirt was frayed. He was plainly impatient, and his mood did not improve when I asked for a reaction to Alabama governor George Wallace's demand that JFK resign the presidency because of his stance on school desegregation. Bobby fixed those icy blue eyes on me and said, as if I were to blame for the governor's statement, "I have no comment on anything Governor Wallace has to say."

I was on duty in the newsroom a few weeks later when the United Press International wire-service machine began to sound its bulletin bells. I walked over casually and began to read a series of sentences breaking in staccato fashion down the page:

THREE SHOTS WERE FIRED AT PRESIDENT KENNEDY'S MOTORCADE IN DOWNTOWN DALLAS . . . FLASH—KENNEDY SERIOUSLY WOUNDED, PERHAPS FATALLY BY ASSASSIN'S BULLET . . . PRESIDENT JOHN F. KENNEDY DIED AT APPROXIMATELY 1:00 PM (CST).

John F. Kennedy, the man I had thought would define the political ideal for the rest of my days, was suddenly gone in the senseless violence of a single moment. In ways we could not have known then, the gunshots in Dealey Plaza triggered a series of historic changes: the quagmire of Vietnam that led to the fall of Lyndon Johnson as president; the death of Robert Kennedy in pursuit of the presidency; and the comeback, presidency, and subsequent disgrace of Richard Nixon.

On that beautiful late autumn November morning, however, my immediate concern was to get this story on the air. I rushed the news onto our noon broadcast, and as I was running back to the newsroom, one of the station's Kennedy haters said, "What's up?"

I responded, "Kennedy's been shot."

He said, "It's about time someone got the son of a bitch."

Given the gauzy shades of popular memory, the invocations of Camelot and JFK as our nation's prince, it may be surprising to younger Americans to know that President Kennedy was not universally beloved.

Now Kennedy was gone, and this man was glad. I lunged toward him, but another co-worker pulled me away.

The rest of the day is mostly a blur except for one riveting memory. As I was speeding out toward SAC headquarters to see what restrictions they were putting on the base, I began to talk aloud to myself. "This doesn't happen in America," I said, still a child of the innocence of the Fifties. And then I distinctly remember thinking, "This will change us. I don't know how, but this will change us." And of course it did.

It was November 22, 1963, and it was, in effect, the beginning of what we now call the Sixties. Kennedy's death was stunning not just because he was president. He was such a **young** president, and his election just three years before had kindled the dreams and aspirations of the young generation he embodied and inspired. His death seemed to rob us of all that was youthful and elegant, cool and smart, hopeful and idealistic. Who now would stir our generation by suggesting we "ask not what your country can do for you, ask what you can do for your country"?

No political pundit or opposition strategist could

have anticipated how JFK's death would be the beginning of the unraveling of the Democratic coalition that had been forged by Franklin Delano Roosevelt in 1932 and had formed the party's electoral base ever since. When Lyndon Johnson emerged from Air Force One as the new president after the flight back from Dallas and stood somberly in the glare of the television lights at Andrews Air Force Base, he was already a familiar figure to most Americans. It would be hard to imagine a greater contrast to JFK than LBJ, the large, ambitious Texan with the thick drawl and the great thirst for whiskey, women, and power. Now he seemed humbled and earnest as he looked into the cameras and said, "I ask for your help—and God's."

With LBJ we were back to business as usual with the old backroom pols, the men who wore hats and had spreading waistlines. To be sure, there was a lot about Kennedy we had not known then or had ignored—such as his chronic illnesses, his reckless ways with women, his Cold Warrior inclinations toward Vietnam, and his temporizing approach to the civil rights struggle.

In June 2007, when the Central Intelligence Agency opened many of its files to the public—those known as "the family jewels"—there were pages devoted to JFK's enthusiastic authorization of a CIA surveillance campaign against a well-known **New York Times** military affairs reporter who had published stories involving classified material. When Richard Nixon became president and authorized a similar leak-plugging operation, it was seen as the first step toward Watergate.

But in the wake of President Kennedy's violent death, America was in a state of shock, and the flaws or failings that were known to us only seemed to make him more human and his loss more deeply felt.

He became the prince of Camelot who left behind a widow whose beauty could not be compromised by grief, a woman not yet forty years old who would remain a part of our lives, in admiration and controversy, until she died in the closing days of the century. And their children, Caroline and John, Jr., now belonged to the nation as surely as the offspring of royalty.

Slowly, the rest of us went back to our ordinary lives, trying to absorb and understand the deep wounds we had sustained and the unimaginable loss we had suffered—and blissfully unaware of all the tragedy and tumult that lay not far ahead. My wife, Meredith, finally found a job teaching English at Central High School in Omaha. We rented a better apartment; this one even had access to a swimming pool, which seemed to us the height of luxury. We watched **The Dick Van Dyke Show** and **Gunsmoke** on our new black-and-white television. We bought our first set of furniture—sofa and matching chair, coffee table, dining room table and chairs, and two lamps—for four hundred dollars.

In the summer of 1964, we drove east to visit Washington, D.C., and New York City on vacation, a couple of Midwesterners curious about life over the horizon from the Great Plains. In Washington, as luck would have it, we were in the press gallery when the House passed the historic Civil Rights Act, outlawing discrimination in jobs and public accommodations. Reporters were shouting into telephones and banging away at typewriters. We saw Roger Mudd, the CBS news correspondent who had been tracking the legislation nightly on the **CBS Evening News,** and Bob Abernethy of NBC News on the phone filing a radio report. I felt like a kid from the sticks who somehow managed to wander into Yankee Stadium while the World Series was under way.

We were thrilled, but a friend who worked for the congressman from Omaha was not; his boss had voted against the act. Another conservative friend from the Midwest insisted, "You can't legislate morality."

Huh? "What about murder?" I asked. "It's immoral to kill someone. If I'm not mistaken, we've passed laws to deal with that."

We took the train to New York and went to the World's Fair in Flushing Meadows. Still bound by the conventions of our upbringing and the customs of the time, I put on a jacket and tie, and Meredith wore high heels and hose despite the sweltering midsummer heat. One night we spent the equivalent of a third of my weekly salary on two drinks and a couple of small crab cakes served on large plates in the Rainbow Room at the top of 30 Rockefeller Plaza, which was also the address of NBC News—an occasion I never failed to remember whenever I returned there years later, under much more prosperous and elevated circumstances.

We were dazzled by New York but couldn't imagine ever living there. We returned to Omaha, where my boss let me roam the Midwest, covering the big campaign events as the presidential election started heating up, including the return of the Democratic vice presidential candidate, Hubert Humphrey, to our common home state, South Dakota. Speaking from the back of a flatbed truck in the small town where he had grown up, he called out the names of old schoolmates he saw in the audience.

I also spent a fair amount of time with the Republican nominee, Senator Barry Goldwater, during his Nebraska campaign stopovers. Like so many, I was impressed by the direct and friendly manner of the handsome, granite-jawed Arizona senator. His best-selling book **The Conscience of a Conservative** had galvanized a new generation of young conservatives by providing a manifesto for taking over (rescuing as they saw it) the Republican Party from its liberal and elitist eastern wing. They had been anticipating a showdown between Kennedy and Goldwater, and some pundits had predicted that it might even be close. But running against Kennedy's memory was all but pointless.

Politically, Goldwater was the antithesis of the Brokaw family's political demigod, Franklin Delano Roosevelt, but he was no ogre, and he was always gracious to the local press. I also met and interviewed Bill Buckley, who filled the role of the national conservative intellectual as a columnist and editor of the magazine he had founded, **National Review**. When I tried my best fastball questions on him, he was like Ted Williams in the batting cage, flicking them away to deep right field. I came away thoroughly chastened and utterly charmed.

Meredith and I were leading young middle-class lives, still comfortable with the contours of the values our parents had imparted. We went to church every Sunday and began to get involved in a black minister's efforts to close the racial gap in Omaha. Our friends also included the local Marine recruiter and his wife. I sent him to see my youngest brother, Mike, and to a close college friend, Gene Kimmel. They both signed up for what we all assumed would be peacetime tours of duty.

Johnson's landslide in November 1964—still the biggest in presidential history—pretty much sucked the air out of politics for the time being, and in 1965 I was stuck on the morning and noontime shift, working six days a week grinding out four newscasts a day and running off to cover big fires or crime stories when we were shorthanded. My bosses counseled me to be patient. Someday, they said, I might be able to anchor the six o'clock news and earn as much as two hundred dollars a week.

One memorable day the phone rang at home, and on the other end I heard a voice that was familiar from television. It was Ray Moore, the news director at Atlanta's WSB-TV, the crown jewel of the Cox Broadcasting Company. He was also a semiregular on **The Huntley-Brinkley Report,** filing reports on various civil rights stories in the South.

A Midwestern friend of his had heard that I was restless and thinking about moving on; they had checked me out and decided that I was ready for prime time in Atlanta. Ray was calling to offer me a job as anchor of the eleven o'clock news with a chance to freelance for NBC News, including **The Huntley-Brinkley Report.** My starting pay would be around eleven thousand dollars a year. This was at a time when a well-known preppy clothing company ran ads for their suits that included the line "For the young man who wants to make $10,000 a year before he's 30." I was twenty-five.

Atlanta turned out to be a brief but important stop for Meredith and me. We experienced firsthand the cosmopolitan qualities of that proud and historic city, while also seeing through our Midwestern eyes the depth and complexity of the place of race in the South. There was so much more daily personal interaction between blacks and whites than in our experience in Omaha, but the roles were also much more clearly defined—and clearly divisive. The plantations were gone but not the attitudes for so many Southern whites, especially those of the redneck variety.

It was always an occasion whenever Dr. Martin Luther King Jr. would return home to Atlanta from the civil rights crusade he was now leading all across the South. I sat in the balcony at the Ebenezer Baptist Church one Sunday when Nelson Rockefeller, the millionaire Republican governor of New York, presented the church with a new organ, and Dr. King's father, Martin Luther King Sr.—who was known by all as Daddy King—presided at the service. When Dr. King's sermons sometimes started to gain altitude, Daddy King was known to lean forward and whisper, "Keep it simple, son, keep it simple."

Among the bravest people I have seen in half a century in this country were the young black men and women who defied death threats, beatings, and jail to march for their rights. In those days the South was already caught between the pincers of race and war, both of which were soon to ravage the whole country. Vietnam was just beginning to become controversial elsewhere, but in Georgia, the home of Fort Benning and of Senator Richard Russell and Representative Carl Vinson—the two most powerful champions of the military in Congress—the South's reputation for going off to war was holding up.

My reporting from the civil rights trail caught the attention of NBC News, and in 1966, fifteen months after arriving in Atlanta, we were moving again, this time to the NBC News bureau in Los Angeles. One of my first assignments was covering Ronald Reagan's first campaign for governor.

To win the Republican nomination, Reagan's friends had hired a pair of California campaign consultants, Stu Spencer and Bill Roberts, who had done winning work for Nelson Rockefeller in New York. They used in-depth polling and took advantage of Reagan's celebrity and acting skills to construct a successful campaign that gave voice to working-class and middle-class frustrations. We didn't know it at the time, but this would be the start of the Reagan Revolution.

Reagan was most effective on television or speaking to large crowds. In smaller groups, and with the California political press, which was largely skeptical about his qualifications, he was the same reserved, almost distant, figure I had encountered in Omaha.

In retrospect, his natural inclinations served him well; he wasn't just another backslapping pol. He knew the power of stardom, whether it was on the big screen or on the campaign trail.

Shortly after we arrived in California, I took Meredith to dinner at a popular restaurant on the beach at Santa Monica. We had been married just four years and had a six-month-old daughter, Jennifer. It was the first time that Meredith had seen the Pacific Ocean, and after dinner with a few glasses of wine, she took off her shoes and waded into the surf. I watched her, my beautiful young bride, splashing in the moonlit waves, and thought, "This is a long way from where we started." We did not know, of course, how the country was about to change so dramatically as well.

By 1968, we were living in a rented three-bedroom home with our own swimming pool on a cul-de-sac in Van Nuys. We had a Buick Skylark and a Ford Mustang in the driveway, and we spent Sundays hanging out on a beach north of Malibu. We bought an elaborate stereo system to listen to my collection of long-playing records by jazz artists such as Dave Brubeck, Chet Baker, Stan Kenton, Count Basie, and Frank Sinatra. I also liked the new sounds in the air— the Beatles, Buffalo Springfield, Crosby, Stills & Nash, the Supremes, the Mamas and the Papas, Glen Campbell—but I was still loyal to my Fifties favorites.

I was making thirty thousand dollars a year in my dual roles as reporter and anchorman on KNBC, the NBC-owned station in Los Angeles. That was a very comfortable salary for a couple our age in an era when gasoline cost about thirty cents a gallon and a custom home in the San Fernando Valley was available for $42,500.

Meredith was now a stay-at-home mom, looking after our firstborn daughter and preparing for the birth of a second. She was taking some graduate courses in linguistics at a local state college, thinking she might like to teach English as a second language when the kids were in school. But she was mostly concentrating on the role of mother as it had been played by her mother and her grandmother before her. All the California trappings aside, we continued to remain true to the Fifties values and conventions of our parents and the way we were raised.

The summer we married, five other couples from our circle of college friends were married as well. All but one of them were following a similar trajectory in the Midwest, the husbands pursuing careers while their college-educated wives were trying to balance the demands of work with the business of having babies. The one exception was the couple that seemed to have rushed into marriage because, well, everyone else they knew was doing it. Even though they were clearly not the best match, we were still a little shocked to hear that they were considering going their separate ways. In the world in which we'd grown up, divorce was a lowercase scandal, not very frequently encountered and spoken of in hushed tones when it was. Divorced women, especially, were perceived as having failed society's standards. "She's a divorcée" carried the unspoken judgment, "She couldn't keep her man, however unworthy he may have been."

Divorce was just one of the many changes about to descend on America. Between 1965 and 1975, divorce rates more than doubled. Equally startling to the puritanical conventions of the Fifties, young couples began openly living together without the benefit of marriage. The phrase "starter marriage" began to be heard. In some ways the changing sexual and marital mores rattled my parents' generation because they were so openly discussed and displayed. They had been raised to believe that sex and troubled marriages should be kept behind closed bedroom doors.

In Los Angeles our friends were a mix of native Californians and others like us who had migrated west, attracted by the expanding opportunities of a sunny meritocracy where pedigree and family connections were much less important than they seemed on the eastern seaboard. They were an eclectic group: journalists, lawyers, real estate entrepreneurs, manufacturers, and politicians.

In our crowd, the men still wore suits and ties to work. The women were, for the most part, still in search of careers or working part-time, while trying to juggle housekeeping and child care at home. We were a Saturday-night-dinner-party-at-home kind of crowd, although we would also enjoy gathering at a hot new restaurant on the west side of L.A. after a day of tennis or playing with the kids on the beach in Santa Monica. We were still the cocktail generation, but marijuana had started showing up around the edges of our circle.

Yes, I smoked a little pot. I even inhaled. A true Southern California Sixties memory for me is visiting some friends' small apartment on the beach south of Malibu. He was Jewish; she was Japanese-American. They called themselves "Jewpanese," and on weekends they liked to frequent nudist colonies. We were all fully

clothed that night, as we listened to Arlo Guthrie's unlikely hippie hit record "Alice's Restaurant." My friend
gave me a headset and a joint, and I was quickly in a
space I had never known in South Dakota.

On another occasion, we were at a poolside dinner
at the home of a prosperous physician in West Los Angeles when pot was served as a dessert course. One
thing led to another, and before long the pool was full
of naked swimmers, including a draft-resistance lawyer
who came headfirst down the slide with a spliff the size
of a Havana cigar clenched firmly in his toothy smile.

Meredith stayed out of the pool, and she was not
amused, so we left early for a concert starring Herb
Alpert and the Tijuana Brass at the Greek Theatre in
Los Angeles. We went from mild bacchanalia to mainstream instrumentals all in one evening.

Marijuana did not replace a growing taste for good
wine or expensive Scotch among those of us who had
grown up with a palate conditioned to chilled rosé and
Seven and Seven, the popular working- and middle-
class cocktail of Seagram's whiskey and 7-Up.

Life was pleasant, but it wasn't Pleasantville. There
was a new ferocity to the war in Vietnam that was ig-
niting a political wildfire back at home. Every week
more Americans, and not just students and hippies,
were joining the antiwar movement. The nation was
becoming starkly polarized over the war and the culture of protest it inspired.

In the summer of 1967, President Johnson made
an appearance at a Democratic Party fund-raiser at the
sleek new Century Plaza Hotel in the upscale and traditionally liberal environs of West Los Angeles. The

Reporting in Lafayette Square, Washington, D.C., the night Richard Nixon resigned as president

At the Los Angeles bureau, NBC News

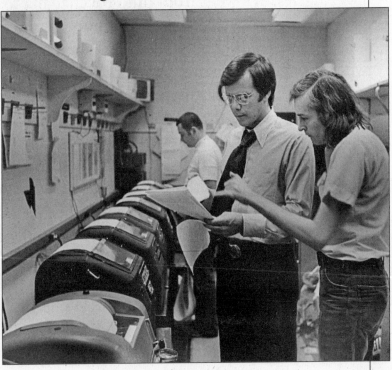

large antiwar crowd filling the street in front of the hotel—with the perfect Hollywood name of Avenue of the Stars—was well dressed and more festive than angry, but their noisy taunts reached the president, who was well protected deep inside the hotel.

Suddenly the situation turned ugly when the LAPD charged the crowd. When the cops gunned their motorcycles and drove the antiwar throng across an empty lot, many of the protestors began throwing rocks and large chunks of sod at the advancing police. The LAPD and some of L.A.'s affluent liberal establishment had suddenly become inadvertent adversaries.

I was part of a team of KNBC reporters broadcasting live coverage for the eleven o'clock news that night, and the viewing audience quickly voted for the cops. The station was flooded with angry calls, blaming the protestors and expressing outrage that police behavior was being questioned.

At the beginning of America's involvement in Vietnam, I had taken my cues from President Kennedy. When he said he believed in the domino theory—that if we allowed Vietnam to fall to the Communists, the rest of Southeast Asia would follow—that was good enough for me. But by 1967 I had serious reservations, fueled in part by the skepticism of my friend Gene Kimmel, who was now flying combat missions. Gene warned me not to believe most of what we were hearing from official sources about how well the war was going.

In California we were living with the contradictions of a raging war abroad and another kind of war— less obvious but no less intense—at home. That was never more clear to me than late one night when I was at Los Angeles International Airport, en route to San Francisco to cover an uprising in a black working-class neighborhood after a police shooting. In one corner of the airport, a squad of U.S. Army infantrymen, in full combat gear, was getting ready to board a charter flight to Vietnam. There were tearful farewells with their parents and wives and girlfriends. But it was like a secret ceremony, well out of sight of the rest of the busy terminal. I thought something along the lines of "What the hell! Here I am, headed to a riot in a black neighborhood in San Francisco, and they're going off to fight someone else's war. Something's wrong here."

When I arrived in California, Watts, a sprawling African-American community in South Central Los Angeles, was still smoldering from the 1965 fires and riots that had rudely countered the nation's easygoing California stereotypes of beaches, blondes, and bikinis. Soon I was in Watts several days a week, reporting on the federal, state, and local programs for education, job training, and housing that were being rushed into the hard-core neighborhoods by the Harbor Freeway that divided South Central Los Angeles.

In my youthful idealism, I imagined the area would be transformed by this long-overdue combination of attention and goodwill and cash, but before very long I began to see that the problems were far more systemic on both sides of the racial barrier than I had realized. Twenty years later, I returned to do a documentary on the sad, violent takeover of those neighborhoods—which had already known so much trouble—by large, well-organized, and ruthless street gangs.

The 1965 Watts riots were a forerunner of the great urban racial riots that by 1967 had escalated and were sweeping the country, from east to west and back again. In Newark, New Jersey, and Detroit, Michigan, small wars were being waged on the streets, with whole neighborhoods ablaze and shooting battles between police and protestors. Other violent protests were erupting in Cambridge, Maryland; Memphis, Tennessee; Durham, North Carolina; and Cairo, Illinois.

Dr. Martin Luther King Jr. who had recently won the Nobel Peace Prize for his philosophy of nonviolence, suddenly found himself marginalized by the raw urban rage being inflamed by the incendiary rhetoric of young black power leaders such as Stokely Carmichael and H. Rap Brown, who mockingly proclaimed that "Violence is as American as cherry pie."

President Johnson appointed Illinois governor Otto Kerner to organize the National Advisory Commission on Civil Disorders to assess the causes of the urban warfare. The Kerner Commission later reported the sadly memorable conclusion that America was divided into two societies that were black and white, "separate and unequal."

In that same year, 1967, however, there was at least some progress. Ed Brooke, a Republican from Massachusetts, became the first black elected to the United States Senate in the hundred years since Reconstruction. Carl Stokes became the first black mayor of a major city when he was elected in Cleveland. The prominent civil rights attorney Thurgood Marshall was nominated by President Johnson to the U.S.

Supreme Court and became the first black justice ever to sit on the nation's highest bench.

That year the president agreed to send another forty-five thousand troops to Vietnam to meet the request from the American commander, General William Westmoreland, who claimed that he was winning the war but needed more men. By the end of 1967, there were 485,000 Americans in Vietnam.

Ronald Reagan was in the first year of his first term as governor of California. It was the beginning of a historic career in American politics. He was a powerful and persuasive new conservative voice after eight years of the liberal policies of Edmund G. "Pat" Brown, the cheerful progressive who had transformed the Golden State by building an elaborate system to divert water to the semiarid southern areas and by building up a statewide system of the finest public universities in the nation.

The California legislature still remained in the hands of liberals, led by the estimable Democratic Assembly Speaker, Jesse Unruh, a brilliant populist who presided over his side of the California Capitol with a hell-raising posse of ambitious young acolytes, including John Burton and Willie Brown, who would remain influential figures in state politics for the next thirty-five years. But politically, the state was turning right, having elected another conservative Republican actor, George Murphy, as a U.S. senator. And Los Angeles mayor Sam Yorty, a Vietnam hawk and a Reagan ally, was a Democrat in registration only.

For draft-age young men, it had become a time of difficult choices. Most answered the summons from the Selective Service System. But with the president pouring more troops into Vietnam and the death toll rising every week, many were frantically trying to get into graduate school in order to be eligible for student deferments, or even contriving medical or physical disabilities that would exempt them from service altogether. Some, like Jeffry House, whom we will meet later, crossed the border to Canada.

California's campuses, particularly Berkeley, the top rung of Pat Brown's highly regarded state higher education system, had already been roiled by the Free Speech Movement during the 1964–65 school year.

There were demonstrations and sit-ins and mass arrests. In the end, the administration backed down and order was restored. Berkeley became the West Coast epicenter of the counterculture and influenced protest movements across the nation. Many of the free speech supporters turned their attention to the war in Vietnam.

Ronald Reagan made the students' disruptive conduct and the restoration of traditional control a central part of his campaign message to the working-class men and women whose taxes helped finance the UC system even though they—or their children—had little direct connection to its campuses. When Reagan took office as governor, Clark Kerr, the bespectacled intellectual whose permissive performance as president of the UC system had been a target of Reagan's campaign rhetoric, demanded a vote of confidence from the university's board of regents. Kerr's demand was rejected, and he was fired.

This set off more demonstrations on the campuses, while it was welcomed in the communities that had elected Reagan by landslide proportions. In covering the story, I developed a good working relationship with one of the regents, who would later play his own distinctive role in history: H. R. "Bob" Haldeman, who came from a socially prominent Southern California family and was the head of the L.A. office of the nation's largest ad agency.

Across the bay from Berkeley—and still in my correspondent's uniform of coat, tie, and trench coat—I began to report from the psychedelic streets of a San Francisco neighborhood called Haight-Ashbury, which had become the destination of choice for druggies, itinerant musicians, and runaways, not to mention the sometime home of Janis Joplin and the Grateful Dead.

In the fall of that year, Meredith and I were invited by my NBC colleague Bob Abernethy to an intimate Sunday dinner at his home with one of our political heroes, Senator Eugene McCarthy of Minnesota. He was our idea of exactly what a senator should be: a sophisticated intellectual, sardonically witty, the kind who would not only notice the books on the shelves of his hotel suite but could mock their titles.

We were charmed and so at ease that Meredith played a home state card, telling McCarthy that Vice President Hubert Humphrey, his former fellow Minnesota senator, had been born and raised in South Dakota. Those McCarthy eyes lost their twinkle as he said coldly, "You can have him back."

I'd like to say I knew then that McCarthy was going to take on the Johnson administration over the war and run for president, but he didn't seem to have the makings of a real candidate, much less the hunger of a politician on the make. He was coolly critical of President Johnson, but much more in the ironic patois of a college professor (which he had been in Minnesota) than in the language of a man with a fire in his belly for the White House.

In retrospect, McCarthy's dismissal of Humphrey was a sign of the unraveling of the unity of the Democratic Party, and of the party itself—a schism that would reach frenzied proportions only eight months later and that would become one of the most complex legacies and consequences of the Sixties.

That Sunday afternoon Meredith and I spent at the Pacific Palisades home of my colleague Bob Abernethy and his wife, Jean, marked the end of one time in our lives and the beginning of another.

It was the last time I can remember having the traditional Sunday midday dinner that had been a ritual of our life in the Fifties. Other changes went well beyond family rituals, racing across a broad spectrum of American life, from the home to the workplace, from politics to the popular culture, from haircuts to hemlines.

More events of 1967, the gathering storm: Muhammad Ali was indicted and found guilty for refusing on religious grounds to be inducted into the Army, a conviction that was later reversed. Elvis married Priscilla. **Hair** opened off-Broadway, and **The Graduate** perfectly captured on the big screen the fracturing of generational mores and values. The Smothers Brothers, a quirky folk-singing comedy act, debuted on CBS and quickly got in trouble with their network bosses for their humorous but pointed needling of the establishment and the president's war policies.

Che Guevara was assassinated while unsuccessfully trying to foment a Cuba-like revolution in Bolivia, although he succeeded in launching a million T-shirts. Fifty thousand protestors marched on the Pentagon on October 21, demanding an end to American involvement in Vietnam (and, reflecting some of the surreal whimsy of the time, intending to levitate the building while they were at it).

Israel defeated an alliance of Arab states in the Six-Day War, a lightning military victory that rearranged the borders of that region in a fashion that is still being contested.

What we did not realize at the time was that 1967 was the overture, as the world accelerated toward the year that would take its place in bold print on history's calendar: 1968.

In 1968 a war in distant jungles would take a fateful turn; a president would back out of office; Richard Nixon would emerge from his cannily self-imposed political exile and rise from the tumult to win the White House on his second try; a weary apostle of nonviolence would be murdered; another Kennedy brother would be assassinated; families would be deeply divided by a phenomenon called the "generation gap." "Sex, drugs, and rock and roll" would become a mantra for some; "America, love it or leave it" would become a motto for others.

One prominent 1969 college graduate said to me when she learned I was working on this book, "Have you cracked the code yet?" She wondered if I had managed to figure out the real message of the Sixties—what was actually accomplished, and what was merely distraction or worse? What have we learned and what loose ends remain to be tied up? No, I said, the code hasn't been cracked and it may not be for some time to come, but isn't it time to explore the possibilities?

As a society we're still trying to sort out what happened and what it means for us in the twenty-first century. As I did at the time, I continue to struggle with the conflicting currents of the Sixties.

Back then, I was outraged by the duplicity of the Johnson and Nixon administrations over Vietnam, but I was also upset by the excesses of those who saw the war as a means of condemning everything about the American political system, and by those who quickly gave up their outrage once they were safely beyond the reach of the draft.

Women and racial minorities made a great leap forward in the Sixties, but gender and color lines obviously didn't disappear. Especially on issues of race, there were unexpected consequences of desegregation: many well-meaning government programs brought about a dependency that locked black families into cycles of government checks, kids, more government checks, more kids, and missing fathers.

When Harvard government professor Daniel Patrick Moynihan began to warn about the destructive effects of the breakup of the black family structure in America in 1965, he was roundly criticized for even raising such an issue.

Artistic freedom expanded profoundly, but the freedom to criticize many of the results contracted proportionately. Rock groups embraced and marketed decadence on records and in public concerts to the adoration of their fans, but when others raised questions about the corrosive effect on the young, they were shouted down.

Drug use, once confined mostly to jazz musicians and hard-core junkies, became a signature of open-mindedness and tolerance for the baby boomer culture. For some it was a passing fancy; for others, a genuinely spiritual enlightenment; for too many others, it was just a crash-and-burn experience.

Grade inflation and liberal intolerance for differing political discourse took hold on many campuses where institutional authority gave way to student demands, regardless of the merits of the demands.

At the same time, prestigious research universities were forced to examine what role they should be playing in the military-industrial complex. Traditional rules of student conduct—dorm hours, no conjugal visits, gender-specific campuses—tumbled.

The environment made it onto the map. Senator Gaylord Nelson of Wisconsin sponsored the first Earth Day in 1970, and conservation awareness started to spread across the land like wildflowers in a mountain meadow. But the curses of the twenty-first century, fossil fuels and no alternative energy, were little remarked upon.

The novelist Tom McGuane was one of the leading young writers of the Sixties with his breakthrough novels **The Sporting Club** and **Ninety-two in the Shade.** He had long hair, smoked dope, and hung out in Key West, but he was also a Stegner Fellow at Stanford, a serious man of letters with a reverence for the literary classics.

He now describes his attitude in those days as "embedded ambivalence. I was against the Vietnam War, but I didn't like the people I was standing next to at the protests. I had been raised in a strict Irish-Catholic family in the Detroit area. Two of my brothers were in the service. My uncles had been in World War II."

McGuane, who graduated from Michigan State in 1962 and did graduate work at Yale before migrating to Stanford for the 1966–67 school term, had a goal: He wanted to make ten thousand dollars a year—but to do it in eleven months so he could spend the twelfth month fishing. He ended up moving to Key West, Florida, where he could both fish and work year-round, abandon his upper-middle-class roots, and hang out with his pals such as novelist Jim Harrison, singer Jimmy Buffett, gonzo journalist Hunter Thompson, and artist Russell Chatham.

Despite (or perhaps because of) his father's disapproval, McGuane began to feel it was okay to be estranged from the mainstream of American life. He says, "I felt everyone else wanted to be in our world. We were the last generation to be cooler than our kids."

McGuane, who has lived on a Montana ranch for the past thirty years, is now, in his own way, a member of the establishment of his adopted state: still a successful writer, a champion horseman, a dedicated fly fisherman, and a grandfather. He's been married three times; his wife, Laurie, is Jimmy Buffett's sister.

As we sit in his writing studio, a tidy streamside cabin filled with books, guns, and the paraphernalia of fly tying, McGuane, now graying but still dashing in his rancher wardrobe of flannel shirt and Wrangler jeans, remembers that something dear to him ended in the Sixties. It was the excitement of waiting for the next big novel or piece of nonfiction. He starts to call the roll: **Desert Solitaire,** by Edward Abbey, the passionate activist and naturalist; **The Armies of the Night,** by Norman Mailer; **The Confessions of Nat Turner,** by William Styron.

The entire decade of the Sixties was rich in literary achievement. **Catch-22,** by Joseph Heller; **Franny and Zooey,** by J. D. Salinger; **To Kill a Mockingbird,** by Harper Lee; **One Flew over the Cuckoo's Nest,** by Ken Kesey; **Slaughterhouse-Five,** by Kurt Vonnegut; **The Bell Jar,** by Sylvia Plath; **The Spy Who Came in from the Cold,** by John le Carré; **Understanding Media,** by Marshall McLuhan; **The Autobiography of Malcolm X,** by Alex Haley and Malcolm X; **One Hundred Years of Solitude,** by Gabriel García Márquez; **The Electric Kool-Aid Acid Test,** by Tom Wolfe; **Portnoy's Complaint,** by Philip Roth, to name just a few.

McGuane sighs and says, "In our rejection of the establishment, we became addicts of esoterica. Overwhelmed by actuality, we turned to Zen, rock climb-

Tom McGuane in the 1960s: "Everyone else wanted to be in our world."

McGuane today, "now graying but still dashing."

ing, happenings, recreational drugs, falconry, and, in my case, avant-garde letters." At least he understands what motivated that rejection. "Most people," he says, "thought LBJ was a crook, Reagan was a joke, and Nixon was coming back."

Peggy Noonan, another Irish Catholic, famous for the eloquent prose she wrote for her hero, Ronald Reagan, was also a conflicted child of the Sixties until, as she has written, she decided to get off the bus.

As she wrote in her book **What I Saw at the Revolution**, Noonan's moment of self-realization came in 1971, aboard a bus going to an antiwar demonstration in Washington, D.C. She was the editor of the student newspaper at Fairleigh Dickinson University, and during the ride from New Jersey she saw the contempt of her fellow protestors for "the nineteen-year-old boys who were carrying guns in the war or in the [National] Guard." Those on the bus thought of those in the military as crude and undereducated. There was, she says, a busload of contempt for America, and that's when she decided to "get off the bus," metaphorically if not literally.

Noonan wrote of her family, "I came from people who were part of the fruits of the FDR realignment—the Catholics of the big cities who fully adhered to the Democratic Party in the Thirties, Forties, and never meant to let go." But in the Eighties Noonan found herself a part of the national political realignment. The party that she had thought of as representing only the "dullards"—the GOP—suddenly became the party of the people.

To her mother's consternation, Noonan crossed

the line over to what she calls "the new party of the people," led by Ronald Reagan, the Midwestern boy who went to California and became a movie star, a television star, and the Republican apostle of America as "a shining city upon a hill."

Now that the Gipper is gone, Noonan worries about the politically obsessed in her party, those who, she says, get their energy from hate. They cannot engage in honorable debate because they cannot see the honor of the other side. That was an affliction of the far left in the Sixties that appears to haunt the right forty years later.

Other alumni of the Sixties have other views. Alan Brinkley, a distinguished historian of twentieth-century America and now the provost of Columbia University, believes the generation in the streets in 1968 got it wrong.

Alan is the son of the late David Brinkley, a man I consider my mentor at NBC News. Over the years Alan and I have stayed in touch, and when I began this project we talked about what he had told Jules Witcover, in Witcover's splendid book about 1968, **The Year the Dream Died**.

Alan, who has written and lectured extensively about the Sixties, said the protestors saw it "as a revolutionary year when in fact it was much closer to being a counter-revolutionary year."

Brinkley said the assassination of Dr. King and the riots that followed "came to be seen by many people as the vision of America's future and gave salience to law and order as an issue."

The various "shocks to the nation's system," he

told Witcover, "far from radicalizing America created a real political reaction which the right was able . . . to exploit."

In our conversation about that time, Brinkley elaborated. He said that the Sixties generation consisted of "unrealistically idealistic people trying to come to terms with realities in the world, in universities, in the workplace, they couldn't understand" because they were so young and so inexperienced. But they pushed on and their elders pushed back by rejecting the embryonic notions of the young.

It is now largely unchallenged political dogma that the chaos on the left delivered the country to the right in 1968. Says Pat Buchanan, the commentator, sometime presidential candidate, and longtime keeper of the conservative flame, who was a speechwriter for Richard Nixon from the mid-Sixties on, "Nineteen sixty-eight was two sides of the same coin. Everything came apart for the Democrats and together for the Republicans. We went on to create a new majority built on the ruination of the Great Society [President Johnson's ambitious attempt to expand on the New Deal policies of President Franklin Delano Roosevelt]."

Tom Hayden, a founder of the SDS—Students for a Democratic Society—and a proponent of a radical remaking of America, thinks that it's wrong to castigate the left for the results of the Sixties, and he dismisses those claims of self-destruction on the left. He told Witcover that the root cause of the Sixties explosion was Vietnam, "because it created a sea of blood that created lasting emotions, feelings and resentments."

Hayden says, "There's a big 'what if' over the Sixties that should keep people from casting blame or causality, and that is the assassinations. . . . Who knows what would have happened if King and Kennedy were alive? It could have launched a liberal period of governance."

Indeed, who knows? **What if?**

As we begin our trip back through the Sixties, the topography can be as instructive for what you don't see as for what you do see.

I recently went to UC Berkeley—to walk through Sather Gate and into Sproul Plaza, which had been ground zero for the 1964 Free Speech Movement. On a sunny day, I encountered three protestors standing with their mouths taped shut to protest the absence of outrage over the war in Iraq. As if to prove the point, waves of their classmates Rollerbladed or walked nonchalantly by, backpacks in place, cell phones or iPods to their ears.

In the library at the east end of the Plaza, a Sixties alum has financed the construction of the Free Speech Movement Café, which has handsome bas-relief plaques depicting the movement's halcyon history of protest. But none of the contemporary students patronizing the Free Speech Movement Café appeared to be thinking about Mario Savio on the day I was there.

Berkeley was also in the forefront of the anti-Vietnam and anti-military protests that marked the Sixties. But now ROTC is back on campus here and at all but four of the Ivy League schools that formerly banned the officer training program.

The town of Berkeley, home to many aging liberals, remains an activist community—often referred to

by the local residents, with varying degrees of seriousness, as the People's Republic of Berkeley—but the
tone today is much more subdued.

As I retraced life in the Sixties, I encountered
other realities that ran counter to the perceptions of
the time. In Chicago, for example, I heard high praise
across the political spectrum for the administration of
Mayor Richard M. Daley, son of the late Mayor
Richard J. Daley, the bitterly despised symbol of everything wrong with the old ways of the Democratic Party
in the eyes of the young protestors who descended on
the Windy City in 1968 determined to make their
mark on the Democratic National Convention.

Wonderbras have replaced burned bras, and men's
haircuts are short again. Communes are out, and trophy houses are in. Britney Spears and Jessica Simpson
have sold many more records than Joan Baez ever did.
School busing was a failure, and conservatives dominate talk radio.

But wait. There are sixteen women in the U.S.
Senate, and one of them is a serious contender for the
presidency of the United States. More women every
year join the ranks of corporate executives. Women
don't yet have a level playing field, but they now make
up roughly half or more of the students in the nation's
medical, law, and business schools. Title IX, mandat-
ing a fair distribution of money for women's athletics,
has changed the game in colleges and universities and,
by extension, in high schools and grade schools.

A young first-term African-American senator has

already energized a large following behind his presidential candidacy, and an African-American woman who needs only one name is one of the wealthiest and most powerful people in America.

The Internet has moved activism from the streets into cyberspace, where the single stroke of a key can send an idea all around the world. I believe that for many, the Sixties, like beauty and bias, is really in the eye of the beholder. The cataclysmic events were so sweeping, complex, and consequential that they cannot yet be encoded into one great truth.

As Stewart Brand, the founder of the **Whole Earth Catalog,** told me, "The Sixties showed us that any generation can try things well beyond the boundaries of what is approved or permitted. We broke through a lot of notions of where the edge is and found some interesting stuff. But there were notions about revolution that . . . were nothing but fantasy."

Yet there are positive consequences we now take for granted, as well as the negative consequences we'd rather ignore. While we were altered radically in some areas of our national and individual interests, we were little changed in others.

When and how we go to war, how we measure and respond to authority, what is culturally acceptable, how we treat each other across racial and ethnic lines, and, most of all, how we live together and advance together, are all questions that linger from the Sixties and still demand our attention and await our answers.

We are profoundly changed in so many ways and yet so much the same in so many others.

Recently, I returned to California to help celebrate

the twenty-fifth wedding anniversary of Kathleen Brown, the youngest daughter of the late governor Pat Brown and sister of Jerry Brown, who matched his father's successes with two terms of his own as governor of the nation's most populous state.

It was a festive gathering of three generations. Of the fifty people there, at least half a dozen had been divorced (including the guests of honor), a number well below the national average. Kathleen and her husband, Van, were celebrating the unalloyed success of their recoveries from broken first marriages. They were the targets of lots of kidding about their odd-couple politics. Van Gordon Sauter, the colorful former president of CBS News, is a Falstaffian figure and iconoclastic Republican. Kathleen is an earth mother and unreconstructed California Democrat.

Van is now a stay-at-home husband, and Kathleen, who went back to school to get her law degree when she was in her thirties, is the breadwinner. She started out first in the family business, winning an election as California's state treasurer before losing a race for governor in a landslide to Pete Wilson.

With her characteristic good humor, she left politics and is now a major figure in the West Coast operations of Goldman Sachs, the top of the Wall Street establishment pyramid.

Her brother Jerry, who was once known as Governor Moonbeam for his new-age ways, was the law-and-order mayor in Oakland at the time of the anniversary party; he's now back in Sacramento, this time as California's attorney general. The former Jesuit seminarian had only recently married for the first time, and he sat quietly at a corner table, accepting the jibes of friends about his long-delayed matrimony. His demeanor is muted, and it's a little startling to remember that at the peak of his political power, he was a symbol of the Sixties sensibilities in his party and a viable candidate for his party's presidential nomination.

Other guests included one long-married pair, Anne Taylor Fleming and Karl Fleming. They met when she was a bright and opinionated flower child aspiring to be a writer, and he was a fortysomething married father of four, a legendary reporter during the difficult days of the civil rights movement in the South. Their wedding ceremony was a full Sixties affair, replete with recitations of dewy poems, flower petals in the hair, and lapels out to here. Their political passions remain intact, but their lives now revolve around the quieter demands of writing memoirs and novels, and the shared nurturing of his grandchildren.

As I looked over the tables and remembered all the personal stories, I was struck by one essential lesson of the Sixties: For all the assaults on convention and all the temptations along the way, strong personal values and affections survived—indeed, thrived—rather than crumbled in the face of divorces, deaths, addictions, rehabilitations, turmoil and triumphs and defeats, fame and wealth, satisfactions and disappointments.

If there were scars from the Sixties, at least on that night in West Los Angeles, they were lost in the cacophony of laughter and heartfelt toasts.

Yet there were some striking omissions that were a commentary in their own way. We were an all-white crowd. In the Sixties, with the determination to integrate the country, most of the guests would have guessed that by 2006 these kinds of social gatherings would be an easy racial mix. There has been impressive improvement over the years, but Dr. King's goal of racial integration remains elusive.

We remain a country still deeply divided along many fault lines. For all the achievements and assimilation of the past forty years, there remain many parts of this immigrant nation that have settled politically, culturally, economically, and geographically into separate—and in many cases still competing— spheres. In Congress alone it is no longer just the Republicans and the Democrats; it is now the Blue Dog Democrats—conservative Southerners—the Black Caucus, the Hispanic Caucus, and the Asian-American Caucus.

He Had a Dream

God bless Dr. King's soul. He was there
to raise our hopes and to give us courage.
He really made us feel it was right to die
for what you believed in if the cause
was good enough.

—REVEREND THOMAS GILMORE

They'd tell me, "Don't get in the way."
Well, in the Sixties, I got in the way. . . .
It's time for people to get
in the way again.

—REPRESENTATIVE JOHN LEWIS

O<small>N</small> A<small>UGUST</small> 28, 1963, there was a massive march on Washington, D.C., on behalf of civil rights. It was a festive, peaceful gathering, bringing together blacks and whites at the Lincoln Memorial, where Dr. Martin Luther King Jr. made a historic speech, a soaring call for racial equality.

With the Great Emancipator looking on, Dr. King called up all of his intellectual and emotional passions and unleashed them in a soulful sermon to his country and his countrymen.

> I have a dream that one day this nation will rise up and live out the true meaning of its creed: "We hold these truths to be self-evident: that all men are created equal."

The "I Have a Dream" speech now has a permanent place in our national consciousness. But Dr. King's dream would not come true with words alone. He would have to mobilize black and white America, and to do that he would need help.

Of all the changes that occurred in America in the

Sixties, none was as important, dramatic, ongoing, or more likely to endure as those involving race. Dr. Martin Luther King Jr. led the way, but lawyers, judges, politicians, and courageous black and white protestors—young and old—in both the North and South were equally important, first in forcing the issue to the forefront and then in forcing America to confront a long history of shameful cruelty and regional hypocrisy in dealing with people of color.

One of those who would help was a poor young man from rural Alabama. When Representative John Lewis of Georgia was growing up in the deeply segregated South in the Fifties, his parents and grandparents would warn him about the realities of being a black boy in a racist society. "They'd tell me, 'Don't get in the way,'" he remembers. "Well, in the Sixties, I got in the way."

Race was the first defining issue of my grown-up years. In South Dakota, we had been insufficiently sensitive to racial issues involving our Indian tribes, and we were largely removed from any kind of regular contact with black people.

My parents, however, had made me and my two younger brothers, Bill and Mike, aware of racial intolerance at an early age. As a child, my father, the youngest of ten children, had been a poor, tough street kid in a small railroading and farm town where work was much more the order of the day than love. He dropped out of school at the age of ten, and no one expected him to amount to much. He was aware of that, and it made him determined to use his natural touch for almost anything mechanical, and especially big machinery, to become a working-class success. His own experience made him a man who always judged others by who they were and what they could do, not by their color or pedigree. Red Brokaw was a champion of the underdog.

As a result, although he wasn't a baseball fan, my father supported my maternal grandfather's proclamation that the family would be Jackie Robinson fans because the Dodgers had done the right thing in signing the first Negro to play major-league baseball. I became devoted to Robinson's life, following it beyond the base paths to learn about his days growing up in Southern California and playing at UCLA. In 1946, following a proud career fighting racism in the armed services in World War II, he started breaking records playing second base for the Montreal Royals. When I realized that this incredible athlete, who was my idol and hero, might have been denied his chance at a major-league career simply because of his skin color, I had my first indelible lesson in bigotry.

At the University of South Dakota and the University of Iowa, there were a few black students, and I was friends with some of them in my classes but not socially. Even in the Midwest, we were separate and unequal in so many ways.

My first real experience with large-scale racial separation came when I started working in Omaha. The city's neighborhoods were divided by de facto segregation, and even Omaha-born young blacks were largely excluded from the professional opportunities that were available to whites from other states.

While Dr. King's campaign for racial equality was

featured prominently on the network news almost every night, there was little social or political discussion of where Omaha or other Northern cities might fit in.

In the newsrooms where I worked, and among my friends at weekend parties, I argued that what King was doing in the South was right and that the nation needed an effective and comprehensive civil rights law.

One of my antagonists was a young Danish immigrant, a news-cameraman whose family had found sanctuary in America when the Nazis were closing in on their country during World War II. I could not get him to acknowledge that the American blacks in uniform fighting against the men who had driven him from his home deserved the same rights as the rest of us—including those who were, like him, newcomers to America.

One day I tried a new tactic. We had a well-liked black janitor who made his daily rounds through the offices, always pleasant but mostly silent. He was probably in his early sixties, so he undoubtedly had experienced a lot of discrimination in his lifetime. His name was Bill, and one day I grabbed him as he walked by. I said, "Bill, we're arguing civil rights. I'd like to know what you think."

It was hard to tell whether my colleagues were more startled or embarrassed. Most of them had probably never talked with a black man or woman specifically about racial issues. They were not alone, of course.

On that day, for the first time anyone could remember, Bill had a lot to say. He began by talking about his sons and grandsons. He said he had worked hard all his life so they wouldn't have to push a broom like he did. Then, looking at the white males surrounding him, he said, "I just hope someday my grandsons can have one of your jobs. I don't want them to be janitors." With that, he left the newsroom and moved on to the other offices he had to clean.

There was a stunned silence from my colleagues. Finally, one of them said, "Well, that old man does make you think."

One of the few Omaha blacks who had a high profile in the city was the director of summer programs for the Department of Parks and Recreation. He had a name to match his personality: Welcome Bryant. We came to know each other when he appeared on the noon newscast to announce the activities for the next day.

He was surprised when I asked him to tell me about black life in Omaha. He said, "Look, you may not be comfortable in my neighborhood hangouts, and I won't be comfortable in your hangouts, so let's just drive around and talk."

So one night in the summer of 1964, we did just that. He told me that if I wanted to know what was happening on the Near North Side, Omaha's biggest black neighborhood, I should check in either at the barbershop, which was the community's equivalent of city hall, or at the funeral home, because that was where the smartest black businessmen gathered from time to time.

Welcome Bryant told me that he and his neighbors were watching the network news every night because they were so interested in what was happening in the South. But they wondered why the local journalists weren't paying attention to the same issues in Omaha. He was right. Neither the local daily newspaper, the **World-Herald,** nor any of the local TV stations made any effort to explore local racial issues as a natural follow-up to the national stories being reported from the South.

Omaha Central, the city's most acclaimed high school, is an imposing gray granite building on a hill in the center of the city. Central's graduates include Susan Buffett, Warren Buffett's late wife; Henry Fonda; and two Nobel laureates. It was a magnet for the city's best and brightest kids because of its strong college prep curriculum, but it also served the black neighborhoods on the Near North Side. It was the alma mater of Gale Sayers, the Hall of Fame running back for the Chicago Bears.

Yet Meredith, who was there as an English teacher in 1963, cannot remember a black faculty member.

Omaha was typical of Midwestern cities. The climate wasn't racially hostile, but neither was it racially sensitive. My view of racial matters took on a new urgency when I was working at WSB-TV, in Atlanta, in the spring of 1965. In those days Atlantans liked to brag that they lived in a city "too busy to hate." It truly was a fast-growing modern metropolis fueled by a unique combination of Southern charm and powerful businessmen, including Robert Woodruff, who single-handedly made Coca-Cola the world's soft drink of choice.

It was also home to branch offices of Fortune 500 companies; the **Atlanta Constitution,** a daily newspaper with generally liberal attitudes on matters of race; a large population of poor blacks who lived in housing projects and neighborhoods called Buttermilk Bottom; and a black middle class personified by the King family.

The local congressman, Charles Longstreet Weltner, a scion of a prominent white family, was the only Southerner to vote for the Civil Rights Act in 1964.

In the city's private clubs, the membership was as white as the gloves on the hands of the black staff serving them there and in their homes.

For all of its claims of racial tolerance, Atlanta in 1964 remained a deeply segregated city with only one black man representing it in the state legislature and just one on the city council. When Dr. King won the Nobel Peace Prize that year, the city's white establishment was divided on whether to sponsor a dinner honoring him. Eventually, the money was raised for the dinner, but few of Atlanta's first families attended.

WSB was headquartered in a re-created antebellum mansion on Peachtree Street. I was excited to be a part of the news staff, which had a national reputation for professionalism and an absence of regional bias when it came to stories about the civil rights movement. It was the only Southern station to be trusted by NBC News producers to provide regular coverage of the movement for **The Huntley-Brinkley Report**. Four of my colleagues and I went on to become NBC News correspondents.

I was a little surprised to discover that there were no blacks on the newsroom staff or in any position of responsibility throughout the television, radio, or corporate offices. The station had taken a chance on me, a twenty-five-year-old Yankee imported from the Great Plains, but no local black citizens had been similarly recruited. That was typical throughout the American workplace in 1965. To my regret, while I noticed it, I didn't dwell on it.

In 1965, when I arrived in Atlanta, the South was going through its greatest upheaval since the Civil War. Late one night I jumped into a small plane for a hurried trip to Alabama to cover the murder of Viola Liuzzo, a mother of five who had driven from Michigan to do her part in what she called "everybody's fight." She was gunned down by Klan members on a lonely road south of Montgomery, the state capital.

On another occasion, in a small town east of Atlanta, my cameraman and I were surrounded and threatened by angry lumberjacks when we followed up a tip that local black students would attempt to board a bus ferrying white students to a segregated school in the next county.

A highway patrolman and the sheriff intervened, saying to the lumberjacks, "Boys, I don't blame you— but if we beat the press, we'll have even more trouble." With that, the sheriff pointed a shotgun at me and said, "Get of town. Now."

In Americus, Georgia, an ugly confrontation between blacks and whites reached critical mass when a young white man was killed in a drive-by shooting. All hell broke loose, inspired in part by a Klan rally and the racial rants of Lester Maddox. NBC News in New York dispatched me to Americus to cover events there until one of its regular correspondents could arrive. I decided to see what the mother of the white victim had to say.

Not quite knowing what to expect, I approached her house in a working-class neighborhood.

A small quiet woman in a plain, faded frock— what we used to call a housedress—opened the screen door just a crack and agreed to be interviewed. I asked her what she thought of all the trouble that had blown up in town, with threats of lynchings and shootings for any black who marched in protest.

In soft tones she said it made no sense. It wouldn't bring back her son. She hoped it would end soon. I found her statement, in its simplicity, tremendously powerful, and an antidote to all the hate-filled rhetoric of the Klan. That night the interview had a prominent place on **The Huntley-Brinkley Report.**

In the meantime, the streets were lined with large white men carrying shotguns, pistols, and clubs. They vowed to kill "any nigger who marches tonight." The local black community was trying to decide what to do.

Gene Roberts, the legendary civil rights reporter for **The New York Times,** and the columnist Nicholas von Hoffman were in town, navigating that awkward space journalists had to chart between our personal feelings about what we were observing and our professional responsibility not to get involved.

Around midnight, the local Negroes, as they called themselves then, broke up their meeting at a small church, and the first person to emerge was a beautiful young woman, about eighteen. I asked her what she was going to do.

"March," she said.

I asked, "Aren't you afraid?"

"Yes," she replied, "but I have no choice."

I don't know her name, but I've never forgotten her quiet courage. She and the others marched that night and while it was tense, there was no violence.

I was on duty at the station helping with the network coverage on March 7, 1965, the day that would become known as Bloody Sunday because of the confrontation at the Edmund Pettus Bridge in Selma, Alabama, when state troopers were unleashed on black and white marchers demonstrating for voting rights. Scores of the marchers were injured by the police, who used billy clubs and tear gas to break up the crowd.

My video editor that day was an affable white Georgian who didn't want to believe what he was seeing. He was sure the crowd had provoked the police. I remember making him rerun the film three times. A young black man could be seen cowering beneath a tree, with violence all around him. He was trying to take cover when he was set upon by a number of troopers flailing at him with their clubs. They hit him again and again, clubbing him to the ground. I said, "You tell me—where's the provocation?"

My editor stared for a moment and then just shook his head. "You're right," he said. "It's wrong, it's wrong."

Representative John Lewis and Julian Bond

One of the leaders of that Selma march was John Lewis. The son of an Alabama sharecropper, Lewis was "country," as they'd say in the South, with a thick rural accent. But he was a true warrior when it came to racial equality, an uncompromising executive director of the Student Nonviolent Coordinating Committee, which was widely known by its initials, SNCC, pronounced "snick."

On Bloody Sunday, Lewis was at the front of the column of blacks marching across the bridge. When the police moved in, the small, somber man wearing a trench coat was an immediate target. They cracked their billy clubs over his head, knocking him unconscious. He was one of ninety marchers hospitalized that day.

When the Alabama police riot played on national television that night, the brutal, unprovoked violence stunned the country. It was a high price for the marchers to pay, but Selma served as a catalyst for the country to adopt the Voting Rights Act before the year was out, a milestone piece of legislation that expanded the number of blacks registered to vote from 30 percent to more than 50 percent in six Southern states in just two years.

No one was surprised that John Lewis had been in harm's way that day. If they had given medals in the civil rights struggle, he would have had a chestful for courage shown and injuries suffered. He was arrested more than forty times, seventeen in Nashville alone, during the lunchroom sit-ins. He was beaten in Montgomery and thrown into a notorious Mississippi state prison. When his contemporaries talked about Lewis, they always began with testimonials to his fearlessness.

Lewis grew up one of ten children on a small, hardscrabble farm without electricity or plumbing in

On Sunday, March 7, 1965, John Lewis (front, right), Hosea Williams (front, left), and others lead marchers across the Edmund Pettus Bridge in Selma, Alabama. The day would become known as Bloody Sunday.

Georgia congressman John Lewis addresses the Democratic National Convention in August 2000.

Troy, Alabama. From an early age, he was interested in learning and preaching. He sharpened his preacher's skills by delivering regular sermons to the flock of chickens he tended, and he conducted funeral services whenever one of them died.

In high school, he began to hear about the bus boycott just an hour away in Montgomery that was being led by a young preacher named Martin Luther King, Jr. He was deeply impressed by a sermon Dr. King delivered on the radio called "Paul's Letter to the American Christians," in which he called for Americans to embrace the values of Jesus.

At the American Baptist Theological Seminary in Nashville, Lewis became a full-time foot soldier in the struggle for civil rights, embracing the philosophy of nonviolence as a means of gaining ground. By 1965 he was a battle-tested commander at SNCC headquarters in Atlanta, but he was little known outside the movement. Short, stocky, and, by his own description, "not handsome," he couldn't compete in that regard with the good-looking and urbane Julian Bond, the son of a college professor who had been raised in the North and was SNCC's communications director.

Bond and Lewis were the classic Mr. Outside and Mr. Inside—the public face and the backroom strategist. That was the arrangement in early 1966 when Lewis decided to issue a statement from SNCC headquarters charging that the United States government had been "deceptive in its claims of concern for the freedom of the Vietnamese people" and expressing SNCC's sympathy for "the men in this country who are unwilling to respond to a military draft."

Bond, who had just been elected to the Georgia state legislature, didn't know Lewis was planning to issue such a radical statement, and instantly found himself the target of outrage throughout the promilitary Georgia white establishment. The Georgia general assembly voted to deny Bond his seat, and the day he appeared in the state capitol to challenge the ruling remains as clear in my memory as if it were this morning.

An angry crowd jammed the corridors outside the assembly chamber. I was a little nervous that there would be violence. Suddenly, Bond appeared, elegantly dressed as always, cool and expressionless as he walked through the hostile onlookers to a holding room where he would await the judgment of his fellow legislators. We were the same age, twenty-five, and although I knew him just slightly, at that moment I was in awe of his courage and composure. Many years later, when I told him how impressed I had been, he laughed and said, "What you didn't know is that when I went into the holding room, I immediately broke out in a terrible case of hives!"

He lost the round that day, but the U.S. Supreme Court later overruled the decision of the Georgia assembly, and Bond went on to serve both there and in the Georgia state senate.

John Lewis was having his own difficulties within SNCC, where Stokely Carmichael, H. Rap Brown, and other young black power activists, frustrated with the slow pace of social change, had taken over the organization. Carmichael forced Lewis out, calling him a "Christ-loving damn fool" because of his commitment to nonviolence.

Lewis moved to New York to work for a foundation, but as an Alabama country product and seasoned activist, he wasn't happy in the buttoned-down atmosphere of the big city. He found a way out when Bobby Kennedy announced his presidential candidacy. Lewis offered his services, and Kennedy sent him to Indiana to help organize the state.

John Lewis was at Kennedy's side the night of April 4, 1968, when, during a campaign stop in Indianapolis, they learned that Dr. King had been murdered in Memphis. The large crowd of black supporters who had gathered to greet Kennedy was unaware that their patron saint had just been assassinated. It fell to Kennedy to deliver the news, which was so shocking and so unexpected that it took everyone a few moments to absorb the enormity of the fact.

As he stood in the darkness, illuminated only by the lights of news cameras, Kennedy talked gently but intensely about the need to resist "hatred and a desire for revenge. We can move in that direction . . . ," he said, "or we can make an effort as Martin Luther King did to . . . remove that stain of bloodshed that spread across our land." He also talked movingly about the death of his brother five years earlier.

It was one of the most powerful speeches of Kennedy's career, delivered extemporaneously. He told the audience:

Aeschylus once wrote: "Even in our sleep, pain which cannot forget falls drop by drop upon the heart, until, in our own despair, against our will, comes wisdom through the awful grace of God."

What we need in the United States is not division; what we need in the United States is not hatred; what we need in the United States is not violence and lawlessness, but is love and wisdom, and compassion toward one another, and a feeling of justice toward those who still suffer within our country, whether they be white or whether they be black. Let us dedicate ourselves to what the Greeks wrote so many years ago: to tame the savageness of man and make gentle the life of the world.

Lewis, devastated by the death of Dr. King, remembers thinking, "Well, at least we still have Bobby." He continues, "Dr. King was the undisputed leader of the movement, but somehow we'd go on. I gave everything I had to the Kennedy campaign."

Two months later, Lewis was in Los Angeles at the Ambassador Hotel when Bobby Kennedy was murdered. This time he was inconsolable. "I broke down and cried and cried," he says. "I felt like it was the end. The next morning I flew from Los Angeles to Atlanta, crying off and on all the way. I just felt like the country was falling apart."

Lewis was aboard the long, mournful funeral train that carried Bobby's body from services in New York back to Washington, where he would be buried next to his brother. "All along the way," Lewis remembers, "I saw people crying, mothers and fathers holding up their children, and signs that said, 'We love you, Bobby.' It was one of the saddest days of my life."

Lewis was hospitalized for exhaustion but recovered in time to join Julian Bond at the Democratic National Convention in Chicago in August, where they challenged the credentials of the official Georgia delegation, which Bond later described as "handpicked, overwhelmingly white, segregationist, and overwhelmingly pro–George Wallace."

I was covering the convention for NBC and said a quick hello to Bond one night as he was preparing to lead his challengers onto the floor. I said something to the effect of "You're always in the thick of it." He laughed and shrugged as if to say, "What choice do I have?" In the end, half the seats in the Georgia delegation went to the challengers. Bond's name was placed in nomination to be the party's vice presidential candidate, but he was just twenty-eight years old and the Constitution requires that vice presidents be at least thirty-five.

With both Bond and Lewis, also born in 1940, I felt a deep generational bond. As a white man, I had received unparalleled opportunities in the boom years after the war. Yet here were two young black men my age who had to fight hard every day just for the basic rights of citizenship and respect.

After 1968 Lewis stayed active in the movement, running the Voter Education Project, which added millions more black citizens to the voter rolls and helped change the face of public officeholders from the local and state level all the way to the nation's capital, where forty-two African-Americans now serve in the House of Representatives.

By the late 1970s, John Lewis felt that he was ready to take his own place in the political arena. He was elected to the Atlanta City Council, a position that gave him a running start for his next, unexpected leap up the public ladder. When the incumbent in Georgia's fifth congressional district decided to run for the Senate, the House seat was suddenly vacant. It was widely expected that Julian Bond would win the nomination and the election. But Lewis decided to challenge his old friend. The conventional wisdom was that Lewis didn't have a chance against the handsome, light-skinned, sophisticated Bond, who was so much better known.

With the same dogged determination that had gotten him through all the violence and tragedy of his early years in the movement, Lewis campaigned door-to-door, night and day. He won the seat, and three decades later it is his to have for as long as he wants. In the House, Lewis is, by his own description, "an off-the-charts liberal." He advocates national health insurance, gay rights, and voting reform. He opposed both wars against Iraq and voted against President Bill Clinton on reforming welfare. He refused to join the Million Man March because it was led by Louis Farrakhan, who would not embrace nonviolence.

While some on Capitol Hill may question Lewis's votes, no one challenges his integrity or moral authority, which have drawn praise across the whole political spectrum. A Republican congressman says, "He's sort of antipolitical, antiego. He's not a glib guy . . . and that's an asset. When he speaks, it's solid, soulful, socially conscious stuff."

Looking back, Lewis now says, "There have been

unbelievable changes for the better in politics and in the economy. But back in the Sixties, people had a sense of hope. I think we've lost that. Something died in America in 1968, and we haven't been able to bring it back. Many of us still believe that good and right will still prevail, but we don't have the same spirit."

That is evident when Lewis talks about the American underclass—both black and white. "We need to build a coalition around poor blacks, poor whites, poor Hispanics. But there's no movement to address that.

"[Hurricane] Katrina reminded us of the permanence of race and poverty in American life, but we don't have the political voice of a Robert Kennedy or George McGovern to address that.

"Barack Obama's candidacy could have a profound effect—if other young black professionals rise up and take their place in public service. I think he should spend as much time encouraging a new breed of leaders as he does in talking about other issues.

"Too many successful blacks have no idea what we went through. Too many black middle-class parents are trying to shield their children from the harsh truths of the past. I read somewhere [that] some young black students didn't really know what Dr. King did. They thought he fought slavery!"

The congressman isn't volunteering to lead any new movements, but his early days taught him that "we need to return to the tenets of nonviolence. It's not old-fashioned to be nice to each other. We need, in the black communities, a revolution of values.

"Too many black males are in jail and not being fathers. Black organizations, such as One Hundred

Black Men, are trying to address that, but we need more one-on-one mentoring to show the way."

Lewis endorses Bill Cosby's message of tough love. The popular and wealthy entertainer exhorts black families to emphasize studying at home, regular attendance in school, and good work habits. "It's important to listen to the Bill Cosbys of the world and others who speak the truth about responsibility, about saving money, about the importance of education," he says. "It's time for liberals to speak out on these issues. Some things need to be said.

"Nineteen sixty-eight," he says, "was a year that changed my life"—and now this aging symbol of personal courage and moral authority plainly believes it's time for a new generation to "get in the way." Recalling how his parents and grandparents had warned him not to "get in the way," John Lewis smiles and says, "Well, it's time for people to get in the way again."

Reverend Andrew Young

John Lewis's friend the Reverend Andrew Young is also a scarred survivor of those early years of the civil rights movement, and the last surviving member of Dr. King's inner circle at the Southern Christian Leadership Council (SCLC), the organization King established in 1957 to coordinate nonviolent protest among local groups throughout the South.

Young, who had been raised in an integrated neighborhood in New Orleans where his father was a dentist, was King's unofficial chief of staff and the mod-

Reverend Andrew Young accompanies
Dr. Martin Luther King Jr. at a press conference
in Chicago, 1967.

Interviewing Coretta Scott King and
Martin Luther "Daddy" King Sr.

erate voice that constantly worried about the firebrands trying to steer the movement into potentially explosive situations. Young understood how important it was to stay on a steady course that would keep sympathetic whites on board.

When the black power advocates such as Stokely Carmichael started to set a different, militant tone for the movement, Young wasn't concerned. "We didn't pay much attention to them," he says. "They were all talk. They really didn't **do** anything. They resented us as old ministers with families who were still getting most of the press."

Young was far more concerned about the push to get Dr. King involved in the antiwar movement and the social problems of the cities in the North. As he says, "I thought we had more than enough to do at home." Many supporters believed that by speaking out against the war in Vietnam—still a controversial stance at the time—Dr. King would undermine public support for the civil rights agenda he was also advancing. King thought otherwise, so in April 1967, during a passionate speech at the Riverside Church in Manhattan, he formally condemned the war, saying, "My conscience leaves me no other choice."

During the speech, he also called the U.S. government "the greatest purveyor of violence in the world today," a charge that, Young recalls, put him at odds with LBJ, the thin-skinned president (who had pushed the Civil Rights Act through Congress three years earlier), and the FBI and its prurient director, J. Edgar Hoover.

What troubled Young was Bobby Kennedy's insistence that the Southern Christian Leadership Conference move into the North. "I resented the fact that Kennedy said we had neglected Northern cities. I thought, 'Well, damn, **you** were the attorney general, with the federal budget and the whole army. What about **your** role?'

"We were about forty poverty-stricken rabble-rousers who were hanging together by the skin of our teeth. Most of us were ministers with families. I was making just eight thousand dollars a year, and I had a wife and three children. So now, suddenly, on a budget of four hundred thousand a year, we're in the Southeast, Mississippi, we move into Chicago—we take on Vietnam—and James Meredith gets shot on his one-man March Against Fear in Mississippi, and Stokely Carmichael is raising his fist and shouting, 'Black Power.' "

The ominous rise of the black power movement galvanized many young African-Americans, but it also scared away many whites who wanted to help.

My memory of Andy Young during the Sixties is always the same. He was the handsome, boyish minister with a frown on his face walking alongside Dr. King. He was the in-house worrier. Forty years later, he tells me, "Black power advocates were always talking about charging the police. That was stupid and suicidal thinking. It's what we called a 'freedom high.' They'd get so emotionally worked up with their newfound freedom and courage that they'd get irrational, and that would get them killed."

Young, sitting comfortably in a private club in the heart of Atlanta's bustling high-rise district, surrounded by an integrated luncheon crowd of business-men, remembers, "We tried to protect them from themselves. We'd say, 'There's a systematic pattern to segregation that is depriving you of your right to vote, your children of their right to an education, your parents to any rights of self-respect, and you're taking it in and doing nothing. If you're planning to do something violent, go away from us and do it elsewhere. If you're not going to do something serious, either join us or get the hell out of the way.' "

Dr. King's Poor People's Campaign—an attack on economic inequality that culminated in the Poor People's March on Washington, a mass demonstration by poor people, black and white, from across the country—was struggling when he decided to defy a federal injunction against demonstrating in Memphis during a sanitation workers' strike. It was April 1968, and King was exhausted by the constant travel and the growing competition within the community between the causes of racial justice and the war in Vietnam.

The night he arrived in Memphis, King wanted to skip a rally at a Masonic temple. He said he was too tired, but his aides, including Andy Young, persuaded him to go, because the hall was already packed with the faithful.

Memphis was on edge. City officials worried that there could be violence, and death threats were a daily concern for Dr. King's traveling band of organizers. That was the setting for what became Dr. King's final speech, in which he said: "I may not get there with you. But I want you to know tonight, that we, as a people, will get to the promised land."

The next evening Young was in the courtyard of the Lorraine Motel, a minority-owned business in the south end of downtown, where Dr. King had spent the day preparing for the SCLC's demonstration on behalf of the garbage workers. In the early evening, Dr. King was standing on the balcony outside his room, chatting with Young and Jesse Jackson, who were in the parking lot below. He asked a local musician to sing "Precious Lord, Take My Hand" at a dinner that night in the home of a Memphis minister.

At that moment James Earl Ray, who had checked into a rooming house on the same street under an alias, fired one shot, killing King instantly.

As Andrew Young rushed to King's side, attempting to stanch the bleeding from a massive facial wound, his worst fears were realized. After all the years of death threats, someone had finally succeeded.

Like John Lewis, Andy Young now sought solace in activity, throwing himself into Robert Kennedy's presidential campaign. At first, he says, "I was very suspicious of Kennedy. He had pushed us into the North when it wasn't wise. During his brother's administration, he often thought we were going too far, too fast. If Martin had lived, and if LBJ had decided to run again that fall, I believe Martin would have supported President Johnson."

But Bobby's reaction to Dr. King's death, and his soulful speech to the stunned black audience in Indianapolis, put Kennedy in a new light with Young.

John Lewis personally escorted Bobby and his wife, Ethel, to Atlanta to meet with King's widow, Coretta Scott King, and attend the funeral. So Young had developed a new caring and regard for Kennedy when the awful news of his assassination came from California on June 5, just two months after Memphis.

Young says, "We never took time after Martin's death to grieve because there was so much to do. We were exhausted and filled with grief, but we kept going, and so when Robert Kennedy was killed, we just fell apart. We were just going through the motions, and that lasted for me for a year."

The death of Dr. King on that April night in Memphis, and the assassination of Bobby Kennedy two months later, was a staggering loss for the country and for American liberalism. Kennedy and King could appeal to the center as well as to the left and mobilize those forces against the conservative tide that was about to sweep the nation.

A year later Andrew Young was, as he describes it, "sort of pushed into running for Congress" from Georgia. No one could have imagined then that Young would go on to have one of the most distinguished public service careers of the second half of the twentieth century. He served in the U.S. Congress, as mayor of Atlanta, and as the U.S. ambassador to the United Nations.

Now the elder statesman of the civil rights movement, Andrew Young has built a prosperous business consulting with American companies hoping to expand in Africa. He continues to make his headquarters in Atlanta, a city he praises as a model for what Dr. King had in mind. "In Atlanta we're just about where we expected to be," he says. "It's working here in business, politics, education, religion. It's open to all people—and Martin would be amazed by some of the homes of the successful black people in Atlanta."

But Young has no illusions about the work still to be done. If Dr. King were starting over today, he says, "He'd begin where he left off—on poverty. He used to say, 'We cannot exist with islands of poverty in this great sea of wealth.' "

Young blames much of the black poverty in America on the well-intentioned but misguided government policies of the Sixties, particularly the controversial Aid to Families with Dependent Children (AFDC). "Young black mothers couldn't get government help if they lived with their mother or if there was an employed man in the house. It broke up the old grandmother network that had served the black community for so long, and it discouraged fathers from taking responsibility, and it shackled young mothers." Those same policies led to a widespread sense of entitlement in the black community, and Young sees this entitlement as a destructive force that is passed along by black parents who had so little that they are too eager to believe their kids are entitled to anything they want.

Young says, "But no one can help us but us."

Throughout his life, Young has been an establishment figure within the black community, a minister of conservative personal values that reflect his middle-class upbringing, his seminary training, and his role as a voice of caution within the SCLC. Yet he's also an astute analyst of the changes in black culture.

When asked about the hip-hop fashions so popular among young urban black males today—the baggy, beltless pants, oversize shirts, elaborate cornrow hairstyles, and disdainful expressions—Young answers, "That's just a reflection of the prison culture, where so many black males are these days. You can't wear a belt in prison or carry a [hair] pick. Rap lyrics grow out of the resentment rappers feel about how they were raised, with no fathers at home and too many mothers who had too many boyfriends."

Young is encouraged, however, by the economic success of black entrepreneurs, including those coming out of the hip-hop culture, such as Russell Simmons, Sean "P. Diddy" Combs, and Jay-Z. Remembering the shortsighted attitudes of Southern businessmen who wanted to keep their lunch counters segregated, he says, "That sends a message about the greater cultural power of blacks. Dr. King used to say, 'When you integrate a lunch counter, you bring more customers.' And it's true. The black consumer market went from eighteen billion dollars to almost eight hundred billion in thirty-five years."

Young is especially heartened by how the opening of Mercedes and Honda auto plants in the South has brought in a new workforce free of most of the old racial stereotypes. "Blacks doing well in those kind of jobs—that's better than what we expected forty-five years ago. The South—places like Selma—it's different now."

Young is a big fan of Oprah Winfrey and her commitment to improving the lot of blacks here and abroad. He thinks she's an important part of the global village that he believes is necessary to raise the fortunes of black people. "She's part of a new model," he says.

He dismisses those who criticized Winfrey for committing forty million dollars to build a lavishly appointed school and leadership academy for poor young black girls in South Africa instead of at home. Winfrey made it clear that she was tired of spending money in inner-city schools, where, she said, "The sense that you need to learn just isn't there. If you ask the kids what they want or need, they will say an iPod or some sneakers. In South Africa they don't ask for money or toys. They ask for uniforms so they can go to school." She has promised to finance the girls' educations through college.

Young sees Winfrey's South African project as part of a global social revolution. "These women will be the leaders of South Africa someday," he says. "We also have Oprah Winfrey Scholars at Morehouse College in Atlanta, training women to be leaders here and in Africa."

Young is disappointed that many successful young blacks in America have no appreciation of all that went before. He was incensed when one of Atlanta's black colleges wanted to honor Dr. King and Malcolm X in the same ceremony. "Dr. King had a Ph.D.," he says, "and did much more for this country and the civil rights movement." But he doesn't seem angry about the absence of understanding among many successful young blacks about how hard it was to create a climate in which they could prosper. He seems more puzzled by it, as when he says, "I'm not sure Tiger Woods has any idea who I am; we've never met."

Nonetheless, Andrew Young remains upbeat. He says, "I'm determined to be an optimist."

Tom Turnipseed

In 1966, as I was driving from Atlanta to Los Angeles to begin my new assignment at NBC, I was stuck for a time on a road in northern Alabama behind a farmer on a tractor. His denim jacket covered the tractor seat, but just as I was about to pass, a gust of wind lifted the jacket to uncover a bold sticker that read WALLACE FOR PRESIDENT.

That would be George Corley Wallace, elected Alabama's governor four times, in 1963, 1971, 1975, and again in 1983. He also ran unsuccessfully as a presidential candidate four times.

Wallace was little known nationally when as governor he first won the hearts of segregationists on June 11, 1963, by standing in a schoolhouse door to defy a federal order to integrate Alabama's public schools. The fact that it was mostly a theatrical gesture did nothing to diminish its effectiveness. If he failed to turn back the U.S. marshals sent by President Kennedy, his standing as a segregationist and champion of states' rights soared among those determined to prevent change and keep black citizens "in their place."

In 1968 the pugnacious Wallace ran for president as the nominee of the American Independent Party. He offered himself as an alternative to the two major parties. As he put it, "Yes, they've looked down their nose at you and me for a long time—the Republicans and Democrats. Well, we're going to show them there are a lot of rednecks in this country."

He was surrounded by a posse of smart, hard-eyed men. These weren't "piney-woods rednecks." They were lawyers and businessmen, shrewd and calculating and suspicious of television networks and mainstream newspapers. They concentrated on the blue-collar neighborhoods of their home region and the industrial North and California, where so many white Southerners had settled after World War II.

During one of Wallace's campaign swings through Los Angeles County, I met his campaign organizer, a genial man with a name that seemed to have been made up: Tom Turnipseed. He was friendlier than the others in the Wallace camp, eager to talk about Alabama football and the Crimson Tide's legendary coach Paul "Bear" Bryant.

He introduced reporters to Wallace, who relished lecturing us on his appeal to "real Americans" and predicting that we would do stories about his country table manners rather than his views, all the while sucking contemptuously on a toothpick.

I often wondered how someone like Turnipseed could work for Wallace and share his views. A few years later I discovered that he had asked himself the same question.

An Alabama native, Tom Turnipseed was the grandson of a wizard in the Ku Klux Klan. When he asked his father about his grandfather's role in the Klan, he was told, "There used to be a lot of good people in the Klan, they did a lot of good." He was about seven at the time, and he failed to ask exactly how his father defined "good."

His grandfather came into sharper focus later, when Turnipseed learned that he had killed a young black man for sassing him at a neighborhood store. The grandfather, known by that ubiquitous Southern endearment "Big Daddy," was convicted of second-degree murder, but was pardoned by the governor of Alabama.

Turnipseed's father was an agricultural scientist at Auburn University and, as Tom recalls, had a different view of blacks. He didn't follow Big Daddy into the Klan, and he often told his son, "Blacks are good people."

Nonetheless, even as Turnipseed proudly recounts his father's moderate views, he freely acknowledges that he was much more the grandson than the son where race was concerned. "I became a very, very rabid racist," he says. "But I was in total denial. I didn't think I was a racist. I would argue, 'I am **not** racist.' But I now realize I was.

"It was all tied up in the Confederacy, our heritage . . . your ancestors fighting for our land. As a kid, I'd go to the Blue-Gray football game in Montgomery, and it was a big thing to cheer for the Gray against the North. I will never forget how big the North-South deal was." The Blue-Gray game, which ended in 2003, was an annual college all-star game that was slow to integrate its teams. Later, it became a showcase for black players from small schools who might not otherwise be seen by NFL scouts. The big college all-star game is now divided between teams from the East and West.

After graduating from the University of North Carolina law school, Turnipseed moved to South Carolina and became involved in the campaign to get tax-exempt status for private all-white academies as an

Governor George Wallace of Georgia during the presidential campaign of 1968, with campaign organizer Tom Turnipseed, wearing glasses, and a supporter from Alabama, Oscar Harper, at his side

Tom Turnipseed today (left), with his cousin Morris Dees, head of Southern Poverty Law Center

alternative to the court-ordered integration of public schools. "We never admitted the race factor," he says. "We claimed we were interested in a lower teacher-pupil ratio—but the real reason was all racist.

"In the low country of South Carolina, where they had huge plantations, you also had an enormous concentration of African-Americans, so when the white professional class set up their segregated academies, they also withdrew their support for the public schools, leaving them poor and still segregated, as they are today.

"They had secondhand books, secondhand everything—the whole idea of public education was not to educate them so they would keep doing menial work. I am not surprised. Hell, it's been going on for 350 years."

Turnipseed's work with the South Carolina Independent School Association got the attention of George Wallace's brother, Jack, who was organizing a similar effort in Alabama. When he invited Turnipseed to join Wallace's 1968 presidential campaign, Tom Turnipseed was flattered and interested.

"I liked him. He was standing up for the South. I was impressed with some of the people who worked for him, real sharp Alabama guys, very professional. You think of the Wallace campaign as a bunch of jerks and rednecks, but some of these guys were much better than that; they just had been brought up in the racist culture."

Turnipseed also affirms that there were hard-core bigots in the Wallace camp—Klan wizards and racist sheriffs, including Selma sheriff Jim Clark, a notorious symbol of bloody attacks on black protestors.

Turnipseed claims that Wallace accepted their support but warned his campaign aides to keep their distance from them. Apparently even extremists could recognize extremism.

The true tone and real intent of the Wallace campaign could not be contained, however. It transcended the South. Turnipseed remembers a conversation with a Polish-American club member in Massachusetts who eagerly signed up for the Wallace campaign. He offered free use of the club hall for a rally and then said he had a question.

"He said, 'One thing I want to know,' " Turnipseed recalls. " 'When Governor Wallace becomes president'—and I swear to God he said this—'he's gonna line up all those niggers and shoot them, isn't he?' And I said, 'Oh, no, sir—we're not that way at all,' but I saw right then, good Lord, this stuff had gone way too far."

Turnipseed says Wallace was a very "skillful politician who knew how to reach out to people—particularly poor white people—and get at their innermost feelings and exploit them.

"During the campaign, his wife, Cornelia, would say, 'Couth him up a little'—move him to the middle, away from being such a racist. But Wallace knew what he was doing. He had all the rhetoric, like: 'They [referring to the media and the so-called eastern establishment] look down their noses at us and call us peckerwoods and lint heads. We're none of that. We're just as cultured and just as refined as they are.' "

Wallace's campaign strategy was to win enough

electoral votes away from Nixon and Humphrey to force the election into the House of Representatives, where he felt he'd have a real forum for his issues.

But the Nixon campaign had other ideas. As Turnipseed says, "We got killed. The Nixon campaign developed a Southern strategy, putting [South Carolina Republican senator] Strom Thurmond on television in a whole bunch of states that were very close. Old Strom'd come on TV and say, 'Well, you know, the governor is a good man, stands for the same things Nixon does—but Wallace can't get elected, and Nixon can. Don't waste your vote.' With the race thing, the Nixon campaign took the Wallace message and co-opted it.

"As a result, the party of Abraham Lincoln became the party of David Duke [the Louisiana Klansman] and Trent Lott. The poor white guys who had voted for Roosevelt went for Nixon. These same poor working-class whites had exactly the same economic interests as the blacks, but they were divided by race.

"That's now your red states—race and religion equals red. It's a powerful combination: a fear of blacks and a fear of going to hell."

Tom Turnipseed's conversion came when he returned to South Carolina and his law practice. He carried memories of what he calls "the raw hatred" on the faces of the Wallace supporters. His racist past began to drop away when he took on a case against utility companies that were charging higher rates for poorer, mostly black customers. Turnipseed could no longer be in denial about his own views when he began to confront the brutal truths about race and oppression. "I knew what racism was because I'd been such a racist, and although I personally didn't like violence, I knew violence and the threat of violence were what held the whole system in place. Some of the folks I met, it got you to thinking, 'God, this is just over the top.'"

He admits that his biggest problem was convincing liberals and rednecks alike that he was sincere in his new beliefs. "Some of these white liberals from way back yonder—I'm even more progressive than they are, but they're suspicious." Turnipseed got involved in politics, at one point even winning a seat in the South Carolina state senate. But whenever he lost a close race, he says, "the vote that would beat me would be the racist redneck vote, because they considered me a turncoat."

His standing with that crowd wasn't helped when he joined forces with the NAACP to call for the removal of the Confederate flag from atop the South Carolina state capitol. He likened flying the Stars and Bars to flying a swastika over the modern German parliament. "That flag is symbolic," he says, "of what happened to black people."

He also worked with the progressive Southern Poverty Law Center on race-related issues across the South, including death-penalty cases. He was the host of a radio talk show and once appeared on the floor of the state senate to sing country songs of protest against rising gasoline prices.

Race, however, is his greatest passion. He believes the United States is doing better in some areas, but not economically—although he's quick to add, "Poor white people are getting screwed, too." Yet he insists that what he calls "the song of the South" is still being sung and listened to across the region today: Divide the races by keeping the poor whites thinking the poor blacks are going to take over.

Though Turnipseed is a John Edwards supporter, he's intrigued by Barack Obama and believes "a lot" of white people would vote for him. "I don't know what chances he's got," he says. "I like the fact he's so new. And with that international background, his dad being from Africa, his white mom, his upbringing in Hawaii, I'm glad he's running."

As for his old boss, Turnipseed says he was disappointed in George Wallace's so-called deathbed apologies on race. "He apologized somewhat," Turnipseed says, "but what I really wanted him to do was to become an advocate for racial justice, which he never did do." It wasn't enough for him that Wallace said "I'm sorry." The former aide and campaign strategist is blunt. "Hell," he says, "what we did, and what I was involved in and I helped carry out, deserves more action than an apology. It deserves justice for the injustices we did."

Turnipseed, who's still attacked as a traitor on racist blogs, claims to have many African-American friends but says, "There's no way to know how they feel unless you're one of them. You try to empathize, but unless you're black and feel the looks and the turn-downs, the put-downs and the discrimination, there's no way to understand it."

Reverend Thomas Gilmore

Tom Gilmore, like Tom Turnipseed, is an Alabama native, but he saw the South from the other side of the racial prism.

Gilmore was born in the heart of the Alabama Black Belt, in Greene County, about eighty miles southwest of Birmingham, in 1941. He lived in an extended family presided over by his grandmother on the forty-acre farm his ancestors had acquired during Reconstruction.

His first memories are of the great postwar exodus of black males, headed north for the promise of good jobs and a better life in places such as Chicago and Detroit. "That was," he says, "the great call of men in my county in my childhood." Gilmore himself had heard of those faraway places, but he knew only the life around his farm, his grandmother, and the nearby white-owned farms where she occasionally worked in the cotton fields. "It was work," he says, "but it was also a lot of love we don't see anymore. I couldn't have had any more love or security. It's the kind of feeling one longs for these days."

He knew the world was a far from friendly place for blacks. "I'm convinced white families in the Black Belt were meaner because we were a threat. They knew change was coming. They tried to keep their feet on our necks." Gilmore's own acute race awareness began when he was about ten and started accompanying his grandmother to a white-owned farm where he played with the owner's young daughters while his grand-mother worked the fields.

Suddenly, one day, the play stopped. The owner in-structed Gilmore to deliver some things to his daughter, whom he now referred to as "**Miss** Betty Jo." That was a signal to Gilmore that the childhood friendship was officially terminated.

There were other, more ominous signs. His grand-mother told about two cousins who disappeared while taking a canoe across the river to visit friends in an-other county. She told that story often, to warn Gilmore against breaking the rules of race that defined their county.

When he was thirteen, a white worker in the cot-ton fields of a neighborhood farm picked a fight with a young black worker. The black man easily defeated his antagonist, but the white man later tipped over a boat in the middle of the river and attempted to drown him. The incident so enraged Gilmore's grandmother that she organized other black workers and encouraged them not to pick cotton on that farm. That was Gilmore's first experience with the tactics of a boycott, and it made a strong impression on him.

In August 1955, a young black man from Chicago named Emmett Till visited his relatives in the Delta region of Mississippi. He allegedly whistled at the wife of a white man outside a country store, and reports of this shocking transgression were soon ricocheting all around the deeply racist area. The woman's husband and his half brothers kidnapped Till, beat him brutally, and threw his weighted body into a river. Till's kidnapping and disappearance mobilized the local black community to demand answers and justice.

The kidnappers insisted they had let him go, but no one believed that. When Till's badly battered body was recovered, his mother instructed the funeral home that she wanted an open casket so the world could see what had happened to her son. **Jet**, the Fifties' most popular black magazine, helped fulfill her wish by publishing graphic photographs of the terribly disfigured young man.

The suspects were brought to trial, and despite the overwhelming evidence against them, the all-white jury acquitted them in just over an hour. Later, the half brothers, protected by the prohibition against double jeopardy, admitted in a paid magazine interview that they had killed Till because they were enraged by his refusal to be intimidated.

Tom Gilmore was fourteen—almost the same age as Till—when he began reading about the fate of Emmett Till. He recalls, "We didn't know much about Dr. King's movement up in Montgomery, but we got really worked up about Emmett Till. I had been baptized the same year he had, and the Lord had been waiting for me to understand. So here I come. I just knew it was one of the ugliest things I'd ever heard of.

"I began to take note of what people said, how they acted. The lady who ran the store near our school, where we spent our pennies, nickels, and dimes, was so rude. I started connecting dots. I started seeing the world differently. I started seeing it better after Till was murdered."

"The Third (3rd) of May Is Gilmore Day"

VOTE FOR

Thomas E. Gilmore

FOR SHERIFF
of Greene County

"GET MORE JUSTICE
WITH GILMORE!"

Subject to Action of the Democratic
Primaries, May, 1966

Pd. Pol. Adv. by Friends of Thomas E. Gilmore

Thomas Gilmore's first bid for Greene County sheriff in 1966: "Every one of these experiences gave me more courage."

Candidate Gilmore (right) speaks with a farmer before the 1966 election in Greene County, Alabama.

When Gilmore left Greene County to begin seminary training in Selma, he came into contact with leaders of Dr. King's Southern Christian Leadership Conference, which had successfully organized the Montgomery bus boycott after Rosa Parks's arrest for refusing to give up her seat at the front of the bus.

Gilmore was so inspired by the SCLC campaign that when he graduated from the seminary in 1962, he went back to Greene County to help organize community reaction against the shooting death of a black man by a local white man. The sheriff wasn't interested in investigating, and when Gilmore and others tried to get the case to a grand jury, they failed.

Gilmore was disheartened and he decided to leave for California, where many Southern blacks had migrated hoping to find a better racial climate. "I wanted to go where racism wasn't so blatant," he says, "but I found out racism was everywhere." He arrived in Los Angeles just three years before Watts blew up. Before that happened, however, Gilmore had already decided to move again—this time to the East Coast—still hoping to escape the all-day-every-day trial by color he was experiencing.

He made a brief stop in Greene County, Alabama, to catch up with family and friends. While he was there, he had a chance encounter with a couple of Alabama state troopers that changed his life forever.

As he drove into a local service station, his car splashed some rainwater on a state police patrol car that was arriving at the same time.

Two white troopers emerged from the squad car,

and one confronted him. "Hey, nigger, you're gonna wash my car!" he said.

Gilmore responded, "I'll pay for your car wash, but I'm sorry, I'm not gonna wash your car."

The trooper slammed him against the gasoline pump and said again, "Nigger, you're gonna wash my car."

Gilmore tried to stay calm and slowly reached into his pocket to get some money for the car wash. The trooper exploded once more: "Nigger, don't put your hand in your pocket!"

As Gilmore tried to explain, the other trooper quietly said to his colleague, "Hey, c'mon—this nigger's not worth it." But Gilmore knew the incident was not over. Everything about him sent one signal to these troopers: out-of-state troublemaker. His car was pointed toward Selma, the scene of many protest confrontations; he had California plates; and he had a full beard. "I looked everything like a civil rights worker," he says.

In fact he had grown the beard because he wanted to imitate his hero, Bill Russell, the peerless center and later coach of the Boston Celtics. But he knew the troopers sized him up as just one more black protestor driving in to cause trouble. His antagonist said, "Nigger, I know where you're headed, and if I see you again, I'm gonna blow your damn brains out."

Unknowingly, that racist Alabama cop turned one black man, who had intended only to spend a few quiet days back home before heading east, into a committed activist who decided to stay on and do what he could to change things. As Gilmore puts it, "That nailed me to

Alabama. I decided to stay and get involved in the movement. **He** made that decision for me."

Gilmore went to the SCLC office, and they put him in charge of expanding the voter registration rolls in his home territory of Greene County. Prior to implementation of the Voting Rights Act in 1965, fewer than 6 percent of the county's black voters were registered. They faced poll taxes and literacy tests, and if they got past those and actually turned up at the polls, they risked losing their homes for some trumped-up reason.

It was hard work, much harder than Gilmore had anticipated. "I didn't know how mean people could be. They knew something I didn't yet know. They knew how important it would it be if black people got the vote. God, they were mean-spirited."

Gilmore was arrested, jailed, and beaten a few times—what he calls his "badges of honor." He remembers that the local sheriff and district attorney ignored pleas to arrest a white policeman who had injured a young black woman during a march. When Gilmore and others organized a sit-in at the sheriff's office, the sheriff, a three-hundred-pound ex–football player, started beating him to the floor. "Every one of these experiences gave me more courage," he says. "And God bless Dr. King's soul. He was there to raise our hopes and to give us courage. He really made us feel it was right to die for what you believed in if the cause was good enough."

After all his traumatic experiences with Alabama law enforcement, Gilmore decided to run for sheriff of Greene County himself. He lost when the incumbent hired a black deputy just before Election Day and won enough of the black vote to stay in office.

In 1970 he ran again. Although he admired Stokely Carmichael, he resisted his suggestion to run as a Black Panther Party candidate. Instead, he joined a ticket organized by the National Democratic Party of Alabama, an integrated political organization. This time he won the election and made a vow to himself. "I knew I was not going to be an everyday, regular sheriff. I didn't know how I was going to do it, but I knew I wasn't going to do it traditionally."

Gilmore credits Dr. King's philosophy of nonviolence, and his own son Ronald, for a decision he made shortly after pinning on his badge.

Ronald had drawn a picture of his dad wearing two big guns and a ten-gallon hat. Gilmore didn't like that image, so he gave up his weapons. "I decided I would try to conduct myself in a way that would reflect my life with Dr. King. I didn't go around telling people I was a nonviolent sheriff. They could see I didn't have a gun. I went out and made arrests without a gun. I thought, 'Man, if you can get through the civil rights movement without a gun, you can get through this.' And it worked because the Lord favored me and the people supported me."

He had an unlikely ally during his tenure as sheriff: Ralph Banks, the same white DA who earlier had refused to prosecute or even investigate the charges of police brutality. It was in Banks's office that Gilmore had been beaten for sitting in as a protest. But when Dr. King was assassinated, Banks came to the SCLC headquarters to express his condolences, saying, "I don't agree with what you guys are doing, or with what Dr. King has been doing, but I know you work for him, and you've been hurt."

When Gilmore became sheriff, he worked closely with Banks and came to respect him. Gilmore says, "We came close to being friends. I liked Ralph a lot, and I think he liked me a lot."

Tom Gilmore served as Greene County sheriff for twelve years before retiring in 1982 to become the minister at Birmingham's Ensley Baptist Church.

He's ambivalent about the state of race relations and the conditions in many black neighborhoods. "I remember when the signs said 'colored' and 'white,' but now I can eat and sleep wherever my money permits me to. So I know how far we've come.

"I am disappointed by the level of integration. I think there's a lot of good stuff happening, but not at the level of Dr. King's dream. We need to work more at getting people together, talking, working together."

Forty years after Dr. King's death, the Reverend Thomas Gilmore still sees in the new South the old divisions that refuse to go away. He remembers sitting at home watching the Florida Gators upset the Ohio State Buckeyes for the national collegiate football championship in 2007. The local station cut to a sports bar to get reaction, and to Gilmore's annoyance, "a young white kid was in the bar . . . and he says, 'We beat them Yankees!' I think, 'What the heck is he talking about? You've got white guys and black guys on both teams, kids from Ohio going to Florida, kids from Florida going to Ohio. What is he talking about—'We beat them Yankees?' "

Gilmore is particularly saddened by the cruel realities of poverty in black communities. "I think if Dr. King is weeping, it is because things have not changed for the poor. The poor are getting poorer, and the rich are getting richer. We're creating a kind of culture where people make it the best way they can, even if it's outside the law, which causes all kinds of havoc in the community.

"Maybe there needs to be another Poor People's Campaign. Government needs to refocus itself—take some of the money being spent in other places and do what Franklin Roosevelt did with the WPA [a Federal program to bring work to the unemployed during the Great Depression by building parks, highways, and other public works projects].

"I'm for affirmative action. Justice [Clarence] Thomas has acted crazy on this issue. He probably got where he is because of affirmative action."

As for arguments that more black people have to assume more personal responsibility, Gilmore asks, "Pull himself up by his bootstraps? A guy might not have any boots, and somebody is probably trying to take away his straps!" He recognizes that, thanks in no small part to his grandmother's strong hand, he got to where he is by taking responsibility for his life. But he remembers that the message was always "Make one step and God will make two." That's no longer heard in the black community, he says. "The world has changed, so you take the shortcut. God is not so important. Family is not so important."

Gilmore grew up without a father, so he knows success is possible in a single-mother household. But the odds are, as he says, "almost zero. How do we overcome that? I've been disappointed at how few black men volunteer to support young black people. Unless it's basketball or football, they don't come out. It's always the mamas and the grandmamas."

Gilmore, who's now sixty-six years old, grew up idolizing Martin Luther King Jr. and the leadership of the civil rights movement. Now, he says, "We could use a whole bunch of role models. It doesn't matter what color they come in."

The Fracture of 1968: The Noisy Masses versus the Silent Majority

So tonight, to you, the great silent majority of my fellow Americans, I ask for your support. I pledged in my campaign for the presidency to end the war in a way that we could win the peace. I have initiated a plan of action which will enable me to keep that pledge. The more support I can have from the American people, the sooner that pledge can be redeemed. For the more divided we are at home, the less likely the enemy is to negotiate at Paris.

—PRESIDENT RICHARD M. NIXON,
IN AN ADDRESS TO THE NATION
ON NOVEMBER 3, 1969

I think we can end the divisions within the United States. What I think is quite clear is that we can work together in the last analysis. And that what has been going on with . . . the disenchantment with our society, the divisions—whether it's between blacks and whites, between the poor and the more affluent, or between age groups, or in the war in Vietnam—that we can work together. We are a great country, an unselfish country and a compassionate country. And I intend to make that my basis for running.

—SENATOR ROBERT F. KENNEDY, THANKING SUPPORTERS DURING HIS VICTORY SPEECH FOLLOWING THE CALIFORNIA PRIMARY ON JUNE 5, 1968

As 1967 GAVE WAY TO 1968, great gaping chasms opened across the political and cultural landscape of America. More campuses were roiled by student revolts. In Washington the debate on Vietnam grew increasingly strident, with prominent members of President Johnson's own party now openly challenging his assurances that the war was moving in America's favor.

The war induced rage, real and exaggerated, that in turn became a license for public behavior that just a year before would have been considered totally out of bounds. Now wherever the young gathered to protest the war or to celebrate their defiance of convention, the heady, sweet aroma of marijuana frequently permeated the air. As thick as the smoke were the four-letter words that suddenly were everywhere.

That year I was at a party in San Francisco where a rebellious young writer was holding forth on the immorality of the war and using the F-word as if it were "and" or "the." Finally, a slightly older matron protested: "I love the word when it is put into practice and as an active verb, but I dislike hearing it as a noun, comma, and exclamation point." The writer was momentarily stunned but resumed his obscene soliloquy a short while later.

Change was everywhere, and the effect was disorienting. Nowhere was the change more dramatic than in the Democratic Party. In retrospect, this was the end of the long-running successful formula that had been cobbled together by President Franklin Roosevelt in

the wake of the Great Depression. After three decades
the New Deal coalition of farm and labor, of urban
Catholics and ethnic minorities, was coming to an
end. While the right side of the American political
spectrum remained rooted to its traditional beliefs,
those on the left turned on one another in a ferocious
internecine fight triggered mostly by Vietnam.

In the simplest terms, it came down to the incumbent party of President Lyndon Johnson and his vice
president, Hubert Humphrey, pitted against the antiwar challengers personified by two Democratic senators, Eugene McCarthy of Minnesota and Robert F.
Kennedy of New York and Camelot.

The battle between McCarthy and Kennedy for
the opportunity to lead the charge against Johnson
and Humphrey was a saga of Shakespearean proportions. The antagonists shared an Irish ancestry and a
Catholic faith but little else.

Robert Kennedy was a tightly bound bundle of
energy and passion with his heart on his sleeve.
McCarthy was cool and cerebral; if it was hard to tell
where his heart was, his brain was always on display.
They didn't like each other, and it showed.

Their contest carried them across America in common pursuit of the presidency against the backdrop of
a convulsive, corrosive, costly war and the murder of
the nation's leading moral proponent of racial harmony.

Among political reporters who covered him in
1968, there was a consensus that the campaign, with its
great issues and its equally great uncertainties, changed
Robert Kennedy. He was no longer just the tough little brother of a martyred president, impatient with

those outside his inner circle and ruthless in his pursuit of what he wanted. He could make fun of himself on the campaign trail—his duets with the pro football player Roosevelt Grier singing "There is a Rose in Spanish Harlem"—were so bad they were hilarious. He spoke movingly about justice, race, poverty, and the consequences of war; his speeches had a raw, emotional quality.

I had heard all about the Kennedy clan's ability to seduce journalists and draw them into their inner circle. But in my first encounters with the senator in the months before he decided to make the run for the White House—reporting on his tour of California Indian reservations and schools and covering his appearances at various campuses—I hadn't exactly been at the top of his dance card. He was manifestly not happy with the crowd of unruly newcomers that had suddenly joined his familiar state and Senate press corps, and that seemed to know hundreds of different ways of asking only one question: Are you or aren't you going to run for president?

At an Indian school in Riverside County, he tried hard to strike up a dialogue with the students, whose reticence made it difficult. As he was leaving, a young Indian with a deformed foot was struggling to catch up so he could get his picture taken with the senator. I caught up to Kennedy and said, "Can you wait a moment so I can take your picture with this young man?" Kennedy glowered at me but waited. I took the picture and the Indian boy retreated, happy with his souvenir. Kennedy walked over to me and said, "Don't ever do that to me again."

I was conflicted. I greatly admired his interest in Indians, and I was sure he was still struggling with the loss of his brother. I had also heard from other correspondents that he was tired of everyone following him around badgering him about his political plans.

Looking back, I can better understand his frustration. He was a man in search of new meaning in his life. Yet wherever he went, and however hard he tried to make a very personal connection to, say, a group of shy Indian students, there we were, this thundering herd of reporters, photographers, and cameramen. We were an unavoidable but unwelcome part of his life during a difficult time.

By the spring of 1968, of course, he was a candidate. He was roundly criticized for opportunism when he entered the race only after McCarthy's strong showing in the New Hampshire primary had demonstrated LBJ's vulnerability. Nonetheless, when Kennedy made his first trip to California as a presidential candidate, he might as well have been a rock star, considering the size of the crowds he drew and the frenzy he created.

Local television news coverage showed the tousle-haired young senator in shirtsleeves in an enthusiastic but unruly crowd of admirers from the campuses and the Hispanic and African-American communities.

On the surface it looked like a hugely successful trip, but his California handlers were worried. A Kennedy campaign insider told me the next day, "We know we can get the Chicano [as Hispanics were called then] and black vote, but we can't afford to turn off the blue-collar vote."

When Kennedy resumed campaigning in California, his appearances were directed more at the working-class families that might have been unsettled by the strong ethnic and student elements of his following.

He even changed his appearance. His hair was still long, but now it was trimmed above his collar and combed into place. During an interview, my colleague Bob Abernethy opened by asking if the shorter hair was a political statement. Kennedy replied, "No, I just got a haircut."

Bob quickly rejoined, "For the first time?"

After the interview in the NBC studio, Kennedy spoke with Rafer Johnson, the former Olympic gold-medal decathlon champion and a novice sportscaster at KNBC. Kennedy wanted Johnson to join his campaign.

I knew that Rafer was conflicted. He had spent a lot of time with Bobby and Ethel and their kids, but his career in broadcasting was just taking off, and it would be hard to restart if he left to be at Kennedy's side.

I had advised Rafer, in the interest of his career, to resist Kennedy's overtures, but as I watched the two of them, I recognized I was wrong. They were as familiar with each other as brothers. I could tell Rafer wanted to work with his friend, so I walked over to say that I had changed my mind about his joining the campaign. Rafer turned to Kennedy and said, "You know, Tom grew up among Indians in South Dakota. He knows a lot about the conditions on the reservations."

When I made a few observations to confirm Rafer's introduction, Kennedy seemed to see me in a new light.

During their visits to the NBC studios, the contrasts between Kennedy and McCarthy were striking. Bobby always arrived in a vortex of activity, surrounded by various aides holding briefing papers, filling him in on the latest developments, while a close friend stood by with a tuna-fish sandwich on a paper plate just in case the senator felt peckish. There were a lot of whispered conversations and a lot of intense rushing around, with the senator, like his staff, in shirtsleeves.

McCarthy, on the other hand, would simply stroll in, accompanied by only one aide. He was pleasant but not chatty, and he never removed his jacket. On the air, he had the demeanor of a dean at a very good small college. When an answer required a date, he would say, "Nineteen hundred and fifty-two" instead of "nineteen fifty-two" or " 'fifty-two." He often avoided direct eye contact with his questioner. He laughed easily, but the joke usually involved a cutting reference to his opponent or some aspect of the campaign.

Jeff Greenfield and Sam Brown

It was not only the two protagonists—Kennedy and McCarthy—that made the 1968 campaign for the Democratic presidential nomination so memorable for those of us covering them. Nor was it just the vital issues of war and peace, race and economic justice. The two campaigns also had the best and brightest of the liberal side of a new generation working for them.

On the McCarthy side, Sam Brown, a twenty-five-year-old Harvard theology student from Iowa, was writing the new rules of campaign organization and getting out the vote.

On the Kennedy side, a bright, quick-witted New

Yorker who had gone to the University of Wisconsin and Yale Law School was writing eloquent campaign speeches against the war and pushing his candidate hard on generational issues. Jeff Greenfield, who went on to become one of the country's best-known broadcast news commentators, hadn't grown up a Kennedy fan. His parents, old-fashioned liberals from the West Side of Manhattan, were more than a little suspicious of Kennedy's early association with Senator Joe McCarthy, a Kennedy family friend. There was also the matter of Kennedy's Roman Catholic faith. Greenfield, who is Jewish, says, "I saw him as the kind of guy that chased me home from school yelling that I killed Jesus."

But by the time Greenfield was at law school in 1965, Kennedy was saying some things he hadn't heard from conventional liberals. "He was challenging big-government liberalism, saying it hadn't worked. He was saying the welfare system was really hurting the people it was supposed to have helped. I remember him saying, 'How can we give Negroes a check and then tell them there are no jobs?' That appealed to me.

"Kennedy had this idea of community development, such as Bedford-Stuyvesant in New York [where he established a project to help the poor black residents of that Brooklyn community help themselves]. He didn't just want the government to write a check, and some of the traditional FDR Democrats had a lot of trouble with that."

Robert Kennedy is remembered now as a martyred symbol of the last glorious days of American liberalism, but as Greenfield reminds everyone, he was also a critic of liberal orthodoxy. "I actually heard him hammer a federal education official for the failure of inner-city schools, telling the guy, 'When I go into the ghetto, two thirds of the people I meet hate two things: the welfare system and the education system. Why can't we do better? We're failing these people, not helping them.' "

That unconventional thinking appealed to Greenfield and also to a nerdy young high school student in Salt Lake City. Karl Rove, who was already fascinated by politics at an age when his contemporaries were much more interested in the opposite sex, told me he found Kennedy easily the most appealing of the Democratic prospects. "I felt the loss when he died," Rove said.

It's doubtful that Rove ever would have worked for Bobby Kennedy, but Greenfield saw the senator's office as an exciting opportunity. He had worked particularly hard in the class of a law professor who had connections in Kennedy's Senate office, and when he applied for a position as a legislative fellow (similar to a law clerk), his professor wrote a glowing recommendation.

In June 1967, Jeff Greenfield, a twenty-four-year-old political greenhorn, went to work for Senator Kennedy. Within a few days, because more senior staffers were unavailable, he was pressed into duty to write a speech on Vietnam. He was told to check out the senator's earlier speeches and to run his finished product past Richard Goodwin, a legendary speechwriter, and Arthur Schlesinger, Jr., the Pulitzer Prize–winning historian.

As Greenfield says now, "I was thinking, 'This is

pretty cool.' " He felt he was prepared for the assignment. After all, as editor of **The Daily Cardinal** at the University of Wisconsin, he had written a much-admired editorial expressing skepticism of the U.S. role in Vietnam. He also admits to writing a commentary that the Beatles wouldn't last six months. "I figure if I had to be right about one and wrong about the other, the war was the one to be right about."

He quickly became very fond of the senator, who, Greenfield remembers, had an impish side. "We were talking about the rigors of law school research, and Bobby joined us." Someone asked him if he also had disliked the drudgery of doing research during his law school days, and Kennedy laughed, saying, "No, I just had someone do it for me," mocking his family's wealth and large personal staff of aides and servants.

"He was kidding," Greenfield says, "but by saying that, he was, in his own way, dealing with what we all secretly thought about his wealth." In another discussion, they were talking about an issue, and Kennedy said, "We couldn't win this if I had a million dollars." He paused, smiled, and said, "Well, I do have a million dollars, and we still can't win."

Greenfield says he most relished seeing Kennedy on college campuses. "And there were a lot of them, even though Kennedy kept saying, 'Don't keep sending me to the students.' He really enjoyed those sessions, and he almost always surprised his audience.

"He would say things like 'I want to know who's for the escalation of the war in Vietnam.' There'd be a big [raising of hands]—half the students. . . . Then he'd say, 'How many of you are for student defer-

Jeff Greenfield at age twenty-four, a speechwriter for Robert F. Kennedy's presidential campaign in 1968

Greenfield, now a CBS senior political correspondent, in New York City in April 2007

ments?' And everybody would raise their hand. He'd say, 'I'm against them.' They'd boo. And he'd say, 'Well, here's why.' And he'd go into the riff about who got student deferments and who didn't. How poor whites and blacks and browns were fighting in Vietnam because they couldn't do this [get deferments].

"At least on one occasion, he actually said, 'You know, when my eldest son is ready for college he's going to get in no matter what because his father is a wealthy and powerful man. But that's not true for a lot of people. And this is a generation that claims you're fighting for justice—well, where's the justice here?'"

Greenfield was there for all the highs and lows of Bobby Kennedy's eighty-five-day presidential campaign, grinding out speeches, staying up late, and getting an up-close-and-personal view of the frequently unprintable on-the-road behavior of the national press corps. On Greenfield's first campaign trip, a veteran correspondent who was a notorious womanizer took him aside and said, "Remember, kid, what happens west of the Potomac stays west of the Potomac."

It was a campaign with an evangelical fervor and an existential id. No one knew how things would end up in August in Chicago, the site of the Democratic convention. Humphrey had all the power of the old politics behind him. He also had the not inconsiderable advantage of being an incumbent vice president. Greenfield says, "I think Kennedy thought he could pull it off. We were working hard to line up the big states—Pennsylvania and Ohio—to go with what we'd won in the primaries. But Kennedy always said, 'Daley is the ball game.'" That was Richard J. Daley, the

Chicago mayor who had been so helpful to John F. Kennedy in his 1960 campaign, delivering Illinois's electoral vote late on election night.

Daley was an old-guard political boss, with enormous power within the ruling circle of the Democratic Party establishment. As mayor of the host city for the 1968 Democratic convention, he would be expected to control the ebb and flow of the floor proceedings.

The mano a mano duel between Kennedy and McCarthy—according to Greenfield, Kennedy considered McCarthy a dilettante—all came down to California and the first Tuesday in June 1968. The week before, McCarthy had swept the primary in Oregon, a progressive state with very few of Kennedy's base of black and working-poor constituents.

The Kennedy campaign was counting on charisma and momentum to make up for the absence of a first-rate organization in Oregon, but they failed to pull it off. It was the first time Bobby Kennedy had ever lost an election—indeed, the first time any Kennedy had lost a political election of any kind—and it was a serious setback as his campaign headed down the coast to California.

Kennedy knew he had to win California to have any chance of capturing the nomination, and his campaign took on an even greater urgency. I remember standing in the back of his headquarters when he made his first California appearance after the Oregon defeat. His volunteers, a mix of Hollywood-starlet look-alikes, scruffy farmworkers, and black union members, were nervous and subdued as he described the task before them. A prominent Southern California lawyer with significant connections to money and star power was standing next to me. "Are you going to get involved with them?" I asked. He smiled ruefully. "If you weren't in the inner circle last week, you won't get in now." The campaign did have an "us against the world, backs to the wall" quality.

On Primary Day, June 5, Kennedy relaxed at the Malibu beach home of filmmaker John Frankenheimer. He had to rescue one of his children from a vicious undertow in the surf. His wife, Ethel, who was pregnant with their eleventh child, prepared for the election-night party at the Ambassador Hotel.

At NBC News in Burbank, the network coverage would be anchored by Frank McGee; Bob Abernethy and I would handle the local coverage. The signs were strong for a Kennedy win, especially after a weekend debate in which he had challenged McCarthy's suggestion to move thousands of residents out of Watts and into Orange County.

Some critics saw this challenge as a betrayal of opportunities for poor blacks. But, as Greenfield says, "Kennedy honestly thought such a move would be a disaster. They'd be transported to an alien culture with no jobs and few friends. Why not concentrate on improving the conditions in the neighborhoods where they already lived?"

As soon as the polls closed, it was clear that Kennedy was going to win. The victory would be uncomfortably narrow—it ended up being 46 to 42 percent. But it was a win, and the stage was now set for a showdown at the Chicago convention. It was the end of Act Two, when, as playwrights say, a gun should go off.

Greenfield was trying on a new Nehru jacket for a victory party at the Factory, a ramshackle but hugely popular nightclub owned by, among others, actor Paul Newman and JFK's former press secretary (and, briefly, U.S. senator) Pierre Salinger. I was at my anchor desk, waiting to go on right after Kennedy ended his victory speech to the exultant crowd in the Ambassador Hotel ballroom with the triumphant exhortation "On to Chicago!" He waved and left the stage, and we began wrapping up our coverage.

Suddenly, the screen erupted into chaos. Someone had been shot. "It's Kennedy! He's hit in the hip. Thank God, he can survive that. No! He's been hit in the head."

I raced to the police station where the assassin, Sirhan Sirhan, had been taken. I could see the California Assembly Speaker, Jesse Unruh, one of Kennedy's close friends, at the end of a long hallway, his head bowed, talking to a policeman. The early description of the gunman was "short, swarthy—looks like a Chicano." It didn't make sense.

I asked Unruh what he knew. "He's an Arab," he said. It turned out that Sirhan was a Palestinian immigrant who had been working in the hotel's kitchen. He had apparently been making "RFK must die" entries in his diary for some time. He had been prevented from firing another shot because Roosevelt "Rosey" Grier and Rafer Johnson had wrestled him to the ground.

Rafer later told me that once he got the small pistol away from Sirhan, he jammed it into his suit-jacket pocket and rushed to the hospital where Kennedy had been taken. "I really did believe Bobby would make it,"

Sam Brown, leader of the "Mobe," the
Mobilization to End the War in Vietnam

Sam Brown today,
still true to his Democratic roots

he said. After a long night Rafer went home to get some sleep. He hung his jacket over a chair and went to bed. When he awoke a few hours later and put the jacket back on, he realized he still had Sirhan's gun in his pocket. He immediately took it to the police.

The area across the street from the Good Samaritan Hospital became a gathering place for the press, the mourners, and the merely curious. It was a surreal scene at the hospital entrance, with the Kennedy family and their famous friends—George Plimpton was among them—arriving and hurrying through the doors.

The networks set up live cameras for updates through the night.

Kennedy lingered for twenty-five hours before the announcement came that he was dead. He was just forty-two years old.

The next day, the motorcade traveled the Santa Monica Freeway, carrying his body to Los Angeles International Airport for the long flight back to New York. David Brinkley said sadly on NBC that for the second time in less than five years, a Kennedy widow was in a car behind her husband's body on a freeway headed west to make the flight east for his funeral.

The year was just half over and across the country Americans were wondering what more could happen. For some of them, the rest of 1968 would be even more trying personally than the first six months.

Sam Brown, a native of Council Bluffs, Iowa, across the river from Omaha, was a Harvard Divinity School student with an undergraduate degree from The University of Redlands in California and a master's from Rutgers. By the time he arrived at Harvard, he had become a disciple of Allard Lowenstein, a seminal figure of the new forms of political activism in America. Lowenstein was a brilliant, charismatic, complex figure, a kind of Pied Piper for the restless young people who were drawn to the great moral issues of the day, first the civil rights movement and then the Vietnam War. Lowenstein had attended a New York prep school, then the University of North Carolina and Yale Law School. He became president of the National Student Association (NSA), an organization designed to put young student leaders in touch with rising leaders in other countries so they could get to know one another on the way up.

The NSA turned out to be a CIA front, organized and funded by the spy agency as a means of getting access to potential foreign leaders at an early stage of their careers. There is no evidence that Lowenstein was aware of the CIA connection at the time of his involvement, and in the early Sixties the association didn't damage his reputation. A few years later, given the manic antiestablishment, antigovernment spirit of the antiwar movement, even the suspicion of any CIA connection might have caused him to be cast out.

Instead, Lowenstein was able to pursue his crusade to deny Lyndon Johnson the Democratic presidential nomination in 1968. It was an audacious—not to say quixotic—undertaking, given an incumbent's almost unlimited power over the nominating convention and its delegates. But Al Lowenstein approached his mission with the physical, rhetorical, and intellectual commitment of a man possessed.

No one was as important as Allard Lowenstein in creating the new political culture that grew out of the American left's opposition to the war. He was a tireless intellectual, racing across the country, mobilizing opposition to the war, and imploring everyone to join the crusade. His speeches were unlike any that seasoned old pols and reporters had ever heard. They were delivered at a rapid-fire pace as he stood before an audience, the bows of his glasses not quite reaching his ears and his small frame all but obscured by the podium. He made the case for opposition to the war and the retirement of Lyndon Johnson with evangelical fervor.

During his first appearance at a California Democratic Party gathering, I was mesmerized by his style and the passion of his challenge to join the crusade against a sitting president. He had no illusions about the difficulty of the task, so he wound up his remarks by asking the audience to recall the last scene in the classic movie **The African Queen**. Humphrey Bogart and Katharine Hepburn have just survived a harrowing journey up a dangerous river and finally made their way into the calm waters of Lake Victoria. They are rescued by a big boat, and when the captain asks where they have been, Hepburn tells him they have navigated the dangerous river. The captain responds, "But that is impossible."

Lowenstein paused. He looked at his audience. And he slowly repeated Hepburn's declarative response: "Nevertheless!"

The young audience was electrified and broke into wild applause. But Carl Greenberg, the venerated senior political correspondent for the **Los Angeles Times** who had been covering campaigns since the 1940s, watched all of this in confusion and walked over to me. "I think I'm getting old. I don't get all this new rhetoric," he said.

Gene McCarthy was more susceptible to Lowenstein's words and ways. When he went to New Hampshire to challenge President Johnson in the state's primary, Sam Brown went along. He was studying at Harvard on a Rockefeller Foundation grant: "The Rockefellers paid for me to go organize against the war."

Brown remembers, "Johnson had dismissed antiwar protestors as lefty, crazy wackos, so we decided to put together student body presidents and college newspaper editors . . . to say, 'Wait a minute, Mr. President. We got elected, and we're the voice of the people. We're not crazies.' We were trying to move everything to the middle."

New Hampshire was ideally located for an organizer such as Sam Brown. It was within easy reach of many colleges, including some of the most politically active in the country—Harvard, Brown, Yale, Amherst, and Wellesley. Sam Brown promised the campaign elders that if they produced the money and the candidate, he'd produce the energy.

But he understood that student energy could cut both ways. Arriving students were instructed to get "Clean for Gene." That meant they would have to look more like preppies than scraggly goatherds just in from a hard season in the mountains. It wasn't always easy to persuade a student after a long bus ride that appearance was as important as message, but "Clean for

Gene" was nonnegotiable, and it quickly captured the attention of the national media and demonstrated that the students were serious.

Brown laughs now, recalling that New Hampshire became a road trip for reasons other than politics. He is persuaded, undoubtedly correctly, that a lot of male students thought, "Hey, I'm twenty-two, the testosterone is running pretty high, and a lot of pretty, liberal women are going to be on the bus." The sexual revolution was well under way.

Brown also says it wasn't an accident that the largest demonstrations occurred in the warm days of early October rather than in the frigid days of December, when final exams were looming. Nonetheless, the McCarthy campaign and the role of the students are now a fixed part of American political lore.

Brown was conflicted about McCarthy, as were many in the campaign. "I liked him very much," he says. "He had a great sense of humor . . . and this complexity and candor. A moral purist's dream." But there were flaws. "He hated the Kennedys, and I wanted to say, 'Get over it. This is not a campaign about you. It's about changing the country.' McCarthy could be enormously appealing—but president? Eh."

By June, Brown had decided that if Bobby Kennedy won the California primary, he would make the switch and join his campaign. On the night of the primary, he was having a late dinner with friends when he heard the news that Bobby had been shot.

Sam Brown stumbled outside and sat down on a curb, fighting for breath. "When you're twenty-four or twenty-five and you don't have a lot of experience with death, even in your own family, nothing can capture how you feel. It wasn't just about Bobby. It was about losing a sense of hope, a sense of what was possible."

The Democratic National Convention was in Chicago in the last week of August 1968. I was riding in the press section of a stretch Boeing jetliner that was carrying the California delegation to the convention. These were not typical boisterous delegates off to choose a nominee and have a good time. They were, for the most part, Bobby Kennedy delegates, still in shock and deep in grief as a result of his murder only six weeks earlier. Now Bobby was gone; McCarthy had all but imploded; and the despised Vice President Humphrey had a lock on the nomination.

Rafer Johnson was a member of the delegation. Rafer, always a quiet man, simply nodded when sympathizers came up to him to express their condolences. He was embarrassed when Paul Schrade, a California union official who had been wounded in the shooting melee, approached to thank him for getting control of the gun, saying, "You saved my life; I was in the line of fire."

Rafer quietly confided to me, "I didn't save any lives." He could think only about the death of his friend and the devastating effect on Ethel Kennedy and their ten children (soon to be eleven), who thought of Rafer as practically a member of the family.

It was an awkward time for the McCarthy delegates on the plane. Their candidate had been characteristically undemonstrative at the time of Kennedy's death, and in the weeks leading up to the convention he had all but disappeared instead of carrying on the challenge to President Johnson. With Kennedy gone and McCarthy light in delegates, the chances of stopping Hubert Humphrey were slim at best. Lyndon Johnson may have gone off to his ranch in Texas, but on the telephone and through his network of party bosses he kept a tight rein on the nominating process.

In retrospect, our flight from California was on a glide path heading toward a monumental crack-up of the modern Democratic Party.

The Democrats had survived the Great Depression, World War II, the Eisenhower years, and the death of their young prince, John F. Kennedy. But another tragic war and a generation of young people coming of age with no connection to, or even memory of, the Depression and World War II were blowing great holes in the party's traditional structure. The LBJ wing was hunkered down. The new, young, and impatient Kennedy and McCarthy crowd mounted assault after assault, but the old guard hung on.

There was a rumor, encouraged all week by the anti-Humphrey forces, that Ted Kennedy would make a dramatic trip to the convention to run for the nomination and carry the family flame back to the White House.

Senator George McGovern offered himself as a surrogate for Bobby Kennedy, a gesture that was welcomed by some but was, in the end, futile.

Mayor Daley had put the Chicago police department on full alert. Streets were cordoned off. Cops were on every corner, watching as long-haired kids carrying backpacks and shouting, "Peace now!" mingled with earnest middle-class couples who had come to show their solidarity with the antiwar movement. At first it was all relatively festive, a movable feast of political theater in the clear and uncommonly comfortable August weather in the heart of one of America's great cities. But the climate very quickly took an ugly turn.

Some of the elders in the antiwar leadership, such as David Dellinger, had counseled the young people to protest with dignity, but that message was overwhelmed by the steadily rising tension between the working-class Chicago cops and the younger demonstrators, most of whom came from college campuses. There were also the provocateurs such as the yippies, led by Abbie Hoffman, a cunning master of public theater, and his sidekick, Jerry Rubin.

They waved Vietcong flags and toted around a pig called Pigasus the Immortal as their presidential candidate. They claimed that they planned to dump LSD in the city water supply, stage mass sexual orgies in the streets, and have yippie women pose as prostitutes to lure delegates. Chicago would be the moment when the whole world was watching, and they were going to make the most of it.

On the first morning, I walked out of our hotel—which was surrounded by Chicago police as part of the security arrangements—to see a white cop arguing with a black mailman at the entrance to an office building across the street. The policeman was ordering the mailman out of the area because he didn't have an official Chicago police credential. The mailman politely explained that he was a federal employee, delivering the mail, and that he didn't need a credential. He refused to leave until he had finished his delivery rounds, so the cop threw him to the ground, handcuffed him, and called in a squad car to haul him away.

I went over to get details and to ask why the mailman had been arrested. The policeman shrugged and said, "He wouldn't leave." "But he's a mailman," I said as the postal worker watched from the ground. The policeman replied, "Well, we have our orders."

By Wednesday night, the fuse was burning toward what would become the lasting, explosive image of the Chicago convention. A huge crowd of protestors gathered in Grant Park across from the Hilton Hotel, many of them waving Vietcong flags and shouting "Pigs, pigs!" at the police. Despite the counsel from older activists to remain nonviolent, many in the crowd clearly intended to taunt the police into a violent reaction, thinking it would help make their case against Mayor Daley and his wing of the party.

Be careful what you wish for. For the next eighteen minutes, the world saw what the official investigating commission would later call "a police riot" as cops chased and clubbed anyone and everyone on the street, including reporters and curious bystanders. The police chased them into restaurants and hotel lobbies, smashing windows and invading hotel rooms. The air was thick with tear gas, and the streets were covered with shattered glass and abandoned backpacks, PEACE NOW! signs, and fragments of tie-dyed shirts. The shocking violent images that played out on television around the world might as well have been coming from Prague or Soweto.

One of the unlikely victims of the tear-gas attacks was Pat Buchanan, the conservative counselor and

Nixon speechwriter who had come to Chicago to be the on-site eyes and ears for his boss. He laughs now as he remembers how the demonstrators all thought he was an FBI agent, dressed as he always was in a blue suit, white shirt, and red tie, with neatly slicked-down hair. "I got gassed right outside what I called the Comrade Hilton," he says, "and ran into the hotel restrooms to get some relief. I found myself standing next to Tom Wicker of **The New York Times** at the sinks, so I thought, 'Well, everyone's getting it tonight.'"

Nixon, who publicly claimed he had no interest in what the Democrats were up to, was with his friend Bebe Rebozo in Florida. They called Buchanan every hour for an update on the mayhem they were seeing on television.

The police said later that they were pelted with ashtrays thrown from hotel windows and bags of urine and feces; sprayed with caustic substances such as oven cleaner; and insulted with cries of "Oink, oink, motherfucker."

Larry Evans, now a retired Chicago police detective, was on riot duty that night, as he had been for most of the week. When we talked in the summer of 2007 just across the street from the Hilton hotel in Chicago, he questioned the decision of his superiors for the police to move in on the demonstrators.

Evans says the situation was tense but manageable up to that point. However, he also strongly defends the police tactics once they did go after the protestors. "We were being hit with everything coming out of the Hilton windows," he said. "My lieutenant was just standing there and he was punched in the face."

Evans, who now has two sons on the Chicago police force, admits it was rough for a while, but he says he went home that night, got something to eat, and went to bed, thinking the police had done their job well.

The biggest loser that night was Hubert Humphrey, who got the presidential nomination but presided over a public relations disaster and inherited a deeply wounded Democratic Party. During his acceptance speech—a moment that should have represented the pinnacle of his political career and his first chance to enlist the American people on his side—the cameras kept cutting away to the scenes of chaos and carnage just outside the hall. Presidential candidates count on a post-convention "boost" in the polls to help jump start their campaigns. Hubert Humphrey had to spend the next two months trying to explain, and get beyond, the debacle that had shocked most of the electorate.

Hundreds of demonstrators were arrested and hauled off to a central holding facility. Robert Pirie, a member of a prominent Chicago family and a senior adviser to the McCarthy campaign, arrived early the next morning, his pockets stuffed with cash, to bail out as many as he could. Pirie remembers, "At first I couldn't get in, but a police sergeant who had worked for my family cleared the way and said, 'You'd better get your people out of here, because these cops know they can do what they want down here.' "

Before the night was out, Pirie had bailed out, as he recalls, seventy-five to a hundred people. When he got back to the Hilton, he saw the full extent of the physical and emotional carnage in the lobby and was furious that Humphrey, who had stayed upstairs, had not intervened to help. "I was so pissed I decided not to support him in the fall," he said. "In retrospect, that was a mistake."

Sam Brown was in Chicago for the convention, still working for McCarthy, when the streets erupted. At the Hilton, he collected the room keys of McCarthy staffers and handed them out to protestors so they could find sanctuary inside. "It was horrible . . . and it left wounds in the Democratic Party that made it impossible for Humphrey to win," he says.

Now, almost forty years later, Brown has a better understanding of the police psyche. "I am still outraged. I don't forgive the police for a second, but I do have some sense they were working-class guys—they'd worked all their lives—and here were these kids, many of whom had elite educations and all the privileges in the world and the freedom to be demonstrating at the Hilton, trying to tear down everything the cops had worked for."

Dan Walker, later the governor of Illinois, headed the commission investigating the riots. He said later, "The FBI took literally all of the wild hippie claims that they would parade naked girls on the beach to distract the conventioneers . . . that they would poison the water supply. All of those were taken as gospel . . . although it was just great drama to Abbie Hoffman and Jerry Rubin. They wanted to drive the police up the wall and they succeeded."

Walker concluded it was a "police riot" but also said, "I don't really fault the police for being worried. What I do fault them for is the failure to make advance preparations. . . . My study showed that the majority of the police department behaved very responsibly. Just some guys got out of hand."

Evans, the retired Chicago detective, just shakes his head when I raise the Walker Commission during our conversation. "He just used that investigation to run for governor," he said, "and then what happened?"

Walker was elected Illinois governor for one term as a reform Democrat who took on the Daley machine. There was talk of a run for the White House.

But when he was defeated in the next Democratic primary by a Daley ally, Walker divorced his wife, married a flamboyant socialite, went into the savings and loan business, and led the high life.

In 1987 he was sentenced to seven years in federal prison for a series of financial crimes committed while trying to keep his businesses and his lifestyle afloat.

Has there ever been a week in Chicago or in any American city where so many lives were set on so many different courses?

I still have many small movies playing in my memory of what I saw as I spent the week moving between the streets and the convention hall.

In a room off the convention floor, Jesse Unruh, Pierre Salinger, Frank Mankiewicz—Bobby's press secretary, who had announced his death—George McGovern, and other antiwar Democrats held a last-minute meeting to see if there were any scenarios by which they could head off Humphrey's nomination.

They were individually and collectively worn out. The conversations were desultory and subdued. Their common sense—and their political smarts—told them that the nomination was locked up. Lyndon Johnson,

Hubert Humphrey, Richard J. Daley, and the other lions of the old Democratic Party had prevailed.

The Democratic Party would never be the same. The LBJ-Humphrey-Daley wing blamed the antiwar activists and counterculture revolutionaries for rejecting the traditional components of FDR's winning electoral coalition. The Southern Democrats, the working class, and the main-street Democrats who had sent four Democratic administrations to Washington felt few ties with the rampaging radicals calling themselves Democrats while they trashed the party's convention and turned the Second City into a combat zone.

That imagery could not have been more striking than the night after the Grant Park melee. Michigan Avenue was now a tangle of concertina wire and armed jeeps. A long row of Illinois National Guardsmen kept the demonstrators on the lake side of the street, and as I walked between them and the crowds in the park, I thought, "This is the dividing line of America." Armed troops in the street, no doubt many of them having joined the Guard for the extra pay, were holding back young people their own age, many of them students in colleges and universities that were beyond the reach of the Guardsmen.

That standoff in Chicago was a precursor to a tragedy two years later at Kent State University, in Ohio, when National Guardsmen, in a similar situation, opened fire with live ammunition on student demonstrators and killed four of them.

Chicago was an exhausting emotional experience for everyone involved, and as I learned when I stopped in South Dakota to visit my family en route back to

California, the emotions were not confined to the Windy City.

When I visited my parents I thought that, given their opposition to the war, they would be sympathetic to the protestors. Instead, my father, a self-made man, was furious with their foul language, the flag burning, and what he saw as the defiance of law and order.

We had a loud, bitter argument that my wife remembers to this day as the most upsetting time in our long family relationship. By the next day I recognized in Red Brokaw's reaction the wounds the Democrats would carry out of Chicago.

Mayor Richard M. Daley and William Daley

Two young men who had front-row seats at that convention are Mayor Richard M. Daley of Chicago and his younger brother, Bill. Now aged sixty-five and fifty-nine respectively, the Daley boys were in their twenties then, the same age as most of the demonstrators and Guardsmen outside, as they sat in the Illinois delegation right behind their father, Mayor Daley, when he had his famous televised exchange with Senator Abraham Ribicoff of Connecticut.

Ribicoff was nominating George McGovern in a last-minute long-shot bid as a stand-in for Bobby Kennedy to wrest the party's presidential candidacy away from Humphrey.

Looking directly at Daley the elder, Ribicoff said,

"With George McGovern as president of the United States, we wouldn't have these Gestapo tactics in the streets of Chicago."

The mayor and his supporters were furious. They began shouting a response to Ribicoff that was out of the range of the microphones but was clear to anyone watching who had even the most minimal ability to read lips and interpret body language. They appeared to be saying: "Fuck you, fuck you!" Others said they also heard anti-Semitic epithets coming from the Illinois delegation.

Richard and Bill Daley, dutiful sons in their suits and ties, sat silently behind their father. When a new generation of activist Democrats began to take over the party after 1968, no one would have guessed that Rich and Bill Daley would not only survive politically but would emerge as two of the most admired, powerful, and influential players in their party without compromising their family ties.

Rich Daley, as he's known, was elected Cook County district attorney in 1980 and to the first of his now six consecutive terms as mayor of Chicago in 1989. He's been in office almost as long as his father was, and he is widely credited with making Chicago a model modern metropolis. He champions school reform, sound environmental practices, and urban development that is both aesthetically striking and user-friendly. He's been featured in **Rolling Stone** as an environmental hero for his work in turning his city a deeper shade of green.

Bill, his younger brother, is a valued behind-the-scenes player. He was secretary of commerce in the

Clinton administration and chairman of Al Gore's presidential campaign in 2000.

He's now the Midwest chairman of JPMorgan Chase, the banking conglomerate, with a penthouse office overlooking the Chicago skyline. As a political operative and as a source for journalists, Bill has a banker's mien. He brings to the arena a clear-eyed assessment of risk and opportunity, value and liability.

Over the years, I've teased Bill about his father's response to Ribicoff, and he unfailingly insists that everyone has got it wrong: "Dad was saying, 'You **faker,** you. You **faker.**' " When the Democrats returned to Chicago for the first time after 1968—for the 1996 convention that nominated Bill Clinton for reelection—Bill Daley had a small lunch for a group of his reporter friends and gave us each a Chicago Police Department cap. That was his droll way of dealing with whatever questions might have been left over from 1968.

When I met the Daley brothers for breakfast on a sunny spring Chicago morning in 2007, we gathered in Bill's private dining room atop the JPMorgan Chase headquarters. Another skyscraper next door tops out just a few floors down, so it doesn't block Bill's commanding vista of the city and the Lake Michigan shoreline.

I said to Bill, "You're lucky that building wasn't higher; it would block your view." He smiled slightly and said, "Yeah, I think they wanted to go up a few extra floors, but for some reason, they couldn't get the necessary permits."

Mayor Rich Daley and his brother don't fit the stereotypes of Irish-American pols. There's no backslapping, boisterous greetings, or gossipy bombast. Politics is the family business, and they approach it in a businesslike way. Their personal relationship is strong but publicly low-key. They know who they are, and they see no need to rearrange their personalities or views to accommodate friends, much less strangers.

I ask when America in general and the Democratic Party in particular will finally get past the fallout from Vietnam. Bill answers quietly, "Not in our lifetime." The mayor nods his agreement, telling me later, "That war . . . tore the heart out of the country. Unfortunately, Democrats were a part of the problem—they didn't respect the sacrifice the men and women who were in the service gave. I hope the party is beginning to realize—and I think it is—we have to honor the idea of patriotism. We have a lot to learn from Vietnam." The mayor's son is in the 82nd Airborne—he joined after 9/11—but Daley honors his son's request not to talk about his service.

The mayor thinks that forty years after the 1968 convention, party membership doesn't mean what it once did. He cites the many different forms for choosing delegates to the nominating convention.

"Some are chosen in caucuses, twenty or thirty people sitting around a room; others are elected; some are appointed." So traditional conventions, in his view, are antiquities. He'd like to do away with conventions and replace them with a series of rallies across the country organized by the candidate who wins the nomination in the primaries. "That way," he says, "people can come together in their regions to see what the party is all about."

The mayor has expressed frustration with the groups that get their members elected convention delegates simply to help protect their special interests.

His Honor also chafes against what he considers the abundance of federal regulation that came out of the Sixties and Seventies. He leans forward and says to me, "We need to expand our airport to compete in the global economy. We're stuck here in all kinds of environmental and other regulations, but I go up to Canada, and Toronto modernized its airport in one year!"

The mayor is a big believer in power from the bottom up and not from Washington down. During our conversation he says, "We're promoting federal answers too much; it becomes too complex for the average person. They wonder, 'How does the federal government really affect my life?' "

He'd like to see the Democratic Party put a lot more emphasis on public education. "That has real value for the future," he says. "That will help take care of poor people—and that should be the soul of the party."

Among other initiatives, Daley has thousands of Chicago kids enrolled in Chinese-language programs because he believes strongly that they'll need Mandarin to be competitive in the coming global economy.

Most of all, the mayor wants his party to emphasize personal responsibility. "We should be talking about parents taking charge of their kids' lives. The people don't want everyone pointing fingers at everyone else."

His brother, Bill Daley, wants the party to be more

attentive to business interests. The morning we met, he was, in his understated way, enthusiastic about a recent appearance by Senator Clinton before an important Chicago business group. "They were impressed," he said. "We need more of that."

Six months later, Bill Daley had a surprise for Hillary. As close as he has been to the Clintons, Bill decided to back Barack Obama, the Illinois senator, for the Democratic presidential nomination.

It was a tough call for Daley to make to Hillary, but as a Chicago guy he felt he had to go with the hometown candidate instead of Senator Clinton, a Chicago native who now is a New Yorker.

He still admires Senator Clinton and he's been known to raise with friends the possibility of a Clinton-Obama ticket. Or is it the other way around? Either way, Bill Daley will be in the game.

I met a large cast of players in Chicago that August week in 1968, including Gloria Steinem. She walked into a room dressed in a leather miniskirt, wearing her trademark aviator glasses and just-so blond hair framing her cool cover-girl looks.

She was there as a journalist and she was just beginning her rise to fame as an advocate for the modern woman who wanted more choices in life. I quickly learned that Steinem may have looked like a model, but it was her writing and her intellectual commitment to advancing women's rights that would earn her a permanent and prominent place in the history of her time.

I also met Warren Beatty, who personified both

the carefully managed glamour of Hollywood's past and the emerging shape of its activist future. The year before, he had produced and starred in the groundbreaking hit movie **Bonnie and Clyde**. Beatty was every inch, and without any apologies, unquestionably a star. He combined the manners of a Virginia gentleman, reflecting his Old Dominion upbringing, with the grace of the athlete he once was (having been recruited to play football at Northwestern University). He was, as the saying goes, tall, dark, and handsome— a gifted actor with a playboy's reputation and a shrewd head for business. He was also just beginning to explore another interest that would become as prominent in his reputation as his movie roles and glamorous girlfriends. He was an increasingly conspicuous presence on the Hollywood left, a proud liberal, and the brother of actress Shirley MacLaine, who was already well established as a Democratic Party activist.

At the end of a raucous convention session the old Democratic Party bosses delivered the nomination to Vice President Hubert Humphrey—a final tribute to President Lyndon B. Johnson, who didn't dare to show his face in Chicago but was working the phones from his Texas ranch. The antiwar delegates faithful to Robert Kennedy and Gene McCarthy organized a candlelight march along Michigan Avenue.

I had arranged to meet Rafer Johnson and Roosevelt Grier to walk back to the hotel. When Rafer and Rosey appeared, they were accompanied by Shirley MacLaine and her brother. Beatty was dressed casually but elegantly—none of the torn jeans or baseball caps and nighttime sunglasses affected by contemporary celebrities. As we started our walk, he was in that zone reserved for the truly famous, part of the crowd but entirely on his own terms, never quite making eye contact with the constantly accumulating groupies and photographers surrounding our little posse.

The other delegates, who, moments before, had been debating the great moral and political issues of the day, interrupted their somber pilgrimage away from the convention to circle Beatty, whispering to one another, "It's **Clyde,** omigod, it's Warren Beatty." But they kept a respectful distance. The photographers were polite, although one of them was momentarily stunned when the massive Rosey Grier suddenly grabbed his camera and turned it on the crowd, scowling at first and then breaking into his familiar belly laugh. It was all light-hearted, and light-years away from the contemporary paparazzi frenzies surrounding even "B-List" celebrities.

That night, as we walked away from the wreckage of the convention and the badly fractured Democratic Party, Beatty was wondering aloud what would happen in the fall elections and commiserating with his sister, who said at one point, "So now I've seen a rigged convention," referring to Humphrey's nomination by delegates handpicked by party bosses.

When we reached the hotel, Beatty knew where he wanted to go next, at least that night. "There's a party at the Playboy Mansion," he said. "Who wants to go?" I was not part of that invitation, but I remember thinking it was a sign of the contradictory times in which we were living. Riots one night, parties at Hugh Hefner's pad the next one.

Beatty offered to help candidate Humphrey produce a campaign film if he would denounce the war, but the vice president hesitated, so Beatty went to Paris to make a movie with Elizabeth Taylor. He was not alone in his decision to walk away from the fall campaign.

Sam Brown refused to help Humphrey, a decision he now regrets. "It was just stupid," he says. "We didn't fully understand the stakes, and we were too focused on a single issue—Vietnam. And we weren't respectful enough of what Humphrey had done in the past, particularly on civil rights.

"But Vietnam was compelling. We had almost half a million troops there, and every community had someone. You could not not talk about it. So maybe the decision not to support Humphrey is understandable—if not defensible."

After the 1968 election, Brown returned to Harvard as a Fellow and volunteered time advising at a local mentoring center for young activists. But he was becoming increasingly disenchanted with the growing mindless extremism of many on the left. He remembers a student, the son of very wealthy parents, bursting into the mentoring center to proudly announce that he and some revolutionary Maoists had just poured sugar into the gas tanks of a local dry cleaner involved in a pay dispute with some of his workers.

Brown says he exploded. "For God's sake. This is a guy with four trucks to his name? This is going to further the revolution?" Still frustrated after all this time, Brown concludes, "It was just that infantile leftism. There was always that unwillingness to draw a line on the left—silly, self-destructive, and childish."

Brown believes the reason the right has been successful in distorting the views of the left is that the right is very quick to say, "This is not acceptable." He continues, "But on the left, you want to identify with the civil libertarian position, to be open-minded. But that shouldn't mean you're so open-minded that your brains fall out."

That was never clearer to him than in the fall of 1969, when he was running the Vietnam Moratorium and preparing for the big demonstration in Washington. A delegation from the radical group known as the Weathermen came to him and said, "We all stand in solidarity. We have a lot of people on the run or with large bail bonds because of a crackdown by the fascist pigs. We can allow this demonstration to go forward if you give us fifty thousand dollars."

Brown says, "I didn't give them the money. It was an example of how far things had gone. I said, 'Enough, already.'"

Pat Buchanan

As the Democrats continued to splinter into many pieces, the Republicans were facing some of their own struggles over the direction of the GOP.

The Republican convention had been held at the beginning of August, in Miami Beach. There had been the predicted but orderly triangular struggle for leadership among New York governor Nelson Rockefeller, the symbolic head of the fading eastern-establishment liberal wing of the party; California's new governor,

Ronald Reagan, representing the rise of a renewed conservative movement in the American West; and the man who cleverly managed to maintain loyalties in both camps, former vice president Richard Nixon.

From the outside, Nixon's nomination seemed almost surreal in light of his famous declaration only six years earlier, on the morning after being drubbed by Pat Brown in the California gubernatorial race, that the media wouldn't have Nixon "to kick around anymore" because this would be his "last press conference." As if to underscore the point, he even pulled up stakes and moved his family east to New York City, the unfriendly home turf of his longtime party rival Nelson Rockefeller.

But Nixon still had strong ties to the Republican Party establishment, and he had plotted his comeback carefully and thoughtfully. He had spent the better part of three years—1964 to 1967—crisscrossing the country, helping to raise money for Republican candidates and cementing ties with local party leaders. By the time 1968 rolled around, he had solidified the support and accumulated the chits that could pave the way to another shot at the presidency for him.

Rockefeller, as before where his great desire to occupy the Oval Office was concerned, showed that he had the ambition but lacked the will. As it became clear that the party had moved well beyond its old eastern establishment ties and that a real fight would have to be waged to wrest it back, he announced that he wouldn't be a candidate. The field was suddenly open to Nixon, the man whose political obituary had been written several years earlier.

The November 2, 1968, issue of the Nixon Agnew Elector, published by the campaign committee, hails Pat Buchanan's thirtieth birthday with a tribute to the "Ink-Stained Jet Setter."

THIRTY!

SKORPIOS IS NOT ONLY AN ISLAND, it's the swinging sign of the Zodiac under which Patrick Joseph Buchanan swung into the swing of life. His horoscope for November 2, 1968 reads: You are in a suspended period of angst, await-ing a major event whose outcome will reshape your life. Hang in there and keep your cool. The tall, dark man with whom your personal future is inextricably linked will emerge victorious in the very near future.

Nixon speechwriter Pat Buchanan at work in the White House, June 1969

Buchanan campaigning for the Republican presidential nomination in 1992

Nixon's campaign team was a mix of loyalists from his days in the Eisenhower administration and political friends from California, as well as some young men such as Pat Buchanan, the talented speechwriter with deeply conservative views and an encyclopedic knowledge of American politics. Buchanan had begun in December 1965 as a ghostwriter for Nixon's syndicated newspaper column and a traveling companion as the former vice president began his purposeful cross-country speaking trips for Republican candidates.

However, the New Nixon was, at heart and in his personality, actually the same old Nixon. Shortly after Ronald Reagan was installed as governor of California, his lieutenant governor, the estimable Robert Finch, a bright and decent man, arranged for a meeting between Nixon, who had been his friend and political mentor for many years, and the new governor.

Finch tipped me to this meeting "at the Grove," as he described it. I was then new to California and wondered why Nixon and Reagan would choose to meet in a famous Hollywood nightclub. Finch, of course, wasn't referring to the **Cocoanut** Grove but to the **Bohemian** Grove, an exclusive secret hideaway in the redwoods north of San Francisco where the rich and powerful gather every summer for fellowship and networking.

When Nixon arrived in San Francisco for the meeting, he agreed to see a few reporters at a side entrance to the St. Francis Hotel (the same entrance where President Gerald Ford was shot at by Sara Jane Moore in 1975). In the crush of cameras and reporters, I was pushed up so tightly against Nixon that we suddenly found ourselves face-to-face. I asked if he was going to discuss presidential politics with the new governor and what he expected the meeting to produce. To my astonishment, Nixon, who was wearing pancake makeup for this "impromptu" news conference, shook his head vigorously and, with his eyes fluttering as he looked at a point somewhere between my nose and my neck, said, "No, no politics. This is just a meeting between old friends." Then a quick, frozen smile.

It was my first close encounter with Nixon, and it reinforced everything I'd read about him. He could have just laughed and said something like "Why, whatever gave you that idea? Just because there's a presidential election next year, you think the popular new governor of California and I would talk politics?" followed by more laughter or even a roguish Rockefeller-like wink.

Reagan had been a model of cheerful and skillful disingenuousness on this same subject for the last eighteen months. Everyone knew that his "kitchen cabinet" of powerful California financial, oil, and automobile barons was already exploring his presidential chances with operatives from his political staff. But by humorously deflecting the rumors—instead of unconvincingly denying them—Reagan maintained the respect of the reporters, who appreciated that his job was to avoid answering the questions just as their job was to ask them.

As Buchanan now describes the Nixon camp's reaction to the rapid rise of Reagan, "We knew Nixon had a clean shot at the nomination in 1968. We thought we could beat Rockefeller easily, but there was that crazy character in California, Reagan. He could ignite, so I spent a lot of time courting the conservative commentators and columnists, mainly Bill Buckley and James J. Kilpatrick."

Buchanan had also developed a letter-writing relationship with Barry Goldwater, who retained a loyal following despite his disastrous landslide loss to Lyndon Johnson. Although Goldwater considered Nixon insufficiently conservative on many issues, he remained grateful for his loyal support throughout the 1964 convention and campaign when others, including the New York governor, hadn't been able to distance themselves far or fast enough from him. The Nixon team also recruited South Carolina's Strom Thurmond and Texas's bright new conservative star John Tower to help them hold the South, which turned out to be a key to beating Reagan at the convention in Miami.

California's Republican delegates chartered a plane with a press section for the flight to their convention in Miami Beach. When they arrived, they wanted to make a visual statement for our cameras. Cesar Chavez and his farmworkers' union had recently organized a California grape boycott against the big growers in the state's central valley. The white, wealthy California GOP delegates emerged from their plane conspicuously eating clusters of grapes.

One of the founding geniuses of modern Republican Party strategies, Stuart Spencer of California, always cringed whenever he saw such a display of disdain—it was, unfortunately, not atypical—within his party for the state's sizable and growing Hispanic population.

Spencer, who had managed Ronald Reagan's campaign for governor and later helped design George H. W. Bush's successful presidential campaign, saw the Hispanics, with their strong families, traditional values, and upfront patriotism, as natural constituents for the GOP.

The Republican convention had the air of a large suburban country club in the Fifties. The delegates were almost all white and male, affluent, and dressed as if Ike were still in the White House. Ralph Abernathy, Martin Luther King Jr.'s chief lieutenant, organized a Poor People's Campaign demonstration, but it received about the same respect among the delegates as the grape boycott. A black rally in Liberty City, one of Miami's poorest neighborhoods, blew up into a violent confrontation with local police, but the Republican delegates were barely aware of it.

Although his position was strong, Nixon was not yet home free when he arrived in Miami. Reagan's operatives still hoped to force a stalemate that could allow their man to present himself as the handsome cowboy riding in from the West to save the party. But the Nixon forces were relentlessly prepared. While Reagan's men tried to peel away delegates behind closed doors, Thurmond and Tower kept the South and Southwest in line for Nixon.

I was covering the California delegation. With the exception of Reagan's innermost circle—his so-called kitchen-cabinet members—most of the delegates spent their time soaking up the South Florida sun and organizing elaborate dinner parties in expensive restaurants.

Pat Buchanan was busy behind the scenes, promoting his choice for Nixon's running mate: Maryland's governor, Spiro T. Agnew. A tall, dapper local pol only two years into his first term in Annapolis, Agnew had no experience that would seem to qualify him to be placed a heartbeat away from the presidency. He had earlier been an active supporter of Nixon's archenemy Nelson Rockefeller, but because of Rocky's withdrawal from the race, the Maryland delegation arrived at the convention officially uncommitted. The Nixon people got to him, and when it was suggested that he might be considered for the number two spot on the ticket, he released his delegation and signaled that he was very interested.

Buchanan remembers that this little-known son of a Greek immigrant "was one guy who had been tough on demonstrators after the Maryland race riots. He could hold down the Wallace states since he was a border-state governor. But when we picked him, a lot of people went bananas. I can still see Mike Wallace ranting and raving." Buchanan laughs again heartily at the consternation the Agnew choice caused.

When the Agnew announcement was made the morning after Nixon's nomination, I was standing in the back of the room and waved to Nixon's press secretary, Ron Ziegler, who had been pressed into the campaign by Bob Haldeman, his boss at a Los Angeles advertising agency. Ziegler had been in charge of the NBC News advertising account, so I'd gotten to know him some.

When I spotted Haldeman at the Agnew announcement, I kidded him about a conversation we'd had a year earlier. I had asked him if he was going to be involved in Nixon's campaign, and he had said he didn't think so. After the bruising and losing '60 and '62 campaigns, he was inclined to sit this one out. In what would turn out to be one of the great personal mistakes of the late twentieth century, he changed his mind.

Haldeman, of course, quickly became one of Nixon's most powerful aides, first in the campaign and then, especially, as his White House chief of staff. With his severe crew cut and cold-eyed demeanor, and his impatience with any questions about presidential authority, he quickly became known, in his own word, as Nixon's "sonuvabitch."

He and I, however, maintained a cordial relationship, and he played a major part in one of the best-kept secrets of my life in the Sixties. Sometime in late 1969, Haldeman asked me to have lunch with a friend of his in Los Angeles. I was mystified but agreed to meet a very cordial man named Cliff Miller at a smart little French restaurant in Hollywood. He got right down to business. Bob, he explained, wanted me to consider joining the Nixon White House as press secretary. The plan was to move Ron Ziegler to the post as director of communications.

I was stunned and stammered something about not wanting to leave NBC News, where my career was moving along nicely, and that I wanted to stay a journalist and not go into the political arena. I didn't add that my family of FDR and Harry Truman Democrats would never understand.

Miller asked me to think it over, and as a courtesy I said I would. I rushed back to the office and pleaded with my boss to get me out of this, and, for God's sake, keep it quiet. A few days later, an NBC executive was at the White House for a meeting and took Haldeman aside to say I had just signed a new contract and wanted to stay in journalism.

It didn't come up again until a few years after I had moved to New York to host the **Today** show. I was participating in a symposium at Hofstra University on the Nixon years when someone grabbed me from behind in a big bear hug. It was Bob Haldeman, not that many months out of federal prison for his role in Watergate. He said cheerfully, "Do you know how many times I've watched you on television and thought, 'I could have put that young man in a position where he could have gotten into a lot of trouble!' "

The final comment on the episode came from Richard Nixon himself. When I turned fifty in 1990, NBC sent a camera crew, unbeknownst to me, to Nixon's office as part of a roundup of birthday wishes. Nixon was in his usual blue suit with that awkward smile on his face when he said into the camera, "I've always thought Tom Brokaw was a man of good judgment. He never showed better judgment than when he turned down my offer to be my press secretary."

The Nixon-Agnew ticket left the 1968 Republican Convention in Miami with a plan. The former vice president would now be the statesman-candidate, while his little-known vice presidential running mate would become the attack dog taking on the antiwar protestors and civil rights agitators. The idea was to attract a target audience of basically conservative working- and middle-class voters who were appalled by the excesses and threatened by the disruption that suddenly seemed to have beset American society and was in the process of ravaging the Democratic Party. This was the so-called silent majority—a phrase often attributed to Buchanan—who trusted the forces and institutions of law and order and who believed in God, flag, and country.

Buchanan recalls a statement he had written for Nixon earlier in 1968, condemning the student radicals at Columbia University who had occupied and trashed the library and administration building for several days before they were finally evicted by the police in a series of violent clashes. "They had released it, and it was really rough; **The New York Times** was attacking us, but when the next poll came out, I think it was ninety-eight to two against the campus riots. The American people were disgusted by what the students were doing, so I knew damn well we were in touch there."

The leader of the striking Columbia students was Mark Rudd, a young man from New Jersey who had arrived on the campus three years earlier with no thought of becoming one of the leading activists of his generation. He joined the SDS—Students for a Democratic Society—and by 1968 he was committed to the radical revolutionary politics of Ernesto "Che" Guevara, Fidel Castro's comrade-in-arms in Cuba and throughout South America.

Rudd organized the student strike to protest Columbia's military-research role in the Vietnam War and what he saw as the institution's racist attitude toward the surrounding community of black and Hispanic working-class families. Rudd's role as the face and voice of the Columbia uprising made him a notorious or celebrated figure, depending on your point of view, in the media capital of the world, landing him on the cover of **Time** magazine.

His politics became more radical when he gravitated to the Weathermen faction of the SDS, a group determined to foment a revolution in America, by violence if necessary.

Three Weathermen, friends of Rudd's, were killed when they accidentally set off a bomb they were building in a Greenwich Village townhouse. Rudd was not directly involved, but the FBI was looking for him, so he went on the run, living underground as a fugitive for the next seven years. When he emerged during the administration of Jimmy Carter, he plea-bargained for a penalty of two years' probation and a small fine.

When I met Rudd on the Columbia campus at the beginning of the 2007 fall term, he was a gray-haired man with a hearing aid in each ear—"rock and roll destroyed my hearing," he explained. He was still committed to the cause of social justice but no longer a believer in violence of any kind, not even for a revolution he could support. "I'm a pacifist now," he explains.

From atop the student center, Rudd looks down on Columbia's now-peaceful and still graceful quadrangle and says he's proud of what he did then, but he concedes the revolution he had in mind failed. "We lost, they won," he says. The conservatives were better organized to move forward and their ranks were filled with people who didn't drift away from their cause, as those on the left did.

He has no explanation for why his generation of activists on the left didn't stay with the cause. He's puzzled, because he believes that with the war in Iraq and what he calls "American empire," the conditions are much as they were in 1968.

Rudd is now a community college professor in New Mexico where he's active in the antinuclear movement. As for Columbia, he says not that much has changed. "It's still the university of the ruling class," he claims, "and there still is military research going on here."

Rudd and his cohorts in 1968 were a godsend to Buchanan and Nixon's other strategists, who saw new opportunities for the Republicans by using Goldwater followers as a base and adding Northern Catholics and disenchanted Southerners. Spiro Agnew, tall, tanned, and blandly handsome in a sleek Palm Springs way, was happy to carry the law-and-order message to those constituencies.

Nixon stuck to his strategy of staying above the fray, even when Vice President Humphrey finally broke with Lyndon Johnson by calling for a bombing halt on North Vietnam. At last, Humphrey's campaign began to pick up some momentum. Buchanan, ever the warrior, went to Nixon and said, "Sir, we've got to attack Humphrey tomorrow. We need to say that it's not Humphrey who's taking the risk, it's the guys up on the DMZ, the demilitarized zone. We got to force the breach back into the Democratic Party between those who want the bombing halt and those who don't."

Buchanan continues, "Nixon wouldn't do it; he stayed with the same old speech. So I asked him if I could go on Agnew's plane. Agnew was in trouble. He'd called a reporter 'a fat Jap' [on another occasion he had talked about 'Polacks']. We helped him get his confidence back with some serious speeches on Social Security and so on.

"But the press—jeez, I'd never seen anything like this before. You'd get on the plane, and all you could see from the press corps were blazing eyeballs." Again that hearty Buchanan laugh.

Despite a closing surge by Hubert Humphrey and his running mate, Senator Edmund Muskie of Maine, Nixon and Agnew won by racking up a substantial electoral-college margin, although they had less than a 1 percent lead in the popular vote. Alabama governor George Wallace, running as a third-party spoiler candidate, actually succeeded in winning over 13 percent of the popular vote and forty-six electoral votes, all in the South.

Richard Nixon had completed his comeback and was now prepared to take office with grandiose plans to secure his place in history. His place in history is unquestionably secure, though not in the fashion he had hoped. As president, he turned out to be an even more complex and enigmatic figure than his enemies had realized. He was clearly capable of significant and worthy accomplishments. He effectively reorganized the executive branch of the federal government to meet modern demands, and introduced a number of enlightened domestic programs. He introduced innovative environmental legislation and established the Environmental Protection Agency. He created OSHA—the Occupational Safety and Health Administration. He signed the Higher Education Act of 1972, and, with the stroke of his pen, Title IX revolutionized the role of women in university sports; its impact on education and employ-

ment and gender equity was immediately felt throughout American society.

He brought the intellectual maverick Democrat
Daniel Patrick Moynihan from Harvard to the West
Wing and endorsed Moynihan's plan to provide a guaranteed annual income to every American family. He
sent a message to Congress endorsing self-determination
for Native Americans, and the executive director of the
National Congress of American Indians said that Nixon
was the first president since George Washington to
honor America's obligations to the Indian tribes. He
mobilized the resources of the government to launch a
"war on cancer."

On the international front, Nixon, the old Cold
War red-baiter and anti-Communist, began a lasting
process of diplomatic détente and nuclear-arms reduc-
tion with the Soviet Union. He boldly opened the door
to China, a daring strategic move that his Democratic
predecessors had not attempted, in part because of the
political risks of giving the Republicans a new opportunity to accuse them of being "soft on Communism."
In the Middle East, he broke new ground by opening a
dialogue with Israel's Arab neighbors. Working in
often uneasy tandem with his national security advisor
and secretary of state, Henry Kissinger—the most unlikely dynamic duo in diplomatic history—he looked
for new answers to old problems.

Not all of his international initiatives were successful. Despite campaign suggestions that he was in
the strongest position to end the Vietnam War, peace
talks with the North Vietnamese quickly stalled, and
Nixon, while withdrawing troops, continued to ex-

pand the U.S. role by invading the neutral nation of Cambodia.

The Cambodian invasion (or "incursion," as Nixon insisted on calling it) set off massive protests across America, and particularly on college campuses, culminating in a hastily organized march on Washington. In a now famous episode often quoted by Nixon critics and dramatized by Oliver Stone, the president went for a predawn visit to the Lincoln Memorial, where many of the antiwar college students were camped out. Accompanied only by his personal valet, Manolo Sanchez, and a small band of Secret Service agents, Nixon must have struck the students as a surreal vision when he suddenly emerged out of the darkness. Nixon, who had been up most of the night before telephoning Henry Kissinger and other aides about the explosive political climate that had greeted his Cambodian decision, began by asking the students where they were from.

Then, according to the recorded recollections of Egil "Bud" Krogh, a junior White House aide who had scrambled to catch up with his boss at the memorial, the president said, "I know that probably most of you feel I am an S.O.B., but I want you to know I understand, that I know how you feel."

He went on to describe his own poor Quaker childhood and how as a young man he had supported British prime minister Neville Chamberlain's attempt at peace with Hitler, saying, "I thought Winston Churchill [Chamberlain's sharpest critic] was a madman . . . but I was wrong." One of the students said, "I hope you realize that we are willing to die for what we believe in." Nixon said he had felt the same way about what he believed in when he was their age, and that he was trying to build a world in which they would be able to live, rather than die, for their beliefs.

As the small knot of students mostly listened, Nixon urged them to travel, describing his own overseas adventures and his hope to see China one day.

One of the students asked for a picture with the president, and while that improbable image was being snapped, three young women told him that they had driven down from Syracuse University. Nixon inquired about the fortunes of the Syracuse football team and then led his small but growing entourage of aides and security men to the other end of the Mall for an early morning visit to the Capitol building.

There were no reporters along on this intensely personal and somewhat bizarre attempt by Nixon to find some connection to the students, so the first press accounts came from one of the Syracuse students. She said, "I hope it was because he was tired, but most of what he said was absurd. Here we came from a university that was totally uptight . . . and he talked about football."

When some of his aides picked up on the football comment as emblematic of the entire encounter, Nixon fired off a memo saying, "We seem to lack on our staff any one individual who really understands or appreciates what I am trying to get across in terms of what a president should mean to the people."

Political pundits, historians, psychiatrists, close friends, and bitter enemies have tried over the years to plumb the psyche of this strange man who arose from a childhood of privation and insecurity to become the twice-elected vice president and twice-elected president of the United States before he dragged the country through Watergate, one of the most damaging constitutional crises in our history.

Because above all there is Watergate. Nixon's legacy will forever be bound with that botched break-in and its clumsy, felonious cover-up. The degree and extent of complicity on the part of the president and his administration in the Watergate cover-up and the myriad offenses that became known as "the White House horrors" were deeply shocking to a nation that still held a special respect for the chief executive.

The fact that everything turned out to have been recorded on tape seemed to add insult to injury.

Having observed Nixon close-up for years—including three years as NBC's White House correspondent—I was endlessly puzzled trying to figure out how a man so essentially unsuited to the rituals of getting elected had not only chosen politics as his career but had risen to its very heights. He was driven to succeed but uncomfortable with success.

His White House staff was filled with bright, hardworking, dedicated young people who were loyal and protective of him to the day he resigned. I could never reconcile the president they admired with the president I found in the White House transcripts of his Oval Office recordings—sordid, bitter ramblings that filled his days and nights in the office he spent his life pursuing.

I always believed that Nixon was a prisoner of Nixon. His personal and physical awkwardness, his ab-

sence of natural grace, made him an easy target for caricature when he really wanted desperately to be seen as
a historic figure, a brave statesman wisely leading the
most powerful nation in the world.

Nixon was finally forced to resign in August 1974,
as a result of the "smoking gun" tape that put the lie to
his assertion that he had not been involved in the cover-
up. I was in the East Room of the White House on that
muggy Friday morning when he made his emotionally
raw but essentially self-pitying farewell speech. He invoked his mother and his humble Quaker roots and instructed his still-faithful staff gathered there not to hate.
He said, "Always remember, others may hate you, but
those who hate you don't win unless you hate them, and
then you destroy yourself." Somewhere along the way,
hate had become a fixed part of Richard Nixon's persona, his visceral reaction to the slights, real and imagined, that he had suffered in a lifetime of achievement
and failure.

Vice President Spiro Agnew had resigned the year
before, when a federal investigation proved he had
been taking payoffs in the vice president's office, a
practice he had begun while governor of Maryland.

The Nixon presidency ended with a degree of
disgrace that not even his many enemies could have
imagined.

For his part, Pat Buchanan, who worked in the
Nixon White House during Watergate but was not personally involved in the scandal, sees that long, sordid
episode as only a temporary setback for Republicans.
"It did not change the fundamental dynamics of the

country, as we saw with Ronald Reagan's forty-four-state victory six years after Watergate. His big win in '84, the big Republican victory of 1988 [George H. W. Bush over Massachusetts governor Michael Dukakis]."

He thinks the Democrats failed to recognize how much they'd been hurt by the fallout from 1968. "The student radicals were always despised. They were considered brats who had privileges that none of the working folks had. Here they were, drinking, smoking pot, demonstrating, hanging out at Woodstock. We capitalized on that."

However, Buchanan believes the Republicans in their own way have succumbed to the temptations of excess and the hubris of power, and that they are now in danger of squandering all the gains made during the years of the Silent Majority and Reagan Revolution. Buchanan was openly critical of the influence of the neocons in the administration of President George W. Bush and their determination to go to war.

He correctly called the congressional elections of 2006, in which the Democrats won control of the House and the Senate, "a referendum on the neocons," the conservatives who turned the Reagan revolution into a rigid theology of what they believe is unassailable moral and political superiority.

The presidential election of 2008 promises to be a climactic showdown between those political forces that were unleashed on the left and the right forty years ago. Whoever is at the top of either ticket, the contest will be waged between candidates who were shaped, to one degree or another, by their personal and political experiences in the Sixties. Are they prepared to move on, to get beyond the politics of separation and get to the politics of unifying purpose?

The larger question is, will either or both candidates attempt to move America to a new landscape that has the contours of common concerns about the future instead of the fault lines of the past?

A Place
Called Vietnam

'Sixty-eight just blew away my self-confidence about what I thought I knew. I said, "My God, look at how all these incredibly smart people screwed up over Vietnam. Look how you screwed up."

—LES GELB, DIRECTOR
OF THE PENTAGON PAPERS PROJECT

I wanted to believe we were there for an honorable purpose, but the other part that was tugging at me was "Why in the world don't we try to do more . . . to solve these issues without tearing bodies apart like this?" It's not just that they die. It's how they die at such a young age.

—NELLIE COAKLEY

You never really leave the battlefield.
I was older at twenty-four than I am today.

—SENATOR JAMES WEBB

We Had to
Destroy the Village:
Captain Gene Kimmel and
Dr. Les Gelb

When I was a senior in college in 1962, most of my friends were about to be commissioned as second lieutenants in the U.S. Army. They were graduates of the University of South Dakota's Army ROTC program, which I had elected to take a pass on because I wanted to be a Navy officer. The regional recruiter was more than happy to make arrangements for me to take the Navy exams.

After I'd breezed through the written and most of the physical tests, the doctor noticed that I had flat feet. "We can't take you—Navy rules," he said. What? Then what about the Army? I volunteered for my draft physical, and the same verdict came back: You've got flat feet, so thanks, but no thanks. I was classified 1-Y, a kind of ready-reserve status.

It was unexpected and a little disappointing. I needed the job, and I had always dreamed of running

PT boats, like John F. Kennedy. But it was also a gift of sorts. My country didn't need me at the moment, and there were few signs that the situation would change anytime soon, so Meredith and I could now proceed with our marriage and career plans.

Three years later, my brother Mike, whose feet were finely arched, was shipping out for Vietnam as a Marine grunt. And my brother Bill, even though he had flat feet like mine, had been drafted to meet the increasing need for boots (regardless of the kind of feet inside them) on the ground and sent to Germany as an Army MP. It was 1965, LBJ was in the White House, and America was now deeply involved in a war—and getting in deeper with every week. It was a startling turn of events that had come about gradually. There was no surprise attack on America to electrify the country and trigger a rush to the recruiting offices. President Lyndon Johnson, Defense Secretary Robert McNamara, and Secretary of State Dean Rusk defended the need to stop Communism in Vietnam in reasoned arguments and speeches.

In a way that only a few people envisioned at the time, we were slipping into a quagmire of tragic proportions and historic consequences. As Bob Kerrey, the former U.S. senator from Nebraska who was a Navy SEAL and recipient of the Congressional Medal of Honor, says, "We'd better never forget the lessons of that time," as we try to find our frame of reference for thinking about Iraq.

If only the lessons had been clearer at the beginning.

It was America's "best and brightest," to use David

Halberstam's succinct description, who saw Vietnam as a crucial test of wills with the Communist powers in Moscow and Beijing. John F. Kennedy and his resident intellectuals—including National Security Advisor McGeorge Bundy, Secretary of Defense Robert McNamara, and Secretary of State Dean Rusk—were traditional Cold Warriors, prepared, as JFK had put it in his stirring inaugural address, to "fight any foe" in the "long twilight struggle" against Communism.

At first it seemed to be a reasonable formula: Prop up the South Vietnamese against their Communist antagonists in the North, and send a signal to Beijing and Moscow that the American people were prepared to draw the line in Southeast Asia.

At the beginning, it seemed to be not only the right thing to do, but a noble undertaking that was widely supported. By now the world knows what history has recorded—that it was to be a long, tragic, losing struggle in a tiny country that cost millions of lives and deeply scarred the American psyche.

However, from the outset it was a mission bedeviled by what General Maxwell Taylor, the World War II hero who helped develop Kennedy's intervention policies, called "fundamental mistakes." Shortly before his death in 1987, Taylor, who served as U.S. ambassador to South Vietnam in 1964, told journalist Stanley Karnow, "First, we didn't know ourselves. We thought that we were going into another Korean war, but this was a different country. Second, we didn't know our South Vietnamese allies. We never understood them, and that was another surprise. And we knew even less about North Vietnam. . . . So until we know the enemy and know our allies and know ourselves, we'd better keep out of this dirty kind of business. It's very dangerous."

Frances FitzGerald, in her Pulitzer Prize–winning book, **Fire in the Lake,** described in illuminating detail the depth of American ignorance about the ancient history of Vietnam and the roots of the movement led by Ho Chi Minh. Her book, considered a classic of reporting and enterprise, traced the complicated rise of Vietnam, its historic tenacity, and its political and economic structure, which, she said, American GIs discovered was neither Communist nor democratic. But by the time her book was published in 1972, more than fifty-six thousand Americans had already died there.

FitzGerald's work and General Taylor's revealing conclusion in Karnow's widely praised book **Vietnam: A History** are part of the consensus about what went wrong for America in Vietnam.

Recently, there have been other versions from a revisionist school of historians. One is called **Triumph Forsaken: The Vietnam War, 1954–1965.** The author, Mark Moyar, is an honors graduate of Harvard with a Ph.D. in history from Cambridge University. Previously, he had written an account of the CIA's campaign against the Vietcong.

Moyar argues that first President Kennedy and then President Johnson missed great opportunities in the early stages of U.S. involvement in Vietnam because of their inconsistent and often contradictory policies. He believes it was a major mistake not to go directly after Communist expansion sponsored by North Vietnam and China in nearby Laos.

In 416 pages of text and 83 pages of endnotes, he marshals his case that principal allies of the United States and strategists in Hanoi and Beijing alike saw Vietnam as a great testing ground in the struggle between democracies and Communism. In 1965, Moyar argues, the domino theory was real and credible.

His other major points include a defense of the leadership of South Vietnam's president Ngo Dinh Diem, the aristocratic Catholic intellectual who lost the Kennedy administration's support by resisting many of its recommendations for reform. Diem was killed in 1963 in a coup organized with the knowledge of the CIA.

Moyar is especially critical of the early reporting from Vietnam by American journalists who challenged the official military view. He believes that many of the reporters had personal agendas and relied heavily on sources that were not credible.

By his reckoning, that created a political climate forcing President Johnson and the military commanders to accept constraints dictated more by domestic politics than by military realities. Twinned with what Moyar calls "faulty intelligence and unwarranted confidence in brainy civilians," the combination forfeited opportunities to deny the Communists the great strategic advantages they were to enjoy for the next ten years.

The consequence, in Moyar's judgment, was "not

to be a foolish war fought under wise constraints but a wise war fought under foolish constraints."

Moyar's work deserves a place on the long list of books devoted to the origins and the execution of the war in Vietnam, but it will remain a distinctly contrarian point of view.

More than three decades after its end, the Vietnam War is still an emotional trigger for those who fought in it, for those who fought against it, and for those who were somewhere in the middle. It lingers, as it should, for it was a deeply traumatic and costly time for everyone.

In 1968 alone, 14,589 Americans died in Vietnam; 87,388 were wounded in action. Five times as many Marines died in Vietnam as in the most celebrated battles of Corps history in World War II: Iwo Jima, Guadalcanal, Tarawa, Palau Islands, and Okinawa. The January 1968 Tet Offensive—in which the Vietcong penetrated the grounds of the U.S. embassy in Saigon and stunned the world with a bold offensive all across South Vietnamese territory that had been thought to be secure—was, in pure military terms, a very costly exercise for the North, but their psychic victory was enormous. It was the beginning of the end for the United States, although it would take seven more long years to get there.

The last desperate act for the United States was the evacuation of the remaining Americans and thousands of South Vietnamese from Saigon and the surrounding countryside as the North Vietnamese took control of their conquered territory. American helicopters lifting off from rooftops; cargo planes jammed with refugees lumbering down runways; U.S. ships rescuing those who had escaped in flimsy boats (the tragic "boat people")—these were the final images of America's longest war. Some nine million young Americans served in the military during the Vietnam era, three million of them in the Vietnam theater. And fifty-eight thousand of them died there and never returned home.

One of those who served in Vietnam was my friend Gene Kimmel. We had hit it off from the first day we met at the University of South Dakota, at a time when we were hardly aware that a place called Vietnam even existed. The bonds of friendship were deepened when Gene married Mary Lou, who had been one of Meredith's college roommates.

Gene had gone from high school directly into the 101st Airborne to earn money for college, and when a knee injury cut short his jumping out of planes, he enrolled at the University of South Dakota, where he quickly became an honors student in political science and a gifted editor of the student newspaper.

Gene had a Steve McQueen quality about him—a little ornery and with a broad streak of the daredevil. When he completed his master's degree in political science and asked for my help in finding a Marine recruiter who would help him become a pilot, I was not surprised.

As I suspected, Gene was a natural as a Marine and as a fighter pilot. And he was thrilled to be in the program.

By 1966 Gene was flying combat missions over Vietnam and I was working for NBC News in Southern California. I heard that he had been evacuated stateside after suffering serious burns when his plane exploded just before takeoff on what would have been his 113th mission. I drove out to Oakland and tried to find him at the naval hospital there. He had already moved on, but the wards were full of other young men who had been badly burned or injured in Vietnam.

"Migod," I thought, "no one even knows about this place." I did a story on the new techniques of treating burn injuries, but it got lost amid the more colorful exotica that people were interested in from the Bay Area in those days—like the be-ins at Golden Gate Park, the drug and free-love culture in Haight-Ashbury, and the concerts featuring the Jefferson Airplane or Janis Joplin that Bill Graham was promoting at the Fillmore West.

Gene, I learned, had recovered. He was now a captain and already contemplating another combat tour. Meredith and I visited him and Mary Lou at their small, government-issue apartment at Camp Pendleton, the sprawling Marine base north of San Diego.

After a dinner of wild pheasant harvested during a hunting trip back home to South Dakota—he was a skilled and serious hunter—Gene and I took big tumblers of whiskey into his small den, where he had prominently displayed the burned-to-a-crisp center console that had been recovered from his A-4 Skyhawk jet fighter after the explosion on the flight line.

By then I was disillusioned with the war and the domino theory that fueled it. I tried to talk him out of returning to Vietnam for the second tour, but he was excited about flying the new OV-10, an aeronautically challenging aircraft that required exceptional pilot skills. Besides, he felt invulnerable after surviving the terrible fire and burns.

As a journalist I was immersed in the politics of the war, and Gene had his own profound doubts about the political decisions being made by the civilian leaders. But he was a warrior and a Marine flier through and through, so a few weeks later he went back. On October 22, 1968, he was shot down over Quang Nam province by a shoulder-fired missile.

A couple of years earlier, in a letter to his parents, he had written: "I'd like to think I have made an attempt, although small it may be, to leave a safer more secure world than the one I had. . . . I don't want you to think this war is for nothing. . . . God made us all different, to think and feel and do what we think is right."

At Gene's funeral, on one of those achingly beautiful golden autumn days in South Dakota, a squadron of Marine jets flew over and one peeled away—signifying the "missing man"—in the traditional formation flown at ceremonies memorializing a lost military aviator. I burst into tears and yelled something about this goddamn war, but my South Dakota friends were typically stoic and my own emotional gauge was tempered by the muted grief of his wife and parents, the mix of patriotism, and a devastating confusion about the loss of this singular young man who had harbored ambitions of returning to South Dakota to run for office one day.

As I was leaving the postfuneral reception, Gene's

father, a weathered auto mechanic, took my hand, gripped it hard, and looked at me through his tears. He said of his only son, "Whatever he done, he done good, didn't he?"

I choked out a response: "Yes, yes—he was very, very good."

I remember thinking, not for the first time that year, that I was living in so many Americas. It was a bewildering, emotional time for American families who had been raised to accept the sacrifices of war secure in the knowledge that it was for a noble and worthy cause.

In Washington, D.C., the Senate was deeply divided over the war. Ernest Gruening of Alaska and Wayne Morse of Oregon were early outspoken opponents, but they were considered mavericks. It was the Democratic establishment, represented by J. William Fulbright of Arkansas, Frank Church of Idaho, Mike Mansfield of Montana, Robert Kennedy of New York, Eugene McCarthy of Minnesota, George McGovern of South Dakota, Abraham Ribicoff of Connecticut, Al Gore Sr. of Tennessee, and Gaylord Nelson of Wisconsin, that was now starting to lead the way, joined by moderate Republicans such as John Sherman Cooper of Kentucky and Jacob Javits of New York.

Many of these senators were old friends of Lyndon Johnson from his days when he had dominated the chamber as the Democrats' majority leader. But the war had first frayed and then severed the strong ties between the Oval Office and the Senate Democratic caucus.

Even Johnson's closest friend, Richard Russell of

Georgia, the Senate's leading voice on military affairs, privately confided to the president that Vietnam was the "worst damn mess I ever saw."

Within the president's national security community, however, the war planning went on, directed by McNamara, Rusk, and Bundy, the holdovers from the Kennedy administration, who inadvertently became the intellectual godfathers of a new generation of tough-minded foreign policy students who were already rising through the ranks.

One of the new young stars was Harvard Ph.D. Leslie Gelb. By 1968 he was working in the Pentagon with the marathon title of deputy assistant secretary of defense for policy planning and arms control. He was an acolyte of Bundy, Henry Kissinger, and the other Harvard scholars who were defining this new field of national security in the post–World War II years.

Les Gelb shared their judgment that the lessons of Munich—the 1938 conference where the French and the British tried to appease Adolf Hitler by allowing him to take over western Czechoslovakia—should not be lost in confronting Communist expansion, even in little-known faraway countries such as Vietnam. British prime minister Neville Chamberlain's failure to stand up to Hitler at Munich was strongly imprinted in the consciousness of American national security strategists.

Gelb says, "Munich was the historical reference point. In our field, there are no proofs. It isn't mathematics. You argue by historical analogy. And the historical events that led to World War II were the dominant experience of those shaping policy. All of those events led to the domino theory. Vietnam was not as important for itself as the effect of losing it and then its neighbors and then their neighbors."

The year before, in 1967, when he had been working on Capitol Hill for New York senator Jacob Javits, Gelb had had his first hint that Vietnam was not just a scholar's exercise. A former Harvard classmate, an honors graduate of West Point, was commanding troops in the central highlands of Vietnam. He wrote to Gelb about a major battle: "My troops fought courageously and brilliantly, but the other guys fought better. Either they were on dope or they were on nationalism. If it was nationalism," he concluded, "we are not going to win this war."

Gelb, a rumpled professorial type, witty and intellectually vigorous, was taken aback, but by the next year he was buried in the bowels of the Pentagon fully committed to the administration strategy, working for Defense Secretary Robert McNamara on a project that came to be known as the Pentagon Papers.

When Gelb went home at night, his wife, Judy, would tell him what she had seen on the news while he was busy writing memos. As Gelb now recalls, "We were so busy in the Pentagon, we never watched the news— and the disconnect became greater and greater."

That disconnect became especially clear on October 21, 1967—the day of the march on the Pentagon, when hundreds of thousands, maybe as many as half a million, gathered to protest the war in Vietnam. There were the ordinary and the famous, including Dr. Benjamin Spock, the baby expert, and novelist Norman Mailer.

Gelb remembers going to work that Saturday, knowing there was going to be a protest of some kind but wholly unprepared for the magnitude of what he found. "Here it is," he recalls, "a huge mob. . . . You watched for a while in a kind of amazement and horror. You didn't know what they were going to do, whether there would be shooting.

"I was not terribly sympathetic to them. Now, if you ask people who were in the Pentagon but not in uniform, most of them will say, 'Oh, I agreed with the protestors. I was already against the war, but I couldn't say it.' " Gelb adds, "That's all bullshit."

Nonetheless, Gelb counts 1968 as one of the most formative years of his life, a year when he began to examine his assumptions about American foreign policy and how it might shape the world. "For me," he says, "and most of the people around me, it was a slow, torturous process. Because it meant examining things that had been lodestones in how you thought about foreign policy and national security.

"It happened very slowly, very incrementally. To me, it was never a case of the good guys against the bad guys. I never thought Ho Chi Minh and his fellow dictators were saints and that we were the sinners. The morality of that war was very confused."

For Gelb, who went on to become an award-winning reporter and columnist for **The New York Times**, his Pentagon years were a life-changing experience. "The main thing I learned in 1968 was about making mistakes. That's a hell of a good lesson. Be-

Les Gelb, a "rumpled professorial type," in 1968, while
working for Defense Secretary Robert McNamara
on a project that would become known as
the Pentagon Papers

cause it makes you much smarter about public policy if you realize just how prone you are to making mistakes. 'Sixty-eight just blew away my self-confidence about what I thought I knew. I said, 'My God, look at how all these incredibly smart people screwed up over Vietnam. Look how **you** screwed up.' "

As a result, Gelb says, "There is no more foreign-policy establishment after Vietnam. A community that had been comprised primarily of moderate non-partisans became permanently divided along partisan lines." It led, he believes, to what he calls the "cut-throat politics" and "frightening logic" of the political conservatives who came to dominate American foreign policy.

When Gelb became president of the very establishment Council on Foreign Relations he brought new, younger voices and fresh ideas to that institution on East 68th Street in New York; but in Washington the partisan polarization continued.

Gelb, who describes himself as more interested in the issue than in the party, registered as a Democrat, he says, only to oppose the policies of George W. Bush. But he also remains critical of the Democratic Party's hangover from Vietnam. "I think," he says, "it was the most intellectually important experience for us. All those policy makers in the Clinton administration, including the president, were reluctant to use American power. Not just military force but power in general. I was not a big fan of the Clinton administration, for which my friends never forgave me."

However, Gelb believes his Clinton friends, particularly the national security advisors Anthony Lake and Sandy Berger, were not paralyzed by a Vietnam syndrome. He believes the problem was their boss. During the 1992 campaign, Clinton was critical of the administration of President George H. W. Bush for not taking a tougher line on Bosnia and China. But, as Gelb says, "As soon as he became president, he looked the other way. I don't think that was Vietnam. I think it was politics—domestic versus foreign policy."

As for Lake and Berger, Gelb believes they were determined not to be accused of being hostage to Vietnam. They were prepared to use force, but President Clinton was not interested during the first two years of his administration. Gelb believes Clinton was too heavily invested in the notion that the Cold War was over and that in the new era of globalization, the use of military force was not as important as economic power and cooperation. The neoconservatives, on the other hand, Gelb says, believed in imperialism, the notion that America in the post–Cold War years can do whatever it wants.

Now that there's ample evidence that both theories are at best flawed, if not dangerously naive, the question is "What next?" Gelb is not encouraged. He worries that the current generation will "overlearn the lessons of Iraq. The reaction will be 'Don't get involved in this stuff.' [Nineteenth-century German chancellor Otto von] Bismarck had a great saying about this: 'Fools learn from experience. Wise men learn from the experience of others.' "

In one way or another, Vietnam still is with us. Whenever I encounter a Vietnam veteran, I ask what he thinks of his experience there. Most of them answer,

"Well, it was really screwed up in so many ways, but I am proud of what I did. No one can take that away from me."

There is no one life that perfectly sums up the angst, loss, turmoil, and myths of Vietnam, but in the experiences that follow, and for some others who lived through it—whether here on the home front, there on the battlefield, or on the run and watching from some neutral distance—there are enduring lessons about when and how to go to war, and how society should treat those who choose to serve in uniform.

Married to Vietnam:
Tom and Nellie Coakley

Tom Coakley didn't want to go to Vietnam.

Nellie Coakley insisted that she be sent there.

That was before they were husband and wife, before they knew each other, before Coakley lost his leg in an ambush near Lai Khe, about thirty miles north of Saigon in 1969, and before they understood how the war would bring them together and define so much of their lives individually and as husband and wife.

Tom Coakley was a handsome, hard-partying hockey star at Brown University, a young man from upstate New York who didn't pay much attention to politics and had only a vague idea of what he would do after he graduated in 1968. He thought maybe he'd try to attend graduate school in Canada so he could continue to play hockey. But Uncle Sam had other ideas.

A few months before graduation, he was alerted that his student deferment was about to expire. "It was kind of a rude awakening," he remembers, "because I was very comfortable living in the present and not thinking about what was going to happen next."

The first thing that occurred to him was that family friends might be able to get him moved to the top of the reserves list. "The reserves then, compared to today, were considered a haven. It was relatively certain that you wouldn't see any action, that you'd do your four to six months and come back home. That appealed to me."

But his father, who had been a major in World War II, told his son that if their neighbors had to take their chances, Tom needed to take his chances as well. Coakley says, "What my dad said had a significant impact on my thinking, and I signed up for OCS—Officer Candidate School—in the Army." He laughs now as he remembers that his eyesight wasn't up to Navy OCS standards, but for the Army, it was good enough to go fire at the enemy.

He recalls that only one of his friends at Brown joined him in his decision to serve. As for those who evaded service, he says simply, "You know what I think? I think in many ways they struggle to this day with their decision." He admits that he struggles some with his own decision. "I think it was a no-win situation," he says. "The choices weren't good no matter what you did."

At about the same time, in Baltimore, Maryland, Nellie Harness had no problem with her choices. When she was in the sixth grade, she was hospitalized with rheumatic fever. Her father was a career Army officer stationed at Fort Leonard Wood, Missouri, and during her five-week stay in the base hospital, she came to admire the nurses so much that she decided, "Someday I'm going to be an Army nurse." Looking back, she says now, "It never changed—which is amazing."

Tom Coakley (far left) in the summer of 1969, at the Fire Support Base Gela near Lai Khe, "just having some fun with the camera"

First Lieutenant Nellie Coakley at her MASH unit in Vietnam, 1968

Tom and Nellie Coakley with their grandson, Peter, in 2005

In high school, when most of her girlfriends were thinking only about getting a college degree and a husband simultaneously, Nellie was still on course to be a nurse. "I might have strayed from that," she says, "if the war in Vietnam hadn't occurred." But while she was a nursing student at the University of Maryland, the war was heating up fast. "I remember watching the soldiers on television, and there was no question in my mind where I belonged, because I had a skill that could be used. I felt a strong identity with those soldiers and the military."

While she was training to be an Army nurse in 1966 and '67, Nellie was appalled by the indifference of her fellow students toward Vietnam. "It didn't touch their lives," she says. "It didn't ask anything of them. I found myself having a hard time with that."

The man who would become her husband was not indifferent to Vietnam, but he wasn't happy with the Army. After reporting for OSC, Tom Coakley signed up for armor, thinking it would be safer than the infantry. But about halfway through the armor course, the Army, under heavy pressure to fill the infantry ranks, pulled a switch. It presented him with a lose-lose choice: Either sign up for the infantry officer training program or take your chances as a regular draftee.

"I felt that I had been abandoned by my government, you know? I was being betrayed. This was early 1969, and I was more aware, more concerned, about what was going on in Vietnam. I wasn't ever comfortable with my decision, but I decided I should serve in Vietnam as an enlisted man, not as an officer. There was also the consideration that continuing as an officer meant an extra year, and I was ready to be done with this as soon as possible."

He transferred to Fort Campbell, Kentucky, and emerged as an infantry grunt with the 28th Black Lions Battalion of the First Infantry Division—the celebrated Big Red One that, in another war, had landed on Omaha Beach on D-Day. But by almost every measurable detail, the war that Tom was entering in 1969 was vastly different from the war that the Big Red One had fought across Europe in the mid-Forties.

Back home, his younger brother was recruited to play hockey at West Point but chose to follow him to Brown in large part because of his opposition to the war. Between 1968 and 1970, the antiwar fever on campuses reached new heights, and looking back, Coakley is sympathetic. "I might not have made the same decision in 1970 that I did in 1968," he says. "Who knows how you would be affected by your environment?"

However, Coakley's decision had been made and he was on his way to Vietnam, where he became a radio operator assigned to a company operating along the Cambodian border, running nighttime search-and-destroy and ambush missions or guarding the perimeter of firebases.

He'd already been in heavy action during the spring and summer of 1969 when, on August 23, his company spotted North Vietnamese troops and received orders to engage them. His battalion commander ordered him to put up the long whip antenna on his radio. He was immediately concerned—"those in the field had advised me never to use the antenna because it served as an obvious target, rising above the brush." But an order was an order, and almost as soon as the antenna went up, Coakley was ambushed with a grenade that landed about a foot away.

There was a tremendous explosion. "I felt myself thrown in the air, and when I landed, I tried to reach for my rifle, but my left arm simply flopped out of control, with both bones broken below the elbow and the elbow severely dislocated. When I sat up, I realized my left leg below the knee would never be saved, and my right leg looked questionable. Just as I lay back down, the soldiers behind me were cut down with AK-47 fire. Had I sat up any longer, I would likely have taken rounds in the chest and head.

"At some point, my old platoon mates attacked the North Vietnamese bunker from the flank, knocking it out with a rocket launcher. The ambush stopped just as quickly as it started. The medic was next to me immediately. I felt like I was burning all over. I was losing it mentally as well as physically, floundering between the prayers I'd memorized in childhood and the worst swearwords in my vocabulary.

"Then, out of nowhere, I focused on my family. All of a sudden I had one all-encompassing thought— I couldn't die over here and leave them in that way. I will always believe that this focus on something more than me in the terror of the moment is what saved my life."

Nellie Harness was a close witness to life-and-death experiences almost every day that she was in Vietnam, from late March 1968 until she was rotated stateside in 1969. At the beginning of 1968, she was getting impatient when her orders for Vietnam weren't coming through, an impatience that became acute after the Tet Offensive in January.

She pressed her case with the chief Army nurse at the Pentagon. "When do I get to go?" she asked. She'll never forget the response: "Don't worry, little one. You'll get your orders." In March she was on her way, and she vividly remembers the soldier sitting next to her on the plane, an African-American. As Vietnam came into view, she said, he began saying the "Our Father" over and over. Nellie wishes she could remember his name because "I'd love to know if he made it home."

Three days after landing in Vietnam, Nellie was on duty at a sixty-bed mobile Army surgical hospital (MASH) near Xuan Loc when a number of civilian casualties began arriving from a nearby village that had been attacked. "Because I was new, the chief nurse didn't put me in triage. She placed me in a holding ward, and I saw this little girl, maybe four or five years old. She had dressings around her head, and I went over to make her a little more comfortable. Then I noticed that half her brain was gone. Obviously, she was going to die. That was my first reality check. The war wasn't just about soldiers. It was a very sobering moment."

There were many more sobering moments to come for Nellie. If they began to add up to some serious doubts, they didn't amount to her complete abandonment of the purpose of the war. "It was very important for me to believe we had a purpose there, and nothing yet was telling me to think of it any differently. I still believed in the politics of the war because I didn't understand them. I wanted to believe we were there for an honorable purpose, but the other part that was tugging at me was 'Why in the world don't we try to do more . . . to solve these issues without tearing bodies apart like this?' It's not just that they die. It's how they die at such a young age."

In February 1969, as Nellie was coming off a night shift, she was witness to a violent death that would stay with her forever. "I was called up to triage, and there was a young soldier on a gurney. I walked over and asked if there was anything I could do, and they said, 'No, he's already dead.'"

Nellie had been on duty for eleven months, and she was due to go home shortly, so she knew the rules: Don't personalize things; don't read the dog tags. But for some reason, she couldn't resist. "We would put a paper tag around their wrist, sort of like a luggage tag. I looked at that. His name was Richard Burns.

"I stroked his cheek. I stepped away from the gurney and looked out the door of the triage unit. It was a gorgeous day, and I thought, 'My God, his mother doesn't even know her son is dead.' The whole war kind of washed down over me. I thought again, 'Why do we do this to each other? Why is this boy dead?'

"I went on duty that night, thinking that Richard Burns was out of my life. He was with the First Airborne up at Phan Thiet, and we had a lot of casualties from that area in my ward that night. Almost everyone was sleeping except this one soldier who kept smoking one cigarette after another. So around one-thirty in the morning, I walked down to where he was and—this was not typical of me—said, 'Are you okay? Would you like to talk?'

"And he said, 'Well, a great guy in our unit got hit

today and I just wonder how he's doing.' I said, 'What's his name? I'll find out for you.' He said, 'Richard Burns.'

"So I had to tell him Richard had died. I could see him just lock down. He got very quiet and very stiff. I said, 'If you need to cry, it's okay. Everyone is asleep, and they're not gonna know.' And he cried—he started to sob.

"He cried and talked about Richard. I stayed at his bedside for an hour and a half. I am so glad I helped him work through some of that grief. He moved out of my life the next day, because surgical hospitals just stabilize patients and then move them on.

"Five days later, I was still on night shift, and we had a young captain from the 101st Airborne. He had been hurt pretty badly. He was in pain, and he couldn't get to sleep. I went to his bedside and said, 'Do you need to talk?' And he started to talk about Richard Burns and what a wonderful young soldier he had been."

Nellie was rotated back to Walter Reed hospital in Washington, D.C. She continued to treat Vietnam casualties, but by the time they arrived at the famed Army hospital, the wounds, physical and emotional, weren't so fresh, and there were no deaths on the gurneys as they were wheeled in.

Nellie had been in Vietnam only a year, but it had been a long, difficult twelve months, far removed from the world she was now reentering. Nellie found her new life back home disorienting at first. "First of all, I had a lot of trouble driving; I hadn't driven in a year. My legs started shaking. I had to pull over." But driving wasn't as hard as attending a party with friends and colleagues from nursing school and the medical center where she had trained. "Not one of them asked me about Vietnam. Not one. I remember standing there and feeling so out of place, leaning against a doorway and thinking, 'These are the most self-involved people I've ever known.' Not one question about the kind of medicine we were practicing, the nature of the wounds. And these were medical people.

"The war didn't ask anything of them. It didn't touch their lives. When I left the party, I knew I would never go back. I would never have a connection with any of them again."

Besides, she had a new population of patients to worry about on Ward 50, where she was head nurse. She made it a point to greet all newcomers personally and welcome them to her ward. For some reason, she specifically remembers a handsome young man who was checking in for continuing treatment on what was left of his right leg. His name was Tom Coakley.

"I absolutely remember Tom, but I don't know why. I remember welcoming him to Walter Reed and telling him we'd do the best we could to make his time comfortable here."

Nellie assigned Coakley to a room with Al Vasquez, another Brown grad, who was depressed because his wounds weren't healing. Coakley had already been in hospitals in Saigon, Japan, and Pennsylvania, so by the time he got to Walter Reed, he was adjusting at a pace that surprised him: "The recovery was easier because you were in an environment with fifty others just like you. There was the typical male humor and dealing with things together.

"I was on the enlisted men's floor, and when Nellie put me next to Al, we became close friends, even though at Brown, we had been extraordinarily different. He was into plays, I was on the hockey team, but we talked back and forth about the high points at Brown, like the best place for pizza and so forth."

When Nellie came around to check on Vazquez, Coakley would try to get her attention with the brainteasers he worked on to pass the time, but nothing worked. Nellie remembers, "I was so conservative. In the military, nurses don't date patients, so there was no way I was going to get interested in someone I was taking care of. Besides, having gone through Vietnam and then being on the amputee ward, I just had my fill of war, so I had a very firm position of making sure, when I dated someone, they were going to have all their body parts."

Coakley was eventually discharged from Walter Reed and started his new life as an amputee and Vietnam vet, not knowing quite what to expect. "I remember coming home for the first time and my dad wheeling me into the high school gym to a basketball game, and the place went silent. It felt a little awkward to be the center of attention like that."

He was also gaining perspective on what was important to him. "Before I lost my leg—when I was twenty-one or twenty-two—I might have thought that dying wasn't a bad alternative to amputation." But he quickly learned that "living is what it's all about." Besides, he was comfortable with his condition. He would go to elementary schools and talk to the students about people with disabilities of one kind or another, showing a film of a young woman skiing expertly and then removing her prosthesis to reveal an above-the-knee amputation. He would then methodically remove his own shoe and sock, pull up his pant leg and disclose his artificial leg, remove it, and set it in front of the class. He wanted the youngsters to be at ease with the idea of a missing body part or two.

He was moving on, with only a few regrets. He admits that when his old Brown hockey teammates showed up at a summer camp to skate, he was sad, even crying, that he couldn't get out on the ice with them. However, within a year he was skating again, although not joining in the body-slamming hockey games that had been such a major part of his younger years.

He also went back to Walter Reed to visit some friends, who immediately told him he should look up Nellie. She had left the Army and was now a civilian nurse in another ward. Coakley found her, and despite her determination to date only men without any missing limbs, they began seeing each other. Five months later, they were engaged.

Curiously, they rarely talked about Vietnam in the first years of their marriage, although Nellie says he was a big influence on her thinking about other matters. She was a self-described conservative Catholic who lived her life by the rules of the Church. Coakley had fallen away from institutional Catholicism, a separation that was widened after he heard a Catholic chaplain in Vietnam bless the troops and then urge them to go out "and have a good kill."

At first Nellie was troubled when he wouldn't attend Mass with her, but slowly, she came around to his way of thinking about God and faith. She said, "Both of us believe in God and have a strong relationship with Him in our mind, but the Church became less important to us."

After Tom graduated with an MBA from the Wharton School at the University of Pennsylvania, he and Nellie began having children and working their way back to his home territory in upstate New York. He held senior management positions with three major corporations before becoming a visiting lecturer in the economics department at St. Lawrence University, near the Canadian border.

Nellie began to do some serious thinking about Vietnam. She felt that she needed answers. How had the United States gotten into this war that she had supported so strongly at the beginning? What were its lessons for succeeding generations? She signed up for a class at St. Lawrence, and before long she became obsessed with the gross political and military miscalculations, the deceptions, and their terrible costs to families who had accepted the statements of those in charge. Tom remembers her bringing books to bed and reading aloud from her texts and pestering him with questions. One night when she was particularly persistent, he doggedly continued reading his own book. Finally, Nellie said, "What are you reading, honey?" He showed her what he remembers as being "a fairly steamy novel" and said, "If I'm gonna dream, I'm gonna dream **good** dreams."

Slowly, steadily, Vietnam reentered their lives. Nellie trained as a counselor and began working with Vietnam vets suffering from post-traumatic stress disorder. Tom became vice president of administrative affairs at St. Lawrence, but he was frequently invited into classrooms to talk about his war experiences. This gave him a chance to measure the differences between his generation of students and their successors.

He says, "There isn't as much activism or the same passion for the things we took on. There is more diversity within the student body and more diversity of opinion overall." He admits that his own views have evolved from great skepticism about authority and the military to accepting the need for a strong defense. "In the early years after Vietnam I was highly skeptical of our armed forces. The skepticism was part political choice and part personal. . . . Over time I evolved to a different place. I reunited with my platoon mates and recognized that I felt a sense of pride in serving with these guys, having made the personal choice to put my own safety second to the defense of my country. I grew comfortable with the paradox of feeling a pride in serving and at the same time believing that Vietnam was a major political mistake allowed to perpetuate itself and multiply in its significance for years and years. Reading Colin Powell's books and listening to his tapes helped me to accept this position.

"On a more macro level I also accepted over time that the world was not all good and that we did in fact need a strong defense and military presence. Furthermore, that defense of our society and way of life was totally dependent upon the continued willingness of individuals to put the defense of our way of life first and their safety second, just as my platoon mates and I had once done."

However, when one of their sons was recruited by the Air Force Academy as a cadet and hockey player, Tom didn't cheer him on. "I didn't try to dissuade him," he said, "but I tried to lay out clearly what his life would be like, and tried to make him understand that it was right for some and not right for others." It's the same advice he gives in the classroom when the subject of military service comes up. Their son decided not to attend the Air Force Academy, and none of their four children has served in the military.

Given Coakley's concerns in 1967 and 1968, he's still a little surprised that the new generation doesn't have to worry about being drafted. He would like to see some form of mandatory national service and thinks that "it's a nonideological issue. If you want to unify a society and culture, it's something we should do. That's what makes me comfortable about my service. Even though I didn't value the war, I had a responsibility to society.

"I think I would have seen the world much more differently if I hadn't gone to Vietnam. I would have been much more shallow. Life would have been much less complex. I wouldn't want that."

He stays in close contact with his old platoon. They have regular reunions, and he says they talk less and less about Vietnam every year and more about what's going on in their lives now. They all went through a difficult passage when one of them had a son-in-law killed in Iraq.

In her role as counselor, Nellie is now seeing Iraq as well as Vietnam vets, and she sees the parallels as sadly familiar. One young man just back from Iraq said to her, "You know, we really don't matter to anyone." She's trying to establish a comfort zone between the community and the Iraq War veterans, reaching out to local nonprofits to find money for additional counseling and outreach programs.

The experience has not been easy. She has had to readjust from the Vietnam veterans, who had the buffer of time between their war experiences and their current situations. Iraq veterans, she says, arrive with their emotional wounds still very raw. The expanded role of the National Guard has added another difficult dimension. "It's very tough for the guy who left a civilian life with a civilian job and family to go to Iraq and then return to that civilian world with no comprehension on the part of those around him about what he'd been through.

"Marriages," she says, "are falling apart all over the place. These guys, like those in Vietnam, were fighting an enemy they couldn't see. They became paranoid. They didn't trust anyone. They're not identifying with their family. They're in pain. The wife is saying, 'Get over it. You're home.' It's very much like Vietnam. And for everything the Army says they're doing, they're just not doing enough.

"I placed a family of an Iraq War vet about three or four houses down from me. A very good friend of mine lives two houses away, and she was upset because the vet was always revving his motorcycle and his dogs were always barking. I went to her and said, 'Maybe he doesn't live like you, but there are things he's working through right now. These guys . . . need help adjusting. They need people to reach out and welcome them to the neighborhood.' " Nellie imagined what the vet must be thinking: "I've held guys in my arms dying, and you're telling me the most important thing in your life is that my dog is barking? That's all you have to worry about?"

Nellie's life will continue to be defined by those searing experiences as an Army nurse in Vietnam, which left her with an enduring empathy for veterans and their families.

Through all the years that had passed since she got back from Vietnam, Nellie had never forgotten Richard Burns. She kept thinking of him and how his mother didn't know when her son died. So she decided to find the family of that young paratrooper from the 101st Airborne whom she knew only from his name tag, his violent death, and the strong impact he had made on some of the men who knew him. With Tom's help, she found a contact on the Internet, a friend of Richard Burns's parents who had left a note about him on a Vietnam memorial website.

Nellie left a note on the same website, describing her role as a nurse the night Richard was brought in. A few days later, the phone rang. It was Richard's brother, Michael, who had been a medic about to ship out for Vietnam when Richard was killed. He told Nellie that his mother had gotten in touch with her congressman and said, "You've already taken one of my sons. You will not take another." Michael was held back.

Michael arranged for Nellie to talk to his mother, who was living in Nevada. Mrs. Burns said she was nervous about the call but very happy that it had been arranged.

Nellie told Mrs. Burns about how Richard had been so beloved by his buddies and how her MASH unit had done everything possible to save him. She was surprised that the official notification of his death had gotten so many details wrong, omitting the loss of his legs and misidentifying the hospital where he had been sent.

After the call, Mrs. Burns was eager to meet Nellie. They made arrangements to get together in Las Vegas, where Tom's platoon was having a reunion. Nellie recalled, "I arranged to have a dozen roses at the front desk for Richard's parents when I met them." Mrs. Burns, in turn, had made a floral arrangement for Nellie, and when they met, it was an emotional moment for all. "It was apparent that Richard's death had all but destroyed the family," Nellie said, "but the mother held it together. She was the strength. As we parted, she kissed me and said, 'To think that I have touched you, who touched my son.'"

Nellie sent the family a photograph of the ward where Richard had died because, as she put it, "If that was my son, I would want to be as close to him as I could be in his death." She also arranged to meet Michael at the Vietnam Veterans Memorial in Washington on February 28, the anniversary of Richard's death.

"He told me he went there every year on that date with two Budweiser beers. He drank one and set the other down beneath his brother's name." Nellie left a rose and a note at Richard's name, saying, "I finally met your family."

Since then she's stayed in close touch with the

Burns family. "They're like part of my family. I think Richard helped all of us to gain closure. There's a little more healing that's taken place."

As for her life with her husband, Nellie says, "We didn't talk about Vietnam for ten years. When we began, he didn't want to go there. But now we've become quite a team."

Oh, Canada:
Jeffry House

Jeffry House didn't go to Vietnam.

He went to Canada.

He's still there, and he plans to stay.

House is one of three sons of a Wisconsin couple firmly rooted in the values of their region and their time. His father was a newspaperman and a veteran of World War II who landed at Normandy and was later wounded fighting in France. House's mother was first an admirer of Dwight Eisenhower, the Allied commander in World War II who returned home to become a two-term president of the United States, and then she transferred her political allegiance to Barry Goldwater, the Arizona senator and the godfather of the modern conservative movement.

They were typical of so many of their generation in their life's experiences and their unquestioning love of their country and its leaders. When House was still in high school, America's role in Vietnam was expanding, but in his family and community, there were no doubts about the need to be there, because of the

Jeffry House as a student at the University of Wisconsin in 1968

Jeffry House today, a citizen of Canada for more than thirty years

domino theory, which held that every Southeast Asian nation would fall to Communism if the United States didn't intervene in South Vietnam.

House grew up under those influences in Green Bay, the home of the storied National Football League Packers and their legendary old-school coach, Vince Lombardi. Lombardi personified the America of the Fifties and early Sixties with his authoritarian manner and hard-nosed homilies. He is famous for the quote "Winning isn't everything; it's the **only** thing."

In 1965 Jeffry House enrolled at the University of Wisconsin, a hothouse of liberal activism, where he was exposed for the first time to a different filter on the image of America, particularly on the country's growing presence in Vietnam. He took a class in Southeast Asian history and, as he now remembers, "Things didn't quite compute. The story I was getting in the course was not exactly the story I was hearing from the government." By 1966 the antiwar movement on the Wisconsin campus was one of the most active in the country, and House had even more doubts about what he was hearing from Washington.

Then came the Senate hearings organized by Senator J. William Fulbright, the erudite chairman of the Senate Foreign Relations Committee and an early critic of the war.

House was stunned to hear George F. Kennan, the Princeton scholar venerated for his insights into Soviet intentions and American foreign policy, express reservations about the war. Kennan was a Wisconsin native and highly regarded by House's father, who had once interviewed him and shared with his sons an admiration for

Kennan's judgment. To hear a fellow Midwesterner with such impeccable credentials question the president's decisions had a special resonance with House.

House was no longer the young innocent from Green Bay. "I slowly awoke to the fact that President Johnson wasn't telling the truth about the Gulf of Tonkin Resolution [which gave him greatly expanded authority to wage war in Vietnam after what turned out to be an illusory attack on an American warship]. He wasn't a god.

"All of a sudden I felt terribly betrayed that they could lie about this and send people off to die thinking they were defending their government. At the university, there were a lot of out-of-state students who were much more cynical than those of us from the Midwest. We thought everything was hunky-dory, so we were surprised when it wasn't what we were told."

Despite his feelings of betrayal, House wasn't particularly active in the campus antiwar movement. "I was marginally involved, I guess," he says now. The one demonstration he remembers most clearly was a memorial on the night Dr. Martin Luther King Jr. was assassinated. "That was a very passionate moment . . . when you didn't know whether to throw yourself in front of a car because America was such a damned country."

As he made his way through his undergraduate years, House had episodic discussions with his father about Vietnam. The elder House would respond to his son's criticisms with something like "The president knows way more than you can ever know."

Jeffry House, however, had different ideas. He was hoping the war would be over by the time he graduated so he wouldn't have to make the difficult decision about whether to dodge the draft. But he graduated in the spring of 1969, and a few months later his draft notice arrived.

He admits that he was torn between the world of his upbringing and the new world that had opened to him in Madison. For a while he felt, "I really don't like this war, but I think I have an obligation to go through with it." As he wrestled with his decision, he came to another conclusion. "Going through with it means shooting people . . . they want you to kill for this cause. I ultimately thought, 'No, I can't go and shoot people.' "

House made his decision after reporting for his draft physical. "I remember very well, all the recruits were treated as pieces of garbage. Those in charge were telling us to spread our anuses, and if we didn't spread them wide enough, 'You're gonna be shipped to Vietnam tomorrow. You won't even have time to go home and see your parents.' Their attitude made it clear I wasn't making a mistake in what I was thinking."

What he was thinking was that he should go to Canada. He had been ordered to report for military duty on January 28, 1970. He spent Christmas 1969 with his family in Green Bay. He waited until the last minute to tell his parents his plans. They were furious. "My mother was really mad. She ran off to her bedroom crying. My dad was also angry. He said he couldn't support my decision in any way, and if I left the country, I was leaving the family for good—I should just forget about them."

After House left for Canada, his father announced

to his two other sons that their brother was persona non grata in the family. The brothers, both younger, immediately took Jeffry's side, telling their dad that they would do the same thing. The dinner hour erupted in a shouting match. House's father, a man who rarely used profanity, was in a rage, pounding the table with his fists, yelling, "Goddamn it!"

The war, which so divided the nation, had an even deeper scarring effect on families, often for different reasons. When my brother Mike, a working-class high school graduate, shipped out for Vietnam, our father called me to complain bitterly about the deferments automatically given to college students. When I tried to defend them, my arguments sounded hollow and feeble. By the end of the call, I told Dad he was right.

Mike returned home safely, and his Marine Corps experience is something he treasures to this day. But if something had happened to him in Vietnam, I'm sure our father never would have forgiven the system that protected the privileged and offered no similar sanctuary for the others.

On the day Jeffry House was to report for military duty, he joined the exodus of many young men his age and left for Canada in his Volkswagen Beetle. It was not easy leaving America. "It was really sad, because the United States is filled with terrific people, great institutions; it's such a beautiful place. But I was not the corn-fed all-American boy I had been four years earlier.

"Still, when you give up your country it hurts in ways you don't expect. I didn't expect to be as sad as I was. I had been thinking, 'They're doing the wrong thing. I won't shoot someone just because the president says so. I'm doing what I know is right, so screw you guys.' But then as I crossed into Canada, I remember thinking, 'Oh, man . . .' "

At first House missed the familiar parts of his old life: watching the NBA on television, or his beloved Green Bay Packers on Sunday afternoons (American sports on television had not yet become a fixture north of the border). For six months no one in his family called or wrote. Then his mother and grandmother came to visit him in Toronto, to make sure he wasn't homeless.

The political debate in America was shifting fast on Vietnam, and House believes his father was undergoing his own transformation. But it was almost two years before his dad finally called to say, "I'm rethinking this. Maybe what you did wasn't so wrong." His father came to Toronto, and they retreated for a week to a cottage in the woods north of the city to reconnect. When I asked House what they had talked about, he said, "Just the normal stuff—we didn't really discuss politics or the war or my decision."

House went back to school in Canada, earning first a master's degree in political theory and then a law degree. He's been in private practice in Canada for over thirty years now, specializing in human rights law. He has no regrets about his decision to run from the draft that could have sent him to a war he so strongly opposed. "I think the United States from time to time betrays its better self, and the Vietnam War was one of those moments. So I personally felt I had to refuse, to maintain what I think are the better traditions.

"I've probably had only two days of doubts the

whole time I've lived here," he says. He consciously did not become part of the Canadian culture of American resisters and draft dodgers. "Mostly, I stayed away from [them]," he says, "because their main orientation was AMEX, Americans in Exile in Canada. I never thought of myself as an exile. I thought of myself as an American who had to emigrate.

"There are quite a few American deserters and draft dodgers still here. The main Toronto radio personality is Andy Berry, an American deserter. Five or six judges in Toronto now are old draft dodgers or in the provisional parliament. So they're all over the country."

House is firmly settled in Canada physically, intellectually, and emotionally, but he's still struggling with his journey north. "I feel more objective about the American culture than when I was in it . . . it's made me more inquisitive. You swerve off the path you always thought you'd be on, and you wonder, 'Was it my mistake? Was it inevitable? What in me—in my parents—drove me to make the decision I did? If I had met the right person at some other time—someone I wanted to marry—would I have made the same decision?'

"I feel my path would have been easier if I had remained in the United States. I had connections with people there. You understand the culture better, having grown up in it.

"Here in Canada I remember during the first few years, I was perceived as loud and pushy, with more Midwestern assertiveness than they have here."

For House, the war in Iraq has brought his life full circle. He's now representing U.S. servicemen who have moved to Canada to avoid service in the latest American war.

He emphasizes that he's not automatically antiwar: "I thought the first Gulf war was fine. Afghanistan, I thought, was in self-defense . . . even the war in Yugoslavia, I thought there was a reasonable basis for that. But Iraq is different.

"I was with the many people in the world who thought . . . it was not justified. When [UN arms inspector] Hans Blix said, essentially, 'I can't find any weapons of mass destruction,' I thought that was very significant. I was opposed to the war in Iraq before Jeremy came into my office."

Jeremy Hinzman is a U.S. Army deserter now seeking asylum in Canada. He was referred to House by a Quaker congregation in Toronto. House saw a lot of himself in Jeremy during their first meeting. "He said, 'This war is bogus,' which is not a word from the Sixties, but it's exactly how I felt when I found out about President Johnson's lies. So I told him my story and how I've been able to make a good life here."

Canada's Immigration and Refugee Board denied Jeremy's petition for asylum on the first pass, and House appealed to the Federal Court of Appeal, which also rejected Jeremy's claims. House has made one final appeal, to the Supreme Court of Canada, and he is awaiting that decision.

Canada's system for dealing with American deserters has changed since Vietnam. The Immigration and Refugee Board is new, and its decisions have a legal rather than a political basis. Another major difference is that while Vietnam-era deserters could argue that they were being involuntarily drafted, Jeremy joined voluntarily, albeit in peacetime.

By early 2007 House had a dozen American military clients, all seeking refugee status in Canada. Additionally, he says, he has informally counseled scores of others, including West Point graduates. "I'm very impressed by these American soldiers," he says. "They take their obligations as human beings and as citizens seriously."

House is married to an Argentinian woman he met at a human rights conference, and they have two teenage sons who, he says, share his critical views of U.S. foreign policy in the Bush administration.

He occasionally visits family in the United States, though he never attends high school reunions or seeks out old friends from the Sixties. House says that earlier, when he did return, most of his friends were supportive of his decision, but some weren't. It didn't bother him—then or now. He's comfortable with who he is—an American by birth, a Canadian by choice.

Semper Fi:
Senator James Webb,
Mike "Mac" McGarvey,
and James Fallows

The first thing you need to know about James Henry Webb Jr., U.S. Naval Academy Class of 1968, is that he is a warrior—physically, intellectually, and culturally. He has fought for his country, often face-to-face in combat. As one of the most highly decorated Marines in Vietnam, Jim Webb has impeccable military credentials. Among his many medals and campaign ribbons are a Navy Cross, which is the service's second-highest honor (surpassed only by the Medal of Honor), awarded for "extreme gallantry and risk of life in actual combat with an armed enemy force," and a Silver Star. He is also a fierce believer in his personal and political compass, which is a product of his working-class Scots-American roots in Appalachia.

I traveled to Vietnam with Jim Webb in January 2006, almost a year before his surprising upset over incumbent Republican George Allen in the race for one of Virginia's U.S. Senate seats. As we walked through Vietnam's prosperous cities and peaceful countryside, he was still trying to decide whether to run.

It seemed a quixotic effort at best for a man who was still a registered Republican to be seeking the Democratic Party's nomination. Allen had been a popular governor and congressman before being elected to the Senate by a comfortable margin in a race against another Vietnam veteran, Charles Robb, the Democratic incumbent and son-in-law of the late Lyndon Johnson.

George Allen, the son and namesake of the legendary Redskins football coach, had his own deep family roots. He was a popular good ol' boy who was already being measured as presidential timber. In fact, his almost universally anticipated reelection was considered the first step on a road that would lead from Capitol Hill to 1600 Pennsylvania Avenue.

Webb decided to challenge Allen only after lobbying the senator to take a more critical view of how the Iraq War was being managed. According to Webb, Allen responded, "I can't go against my president." That was when Webb concluded that Allen was more interested in protecting his partisan interests than in representing the broader national interest. Still, when political pundits and campaign consultants heard he was considering a run against such a popular incumbent they gave him little chance. He was, not surprisingly, undeterred. For Jim Webb, the Virginia Senate campaign was only the latest chapter in a highly unconventional life of military service, literary success, contrarian views, and a confrontational personal style.

He was not a natural as a candidate. He is what the

British would call an "unclubbable" man who doesn't fit in easily with social conventions or have much patience with glad-handing and small talk—the traits that most people consider prerequisites for any politician. One of his longtime friends is Bob Kerrey, who tried to prepare him for the rigors of the campaign trail. "Man, you've got to get up every morning and stand in front of a mirror and practice smiling for thirty minutes," Kerrey joked. When someone told Kerrey that despite their tough exteriors, the two shared similarly "impish" characteristics, Kerrey was skeptical. He quipped, "Jim's a dark imp, the kind who says, 'Fuck with me and I'll kill you.' "

The campaign was unconventional from the start. Webb arrived at campaign appearances in a Jeep driven by one of his old squad members. He wore suits and the beat-up combat boots that his son, Marine Lance Corporal Jimmy Webb (aka "Webb-stah"), had worn through basic training before being shipped off to Iraq.

Webb was the neophyte in the race, but it was the incumbent who made the big mistakes. Most famously, he referred to a Webb campaign worker assigned to follow and videotape his appearances as "macaca"—an African expression for "monkey" that could also be a racial epithet. The young man, a Virginia resident, was of East Indian descent. A video of Allen's mocking comment quickly showed up on YouTube and was replayed constantly throughout the campaign.

Webb, a passive and rather undemonstrative campaigner, was the beneficiary of his opponent's continuing stumbles. When Allen was asked about reports that his mother was Jewish, he said he had only recently become aware of it and then added, inexplicably, "I still had a ham sandwich for lunch." It was also disclosed that apparently he had a fondness for the Confederate flag, and that he had once hung a noose (which he described as "more of a lasso") on a ficus tree in his law office.

Webb had his own difficulties, having to explain a long, contentious article he'd written when women were admitted to Annapolis. The essence of it was that the academy's mission is to train men for combat and women are simply not suited for that kind of fighting. He refused to say he was wrong, but he took the edge off the issue with references to the number of women he had assigned to important positions while he was secretary of the Navy.

Webb, positioning himself as a conservative Democrat out of what he calls the "redneck school," was decidedly an acquired taste for liberals such as Charles Schumer, who was in charge of the Democratic Senate races. But the New York senator completely understood the importance of Webb to the party's attempt to broaden its appeal among white Southern males and promilitary voters. Webb so hated making fund-raising calls, and was so ineffective at them, that Schumer would grab the phone from his hand and up the ante with whomever was on the other end of the line.

Now a member of the United States Senate—"the most exclusive club"—Jim Webb remains refreshingly unclubbable. One of his aides was briefly detained when he absentmindedly carried a sidearm into the Capitol.

In an exchange of e-mails with me, Webb expressed his frustrations with what he called the politically correct debate being conducted over immigration and global warming while what he considered the more important concern of economic fairness for the working class and underclass was being ignored. He expressed frustration that his side doesn't know how to fight. He recalled what someone said about liberals: "They leave the room when a fight breaks out."

During our trip to Vietnam I came to know how Webb fought for what he believed in during the war, and how that war and its politics formed so much of what he is now.

When I arrived in Saigon at midnight, he was there to meet me at the airport on what he later called "a successful blind date." After all, we knew each other only slightly, and here we were in a country where he had been under fire almost every day for a year in 1969, while I was half a world away living a comfortable life in California and covering the antiwar movement that he thoroughly despised. A former Golden Gloves boxer who still has a tight, solid middleweight build, he led the way through the crowded terminal, chin and chest out, as if answering the bell for the next round.

Outside in the mild muggy January night, he used his fluent Vietnamese to arrange for a taxi and to get my luggage stowed. This was his fifteenth trip here since the war ended, and each time he has been struck by the tremendous changes that have taken place. Saigon (officially called Ho Chi Minh City since the Communists took over in 1975) and Hanoi are lively cities, buzzing with the constant hum of motor scooters and merchants eagerly beckoning Western tourists

"A warrior—physically,
intellectually, and culturally."
Lieutenant James Webb on patrol.

Virginia senator Jim Webb taking the oath
of office, as administered by a political
adversary, Vice President Dick Cheney.
Webb is accompanied by his wife, Hong Le, and
daughter, Georgia LeAnh, born just weeks before.

into their small shops stocked with silk goods, electronics, cameras, and pirated and local folk art.

The bright red Communist Party banners hanging from light poles and gateways to public parks are reminders of the continuing political reality of Vietnam, even as they present an incongruous contrast to the throbbing free enterprise flourishing on the streets below them. It's almost impossible to believe this is the same grim country where so many Americans died.

As we left Hoi An, the historic old city along the central coast, Webb said, with sudden feeling, "You know, I love this place. I also hate it." The view out the van's windows in the winter of 2006 was very different from what Second Lieutenant Webb would have seen when he arrived as a freshly minted Marine lieutenant in 1969. After graduating from Annapolis, he was the top man in his class at the combat training command center at Quantico, the big Marine base in northern Virginia. His superiors had very high expectations of Lieutenant Webb—but none higher than the standards he set for himself. He arrived in Vietnam to fight a war he believed in deeply. And he was fully aware that he would be carrying on the traditions of his ancestors who had worn American military uniforms since the Revolutionary War.

He says, matter-of-factly, "The concept of what your country is, and what it meant to your ancestors, is very basic to me." Two of his forebears died fighting for the South in the Civil War, and when he was asked to speak at the Confederate Memorial in Arlington National Cemetery a few years ago, he accepted in part because he believes so strongly in the definition of service that is carved around it:

NOT FOR FAME OR REWARD
NOT FOR PLACE OR FOR RANK
NOT LURED BY AMBITION
OR GOADED BY NECESSITY
BUT IN SIMPLE
OBEDIENCE TO DUTY
AS THEY UNDERSTOOD IT
THESE MEN SUFFERED ALL
SACRIFICED ALL
DARED ALL—AND DIED.

For his speech that day at the Confederate Memorial, Webb invited along one of his oldest and closest friends, Nelson Jones. Jones, a fellow Marine and Vietnam vet, is a black man. Introducing him to the large audience, Webb said, "Those Americans of African ancestry are the people with whom our history in this country most closely intertwines, whose struggles in an odd but compelling way most resemble our own, and whose rights as full citizens we above all should celebrate and insist upon." It was the kind of counterintuitive moment you get used to if you spend much time with Jim Webb, a complex and iconoclastic man who lives in many worlds.

The Vietnam War, Webb believed then, and still believes today, was both just and justified. Communism, led by the awakening giant of China, was a spreading menace throughout Southeast Asia. "Look at what had gone on in Indonesia," he says, referring to the rise of the PKI, which had become the third-largest Communist Party in the world before it was wiped out in 1965 following a failed coup.

But he also believes, just as strongly, that the execution of the Vietnam War was a disaster, and that the divisions at home—especially those separating the elite class from the obligations of service—are destructive and consequential to this day.

Jim Webb is now sixty-one. Married for the third time, he is the father of four grown children and a toddler. He has a law degree from Georgetown University. Before Ronald Reagan appointed him secretary of the Navy, Webb was already the author of seven books, including his seminal novel **Fields of Fire**, which is widely regarded as one of the few fiction classics of the Vietnam War. He has been a Hollywood screenwriter and producer and a newspaper columnist on national security issues. He is the best-known Marine to come out of Vietnam—except, possibly, for Oliver North, his Annapolis classmate. They share an alma mater and the Corps and little else.

Jim Webb and Ollie North were two alpha males who were bound to clash. They were Naval Academy rivals and Marine officers during the same period. They both served in the Reagan administration: Webb worked for Defense Secretary Caspar Weinberger while North was a junior aide in the White House and self-appointed swashbuckler who became a pivotal figure in the Iran-Contra scandal. Subsequently he ran for the U.S. Senate and lost to another fellow Marine—and Webb's predecessor—Chuck Robb.

Webb plainly is neither friend nor fan of Oliver North, but he's resigned to the fact that their lives will be forever linked by the academy, the Marines, combat, politics, and the contrasts in their ethical standards and personal conduct. Webb wins on every measurable count, but it's not a contest he welcomes. He says, "North was a fine combat platoon leader." But he won't say anything more, and, like so many others, he has no patience for North's self-aggrandizing ways, which he feels too often fail to line up with the truth.

The enduring and defining truth in the life of James Webb began when, at the age of twenty-three, he got on a plane in America and stepped off it into the fields of fire called the An Hoa Basin. He took over a platoon on the run—literally—as it was returning from patrol without a lieutenant. Webb says dryly, "I think they'd had three lieutenants in three months."

He was ready. Robert Timberg, a fellow Naval Academy graduate and Marine veteran of Vietnam, wrote an insightful character study of Webb in his book **The Nightingale's Song**. Timberg described Webb's arrival in hostile territory:

A battle-hardened young lance corporal watched the youthful Webb emerge from a helicopter and muttered, "Boot" as the new lieutenant hustled by him. Webb recognized the contemptuous term for "rookie." He turned back to the enlisted man, got right up in his face and said, "Do you know who I am?"

"No, but it doesn't matter," came the reply.

"I happen to be Lieutenant James H. Webb, Jr. You can call me 'Lieutenant,' or you can call me 'sir.' You got that?"

That night, with only one day of field indoctrination, Webb led a patrol into a heavily fortified North Vietnamese stronghold. A major firefight broke out. As the brigade commander watched from his compound, he thought he'd lost his new Naval Academy graduate on his first night.

But Webb was coolly directing his troops—calling in mortar, artillery, and air strikes—and before long, the fight was over with no American casualties. He had a repeat performance the next night, and within a few days, his troops and commanders knew they were in the presence of a Marine's Marine; more important, an officer who could lead them into battle and bring them home alive.

One morning we drove to the An Hoa Basin, the broad valley and delta where two big rivers drain down from the surrounding mountains. This had been Jim Webb's home base for a year of almost daily fighting. The backcountry roads were narrow but now paved as they wound through the rural villages and rice paddies where farmers bent to their labor with simple hand tools. On this mild morning, the scene, some twenty miles west of Da Nang, was undeniably beautiful. But the first time Jim Webb saw it, An Hoa was a charnel house that chewed up anyone who entered. After driving into the valley we stopped at a memorial to the North Vietnamese and local war dead. A two-story ceramic tower stood atop a small knoll in the village of Dai Loc, flanked by fifteen-foot-high panels. We did a rough calculation and determined that the eighteen big panels bore at least six thousand names.

Webb took it all in and then said in a low, forceful tone, "We did our job, Mr. Brokaw." It was as if, all these years later, he was back on active duty, a warrior checking in, making a formal report on his activities. We stood in silence, looking out over the lush green valley, with this stark reminder of the cost of war in front of us. "In the military, they say, 'Marines know how to die,'" Webb said. "These people knew how to die."

In his six months as a platoon and then company commander, Webb was in combat almost every day, fighting everything from pajama-clad guerrilla Vietcong patrols to regular regiments of the North Vietnamese Army. It seemed as if they just kept coming out of the mountains to the north and west and out of the small farming villages all around.

Now, as we moved west along the road connecting these same villages, Webb became pensive, taking in the improved conditions—the new wells, the efficiently designed concrete and tile houses, and the thriving markets spilling over with local farm products and modern appliances for sale.

He remembered when the north side of the river was a North Vietnamese Army and Vietcong hot zone and he was ordered to pull his platoon back two miles so the area could be carpet-bombed. After the planes had gone, his team was sent in to assess the damage. "It still gives me chills," he said. "Those people suffered so much. Even now, on that side of the river they hate us." In the target area and throughout the valley, the combat was so fierce that there were no trees left standing. Today it is a lush verdant postcard of Southeast Asian tranquillity and emerging prosperity.

Webb remembered another time when he was returning with his squad from a patrol. The American commander in the area had organized a kind of town meeting with local village officials to discuss the prospects for political reform, including the possibility of conducting more elections. "They were all in one hooch," Webb said, "when suddenly, out of the trees, a Vietcong squad materialized and just massacred everyone in there. Someone had leaked details of the meeting, and the last thing the VC wanted was a real democracy.

"You didn't hear the antiwar protestors back home complaining about that kind of behavior."

Even today, with Vietnam rushing headlong into the twenty-first-century world of free global markets, Webb is still aware of old sensitivities. There are some memories he doesn't want to share publicly because many of the senior local government officials in Quan Nan Province are former members of the North Vietnamese Army, and the warrior-to-warrior camaraderie, he worries, would go only so far. There were operations that had targeted key NVA personnel, and they may still have friends in the area.

At a local government headquarters, we met one former NVA soldier, now a very senior provincial official. He was polite but wary as Webb tried to gauge his interest in an ambitious project he is interested in developing on the former site of a massive Marine fire-base at the western end of the valley. Webb would like to build a complex that honors both sides in the war and explains the different reasons why they were fight-ing. He envisions a school, a history center, and a re-creation of a typical small village of the period. This is one of Webb's ceaseless efforts to validate, as he puts it, the service of those who fought and to honor the sacri-fice of those who died, on both sides.

The ex-NVA soldier was, at best, distantly non-committal. He said he would like to see some formal plans, and then he assigned three young plainclothes-men to follow us the rest of the day. Not a good sign, Webb concluded.

We drove on to the head of the valley, to a broad grassy plain that had been the site of the main Marine base—a sprawling compound of artillery positions, ammunition depots, bunkers, a hospital, communica-tions centers, mess halls, and a long single-lane airstrip for helicopters and cargo planes. The airstrip is all that has survived, apart from a few remnants of sandbags and C-ration packages.

As Webb stood on the airstrip, he said, "God, it's so easy to get back into it because of the intensity of my time here. I know this place as well as any place I've ever been in my life. I was constantly thinking, 'What do I do if X or Y happens? Where are we? Where do I go next?' "

He recalled one particular day: "There was a light rain. Mists were pouring down the mountains. It was gorgeous. I was saying to myself, 'I could stay here forever.' You hate it on the one hand, and yet on the other, you know this is what you do well. And I had no idea what I was going to do with the rest of my life."

In a way, Webb did stay forever. He will never completely put Vietnam behind him; nor does he want to. He laughs and says it's all James Michener's fault. He read **Hawaii** when he was a teenager and instantly became fascinated with the tropics. By the time he got to Vietnam, his curiosity about Asia had become boundless, and looking back, he says, "It's kind of funny, because we fought every day, and in the villages there was always tension, but I thought I understood this place and these people better than I ever understood anything in my life."

Webb's third wife, Hong Le, was born in February 1968, during the Tet Offensive, and she was just seven years old when she fled Vietnam in a fishing boat in the middle of the night just ahead of the Communist takeover in 1975. Her family, penniless and uneducated, settled in New Orleans, where her mother opened a small Vietnamese restaurant.

Hong's is one of many inspiring Vietnamese refugee success stories. She graduated from the University of Michigan with distinction and attended Cornell University Law School. A beautiful, petite woman, she now practices securities law in Washington, D.C., where she met Webb through their mutual interest in the developing business climate in Vietnam.

At one village, while Webb and I wandered off to survey old battlefields, Hong was approached by villagers who, not knowing her relationship to us or her family background, warned her to be careful. "They told me the Americans might kidnap me," she said, laughing.

Webb chuckled, but he's not a man given to light moments, especially here, where there are so many memories. As we walked past a villager's garden, he pointed. "That was a good place to sleep. You could get comfortable in the furrows." But only for so long. The valley was never a truly comfortable place.

He won the Navy Cross when he led a platoon against a Vietcong bunker complex. As they approached, three guerrillas jumped out, and Webb personally captured all of them. At the next bunker, he called for the enemy to emerge, and when they responded with a grenade, he answered with a claymore mine and took two casualties. At the third bunker, he and his men again came under assault by grenades. Webb suffered fragment wounds as he shielded his men while managing to fire into the bunker and detonate a grenade.

During our visit, he took me to a cemetery on a small hummock rising out of the delta. He recalled one of his worst moments as a commander. Earlier, a Marine company had been pinned down there during an eight-day battle, so when Webb arrived with his squad, he very carefully positioned his men, including Mike "Mac" McGarvey.

While Webb was directing his troops at the other end of the cemetery, someone told McGarvey to move to the top of the mound. An NVA land mine exploded, and McGarvey was thrown through the air, shrapnel severing his arm in the process. When Webb rushed over, he was so shaken by the wounds to his friend that he uncharacteristically began to cry. Mc-Garvey said, "Knock that shit off, Lieutenant, it's just an arm."

Mac McGarvey had joined the Marine Corps as an eighteen-year-old high school dropout. When he returned to the United States, he moved to Nashville and started adjusting to life with a missing limb and a lot of memories. He worked his way up to one of the coolest jobs in Tennessee—the manager of the legendary Tootsie's Orchid Lounge, where greats like Roger Miller, Willie Nelson, and Kris Kristofferson could always count on a cold brew and a hot meal when they were starting out in their careers.

Mac has long been a civilian, but he'll always be a Marine. "I can't imagine anyone ever wanting to be anything but a Marine," he says. "My older brother was in the Air Force, and after I'd gone through boot camp and the indoctrination of the Marine Corps history, I thought, 'Why in God's name did he join the Air Force?' "

McGarvey was Webb's radio operator, which meant he shadowed the young officer's every step into hostile territory. "We literally ate together, slept together; every step he took, I was right in back of him." McGarvey admits that he's blocked a lot of the Vietnam days from his memory, but Jim Webb will always stand out. "He's a person that you want to know. I knew almost immediately that if it weren't for rank, we were going to be friends. There was a kind of automatic trust with Jim. He was a straight-up dude."

They were separated when the medevac chopper took McGarvey out on the first stage of a long recovery that led from Da Nang to Japan and eventually to Philadelphia for treatment of his wounds. In 1977 the phone rang in the home of McGarvey's mother in Tennessee. A voice on the other end said he was looking for a Mike McGarvey who had been a Marine. McGarvey said that was his name and that he had been a Marine. The caller then asked how many arms he had. When McGarvey answered, "One," the voice said, "Mac, this is the skipper."

Webb invited McGarvey to join him at a ceremony awarding a long-delayed Silver Star to one of their buddies, Dale Wilson, who had lost three limbs in combat. For McGarvey, the phone call was like "a child or a parent contacting you after all those years. Because you learn not only to trust other Marines, you learn to love them."

Webb and McGarvey have been in almost constant contact since that time, and every year they spend time together somewhere. McGarvey moved to Virginia for the Senate campaign and drove Webb around in the Jeep. When Webb was elected, McGarvey became his legislative assistant for veterans' affairs. He quit after six months, explaining, "It's just not where I want to be right now. You put your life's energy into a bill and it might pass six months from now but it might be six years. I'm at a point where I want to slow down."

McGarvey's decision cost Webb some bragging rights. He liked to say that "Mac" was the only senator's aide with a nipple ring and a tattoo on the stump of his missing arm that reads: Cut Along Dotted Line.

McGarvey moved back to his small hometown,

Grayville, Illinois, where cold beer is just a dollar-fifty a bottle and you can still get credit at the grocery store. His son plans to open a restaurant in Grayville, and McGarvey's brothers and sister are within a day's drive.

The skipper would like Mac to consider returning to Washington but he doesn't think he will, even though he "would do almost anything for Jim Webb . . . the relationship we have is sealed in blood. We're just a part of each other."

McGarvey and Webb had arrived in Vietnam from what amounted to two different worlds. As McGarvey puts it, "He had a degree from Annapolis, and I had quit school in a small town in Illinois. The people on my level were tobacco-chewing and beer-drinking—the kinds of guys whose fathers had fought in World War II. The guys Jim was dealing with, especially in that Washington zoo—Disneyland East, we call it—they came from a sort of privileged background. You don't have too many poor kids going to Georgetown University."

Webb did return to a different world than the honky-tonks of Nashville. He admits he didn't seriously consider the politics of the Vietnam War until well after he returned stateside and enrolled at Georgetown Law School. When he had graduated from Annapolis in 1968, as he described it, "my feelings about what was going on were personal and military rather than political." He had a job to do in Vietnam, and his biggest worry was whether he'd be up to the challenges of fighting a tenacious enemy, staying alive, and keeping his men safe while they were under constant fire on the enemy's home turf.

In law school, Webb encountered some of the antiwar feelings that had unfortunately spilled over into contempt for the men who were fighting the war. He was enraged by an exam question at the end of his first term. One of his professors, an outspoken critic of the war, had created a hypothetical case in which a fictional sergeant he provocatively named "Webb" was accused of shipping illicit jade home from Vietnam in the bodies of dead Marines. Webb completed the exam in a cold fury and spent an angry, tearful night trying to decide how to react. Later, he confronted the professor, saying, "I just want you to know it wasn't funny. I went over to Vietnam with sixty-seven lieutenants, and twenty-two died; and it wasn't funny."

Webb learned two big lessons in law school: how to fight with your brain, and "never to take any shit again." After school, he stayed in Washington and went to work for the House Committee on Veterans' Affairs. His curiosity was piqued by the many conflicting reports about Vietnam—about who had served and who hadn't—so he began to dig into the facts. What he found troubles him still. "This was the first large-scale war in American history where the elites didn't go," he says. "I called Harvard, Princeton, and MIT, and I asked the registrars very specific questions. This was a war fought by the poor, by minorities, and by the middle class—not the elites."

His friend McGarvey saw that disparity from the perspective of his country-boy roots. "It certainly seemed unfair, but you know the world's not fair. The privileged are the privileged. Those people know what they did. They have to look in the mirror and deal with that today."

In fact, there is very little dialogue or public reflection on the part of those who chose not to serve, by whatever means. The same is true for the consequences of the end of the war. But for the Vietnam veteran, these issues never completely fade.

The fall of Saigon in 1975—the images of people holding on to the skids of the choppers leaving the American embassy, the dramatic mass migration of millions of South Vietnamese, and the dire fates that befell many of those who had to stay—had a profound effect on Webb. When he was fighting, he hadn't had the time to figure out the politics of it all. But "watching the boat people jumping into the sea, half of them dying, just to get away, that gave meaning to what the U.S. had been trying to do, far beyond what many Americans were willing to understand or acknowledge."

It wasn't just the South Vietnamese who affected Webb in 1975. He was also concerned about justice for another class of refugees from the war—the rank-and-file grunts, the young men who had been drafted or had enlisted out of a sense of duty or because they had no other way out of what was supposed to be the universal obligation of military service.

"When Saigon fell, a lot of Americans just wanted to sweep the whole experience under the rug. A lot of us who had college educations when we went to war returned to assimilate in a certain way. But I saw so many guys I cared about—eighteen-, nineteen-year-olds for whom the war was their first adult experience—and when they got back, they were wrecked. No one seemed to care."

In the worst cases, returning veterans still in uniform were called "baby killers" or shunned in public places by young men and women their own age who had escalated their personal opposition to the war into a license to attack anyone in uniform. It has always been difficult to quantify the extent of that vile and inexcusable behavior, and some veterans may have exaggerated it, but over the years I've heard from enough thoughtful veterans to know it wasn't one or two isolated incidents.

One of them, Nebraska senator Chuck Hagel, a working-class kid and college dropout, was severely wounded twice in Vietnam. He remembers the jarring transition of being on patrol in the jungle one day and then, three days later, being flown to San Francisco, where he was mustering out of the Army.

"There was no goodbye or thanks or anything of that order," he says. "They just told us, 'Don't wear your uniform into San Francisco; that will get you in trouble.' " He was given a bus ticket and told that he could go home to Nebraska. His only other memory of leaving the Bay Area was a new song on the radio by Dion and the Belmonts—"Abraham, Martin, & John," about the assassinations of Lincoln, King, and Kennedy.

The Vietnam veterans were returning to a different country from the one they had left, and their treatment at home at the hands of some created strong bonds. As Webb's friend McGarvey puts it, "I don't care what your politics are, but when you start coming down on the warrior, I am not a pleasant person to deal with. I can swell up pretty quick. I saw too many people wounded and dying to tolerate anyone even beginning to talk bad about the warrior."

It is a wrong that Webb is determined to right. His mission reaches all the way to Saigon and those who served in the South Vietnamese Army. He suggested that we stay at the Rex Hotel, a stately old colonial-style structure in the heart of Saigon that had been a familiar watering hole for Americans during the war.

He wanted me to meet a cyclo driver, one of those ubiquitous figures on the streets of Vietnamese cities trying to attract tourists into their bicycle carriages. They're at the bottom of the transportation chain, earning maybe the equivalent of ten U.S. dollars on a good day for putting in a lot of hard work.

Webb's friend goes by the name of Louie. He's a charming, droll man, a heavy smoker, and a veteran of the South Vietnamese Army's elite airborne brigade. When the Communists won, Louie was sent for several years to a "reeducation" camp, part of a grim gulag of indoctrination and hard labor not unlike the ones spawned by the Cultural Revolution in China. For whatever reasons, too many Americans who had been strident in their denunciations of the corruption of the South Vietnamese government during the war had too little to say about the cruelties of the victorious North.

Louie organized three of his fellow cyclo drivers to give us a tour of District 4, which is Saigon's ghetto for the war's losers—the South Vietnamese Army veterans and former government officials. District 5 is the flourishing Chinese neighborhood. As Louie put it, "You go to District 5 to live. You go to District 4 to die."

We were pedaled through alleyways choked with people and debris, across open sewers and past markets that were little more than lean-tos with sparsely stocked shelves. District 4 is a permanent squatters' camp, not unlike those I saw in South Africa while apartheid was still enforced. Webb, with a wad of Red Man chewing tobacco tucked into his lower lip, thought it important that I see how the North had treated their fellow Vietnamese. Thirty years after Saigon fell, the wages of war are still being paid by the losing side.

Webb also wanted me to see what is now called the War Remnants Museum, formerly the Museum of Chinese and American War Crimes. The rebranding was apparently made with an eye to the growing Western tourist trade. In its previous incarnation, Webb said, it was so outrageously heavy-handed that he walked out. Now the displays and the language are slightly more tempered. The courtyard is jammed with disabled American tanks and artillery pieces, bomb casings, and wrecked U.S. helicopters.

In the main hall, large black-and-white photographs show people purported to be victims of American torture. The most prominent display features Webb's friend Bob Kerrey. As we approached the photo, Webb murmured, "Kerrey made the big board—but not in a way he would like." The display recounts a controversial nighttime raid that Kerrey led on a Vietnamese village in which a number of women and children were killed in a firefight and a village elder had his throat cut.

A member of Kerrey's team later claimed that the raid, and the atrocities that he charged had been committed during it, had been covered up. Kerrey and the other members of his squad have all denied this. Regardless, the Vietnamese have used the incident as an example of American cruelty. In the museum, they also claim, "Not until April 2001 did former U.S. Senator Robert Kerrey confess his crimes before international public opinion."

That is not true, and Webb believes the U.S. government should lodge a protest to Vietnam, not just for Kerrey but to assure veterans of other wars, including Iraq, that they will not be abandoned to the propaganda of the enemy after the fighting is over. This is a continuing crusade for Webb, and it is not confined to Vietnam. He was critical of the early American involvement in the Persian Gulf, well before Saddam Hussein invaded Kuwait and the United States launched Operation Desert Storm on January 17, 1991. He felt the Navy was stretched to dangerous limits, protecting Kuwaiti oil tankers against Iraqi mines and warplanes. On March 17, 1987, an American frigate, the USS **Stark,** had been attacked by Iraq, killing thirty-seven U.S. sailors.

He told **The New York Times** in 1988, "We commit our forces to an operational environment and then become paralyzed by the political debate that follows." He was secretary of the Navy at the time and became an outspoken critic of the operation, both inside the Pentagon and publicly.

During our trip to Vietnam, I told Webb that the mere mention of his name causes some of the best-known officials in the American military and national security circles to roll their eyes. He looked at me for a moment and said simply, "When I fight, I fight. It's always been my way."

Combat in Vietnam shaped Jim Webb's life then and now. As he puts it, "You never really leave the battlefield. I was older at twenty-four than I am today." His wife believes his experience as a platoon commander instilled in him a lifelong obsession with taking care of people. For Webb, that means speaking out against the injustices he sees to a far greater degree than when he was himself a young man with dreams of a life in uniform.

He returns again to the class lines that divide the civilian population from the uniformed services. He sees the same troubling patterns in Iraq as he did in Vietnam. The elites (as he describes them) are still successfully manipulating public and congressional opinion but still not personally paying the price when their policies go awry. "Iraq," he says, "is the worst event to happen in my adult lifetime. It was promoted with very little examination by the public or the legislative branch, and it will take us a good twenty years to get out of there—if we ever do."

He thinks that America is in more trouble now than it was in 1968. "I worry a lot more about the country now than I did then. We've evolved into this notion of class and the sense of entitlement that come out of American elites—how it affects who serves and who decides." For him, it is simply a matter of the elites not having a sense of duty to their country, while the lower classes, for reasons of economics and family tradition, continue to sign up and march in the direction they're pointed.

One of those elites who avoided serving in Vietnam is now one of Webb's close friends. He is Jim Fallows, an editor of **The Harvard Crimson** and Rhodes scholar in the late Sixties, and one of the best long-form journalists over the last thirty years.

When Fallows arrived at Harvard in 1966, he was still a Goldwater Republican from a socially conservative family in Southern California. He remembers how great he had felt about the election of Ronald Reagan as governor. By 1968 his worldview had changed 180 degrees. He was swept up in the antiwar movement and appalled by the assassinations of Dr. Martin Luther King Jr. and Bobby Kennedy. At the **Crimson**, however, he was still viewed as a conservative because, as he says, he believed in the elimination of ROTC from campus but not in blowing up the ROTC building itself. He even thought that American disengagement from Vietnam was preferable to a Vietcong victory.

As he says, "It's true the antiwar movement was way more right than wrong. But there was this inconvenient reality that people didn't want to face." That reality was that it was a war being fought largely by the working and middle classes, not the privileged at places such as Harvard. Fallows came face-to-face with that ugly reality when he drew a low number in the lottery and realized that he "must either be drafted or consciously find a way to prevent it." He wrote about his decision six years later in a long piece for the **Washington Monthly** entitled "What Did You Do in the Class War, Daddy?"

In the atmosphere of that time, each possible choice came equipped with barbs. To answer the call was unthinkable, not only because, in my heart, I was desperately afraid of being killed, but also because, among my friends, it was axiomatic that one should not be "complicit" in the immoral war effort. Draft resistance, the course chosen by a few noble heroes of the movement, meant going to prison or leaving the country. With much the same intensity with which I wanted to stay alive, I did not want those things either. What I wanted was to go to graduate school, to get married, and to enjoy those bright prospects I had been taught that life owed me.

In preparation for his Army physical, Fallows starved himself so his weight was dangerously low and told an induction center inquisitor he had suicidal tendencies.

The Army decided to pass, so Fallows was free to return to the sheltered confines of Harvard Yard. On the bus ride out of the induction center, however, he saw another bus entering, filled with the working-class kids of Southie, Boston's traditional Irish neighborhood. It was a jarring moment for this son of a Southern California physician.

Most of them were younger than us, since they had just left high school, and it had clearly never occurred to them that there might be a way around the draft. They walked through the examination lines like so many cattle off to slaughter. I tried to avoid noticing, but the results were inescapable. While perhaps four out of five of my friends from Harvard were being deferred, just the opposite was happening to the Chelsea boys.

We returned to Cambridge that afternoon, not in government buses but as free individuals, liberated and victorious. The talk was high-spirited, but there was something close to the surface that none of us wanted to mention. We knew now who would be killed.

Fallows, briefly a speechwriter for Jimmy Carter, was very enthusiastic about Webb's candidacy, thinking it was exactly what the Democrats needed. He has long believed that his party of preference is politically vulnerable because it is "chronically weak on military issues," a throwback to the political angst and confusion growing out of Vietnam.

Besides, as Webb describes their bond, "Jim and I had really strong discussions for years. . . . I think we tried to engage our intellect in problems . . . and today the extremes in politics won't allow that to happen." Fallows believes their intersection demonstrates "a general sense of responsibility, of taking things seriously, not being arrogant or flip about the really big decisions facing the country."

For example, they share a common view that affirmative action should be continued, but not based only on race. Webb cites a bright but poor cousin on his mother's side in Arkansas who became the sole support for his family when his father died. When the young man graduated at the top of his class from high school, no colleges were competing to make room for him, as they might have been if he had been a minority, so he joined the Air Force. Subsequently, he developed a debilitating eye disease from a chicken virus that left him blind. He was, in Webb's view, a symbol of the abandonment of white working-class America.

Webb says, "If you're going to have diversity, you've got to include the white culture that's on the bottom economically." Fallows quickly agrees, adding, "The essential class unfairness of life . . . it's not even given lip service when it's the white underclass."

They also agree on abortion being a woman's choice to make, and on gay rights, although they haven't completely sorted out the difference between a civil union and a marriage outside the church.

They diverge, however, where guns are concerned. Webb, who is licensed to carry a weapon—and does—says bluntly, "I'm proguns. No one is going to take my guns." Fallows responds, "I'm not from the gun world at all, so I have no personal stake. I do think it would be better if we could disinvent the four hundred million guns or whatever that are already in circulation, but I know that's not about to happen."

He also admits that it is unlikely that he would have been on the boxing team with Webb if he had gone to a service academy. "I was on the tennis team," he says, laughing. Fallows believes strongly that Webb is just the man the Democrats need on their national security team. He sarcastically recalls the emphasis on John Kerry's military record at the 2004 Democratic convention. "They had to say, 'Well, we're not **all** weak. In fact, we have someone who was in combat.'"

Webb's son, Jimmy, dropped out of Penn State to enlist in the Marines after accompanying his dad on a reporting trip to Afghanistan. He was continuing a family tradition dating all the way back to the Revolutionary War, a legacy Webb chronicled in his book **Born Fighting: How the Scots-Irish Shaped America.** He says, chuckling, that with all the buddies who visited him at home, and all the Vietnam reunions, his son had about "three thousand hours of military leadership tutorial," so enlisting was a natural step for him.

On election night, Jimmy was in Iraq on duty in Ramadi, a particularly dangerous assignment. As a new senator, Webb was invited to the White House for a reception, and President Bush singled him out for attention, asking, "How's your boy?" Webb responded, "I'd like to get them out of Iraq, Mr. President." The president shot back, "That's not what I asked you. How's your boy?" Webb answered stiffly, "That's between me and my boy, Mr. President."

It became a highly publicized and controversial exchange, but Webb has no regrets. "We had tons of e-mails," he told me, "praising me for standing up to him. I think they were trying to set me up for a little sympathy for themselves."

One of Webb's military pals said the exchange was an example of how Webb uses his combat training to go through life: One of the basic rules when you're ambushed is not to run but to counterattack immediately.

A few weeks later, Webb was asked by the Democrats to give the party's response to the president's State of the Union address. He insisted on writing his own speech, and it was the kind of message rarely heard from Democrats on these occasions. He is not a natural-born television performer, but his authenticity cannot be denied in any setting. He showed the audience a picture of his father in his Air Force uniform and talked about what the family had gone through at home while his dad "gladly served his country."

He also described how he and his brother had served in the Marines in Vietnam, adding, "My son has joined the tradition, now serving as an infantry Marine in Iraq." Looking more like a recently retired Marine than a recently elected U.S. senator, Webb stared into the camera and said of the leaders who had sent his family to three wars, "We owed them our loyalty . . . but they owed us sound judgment."

When Jimmy returned safely from Iraq in the spring of 2007, I got an e-mail from his proud father that began with an old expression to mark the safe return from a patrol outside the base: "Marine safely back inside the wire," it read.

If Webb had his way, America would make public service mandatory for all young men and women. He wonders, "Why couldn't we say that to every single person in this country—if they're in a school that receives federal funds—that before you finish high school, you have to do a semester of community service. It's a small step to get kids in the mind-set [that] they have to get out there and give something back."

As for his own life, Webb has no regrets. He loved being a Marine; loved leading men in combat and defending their service when he returned; loved criticizing the government from inside the Pentagon, writing books about war, and returning to his old battlefields. Now he's trying to decide whether he'll ever love the political life as much. He is engaged by the policy opportunities that being in the Senate offers, but he has little patience for the compromises, the schmoozing, and, especially, the fund-raising.

He's still an angry man who is more likely to be respected than loved. But the ironies of his life are not lost on him. As I was walking back from dinner with Webb and Hong on our final night in Hanoi, we passed a street vendor selling bedsheet-size posters of Britney Spears. What greater symbol could there be of the changes that had taken place since 1968? I laughed and, motioning to the image of the suggestively clad singer, said, "That's what you fought for, the right of Britney Spears to be displayed on the streets of Hanoi."

Jim Webb paused for a moment in front of the pouting Ms. Spears, slipped his arm around Hong, and smiled while we continued our stroll back to the hotel.

A Woman's Place

What am I doing spending three hours a day on a cake?

—Joan Growe,
former Minnesota secretary of state

I used to think you could have it all. Now I believe
you can have it all, but not all at the same time.
There are costs to every decision.

—Dr. Judith Rodin

Our education was a dress rehearsal
for a life we never led.

—Wellesley classmate to Nora Ephron

I imagined that if we could get a majority
of Americans to support the issues of equality,
it would happen. I didn't anticipate that after decades,
it would still be unrealized. I thought we had more
of a democracy than we do.

—Gloria Steinem

I was raised in a family of three sons with a red-haired construction-boss father. The testosterone ran high through the heavily male Brokaw clan, but each of us knew that the center of gravity in our family was our mother, Jean Conley Brokaw. She had the best judgment, management skills, and intuition. She laughed at our locker-room humor but always knew where to make us draw the line. We relied on her for personal and professional advice and for her ability to resolve the inevitable intrafamily disputes.

Since she worked full-time, first as a postal clerk and then managing a shoe store, she expected us to share household chores, including learning how to iron shirts and sew on buttons. My father, who had been raised by equally strong sisters in a small, run-down family hotel, knew his way around the kitchen and didn't hesitate to pick up a vacuum cleaner or dust mop.

Mother and other women like her in the Great Plains culture of agriculture and Main Street sensibilities were as critical to the success of farms and ranches, small businesses, and education as the men engaged in those enterprises, yet they rarely if ever shared the title we used to hear so often: "head of household."

That was reserved for males and was used to deny, for example, equal pay to single women who were superior schoolteachers because they weren't the head of household. It was not unusual for merchants who relied on their wives to do the accounting, the clerking, and the merchandising to lock up at the end of the day and go to the Chamber of Commerce meeting without inviting along the women who got them there in the first place.

That did not go on in our family. By deed if not by word, Dad let his three boys know that he considered Mom his full partner in the title "head of household." Having grown up in this uniquely enlightened environment, it wasn't until Meredith and I had three daughters—born in 1966, 1968, and 1970—that I came to a much more complete understanding of the place of women in American life and how it needed to be changed.

The place of women in America in the Fifties and early Sixties has been described starkly by historian Ruth Rosen in her book **The World Split Open: How the Modern Women's Movement Changed America:**

Newspaper ads separated jobs by sex; employers paid women less than men for the same work. Bars often refused to serve women; banks routinely denied women credit or loans. Some states even excluded women from jury duty . . .

As late as 1970, Dr. Edgar Berman, a well-known physician, proclaimed on television that women were too tortured by hormonal disturbances to assume the presidency of the nation. Few people knew more than a few women professors, doctors, or lawyers.

Change began in 1963, when Betty Friedan, a little-known magazine writer who had grown up in Peoria, Illinois, in the Twenties and Thirties, published a book that gave a generation of American women a public voice for their frustrations. It was called **The Feminine Mystique.**

The opening paragraphs neatly summarized an essential truth about the place of women in what was universally—and not unjustly by the lights of the times—considered the most progressive society in history. Friedan wrote:

> The problem lay buried, unspoken, for many years in the minds of American women. It was a strange stirring, a sense of dissatisfaction, a yearning that women suffered in the middle of the 20th century in the United States. Each suburban wife struggled with it alone. As she made the beds, shopped for groceries, matched slipcover material, ate peanut butter sandwiches with her children, chauffeured Cub Scouts and Brownies, lay beside her husband at night—she was afraid to ask even of herself the silent question—"Is this all?" . . .

By the end of the 1950s the average marriage age of women in America dropped to

20, and was still dropping, into the teens.
Fourteen million girls were engaged by 17.
The proportion of women attending college
in comparison with men dropped from 47
per cent in 1920 to 35 per cent in 1958.

The Feminine Mystique was an important, long-
overdue book, and it quickly became a best seller. It
spoke mostly to the well-educated suburban housewife
and mother. It made those same suburban women realize that they were not alone and encouraged them to
change their lives. It did not, however, cause women to
take to the barricades. It was the beginning of a new
consciousness among women, but it was not yet a
movement or a revolution.

The trends Friedan described continued to develop
slowly but surely just beneath the surface of America's
busy life. Women continued to marry young. They
were still paid at a lower scale than men in the same jobs
because, of course, they weren't the head of household.
Their voices were rarely heard in the big decisions in the
country or, for that matter, even in the progressive are-
nas of the civil rights or antiwar movements. Most
women in the movements were expected to do the clerical work or organize the lunches.

Stokely Carmichael, the angry leader of the Student
Nonviolent Coordinating Committee, put it bluntly
when he said that "The only position for women in
SNCC is prone."

Some women were showing up in conspicuous
roles in the big left-of-center movements, including
Dolores Huerta, a political and labor organizer who

was a passionate voice alongside Cesar Chavez in the farmworkers' movement. Gloria Steinem was a serious journalist whose glamour, ironically, helped draw attention to the emerging power and agenda of women.

In the age of so much activism, the women's movement was slow to lift off. Looking back, many women who felt as strongly about the issues as men did are understandably bitter about the way they were treated. After all, they worked no less hard and played no less historic roles as they walked the precincts for Gene McCarthy and Bobby Kennedy. But they were coming of age just as the Democratic Party was beginning to separate from the old system that was dominated by white males.

As late as 1968, women were still taking more baby steps than making great leaps forward into the leadership ranks of politics, culture, business, and academia. No woman was seriously considered for the national ticket in either party. There were no women in President Lyndon Johnson's cabinet. There were no women columnists on the op-ed pages of the leading American newspapers. Apart from the traditional women's colleges, no major university had a woman president. And Title IX, the federal legislation that mandated a more equitable distribution of funds for women's athletics in intercollegiate sports, was still four years off.

Women were few and far between in senior management positions in American corporations. They represented just under 8 percent of the graduating medical school classes and 4 percent of the graduating law school classes in 1968, compared with 46.8 percent and 48 percent, respectively, in 2006.

When women first began to organize and to attempt raising the consciousness of society, a small number of radical feminists unfurled their banner in a fashion so strident and extreme that they actually aided those who were determined to keep things exactly as they were.

One, Shulamith Firestone, called for the end of what she described as the "tyranny" of the biological family through alternative means of reproduction. Writing as a member of a group called New York Radical Women, she declared, "The end goal of feminist revolution must be . . . not just the elimination of male privilege but of the sex distinction itself: genital differences between humans would no longer matter. . . .

"Marx," Firestone continued, "was on to something more profound than he knew when he observed that the family contained within itself all the antagonisms that later develop on a wide scale within the society and state. For unless revolution disturbs the basic social organization—the biological family . . . the tapeworm of exploitation will never be annihilated."

Feminist writers and commentators with views similar to Firestone were not representative of the wider women's movement, but their negative views about the place of motherhood were often cited by conservative critics in their claims that feminism wanted to destroy the nuclear family.

Firestone also deconstructed the women's rights movements of the nineteenth and early twentieth centuries. She judged them to be failures because they were insufficiently militant, and because they had been too accommodating to entrenched political and cultural interests.

Setting aside her rant against the place of the biological family, her conclusions about raising the general consciousness of women in the areas of job opportunity, equal pay for equal work, and broader legal rights should have been welcome news to women who longed to have a greater role in life beyond the kitchen and the classroom.

By 1966 the women's movement was expanding at a quickening pace. Betty Friedan and some other like-minded activists met in Washington to review what the government was doing—or, as was more often the case, not doing—about gender discrimination. Unhappy with what they learned, they met in Friedan's hotel room and formed NOW—the National Organization for Women.

Today the largest women's political organization in the country, NOW got off to a very uncertain start. The younger members wanted more confrontations with institutions they considered oppressive—such as the Catholic Church—while the older members were more interested in traditional legal and political strategies such as class action lawsuits and lobbying efforts. There were also other divisions in the women's movement along ethnic lines and over sexual orientation. The African-American writer Alice Walker referred to women of color as "womanists" and white women as "feminists."

But however erratic the trajectory, the women's movement was constantly expanding and moving forward. When there was a strong reaction against the

U.S. Supreme Court's **Roe v. Wade** decision upholding abortion as a constitutional right, NARAL—the National Abortion Rights Action League—responded by mobilizing support for women's reproductive rights.

The very public campaign to elevate women's rights was not universally popular. When I would raise the issue of feminism with many female members of the World War II generation, I almost always got a response along the lines of "Well, I think women should have more opportunities, but I'm **not** a women's libber." These were women who were running the PTA, the local Red Cross, or the Girl Scout Council. They included lawyers, doctors, school principals, or partners with their husbands in running small businesses. They were strong and accomplished, but they didn't like the representation of feminists and feminism that they were seeing play out on their television screens.

Part of the problem was that the mainstream media were in the hands of middle-aged white male members of the establishment who were more amused than enlightened by women's rising consciousness about their rightful place in business, politics, education, and the professions. Those editorial gatekeepers too often treated women's issues as a bra-burning sideshow, always good for some entertainment but not serious enough for the front page or the lead story in the network newscast.

Although women's health issues such as breast cancer and other gender-specific conditions were beginning to get more attention in the medical community in response to the demands of afflicted women, male-dominated newsrooms were still slow to respond.

In 1976 my NBC News colleague Betty Rollin wrote **First, You Cry,** a poignant, revealing, and best-selling account of her ordeal with breast cancer. But she wasn't even asked to report her own story on the evening news. As late as 1980, when toxic shock syndrome—a potentially lethal condition that can be caused by tampons—suddenly appeared as a serious health issue for women, one of the senior male NBC News commentators loudly announced, "I will not say 'tampon' on the air." He was persuaded that the possible life-and-death importance of the story to some women had to trump his own discomfort with saying a word.

Women pioneers in network television, such as Nancy Dickerson, fought hard to cover national politics, but in Nancy's case she was also assigned a midday newscast called **News with a Woman's Touch,** sponsored by Pure, a hand cream. As late as 1972, Cassie Mackin, a tough, independent, beautiful, and accomplished correspondent for NBC News and, later, ABC News, served as the object of endless speculation about her romances, her wardrobe, and her occasional diva tendencies—the kind of gossip that was never visited on any of her equally temperamental male colleagues. When Barbara Walters, who had started as a writer on the **Today** show, was promoted to the big set alongside veteran correspondent Frank McGee, she was instructed not to ask the first question in serious interviews. When McGee died of cancer, Walters scored a number of exclusive interviews with big-name newsmakers but seldom received credit in the newsroom.

Still, things were changing and women throughout the country were no longer being forced to choose between a life of protest or a life as the perfect stay-at-home mom of the kind depicted on the popular television show **The Adventures of Ozzie and Harriet.**

Women who were just coming of age in the Sixties were both witness to and part of a new determination to start addressing personal grievances with collective action. The civil rights movement, the antiwar protests, even the music of the time, said: "Listen to **me.** I won't take this any longer." A new axiom of American politics was established: The **personal** is **political.**

Nora Ephron

One woman who watched all of this, and commented on it in her own inimitable way, is journalist, essayist, screenwriter, film director, best-selling author, and sharp-eyed observer of her life and times Nora Ephron. In our family of four strong women—Meredith and our daughters, Jennifer, Andrea, and Sarah—Nora has long been both a muse and a gold standard of smart thinking. How many times have I heard one or all of them ask, "What do you think Nora would have to say about this?"

Like me, Ephron was born just a few years before the baby boom. She graduated in 1958 from Beverly Hills High School, where she was editor of the school newspaper and voted "most likely to succeed."

"I was the one who wanted to get out of there and write," she says. "I was one of only two classmates that I can remember who had a working mother [her mother and father were well-known screenwriters]—and the other classmate's mother 'had to work' because she was divorced. I was fortunate—I had a role model before we had that expression."

She understood that her ambitions and her family experiences were not typical. When she started college at Wellesley in the fall of 1958 (seven years before Hillary Rodham arrived), it was still a world defined by the conventions of the Fifties. Bright and gifted young women were there to get an education and to earn a degree that was jokingly referred to as an "MrS." Ephron was among them, although she was also one of only two students who joined a sit-in at the local Woolworth variety store in solidarity with the civil rights workers who were doing the same at lunch counters across the South.

She was briefly engaged to a Harvard law student, but it didn't work out. "Our class graduated in 1962, on the cusp of all the changes that were coming, and a huge percentage of them just went off and got married. I was unbelievably lucky I didn't. My classmates who did went into the world with one strike against them because they got married before they knew who they were. The Wellesley women who were interested in medicine married doctors; the ones who were interested in law married attorneys. They all thought they were going to be Fifties housewives, but then they discovered the horrible truth—that their husbands weren't going to be successful enough to support them. A lot of them went to work in jobs that were far less challenging than they deserved."

One of Ephron's classmates later said, "Our education was a dress rehearsal for a life we never led."

Ephron went to New York and got a job in the mailroom at **Newsweek** and then, in short order, at the **New York Post,** which was then the afternoon liberal yin to the **Daily News'** morning conservative yang. The **Post** was in a dreary building, but the staff included such colorful individuals as Jimmy Breslin, Jack Newfield, and Pete Hamill, who were already in the front ranks of American journalism.

"There were a lot of women at the **Post** for several reasons—one was that the **Post** had a long, sob-sister tradition, and the other was that women could be hired cheap," Ephron recalls. The pay differential between men and women was significant, and the women knew it. But they rarely protested; what was the point?

One of Ephron's friends was working just across the Hudson for the Bergen **Record.** She was pregnant, and she discovered that a male co-worker with the same duties was making more money. When she went to her boss, he explained, in the protocol of the day, that the male co-worker needed the extra money because he was about to become a father. Now Ephron just shakes her head and says, "We didn't complain. We didn't say, 'What are you talking about?' "

Ephron remembers discussing **The Feminine Mystique** with Dorothy Schiff, the wealthy liberal socialite who owned the **New York Post.** Schiff stayed in her elegantly decorated fifteenth-floor office and rarely connected with the nitty-gritty of the newsroom below. When Ephron asked Schiff about Betty Friedan's breakthrough book, the publisher's only com-

Nora Ephron, with pad and paper, during Bobby Kennedy's visit to New York's Lower East Side in 1965

ment was that it would result in more husbands asking for bigger salaries to support the elevated expectations of their wives.

The women's movement began to rise up in a hit-and-miss way just as Ephron began to write about women for **Esquire** magazine. Her professional responsibilities mingled easily with her personal interests, and her distinctive voice made her monthly column rich and memorable. She was able to pull off the journalistic hat trick of reporting the big picture, commenting on the telling details, and leaving just enough of herself in the piece so the reader knew that the writer had a personal stake in the story.

Now, as Ephron and I talk about those times, she says the rivalry in those days between Gloria Steinem and Friedan was not helpful. For all of her brilliance and her historic role in raising the consciousness of women, Betty Friedan simply couldn't compete with Steinem's youth and media star power. Steinem was so much more representative of the new generation, with her perfect straight blond hair, her hip wardrobe, and her svelte figure. She was also a natural on television.

When I ask Ephron what she thought of Friedan, she pauses and says, "She was problematic," a discreet description of Friedan's famous petulance and outsize ego. And Steinem, what of her? "A rock star, some combination of brilliant, funny, and misguided in all of her Gloria-ness."

In **Crazy Salad**, Ephron describes a scene she observed at a meeting of the National Women's Political Caucus at the 1972 Democratic National Convention in Miami. Steinem was the star at a news conference, and Ephron watched Friedan's reactions. "Betty's eyes are darting back and forth, trying to catch someone's attention, anyone's attention. . . . Betty's lips tighten as she hears the inevitable introduction coming, 'Betty Friedan, the mother of us all.' That does it. 'I'm getting sick and tired of this mother of us all thing,' she says."

Ephron mordantly observes that, in the women's movement, to be called the mother of anything was rarely a compliment. Moreover, she wrote, it meant that "Betty, having given birth, ought to cut the cord. Bug off. Shut up. . . . Betty Friedan has no intention of doing anything of the kind. It's her baby, damn it. . . . Is she supposed to sit still and let a beautiful, thin lady run off with it?"

While Ephron admires many of the qualities of that "beautiful, thin lady," she thinks Steinem made some strategic mistakes. "She wanted the movement to be leaderless, when it seemed to me it needed leaders. She wanted the movement to be seen as loving and united—like many others, she wasn't willing to admit the dirty little secret that the movement was consumed by petty jealousies.

"A huge amount of energy was spent debating issues that were the equivalent of angels dancing on the head of a pin. There was way too much discussion about who did the dishes in the household."

Yet the movement, however disorganized and uneven, did release the genie from the bottle, and Steinem deserves a great deal of credit for uncorking the bottle. As Ephron puts it, "Even the discussion about who does the dishes was helpful. It was another way to think about divorce. Divorce—getting out of a bad marriage—was the main thing. It was no longer a stigma."

Then there was abortion—the debate, the 1973 Supreme Court **Roe v. Wade** decision, and the political and cultural realities. "Abortion is still an issue," Ephron says. "I don't think it will be rolled back, but I don't know. We're just one Supreme Court justice away from that happening."

Abortion as a choice and as an issue came out of the shadows in dramatic fashion. It had long been a reality, but even in the best of circumstances, it had a back-alley quality.

Ephron recalls joining a demonstration for abortion rights organized by Planned Parenthood sometime in the late Sixties. It was a two-bus caravan from Times Square to Albany, where Governor Nelson Rockefeller was considering legislation dealing with the growing demand for easier access to legal abortion.

Ephron smiles and shakes her head as she remembers: "When we got there, feeling very good about our personal commitment to this issue, we discovered, oh, I don't know, maybe forty-seven buses of pro-lifers! And I realized then how much passion and energy there was on the other side. And it's not going away."

By 1972 Ephron was writing about vaginal politics, which was the title of a breakthrough book by Ellen Frankfort. "Vaginal" had been a word confined to ob-gyn offices until the women's movement came roaring out of the cloistered confines of screened-off examination rooms, suburban kitchens, secretarial pools, and female dormitories. Suddenly it was being used at dinner parties and on some radio shows. And for television, a medium that had been squeamish about using the word "tampon" as part of a medical story, the stakes were suddenly ratcheted up.

Ephron, who's known professionally and personally for her cool sophistication, was wide-eyed as she recounted Frankfort's story in **The Village Voice** about a new campaign for women to "know what your uterus looks like." It was part of a self-help organization demonstrating to women how they could use a plastic speculum to perform their own gynecological examinations and, if necessary, their own abortions.

Ephron was fascinated by the boldness of the book, which she found important but flawed. The do-it-yourself abortion tools left her furious. She wrote, "If doctors were prescribing equipment as untested as these devices are, equipment which clearly violates natural body functions, the women's health movement would be outraged."

Ephron gave Frankfort credit for the larger point that women were resorting to these radical ideas in part because of their treatment at the hands of mostly male doctors who talked to them as if they were children. One of the unheralded developments of the women's movement was the profound change in the relationship between women and the medical community, helped in no small part by the greatly expanded population of women doctors.

In our family, Meredith and I still remember with astonishment and anger the circumstances of the birth of our first child, Jennifer. Meredith's Atlanta doctor had known for some time that the baby was in a severe breech position, and yet he never mentioned it to either of us. When Meredith went into labor, he gave her general anesthesia without telling her what he was doing or why. Only after Jennifer was in the nursery did he mention that it had been a difficult birth.

As for Ephron, how would she describe the women's movement today? "There is no women's movement today," she says flatly. "It's tragic. There is no one who stands for women's rights and stands for that alone."

Gloria Steinem

Gloria Steinem, like Hillary Clinton and Jane Fonda, is a woman who provokes strong reactions—positive and negative—for her role in the Sixties and beyond. Indisputably, Steinem was a seminal force in the modern women's movement. But she didn't set out to be an activist. She just wanted to be a writer.

Steinem grew up in Ohio, the daughter of an itinerant antiques dealer who left Gloria's mother when Gloria was just ten years old. It was not a happy childhood, as Gloria had to care for her ill mother and help support the family as a teenager. When she was fifteen, she moved to Washington, D.C., to live with an older sister.

Steinem graduated Phi Beta Kappa from Smith College and won a fellowship to study in India for two years. She returned with a heightened awareness of social injustice and of how Americans took for granted their standard of living.

When she was twenty-six, she moved to New York

to begin a career as a freelance magazine writer and landed an assignment that remains a familiar part of the Steinem biography.

A now-defunct magazine called **Show** hired her to get a job as a Playboy bunny in the Playboy clubs Hugh Hefner had established to complement his magazine empire. After three weeks on the job in the standard costume of a formfitting and revealing satin chorus-line outfit, bunny ears, and a bunny tail, Steinem quit to write a two-part article that detailed the sexual insults, low wages, and dismal working conditions of the Playboy club waitresses.

By her early thirties she was successful enough as a writer to be invited to join the staff assembled by editor Clay Felker for **New York** magazine, a breakthrough publication that in 1968 launched what came to be known as New Journalism, another by-product of the Sixties.

New York magazine was sassy, hip, and opinionated, the home of writers such as Tom Wolfe, Nora Ephron, and Gail Sheehy, who were joined by homegrown writers such as Pete Hamill and Jimmy Breslin. They broke all the old rules of who, what, where, and when, producing pieces that reflected their personalities and took readers on rollicking rides into places they hadn't been before.

Steinem wrote about local and national politics, the big themes and the big players. It was a radical change from her earlier assignments at, say, **The New York Times Magazine**, where she had been asked to write about "textured stockings and the wives of the candidates, but not the candidates themselves."

When I first saw Gloria Steinem in Chicago at the 1968 convention, she was not yet known as a high priestess of the women's movement, but instead as a smart, new-age political reporter from **New York**.

She now says she was not initially drawn to the women's movement in 1968. **The Feminine Mystique** didn't speak to her. "It was directed to women living in the suburbs who had college educations and who were standing by their kitchen sinks saying, 'There must be more to life than this.' I was already in the workforce, so it didn't seem directed at me."

As she was doing her political reporting, Steinem realized that "women in the civil rights movement and the peace movement were stirring," as she puts it, "because even within those admirable movements, women were still getting the coffee . . . and being sexually available to the leadership. But they began to speak out, to write, much in the same way the early suffragist movement came out of the abolitionist movement."

For herself, Steinem says that rather than relying on the women's movement for help, she counted on women friends already in various professional positions in New York. "I suspect," she says, "I was hoping that if I was very good and worked very hard—the good-girl complex—I could overcome these biases.

"I wasn't doing what I was supposed to do. I wasn't getting married. I wasn't having children. I didn't have a 'real job'—I was freelancing. I was not leading the life I was supposed to be leading, but I suppose I thought I could manage, if not by myself, then at least with the help of friends.

"Even then there was an underground of women

in journalism who helped each other. If someone new came to town, I would give them the name of editors who wouldn't ask you to stop by a hotel room on your way to deliver a manuscript."

Her own epiphany, as she describes it, came in 1969, in the earliest stages of the abortion rights campaign. New York legislators held a hearing on a proposed liberalization of the state's abortion laws and invited as witnesses twelve men and one woman—a nun.

At the same time a radical feminist group called Redstockings held its own abortion hearings in the Washington Square Methodist Church and Steinem covered them for her **New York** magazine column.

"I had never heard women stand up and tell the truth publicly about their own experiences with abortions. I thought, 'Wait a minute, if one in three or four women has had an abortion in her lifetime, why is it illegal? Why are we forced to risk our lives in a criminal underground?' I also had an abortion, but in London, where the rules were more humane."

When Steinem wrote about the Redstockings event, her male colleagues, she says, were alarmed. "One by one they pulled me aside and warned me not to get involved with these 'crazy women. . . . You've worked too hard to be taken seriously.' "

Those warnings from well-meaning male friends played a significant role in Steinem's evolution from journalist to feminist activist. "Suddenly I realized they didn't know who I was—they couldn't know because I hadn't told them.

"I started writing about things I could uniquely

write about. Before, I had been writing about the farm-workers' movement, but not about the fact that Cesar Chavez didn't allow contraception in his clinics.

"It became evident, however, that magazines, including **New York**, didn't want new kinds of articles about women, so when I couldn't write what I wanted to write about I began to speak out in public. Dorothy Pitman Hughes and I became a sort of black-and-white team . . . and in our lectures, where only hundreds were expected, thousands began to turn out. You realized there was a great hunger for anything that took the women's experiences seriously."

That experience led her to think about starting a new magazine with feminism as its primary theme. Her enthusiasm was not shared by financial backers, and the idea stalled until Clay Felker, her entrepreneurial patron at **New York**, offered to publish the new magazine in exchange for excerpts he could run in his own year-end edition.

Ms. magazine hit the newsstands in January 1972 and sold out its entire 300,000 press run. Steinem says **Ms.** became a kind of group therapy for women across the country who wrote to share their stories. She says the common theme was "At least I know I'm not alone. And I'm not crazy. The system is crazy."

Ms. received a good deal of attention, and Steinem became even more famous as she promoted the magazine and its cause on talk shows and in public appearances. **Ms.** was a troubled business proposition from the start and never fulfilled the promise of its early editions.

It can still be found on some newsstands, but it

was never a star in a galaxy of publications such as **Cosmopolitan, Elle, O, Martha Stewart Living, In Style,** or other popular women's magazines that celebrate the gender with career and style tips, gossip, and health news in lieu of issues or politics.

In addition to her advocacy journalism, Steinem co-founded the National Women's Political Caucus and the Coalition of Labor Union Women. She is also a member of the Women's Hall of Fame.

Steinem remained single until the year 2000, when she married David Bale, a native of South Africa and the father of actor Christian Bale. Bale was an entrepreneur and commercial pilot and was active in African environmental movements.

When he died of brain lymphoma just three years after their wedding, Steinem said, "He had the greatest heart of anyone I've ever known."

As for the state of the women's movement, Gloria Steinem sees the results of the activism of the Sixties and early Seventies as mixed. "I imagined that if we could get a majority of Americans to support the issues of equality, it would happen," she says. "I didn't anticipate that after decades, it would still be unrealized. I thought we had more of a democracy than we do."

Steinem blames outside forces rather than women who are making other choices for themselves. "I probably underestimated the depth of the problem," she says. "I felt if people understood [the inequalities of pay and power for women in the workplace], they would want to do something about it, forgetting that much of corporate America functions off cheap labor, that controlling reproduction is one of the pillars of American capitalism."

While Steinem was launching **Ms.** and appearing on the evening news or in public forums promoting the women's movement, other women across the country were finding their own ways past the conventions of their gender.

Joan Growe

Joan Growe, born Joan Anderson, was a typical small-town Minnesota girl growing up in the Fifties, a product of a solidly middle-class family in which the expectations were that she would go to college, find a husband, have children, and stay at home as a wife and mother.

She remembers that her father was the mayor of their town, and friends would often say to her brother, "Oh, I suppose you'll go into politics, too." They never suggested that Joan might also have political aspirations—and in fact, she didn't. She was so invested in the mother-and-wife model that she accelerated her college plans to graduate in three years with a teaching degree so she could get married and support her husband in his final undergraduate year and during three years of law school.

She also became a mother. "Like a good Catholic girl, I had three children in less than three years. He's going to law school, and I'm going along with life, thinking, 'This is the way everyone does it.'"

When her husband graduated, they moved to his hometown, where he set up a law practice. Her life, she says, quickly became a nightmare of abuse brought on by his alcoholism. In the small towns of the Midwest during that time, abuse and alcoholism were not uncommon, and were kept well buried in the local culture.

Growe says, "Growing up, I was never aware of abuse or alcoholism, but now I was being abused, and I didn't tell anyone, because you never spoke of such things."

Finally, she couldn't take it anymore. "I woke up one morning and thought, 'I might die . . . I have these kids, and what will happen to them? I've got to get out of here.'" She had only seventy dollars in what she described as "the Mrs. Mitty fund," in which wives of her era appropriated cash from their husband's wallets from time to time to cover their expenses.

She dropped off her children with an aunt and drove to the Twin Cities, found an apartment, got a teaching job at a Catholic school, and moved the kids in with her, well away from her husband. Then she began divorce proceedings.

"I made three hundred dollars a month," she recalls. "A hundred and twenty-five went for rent, a hundred for child care, and the remaining seventy-five for the necessities of life." She went to school at night to renew her teaching credential so she could earn a little more, but at the end of the first year of this new life, she had to go on welfare to make ends meet.

By 1965 she was married again, this time to a steady, responsible man who loved her children and wanted to provide for them. That was the beginning of what Growe now calls "my other life . . . we lived in the suburbs, my husband went to work every day, I played bridge with the ladies. All the things women did in that era."

Sometime in the late Sixties, she saw an advertisement for the League of Women Voters that struck a chord with her—although she's still not sure which one. "I knew I wanted to do something other than be at home with the children all the time, to do something more stimulating than going to coffee parties and playing bridge. I was looking for more, but I was unclear about what it was."

She dove into League activities, studying local issues intensely, working on local school board elections, moderating candidate debates, and organizing voter registration efforts. At the same time, she began to immerse herself in the antiwar campaign. "I wore my 'Another Mother for Peace' button, did a few antiwar marches . . . just the usual stuff." She attended a precinct caucus for Senator Gene McCarthy in 1968 because of his antiwar stance, but she couldn't be a convention delegate because of her position with the nonpartisan League of Women Voters.

Still, a political life was not on her agenda. She took time out from her League duties to get the family relocated to another Minneapolis suburb, but by 1971 she was restless again. What she calls "the birthday-cake moment" provided the motivation to get out of her rut. "Every year the kids could choose a birthday cake from the General Mills cookbook. One daughter picked the castle cake, and I spent a week making it— with marshmallows, gumdrops, icing—and it was gorgeous. And completely inedible. I thought, 'What am I doing spending three hours a day on a cake?' "

She reentered the political arena just as the Democratic Party was making a concerted effort to raise the profile of women in a meaningful way. "The county chairs were always men and the associates were women, and the women did all the work and the men got all the glory," she remembers.

Suddenly, Growe found herself at a new level of politics as a result of her activities on behalf of gender equality. When the local Republican Party shoved aside a highly qualified woman candidate for a new legislative seat in favor of a local businessman, Growe and her friends in the League were incensed. A group of activists approached her about making the race as a Democrat. The district was solidly Republican, so it wasn't a question of winning. Their goal was mainly to force the GOP candidate to focus on issues important to women. Growe said, "If I can get a babysitter, I'll go to the local Democratic convention and try to get nominated."

She laughs now as she remembers: "My husband was out of town at the time, and I didn't even call him about it. It seemed like no big deal. I had no idea what I was getting into. I was nauseous when the party leaders told me about fund-raising and getting to know the issues and organizing the campaign." Echoing Robert Redford's famous last line in **The Candidate,** after he has just been elected to the Senate, she corralled her friends and asked, "What do we do now?"

Many of her friends were schoolteachers, so they attacked the campaign as if it were a school term, lay-

Joan Growe (center) meeting with voters
at a "campaign coffee party" during her 1972 bid
for the Minnesota state legislature

Minnesota secretary of state
Joan Growe in 1996

ing out campaign strategies in documents that closely resembled lesson plans. One of her friends, Gretchen Fogo, drew up charts and graphs to assign workers to neighborhoods where they were expected to personally visit at least eighty homes. Growe figures that during her seven-day weeks on the campaign trail, she knocked on the door of every home in the large suburban district. "I worked myself to death, even campaigning in the middle of a blizzard—and so did the other women." She'd often hear the comment "Oh, are you campaigning for your husband?" When she explained that she was the candidate, a lot of women were puzzled, and their husbands were sometimes hostile.

"School financing was the big issue," she says. "The ERA, which I supported, was a little issue—and I don't think anyone asked me about the abortion-choice issue." She was prepared to lose. But when the returns came in, she had won with 55 percent of the vote and become one of only six women in the 201-member Minnesota state legislature.

It was hardly a windfall. The job paid just twelve thousand dollars a year for five days a week during the January–May legislative session. Growe loved it from the beginning, even though it was hard to juggle child care and her marriage while immersed in the public policy issues of the state. Neighbors looked after the children if she had to leave the house early or get home late.

Her husband didn't like the changes in his wife, and their marriage slowly began to fall apart. She says, "When I married him, I had three kids, and here was someone who took care of me. But as I became more self-sufficient and independent, I had time to think, to be me. He didn't like that."

Joan Growe's way out of her marriage was to do something no woman had ever accomplished in Minnesota before: get elected as secretary of state. When the political establishment told her she'd have to get permission from the party elders to run, she asked for a meeting with the governor and, as she puts it, "I told him I was running."

She adopted the model of her successful campaign for the legislature, calling all two thousand delegates to the party convention to win the nomination and then campaigning in all eighty-seven Minnesota counties. She won in 1974, beating the incumbent, and became the first woman to be elected to any statewide office in Minnesota.

Growe held the office for the next twenty-four years, winning a national reputation for her voter registration reforms and advances in record keeping. She also wrote the social responsibility policy for the state board of investment, which had the responsibility of managing Minnesota's public money.

When she retired in 1999, she looked back on a life of many unexpected turns. "When I was growing up," she says, "my mother said, 'You have to have an education in case something happens to your husband.' It never occurred to me that I would get divorced or run for office.

"Do I wish the two marriages had not failed? Yes, but if I had not gone through that early trauma, I might not be where I am today. I must have drawn on some reserves I didn't know I had."

Growe's first campaign also empowered her friends who helped her win. Gretchen Fogo became a Methodist minister. Two others returned to school and earned doctorates. Growe says, "My friends went all out in that campaign, and it changed their lives. That wasn't the plan, but we were beginning to realize we weren't just 'Mrs. Glen Growe' or whoever." They discussed the Equal Rights Amendment and began to see other possibilities for their lives, but they weren't hardcore feminists. Growe describes her friend Nancy as the biggest feminist among them because she went well beyond the Midwestern marriage ethos by making her husband do his own ironing.

Growe, who had such a long and successful public career, looks back on that first campaign with great pride because, she says, "It was not **my** campaign. It was **our** campaign. It was a group effort."

Muriel Kraszewski

Like Joan Growe, Muriel Kraszewski is a native of Minnesota who has had a profound effect on the fortunes of working women in America, yet she is little known or recognized for her contributions. Kraszewski is now in her early seventies and living in San Clemente, California, but she was raised on a dairy farm in rural Minnesota, where her early life was defined by the hard work required to keep the family enterprise going.

"My parents were like Ozzie and Harriet. They had no problems between them, and my father never

An unlikely Sixties activist:
Muriel Kraszewski and her husband,
Robert, in 2004

bossed her around, but my mother spent every day doing something for him. That was her whole life, taking care of her family. She was totally a mom."

That was the nurturing Kraszewski took to school, where, in the early Fifties, she followed the unspoken rules for young women of the time and took shorthand and typing, hoping to become a secretary. It paid off when she was hired by the Santa Fe Railroad in Chicago. "But it was not what I thought of as a career. I thought I would get married and stay home with a family. That's how I was programmed."

She met her husband, Robert, an optometry student in Chicago, and after they were married, they moved to Southern California, where their only child, a son, was born. Muriel was content to stay at home and fulfill the role of a traditional mom and housewife while their son was in his preschool years, but as soon as he headed off to first grade, she became restless. "I couldn't stand it; I can only clean house and cook so much. I was going crazy. 'What am I doing? What am I doing?'"

She found a job with a two-agent State Farm insurance office and quickly became a whiz in what used to be called a "girl Friday" position—the women in businesses large and small who made them hum with efficiency by applying multiple skills, from typing and shorthand to answering the phone and covering for the absentee boss.

"I loved what I was doing," she recalls. "An insurance agent wants someone who likes talking to people. They taught me how to give quotes on policies and fill out applications, so even though I did all the normal secretarial stuff, I also took in payments, explained policies, and did whatever the agents did."

She continued to work in State Farm offices, always impressing her immediate bosses with her energy and efficiency. Because she was so on top of office matters, the agents began to take advantage by spending their days on the golf course. "At first they really had me psyched out because I was so programmed to be a wife and a mother and do what people told me to do. But I started thinking, 'Why can't I do this for myself?' "

When Kraszewski went to State Farm's district managers and asked to become an agent, she was abruptly turned away. "They were very negative. They said, 'A woman can't do this job. We can't protect a woman when she's out at night showing a property.' I knew better. The agents I worked for never put in nighttime hours."

She persisted, but the managers kept coming up with new excuses. She didn't have a college degree; but when she responded that none of the agents with whom she'd worked for twelve years had a college degree, they said, "Well, now you've got to have one. That's it. We can't hire you."

She was so fed up that she went to a rival firm, Farmers Insurance, and quickly became a successful agent. She was making a handsome salary and having a good time doing a job she loved, but she could not get over State Farm's treatment of her. Someone suggested she go to the local chapter of the National Organization for Women (NOW) to get some guidance on how to file a discrimination claim. "I went to a NOW meeting, but no one seemed interested in fighting the case."

Instead, Muriel Kraszewski took her case to the EEOC, the federal government's Equal Employment Opportunity Commission, which was created in 1964 to deal with exactly this kind of discrimination. The EEOC filed on her behalf, and State Farm responded with a claim that made her angrier still. "They said they couldn't hire me as an agent because my husband had too much control over me. This after they had earlier admitted that my bosses thought highly of me and that I had been doing a good job running the office."

Kraszewski decided to sue. At first, her husband was skeptical of her involvement in the case, but she countered, "You know what? That's stupid, because I am working for a tenth of what I should make. What's wrong with you?" As she says, he was caught in the same conditioning as she was, having been raised in the Fifties. In 1979 she became the primary defendant in a case called **Kraszewski et al v. State Farm**. Her lawyer, who was already working on discrimination claims against the company, named Kraszewski in the case because she had already demonstrated at Farmers Insurance that she was up to the job.

It was a tough, long, drawn-out case. "State Farm threw every block they could. My lawyer and his partners had to refinance their homes three times to keep the case going." The case didn't go to trial until 1983, and the verdict wasn't handed down until 1988, almost ten years after the claim was made. But the effort and the time were worthwhile because Muriel Kraszewski and her two co-plaintiffs won hands down. State Farm was ordered to pay each of them $431,000.

She had her fifteen minutes of fame, appearing on **The Phil Donahue Show**, on the **CBS Evening News**, and in **People** magazine. "It actually turned out to be a lot of fun. I got so much mail from women across the country." Her case also encouraged more than eight hundred other women to file a class action discrimination suit against State Farm. That suit was ultimately settled in 1992 for $157 million, the largest settlement of its kind up to that point.

It was not what Muriel Kraszewski had set out to do in life. She was not a Sixties activist. She didn't protest against the war or, apart from that one NOW meeting, get involved in women's organizations. She just stood up for her rights at a time when the laws of the land were beginning to reflect the changing status of the rightful place of women in society. "I had no expectations of anything like that. I thought I would get married and have a family and be a housewife."

Dr. Judith Rodin

Judith Rodin set out as a scholar in pursuit of a teaching and research career in psychology. She wound up as president of the University of Pennsylvania. How she got there is a commentary on the objective realities of the Sixties, the myths, and the outrages across a wide spectrum.

Rodin enrolled at Penn as an undergraduate in 1962; when she graduated four years later, the world around her had already changed profoundly. The first two years of college, she says, were the Fifties extended. "Students were very concerned about their own lives, social events, and classroom performance, but they were neither politically nor socially active." The Kennedy assassination, the civil rights movement, and the Vietnam War changed that. As she describes it, "my college years went from fraternity parties to protests. It really felt as if it happened overnight. You could just feel it."

Rodin took a very active role as president of Women's Student Government, forcing the end of separate-gender student government groups on campus and merging them into one organization. She used her newly acquired skills and confidence to organize voter registration drives in the South during spring break, and she took part in campus protests against Vietnam.

That political activism, in turn, helped end the myth that gender equality meant "separate but equal" at Penn. The campus was Rodin's frame of reference. She says she wasn't influenced by the broader, national women's movement. "Women at Penn," she recalls, "made up only about a third of the student body, maybe even a smaller fraction. So we thought we were very brave and very avant-garde."

Fortunately the attitude of the Penn faculty helped. Rodin discovered in her freshman year that she had a passion and an aptitude for psychology, and by the time she was a sophomore, she had been encouraged by professors who, as she puts it, "didn't ask whether I was going to graduate school; they asked 'Where?' "

When she arrived at Columbia University to

Judith Rodin's
high-school
graduation picture.

The first female president of an Ivy League
university, Dr. Judith Rodin presided over the
University of Pennsylvania from 1994 to 2004.

begin her master's and doctoral work, she was not prepared for what was then the prevalent attitude in the male-dominated ivory towers of academia. "I was so intellectually pampered by the faculty at Penn, I never thought there would be obstacles because of being a woman," she says. Her illusion quickly ended when she found that some Columbia faculty members refused to work with women Ph.D. candidates, saying women would never seriously pursue a career. Since Rodin was married, one of her supervisors felt he could ask whether she was using birth control, signaling that he didn't want to be professionally involved with a student who might go off and have a baby.

There were other unexpected obstacles at Columbia. The campus was a hotbed of student activism led by Mark Rudd. In 1968, Rudd led the strike that ended with a violent confrontation with New York City police when students occupied the university's library and the office of the president. Rodin was conducting a major psychology experiment that involved laboratory animals. They were housed in the basement of the mathematics building, which was closed by the student strike and guarded by protestors.

"I had a personal ambivalence," she says. "I was completely against the Vietnam War, but I loved my academic work, I was deeply committed to it." Despite her pleadings, the student guards wouldn't let her in to continue her experiments. "So I lost all my research, about a year's worth. I learned there are no easy answers in life, that loyalties can be divided. It also taught me perseverance, because I had to get rid of the dead animals and start all over again. I had to work twice as

hard for the next six months, and that gave me perspective."

One of the lessons for Rodin was that, as she puts
it, "the protest was protest largely for the sake of drama.
It was extremely male-dominated, so the women in the
movement were relegated to making sandwiches, getting food, delivering drinks.

"That was very unpleasant, because it showed the
protestors weren't mature enough to really think about
the broader context of what they were searching for
and what they were trying to address. If you're not fair
at home, it's hard to protest not being fair abroad."

Rodin was determined, however, to keep her eye
on the larger goal. "It made me tough in a positive way;
it made me very, very determined. At the beginning,
my strategy was to achieve and demonstrate what I
could do. But when I saw that a lot of women who focused only on getting to the top pulled the ladder up
after them, I intentionally worked harder at being a
mentor. I wanted to be the best at what I did so when
I got there people would listen."

She did get there, part of the vanguard of her generation that went to college to get a Ph.D. instead of an
MrS. degree, and to make the most of it. When she finished her doctoral work at Columbia, she joined the
psychology department at Yale. In New Haven, she
began to take the lessons of her formative years beyond
the classroom and introduced them into the administration of what had been an all-male student body
until 1969.

She was appointed provost at Yale in 1992—the
first woman to hold what is effectively the second most

powerful position in the Yale hierarchy. She was, by her own description, driven. She became so focused on her career and research that her first marriage came apart. "I used to think you could have it all," she says. "Now I believe you can have it all, but not all at the same time. There are costs to every decision. Mine weren't cost-free. I had only one child and two divorces. That's a cost."

She learned that lesson in part from her Yale graduate students. When they gave her a party as she was leaving to become the first woman president at Penn, she realized that the male students, on average, had done better than the females despite her dedicated mentoring of the women.

At the party, Rodin wondered why this should be so. "A lot of the women," she said, "looked at how I led my life and decided they didn't want to live at that level of drive and anxiety, with no free time, forgetting to breathe!" She laughed as she recounted the moment. "So you think you're a role model, and they turn around and tell you you're a **negative** role model. So who knows?"

When I asked her if there was a memorable moment during her first marriage when she personally confronted the differences between being a traditional wife and being a modern partner, she quickly recalled a trip she was about to make to Stockholm for a conference on women and work.

"We had just collected data," she says, "showing an equal amount of stress between males and females during working hours on white-collar jobs. The study also showed that stress for males went down at the end of the workday, while it went up for women, who went home to a whole new set of duties. Late the night before I left for that conference, I was standing in the kitchen, preparing a week of meals for my husband. I suddenly thought, 'What am I doing? He can fix his own meals!' "

She cites that as an example of how times have changed for many young couples she knows. "They don't have that pressure, because they've worked out the roles."

Rodin recognizes that other aspects of women in the workplace have not changed as much as she might have anticipated twenty-five years ago. "Child care in the workplace didn't take on the way I thought it would," she says. "There remains tremendous opposition to the so-called mommy track in the workplace, in which a woman wants at some point to go off and have babies and then return."

When she was president of Penn, Rodin introduced a number of what she called "very family-friendly initiatives," but she was amazed at how many people failed to take advantage of them, fearing that to do so could have a negative effect on their careers. "They worried the gains they had made would be taken away," she says. "Women, particularly, were uneasy when they saw how easy it was to fill in around them."

Now the head of the Rockefeller Foundation in New York, Rodin works in the rarified climate of an institution that is charged with determining how to spend approximately $140 million a year on making the world a better place. It is a quintessential establishment foundation, but she brings to it some of the sensibilities she learned as a self-described ambivalent veteran of the Sixties.

"When Lyndon Johnson decided not to run for reelection in 1968," she says, "we felt we had changed the world. Whether it was true or not . . . it was an extraordinarily heady experience for my generation, and it influenced us for a long time."

She recognizes that the current generation of college students doesn't feel particularly empowered. "I wish I had the answer," she says, "but I don't, and neither do they. Maybe it's because they haven't experienced the kinds of consequential events we participated in. I also think the intervening years have led to a mistrust of the broader political processes, so it isn't surprising that they're moving out of the mainstream way of doing things and finding their own projects, away from the conventional political structure. They're more into tutoring and community volunteer projects, that sort of thing."

If it weren't for the Sixties, what about Rodin's life? She laughs and says, "Oh, who knows? I would have been a happily married housewife!" She knows that wasn't a likely prospect for her, with or without the influences of the Sixties on her life. "Could there have been other ways I would have changed? Probably. But certainly living through that time is a core part of who I am today."

Carla Hills and Joan Didion

Two women I came to know and greatly admire during my pilgrimage through the Sixties were native-born Californians, one from the South, the other from the North, one a Stanford graduate, the other a Berkeley alum, both Republicans, one a champion athlete and hard-driving lawyer, the other a frail woman of letters, and neither of them baby boomers.

I knew them well, but they didn't know each other. They existed in distinctly different orbits and yet in their lives, their work, and their influence, they were making profound impressions without taking the approach or voicing the demands of many in the women's movement.

They are Carla Hills, a powerful presence in the law, American foreign policy, and Republican Party politics; and Joan Didion, the novelist, essayist, and award-winning writer of, among many works of fact and fiction, **The Year of Magical Thinking**, a beautiful and timeless book about coping and grieving after the sudden death of her husband, John Gregory Dunne.

Hills and Didion were already well launched in their professional and personal lives when 1968 swept across the American landscape, challenging the core values and conventions of the old order. They were not impressed.

Didion, a Berkeley graduate, was living in Southern California with Dunne and both of them were working as writers. When the social ferment we now call the Sixties first began to get attention, she recalls,

"I was in my early thirties; they were in their twenties. They came from that huge generation that believed it had the power to do anything. I came from a tiny generation. We wanted to be grown-ups and go to the Blue Angel."

In 1972 she wrote about the women's movement in an essay later republished in her book **The White Album:**

> Along came the women's movement, and the invention of women as a "class." . . . They had invented a class; now they had only to make that class conscious. They seized as a political technique a kind of shared testimony at first called a "rap session," then called "consciousness-raising" and in any case a therapeutically oriented American reinterpretation . . . of a Chinese revolutionary practice known as "speaking bitterness." They purged and re-grouped and purged again, worried out one another's errors and deviations, the "elitism" here, the "careerism" there.

She also wrote scathingly of the movement's conclusion that cooking a meal "could only be 'dog-work.' . . . Small children could only be odious mechanisms for the spilling and digesting of food, for robbing women of their 'freedom.' "

Looking back, Didion says, "I wasn't particularly wrapped up in the expression of the women's movement, which seemed totally caught up in the dumb little arguments over who did the dishes. I thought it was a genuine political movement that got messed up in a lot of trivial offshoots, and it got stuck there."

She does acknowledge that the movement was the catalyst for vast improvements in the workplace. She described a niece who works for a large pharmaceutical company in California where child care and equal opportunity are now a fixed part of the company offices.

Carla Hills was a founding partner, with her husband, Rod, of the highly regarded Los Angeles law firm Munger, Tolles, Hills & Rickershauser. The firm, established in 1962, quickly gained a reputation as a hot shop, a productive law firm with a progressive soul. It attracted the best and brightest from the top law schools of the day—Yale, Harvard, Michigan, Stanford, Penn—and put them on a fast track to a partnership.

Carla had grown up in Beverly Hills and attended school in the Waspy Hancock Park section of Los Angeles, a gifted tennis player and a tomboy so competitive she was known as "Butch" in her prosperous Republican family headed by her father, Carl Anderson, a successful building supplies executive, for whom she was named.

When Hills graduated from Stanford in 1955 and announced that she wanted to go to law school at Yale, her father refused to finance any additional education; after all, she was marrying Roderick Hills, a fellow Stanford student and a young man with big ambitions of his own in the law. Besides, if she went to Yale, she might decide to stay on the East Coast, and Carl didn't like that idea at all.

So she paid her own way through her first year at

Writer Joan Didion in April 1967, at a hippie
gathering in Golden Gate Park, San Francisco

Award-winning
novelist and
essayist
Joan Didion
in 2000

Yale. Back in Southern California, her father's friends in Rotary or at the country club would say, "You must be so proud of Carla. At Yale Law School!" That became a form of validation for her, and when she returned home that summer, he agreed to finance the rest of her education.

Hills was one of a handful of women who graduated from Yale Law School in 1958, a time when Yale College was still all male. Her time there remains a cherished memory. "There were women who had preceded me at Yale Law, so that wasn't a problem. The men wore coats and ties, and civility was high."

Her career choice was characteristically unconventional. "When I came out of law school," she remembers, "women lawyers typically went into estates and divorce, that kind of practice, not frontline litigation—which is where I wanted to be."

She applied for a position in the U.S. Attorney's Office in Los Angeles, which was headed by Laughlin Waters, who later became a federal judge. Hills was instantly impressed by Waters because he didn't ask for her party registration, and he quickly hired her to work in the civil division, where she became a successful advocate in federal court.

In those days, if a woman became pregnant, Hills remembers, the expectation was that she would submit her resignation. But she wanted to continue practicing. So they kept her pregnancy a secret. She bought what she describes as "boxy suits" and watched her weight so carefully that she gained only seven pounds.

When their daughter, Laura, was born on a Sunday, her husband called her boss and said, "Carla just had a baby and won't be in this week." Waters and her co-workers were stunned. Two weeks later, she was back on the job; the U.S. Attorney's Office had no maternity leave at the time. "We did live close to work," she says, "and I did come home at noon to nurse Laurie."

Rod remembers a similar situation when their second child, Rick, a son, was born. Hills, by then in private practice, was about to go to trial with a major case. Lawyers had assembled from all over the country, and the night before the proceedings were to begin, she gave birth. Rod went to the courtroom to explain the situation and to suggest a short delay in the start of the trial. How short? the judge and other lawyers wanted to know. Rod said, "She can be here a week from today."

Her old boss, Laughlin Waters, was in the courtroom and jumped up to say, in mock anger, "What? Only a week? When she worked for me, she required two weeks!"

The proceedings were delayed a week and Hills was in the courtroom when the trial began the following Monday morning.

Throughout her life as a superlawyer, Carla Hills has also been a devoted mother. She understands the challenge of balancing the roles, but she believes it's about choices and organization. "Having children changes your life, and you have to like that change," she says.

She has little patience with women who worry about what they should "do." For her, "it isn't an ethical question. It's a question of how are they going to move forward. There was a wave of sentiment that you

Carla Hills (right) with her family in 1974,
soon after being appointed assistant
attorney general, civil division

were somehow diminished if you didn't work. My view has always been, work if you want to. If your job repels you, move on to something else. Be good at what you want to be."

As a young lawyer, Hills paid an economic penalty because she was a woman, even though she was a full partner with her husband in a successful Los Angeles law firm. In the early Sixties, the partners would meet at the end of the year to decide on compensation. Even though she was a star in the firm, bringing in big fees, the senior partner, Charlie Munger, would say, "You know, Carla doesn't need the money; Rod has plenty. And this year we want to pay the associates a little more."

Hills laughs now, recalling that she accused Munger of being a little communistic, an unlikely instinct for the man who later became famous as Warren Buffett's business partner. Still, she went along, although she would have been happier if she had volunteered for the lesser amount instead of having her fellow partners impose it on her.

She continued to be a star as a lawyer, and before long, the other partners were voting her an equal share. That was an object lesson for her. "I believe hard work, not protest, was the most effective vehicle for the women's movement."

That was never more clear to her than when she was summoned to New York to represent a big Wall Street firm in a major case. She was in a hurry to get to the firm's offices, but no cabs were available on Fifth Avenue because there was a big rally for women's rights in Midtown. She remembers thinking, "You think you're helping me? I can't get a cab to get to my meeting."

Stating the obvious, Hills says she was never a big public feminist. She preferred to lead by example. "I felt writers should write and lawyers ought to be lawyers and win their cases and establish good law, and that would make it all the easier for others to follow. "I'm sure the Gloria Steinems did some good for women, but I'm not so sure women couldn't have done as well—if not better—if they showed their excellence rather than shouting. And 'burn your bra'? What does **that** prove?"

Her daughter, Laura, now also a lawyer, at one time sought her mother's counsel when she wrestled with the correct nomenclature of "chairman" in the changing world. Should it be "chairman," "the chair," or "chairperson"? she asked her mother. Hills replied, in typical no-nonsense fashion, "Call me whatever you want. Just give me the job!"

Laura, the eldest of the four Hills children, now has her own law firm and is the working mother of two. She has modeled her life after her mother's, but she has a slightly different take on the effect of the women's movement. She appreciates the role of the noisy protestors in the early days of feminist activism, saying that every movement has a boisterous element. Besides, she points out, if there hadn't been loud, even unruly, demonstrations for women's rights, maybe her mother would have been labeled an extremist, given how much she was changing the role of women in what had been mostly an old-white-boy profession.

By the time Laura was ready to have children while she was working in a big law firm, conditions had changed for women attorneys, but she still didn't advertise her pregnancy. "I worried I would be regarded as a short-termer in the firm and not get particularly interesting cases." Laura had heard the phrase "baby brain," a pejorative for pregnant women, suggesting they lose some of their intellectual edge when shifting their attention to the forthcoming birth and all that goes with it. "I just didn't want to go there," she says. "I didn't want anyone to think I was no longer interested in the law as a vocation."

She thinks that characterizing issues related to family as "women's issues" guarantees failure. "These are universal social issues that involve men, women, and children. If you want to raise a family, it takes time and energy, and it requires life adjustments—remember what every expecting parent hears: 'It will change your life!' And it does. When 'family' is only a woman's issue, then it is women who will be expected to make the adjustment."

Laura is a mainstream beneficiary of the women's movement, a working mom with a measured perspective on the advantages and shortcomings of the feminist revolution, while her mother and Joan Didion, both seventy-three, have their own unique places. They're accomplished professionals who made it to the top of their chosen fields through the sheer force of their talent and determination. Although they didn't apply for the title, they are role models for women of any generation. They're confident about who they were then and who they are now.

Didion, who was sharply critical of social action in the Sixties, has softened some. Back then she wrote, "If I could believe that going to a barricade would af-

fect man's fate in the slightest I would go to that barricade and quite often I wish I could, but it would be
less than honest to say that I would expect such a
happy ending." Now she says, "I am older, so I am
generally more understanding. I'm not quite as doctri-
naire. I'm softer on their desire to do something. I understand why people try."

She remains impatient with the discussions still
going on today about career versus family. "I kept reading these stories about women who had gone to law
school and become this or that, and now they were giving it up to raise a family. And to them that wasn't the
deal. There was an awful lot of self-indulgence around
the movement."

Neither self-indulgence nor self-pity is in the
Didion DNA. She lives alone on the Upper East Side
of Manhattan, a wisp of a woman with a voice so soft
she can barely be heard. But her emotional and intellectual strengths are undiminished by time and trial.
The Year of Magical Thinking is already considered a
classic of the literature of grief. She wrote it after experiencing, within less than two years, the death of her
husband, John, and her daughter, Quintana. She
adapted the book for the stage, and it became a critically acclaimed one-woman show on Broadway starring Vanessa Redgrave.

Lissa Muscatine

Lissa Muscatine, another California woman, grew up
and flourished in the foothills of Berkeley, overlooking

the university campus where her father, Charles, was a distinguished professor of English and a highly regarded arbitrator in the disputes between the university administration and the Free Speech Movement over the rights of the students to use the campus as a forum for promoting non-university causes.

Muscatine's teenage years included walking home from school with the strong scent of tear gas in the air and maneuvering her car during driver's education to avoid the streets blocked by National Guard units called in to control the student demonstrations.

Her parents were old-school intellectuals who had moved to California from the East just in time for the loyalty-oath frenzy of the Fifties when government officials, university professors, and even corporate employees were required either to swear they were not a Communist or lose their job.

Professor Muscatine was fired from the Berkeley faculty for refusing to sign a loyalty oath, puckishly citing, among other reasons, the grief he would get from Lissa's mother, Doris. They built a California modern home in the Berkeley Hills. Charles won his appeal and rejoined the faculty.

That was the quiet, introspective family culture in which Lissa Muscatine grew up as a bright young student and precocious athlete. Her mother had attended Vermont's Bennington College at a time when William Carlos Williams was teaching poetry, Erich Fromm was teaching psychology, and Martha Graham was teaching dance there.

Muscatine says, "My mother had feminist sensibilities, but she grew up with different expectations. She had to keep the new world and the old world together. She had kids fairly quickly after getting married. I think she was pretty frustrated, but she wouldn't admit it."

Muscatine sees her mother as very much a product of her generation: "She was incredibly active in the community, and she was a very successful author who wrote six books. But she could do that within the confines of the role that was expected of her. She certainly wasn't going to run off and pursue a career independent of children and family, or make those things secondary."

As for her father, Muscatine says he lived with that model of the role of women even though he was a supporter of feminism. As she concludes, "Even if you fully understand how limiting that is, you can't fully escape it. My mother lived with these contrasting constraints. She was caught between different times. She was the most proper person I've ever met, and yet she had this streak of free spirit."

For example, her mother encouraged her children to attend antiwar protests but insisted they dress nicely and wear good shoes so the public would know the movement involved more than hippies. Muscatine went along with that, but she bridled at a rule in her elementary school that girls couldn't wear pants.

Lissa Muscatine was a jock, "probably the best baseball player in my school—but how could you play ball in a dress?" Her dad recalls her being left out of a ball game at a birthday party because she was a girl. Fi-

Lissa Muscatine in 1976, the year she graduated
from Harvard University

Lissa Muscatine, then a White House speechwriter,
with her children and the first lady in December 1994

nally, one of the parents relented and let her take a turn at bat. She promptly hit one over the fence. Her dad summed up the moment: "Lissa's revenge began early."

Women and sports became her special province in advancing the rights of her gender. She arrived at Harvard in 1972, just in time to take advantage of Title IX, federal legislation that guaranteed women equal opportunities in sports programs. As a tennis and basketball star, she brought firsthand experience to the job when she was appointed to Harvard's Standing Committee on Athletics.

As a member of the women's basketball team, she had to help pay for their trips to away games. One incident that still rankles involved a basketball practice for the women's varsity. A men's intramural team showed up and claimed the gym, aided by a maintenance man who turned off the lights until the women left.

When she conferred with a Harvard vice president about letter sweaters for women athletes, she had to be persistent because "he kept saying things like 'But don't women want a daintier H on their sweaters? Or what about some pink trim?'" When she said they wanted only a traditional black sweater with the crimson "H," he had a hard time accepting it. Later, she said, he apologized.

She was also captain of the Harvard women's varsity tennis team, and when the celebrated **Harvard Crimson** failed to take notice of their undefeated season, she led all the players to the paper's offices to protest. From then on, women's tennis at Harvard received the coverage it deserved.

After she graduated in 1976, she became a Rhodes

scholar in the first class of that prestigious program to accept women. When she returned home from Oxford, she went to work first as a staff writer for **The Washington Star** for two years and then as a metro reporter and, later, a sportswriter for **The Washington Post,** where she met her husband, Brad Graham, a longtime military and foreign affairs correspondent.

Journalism was not a natural field for Muscatine. She chuckles, "I didn't like the objectivity part. I was too much of an activist." When Bill Clinton was elected president in 1992, she thought it might be her last chance to work for a Democrat in the White House, so she applied for a job as a presidential speechwriter who would also have responsibility for the first lady's speeches. There was a long list of applicants, and Muscatine was anxious about her prospects, a condition that was not improved when she discovered she was pregnant just as the job search moved into the final round.

She volunteered to take herself out of the running, but Hillary Clinton's staff encouraged her to stay in, assuring her that there was a new attitude in the White House about women and work. She got the job, and not too long after starting, she was off on a four-month maternity leave.

She returned to become the chief speechwriter and, later, the first lady's director of communications. At the end of the administration, she became a stay-at-home mother for her boy and girl twins and a younger son while also working as a freelance writer.

At home, Muscatine says, "We talk about women's issues when they come up in the news, but it's not a constant in the house."

At the age of nine, her daughter, Wynne, gave a speech on Capitol Hill at a ceremony commemorating the passage of Title IX. Now thirteen, she is a talented center midfielder who recently helped lead her school's soccer team to the Maryland state championship.

Wynne shares her mother's admiration for Billie Jean King, the feisty and gifted tennis player who put her sport on the front page in the Sixties by demanding larger purses for women in tournaments and, later, emerging victorious in the televised showdown with Bobby Riggs, the loudmouthed tennis veteran who bragged that he could beat any woman.

That match in the fall of 1973 was, in its own way, the Super Bowl for women's rights. Women who didn't know a set point from a second serve were suddenly riveted to their television sets.

King's electrifying victory also changed the way women played tennis, giving rise to a more athletic game. Now, as Muscatine says, "these days there are all these female icons of athleticism and achievement that once seemed taboo for women. Look at Venus Williams and [Maria] Sharapova. Who would have thought they'd be seen as athletic and feminine at the same time?"

Muscatine also sees contradictions, however. "At the same time, there's been a backlash in mass culture against this notion of the independent woman who kind of expresses her femininity individually and how she chooses. The mass culture has instead exacerbated the idea of women as subservient, as only physical specimens. And so I think the younger generation ends up with this tension between the possibilities that are available because of the women's movement and yet this constant barrage in popular culture that asks them to behave completely differently."

Forty years later the women's movement still is making its way across uneven terrain. Women may be discouraged by many of the inconsistencies, but Gloria Steinem, now seventy-three and a widow, is heartened by the overall progress.

"You can't go into any town that doesn't have a battered women's shelter or a women's art gallery or a women's rock band, or a campus that doesn't have a women's history program." She is mystified and angered, however, by the political successes of those who haven't fully embraced gender equality, and especially the administration of President George W. Bush. "We've never had a more hostile administration to women than this one," she says.

Warming to her subject, she blames the Bush presidency for not doing more about international sweatshops and the exploitation of women as cheap labor. "From country to country," she says, "you find eighty percent of the cheapest labor are women and there is no outrage."

Conservatives are equally outraged by the failure of feminists to condemn the previous president, Bill Clinton, for the Monica Lewinsky affair.

Steinem's rejoinder is that what Bill Clinton did was "stupid . . . terrible judgment but not sexual harassment because it was welcome [by Lewinsky]. As for Hillary, it was clear their marriage was one of love and mutual in-

Gloria Steinem in her New York apartment in 1970

Feminist activist Gloria Steinem speaks to thousands of demonstrators during the March for Women's Lives in Washington, D.C., in 2004.

terest and intellectual respect but not fidelity. Therefore it's none of our business."

When Steinem wrote an op-ed piece in **The New York Times** to that effect, she was bombarded with angry letters, including one from a businessman who said, "That's what you feminists stand for—women under the desk giving oral sex." Steinem believes the root of the rage against the piece was the frustration of conservatives who couldn't make their charges against Clinton stick.

Steinem prefers to concentrate on continuing issues such as the difficult choice between motherhood and career. The dilemma, she believes, is "that women's standards are too low, and none of this will have real meaning until men are caring for infants and little children the same way women are. It won't work until we have a system of national [child]care. No story I've seen about a family-friendly workplace includes the role of men."

When I ask Steinem about the maternal bond and the conflicted feelings that women have about returning to work, and, especially in the first year, the complex feelings of a mother leaving an infant whom she's carried for nine months, given birth to, and nurtured, Steinem says, "Women are not solely responsible for children. It's not a punishment for men to stay home, it's a reward."

Hearing that, a female colleague said to me, "Before I had my own child, I would have taken her position. But once I had my baby, I understood the unique bond between mother and child."

Our eldest daughter, Jennifer, an emergency-room

physician and mother of two daughters, read what Steinem said to me and reflected on her own life. "I think my generation of women is constantly anxious about balancing working and motherhood. We don't want to completely give up one for the other, and we're such compulsive mothers that we're going eighteen hours a day between the office and our kids—taking them to music lessons and soccer games, to museums and swimming. The dads help a lot, but the moms want to be there for their kids and for their jobs. It's tough."

Something's Happening Here

There's something happening here
What it is ain't exactly clear
—Buffalo Springfield,
"For What It's Worth"

SOMETIME IN THE SPRING OF 1967, I was in a taxi in San Francisco, returning from a late dinner following another day covering the student demonstrations across the bay at Berkeley. My haircut was fraternity-boy short. The counterculture was in full swing, but I was still way at the back of that particular bus.

The cabbie asked what I did for a living, and when I told him I was a reporter, he said, "Mister, do you know what's going on over on Haight Street?" I replied that I didn't even know where Haight Street was, much less what was going on there. He said, "You won't believe it. Hippies everywhere. Want me to take you there?"

Why not?

Fifteen minutes later, I got out of the cab and found myself in a twilight zone between the ordered world of a young NBC News reporter, married with children, and the strange new universe of the flower children floating through their Summer of Love. Haight and Ashbury streets, just down the hill from the University of California Medical School, had been taken over by a movable mass of hippies in tie-dyed shirts, peasant skirts, caftans, sandals, long hair, love beads, and backpacks. They seemed to be arriving every fifteen minutes on some unseen underground train serving runaway America, and each new arrival seemed to be younger than the one before.

It was almost midnight, and yet the head shops and coffee bars were wide open. Guitarists were playing on street corners, accompanied by the ubiquitous bongo drummers. There was a lot of talk about love solving all the problems of the world. Everyone looked either completely stoned or well on their way. A young girl, no more than sixteen, approached and asked if I wanted to buy some hash, an offer I found oddly naive and trusting, since I looked more like a narc than a user.

When I said no, and by the way, what's going on here? she said, "It's the Haight, man," as if that were all that needed to be—or could be—said. And then, as if to prove her credentials, she added proudly, "I've slept with all the Byrds," one of the hot rock bands of the day.

I wandered around for a while and then retreated to the familiar sanctuary of the Fairmont Hotel, that Edwardian mass on top of Nob Hill, where, as I recall, Ella Fitzgerald was performing in the Venetian Room. Ella I understood. What I had just seen was intriguing but bewildering.

As a reporter, I was fascinated by what was happening, but I was not tempted to dive into that pool. My ambitions were counter to the counterculture. When I did let my hair grow long, and when I abandoned my straight-arrow wardrobe on weekends, I always felt as if I were in costume, just playing a role.

When I started returning to the Haight to file follow-up reports, I soon discovered what was effectively the nerve center of the neighborhood: the Haight Ashbury Free Clinic, organized and run by a young physician and graduate student in pharmacology from the nearby medical school.

Dr. David Smith

David Smith was the grandson of Okies—refugees from the Dust Bowl who migrated to California's rich central valley during the Depression. He was the first in his family to attend college, and his motivation was to achieve the kind of academic success that led to financial success. "I was the least likely person to get involved in social action," he says now. "I wanted to get beyond the limits of my family."

However, walking home from the medical school through Haight-Ashbury in 1965, he was appalled by the problems he began encountering involving drugs, sexually transmitted diseases, and alcohol. He was equally appalled by what he described as the medical community's indifference to what other physicians dismissed as "the voluntary indigent." Smith says that at San Francisco General Hospital, the city's large all-purpose treatment center, the kids were "treated like garbage, likely to be asked, 'Why are you coming here? You're voluntarily poor. Besides, you use drugs—and dress weird and listen to weird music.'"

In fact, David Smith had another connection to

the hippie kids he saw in the streets, but it was one that he didn't discuss in those days. "I had a drinking problem in 1966—and I took LSD. I was studying the psychopharmacological effects of drugs on the mind, and I must say, taking LSD was an incredibly positive experience. I had this big spiritual experience. It opened my mind. To be truthful, I wouldn't have opened the free clinic if I hadn't been taking LSD. And I smoked marijuana every day for twenty years. I was part of that Sixties drugs-are-romantic thing."

Now, however, he counsels young people that there is nothing positive about drug use and that whatever feelings of liberation come with drugs can be found in other safer ways—from exercise, meditation, and yoga, for example. He regrets that the casual abuse of drugs and all that came with it in the Sixties—overdoses, addictions, violence, physical and psychological damage—short-circuited the chances of having a rational, scientific discussion about the appropriate place of drugs in research. He says when LSD became a routine part of the street drug scene—when Timothy Leary, the Harvard psychologist, became the guru urging everyone to "turn on, tune in, drop out"—all the promising research on LSD in controlled circumstances was stopped.

Leary was a charming and manipulative hustler for what he saw as the societal benefits of hallucinogens, particularly LSD. He was a merry medicine man—although a Ph.D. and not an M.D.—peddling his message and his tabs of LSD from coast to coast, often just a step ahead of the law. Some wealthy benefactors set him up in a large mansion just outside of the Waspy enclave of Millbrook, New York, where he gathered worshipful disciples around him.

Through a friend I am familiar with the case of at least one of Leary's Millbrook acolytes. He was the son of a local couple with a modest income, and the brother of a man who became a very successful businessman. The acid-dropping son struggled to recover from his days with Leary. He disappeared to South America for several years, and when his parents finally found him he was a distant and befuddled figure. They persuaded him to come home, and after years of therapy he's now stable, but it has been a long ordeal. His wealthy brother supports him financially.

Back in San Francisco, David Smith began to see his free clinic as more than just an emergency room for hippies with a variety of ailments, from drug overdoses to hepatitis to sexually transmitted diseases. He came to see his work in wider terms. He began to lecture the medical establishment on the need to think of health care as "a right, not a privilege," and he encouraged doctors in other cities to follow his model. He envisioned a nationwide network of free clinics to serve the poor.

When we met again in 2005, still in his original crowded offices on Clayton Street in the Haight, he was at once rueful and proud of the Free Clinic's history. Rueful because drug abuse is a lasting legacy of the Sixties. He's seen the cycle go from marijuana and LSD to heroin and amphetamines, then to powdered cocaine and crack, and now back to heroin and crystal meth.

Dr. David Smith in his office at the Haight Ashbury Free
Medical Clinic, surrounded by psychedelic artwork

Dr. David Smith outside the clinic
with his wife, Millicent Smith,
and an associate in March 2006

He says a big part of the initial appeal of drugs in the Sixties was their antiestablishment flavor. "You're living through chemistry. If you're not, so the thinking went, your mind has been programmed by the government. That's why we have the war in Vietnam. That's why we have racism and all that stuff. Grace Slick of the Jefferson Airplane, who is now in recovery, said at one point, 'If we just take enough drugs, protest hard enough, play our music hard enough, we can change the world.' They actually believed that.

"Then it **all** went wrong. Speed hit the Haight, and terrible violence. I know how bad it was. I lived through it. Any philosophical movement fueled by drugs is doomed to fail. Janis Joplin helped save the Free Clinic in 1967 and then died of a drug overdose in 1970. I know all of the bad stuff."

Smith doesn't dismiss the drug scene entirely, however. "A lot of creativity came out of it. The first light show I ever saw was in 1965. It was a simulated LSD experience, and now that is routine on television, at concerts, even at big corporate events."

But his larger message concerns what he considers the sad state of American health care. "When I first started the clinic, they called me a Communist," he remembers. "I'd respond, 'All we're doing is giving health care to the poor. How is that un-American?' "

He tried to keep politics out of the Free Clinic, concentrating solely on the immediate needs of his steady lineup of clients. I remember that whatever time of the day or night I stopped by the Free Clinic the lines outside were long, and everyone was greeted by a bold sign at the top of the steps:

NO DEALING! NO HOLDING DRUGS.
NO USING DRUGS. NO ALCOHOL.
NO PETS. ANY OF THESE CAN CLOSE
THE CLINIC. WE LOVE YOU.

Today the main office is the headquarters of a network of twelve free clinics scattered around the Bay Area, offering a wide range of medical services, from pediatric and women's care to AIDS treatment and increasingly—a sign of the times and the march of time—care for diseases related to aging, such as hypertension and arthritis.

Smith is convinced that his original clinic was a catalyst for a number of positive medical developments that came out of the Sixties. "Health care reform—a part of that came from the clinic. The gay rights movement—also an important part of the clinic. The origins of addiction medicine. Women's health care. The explosion of the whole free-clinic movement—ours was the first."

The Free Clinic, which has treated going on two million patients in forty years, now gets funding from the city and state and a variety of other sources. But in the early years, it was touch and go financially. When the legendary rock impresario Bill Graham and artists such as the Grateful Dead, Creedence Clearwater Revival, George Harrison, and Ravi Shankar realized that Smith and his colleagues were treating the young who were buying their records and attending their concerts, they organized a series of benefits that saved the Clinic from going under.

When Vietnam veterans started coming home strung out on drugs, the Veterans Administration was not prepared to cope with their needs, so it provided grants to the Free Clinic, and vets became an important part of the patient base in the early Seventies.

An unanticipated legacy of the clinic and its approach to treating patients and conditions shunned by the medical establishment of the time is that it inspired a new generation of physicians to specialize in addiction or take a more unconventional route in their practices. Smith remembers that when he first opened the clinic, one of his professors confronted him and said, "David, where did you go wrong?" Now, he says, physicians who become fed up with the constraints placed on medical care by the government and insurance companies volunteer at free clinics or even start their own when they retire. Or they join Doctors Without Borders, the international physicians' group.

In 2007, four decades after he founded it, the paths of David Smith and the Free Clinic suddenly took an unexpected turn. After a major falling-out over its management and budget issues, he left and opened a new office, called the Prometa Center for Addiction, on Montgomery Street, in the heart of San Francisco's financial district. He is running the Prometa Center for Hythiam, Inc., a publicly traded company that claims its cocktail of three drugs can help resolve drug and alcohol dependency. Prometa is not free; its outpatient sobriety program costs between twelve and fifteen thousand dollars. The high cost, the public marketing of Smith's reputation to promote the center, and the untested use of these drugs for dealing with addiction combined to ignite a firestorm from medical groups and the therapeutic community.

Smith is unfazed by the criticism. He still lives on the edge of the Haight, walking his dogs through the old neighborhood, pointing out the houses where Jerry Garcia and the Grateful Dead once hung out, just across the street from where Janis Joplin was living high when she died.

Judy Collins

Judy Collins remembers the Sixties drug scene all too well.

We first met at the peak of her fame, when I was the host of **Today** and she was booked as a guest. She had just posed naked for an album cover, and she showed up at the studio with her piano player, who was dead drunk. She was difficult to deal with, to put it mildly, and I was not happy. Finally, before the segment could be taped, I walked off the set. Many years later, we met again and she apologized, saying she had been deeply embarrassed by the incident at the time but felt she had no control over her behavior. I admired her honesty, and we've stayed in touch since then.

Judy Collins, one of the true marquee musical artists to emerge during the Sixties, was the daughter of a popular radio personality in Denver who hosted some of the biggest names in music. "My dad was blind," she says, "and a very good singer and very liberal. He railed against the McCarthy hearings, and he was so outspoken, I'm surprised he didn't get thrown off the air, but I think people felt sorry for him because he was blind."

Charlie Collins encouraged his gifted daughter to take up the piano, and by the age of thirteen she was playing the classics—Mozart, Rachmaninoff, Debussy—with an orchestra. Two years later, she discovered folk music, and her life took a turn that eventually led to world fame and generations of fans.

It has not been an easy road, however. At the age of twenty, she dropped out of college to marry her hometown sweetheart, a Navy veteran who was teaching at the University of Colorado. Judy's musical talents were set aside, and she got a clerical job at the school—the kind of bad bargain that many talented young women of her generation were forced to make.

To his credit, her husband thought it was a mistake for her to abandon her music and encouraged her to pick it up again. In short order, she was a hit at a local club as what we used to call a troubadour, singing traditional folk songs such as "Maid of Constant Sorrow" and "John Riley." Her fame spread quickly and she was booked into clubs beyond Boulder. Her husband was willing to stay home and care for their infant son. "We were an enlightened bunch," she remembers. "We read Camus, Sartre, the French intellectuals. We believed in individual direction. But it was a strange mix of Fifties-style kitchens and television sets to go with our far-out ways."

By 1961 she had a recording contract with Elektra and was living in New York. "I developed a real taste for the politically active stuff. I was recording Brecht and Weill, Dylan and Pete Seeger. I was also going on a lot of protest marches. When you move to New York, you get into a lot of activity. Maybe if I had lived elsewhere, it would have passed me by."

She was also drinking a lot and doing drugs. "I took LSD in about '63," she says, "and I didn't come down for two days. It was a terrible trip." Drinking became a constant in her life; she recognized her addiction but couldn't find a way out. "I tried everything. Hare Krishna, meditation, yoga. I went to a doctor who was supposed to get you from hard liquor to beer. No one was on **Oprah** talking about recovery. There was this general lack of education."

She was also going through a bitter personal battle with her husband over the custody of their son, Clark. She initially lost custody of Clark but was able to win him back in 1969, at the peak of her career. By then she was not only a hugely successful artist but a deeply engaged activist.

In the fall of 1969, during the trial of the Chicago Seven for inciting violence and riots during the Democratic convention the year before, defendant Abbie Hoffman asked Collins to be a character witness. She took the stand and, instead of testifying, she began singing her hit antiwar song "Where Have All the Flowers Gone?" Judge Julius Hoffman ordered her to stop. When she didn't, a court marshal put his hand over her mouth. She only remembers the judge saying, " 'We do not sing in court.' The rest of it is all a fog."

Were you stoned or drunk? I asked her. "No, it was just a crazy time." It was also a time when, as she says, "We got to tell our stories in our music—and people

Judy Collins,
one of the
marquee musicians
of the Sixties:
"Beautiful work
was done during
that period. . . .
Maybe breaking
the rules helped.
But we were lucky
to live through it."

wanted to hear them. What could be better for an artist than that?"

Personally she was still struggling with alcoholism, but when it came to her music she stayed on the straight and narrow. "I didn't show up late or drunk at recordings, and I was extremely agitated and uncomfortable when others were—what?—three hours late because they were stoned or strung out on heroin. No one came roaring in and said [to them], 'You're fired.'

"We were innocent. We didn't get it. There were a lot of drug addicts and alcoholics in those days. Those who recovered and those who died. I think it was part of the chaos. It was the least favorite part of it for me, even as I was participating. I was revolted, if you know what I mean."

She feels she was not a willing participant. "It was not my choice. I had an illness. Alcoholism and drug abuse." It wasn't until 1978 that she began to get effective treatment. "I don't know, maybe I saw a poster for the National Council on Alcoholism or something. Before that, I didn't get much help from doctors because I don't think they knew, but now they do know about addiction. I feel so strongly about education in this area."

In 1992 her son, Clark, committed suicide after a struggle with drug abuse and depression. He was just thirty-three, and it was a devastating blow for Judy. She wrote a book about the experience, called **Sanity and Grace,** in which she described the help she got from meditation in getting through the ordeal.

She has offered to others affected by suicide a therapy she calls the Seven Ts: truth, therapy, trust, try, treat, treasure, and thrive. Truth is recognizing there is no guilt in suicide. Try means to stay away from drugs and alcohol. Treasure and thrive mean to treasure every moment and be positive, knowing you can get through this.

Looking back on her musical career, she is astonished at "how much beautiful work was done during that period, the Sixties and Seventies. Maybe breaking the rules helped. But we were lucky to live through it." The place of drugs and the consequences of extensive drug use during the Sixties remain a mixed legacy for artists and others who were involved.

Arlo Guthrie and Tim Russert

Arlo Guthrie, son of Woody and popular troubadour in his own right, says, "There was a time when drugs . . . really opened the doors to perceive a larger—or certainly an alternative—reality. There was more to the world. This was something shamans and priests and priestesses had known for years, and all of a sudden we got ahold of that," he laughs heartily.

Guthrie didn't set out to be a folksinger like his famous father. He wanted to be a forest ranger, so when he graduated from high school he enrolled in Rocky Mountain College in Billings, Montana. It wasn't just the lure of higher education.

"In those days you were either in college or visiting Asian nations, all expenses paid [in the Vietnam War]," he recalled.

But after less than one semester in Billings, Guthrie was ready to leave. "I heard Bob Dylan's 'Positively

Folk-singer Arlo Guthrie
in October 1968, shortly after
the release of his cult hit,
"Alice's Restaurant"

Arlo Guthrie (right) joins David Crosby
at the thirtieth anniversary of the Woodstock festival
in Bethel, New York

Fourth Street' on the radio. It wasn't a country song, and I thought it was indicative of the times: [its] being played in Billings meant something was going on.

"I just thought, 'There's too much going on. I can't stay here in Billings, even if there's the threat of the draft.' "

By 1965 he was back in New England, visiting friends in western Massachusetts. On Thanksgiving Day he helped a friend dispose of some rubbish on private property since the town dump was closed.

The local police chief—Officer Obie—tracked down the culprits and had them arrested. They were fined twenty-five dollars and returned to the home of their friend Alice Brock, who ran an open house for traveling musicians.

After dinner they decided to write a song about the incident, embellish the details, and call it "Alice's Restaurant."

It took nine months to finish.

It was eighteen minutes and twenty seconds long—as Arlo likes to say, "the length of the gap in the Nixon Watergate tape"—and it became one of the big hits of 1966–67, despite its length.

In Guthrie's generation, "Alice's Restaurant" became an epic poem, a counterculture **Beowulf** of the times. As Guthrie says now, "Nobody writes an eighteen-minute dialogue to become famous. In those days nobody was playing any song over two and a half minutes long.

"I just did it because I liked doing it."

When Arthur Penn made a film based on the song in 1969, Guthrie and Stockbridge, Massachusetts, police chief William Obanhein, "Officer Obie," played themselves.

Guthrie says they were putting in long days together on the set, sometimes from four in the morning until eight at night. Finally, one day Obanhein approached Guthrie and said, "If you keep getting up at four in the morning and work all day long . . . you hippies can't be all that bad."

They became what Guthrie calls "very close and dear friends. He was a wonderful, wonderful human being. I thought how interesting that fate brought us together."

"Alice's Restaurant" made Guthrie a cult figure in the widening world of Sixties music, so he was invited to perform at the 1969 Woodstock music festival in New York.

His stoner rap between songs is still considered a defining moment by students of that celebration of rock music, alternative lifestyles, dope, free love, and high times amid the rain and mud.

Guthrie was recorded saying "Yeah, it's far out, man. I don't know if you . . . I don't know, uh—like how many of you can dig how many people there are, man. Like, I was rappin' to the fuzz—right? Can you dig it? Man, there's supposed to be a million and a half people here by tonight. Can you dig that? Thruway's closed, man. Yeah! Lotta freaks."

No one knows for sure just how large the crowd was at Woodstock. It was a mass of hippie humanity, glorying in the sky above and the mud below, cold and wet, with good grass and bad acid. Over the years the gathering has taken on mythic proportions. If every real or role-playing hippie who now claims to have been there actually attended, the population of New York would have doubled.

One who really was there that weekend was a college student from upstate New York who today seems an unlikely rock groupie: Tim Russert, the Washington bureau chief for NBC News and the host of **Meet the Press,** the most popular Sunday morning interview broadcast in Washington.

Russert and three pals arrived on the first night, Thursday, with eight cases of beer stacked atop their car, which displayed a banner advertising WBTA 1490, a Buffalo, New York, rock station. "The traffic was heavy," Russert remembers, "but we paid eight bucks apiece for our tickets and got up close to the stage. We were wearing Buffalo Bills jerseys and thought we'd throw a football around, but it wasn't that kind of a crowd. The early arrivals were hard-core druggies, and the drug use just got wilder and wilder as more people began to arrive. You'd meet someone, and they'd hold out a tab of acid or a joint and say, 'Be my guest.'

"It got cold, so someone built a bonfire, and this one kid, completely stoned, kept trying to throw himself into the fire. It was scary. We kept drinking our beer, and then the rain came, and it was a mess. We couldn't get back to our car, so we sorta camped out, like everyone. We took a bath in a swimming pool one night—and the next day we discovered that after we left, other kids began to use it as a toilet.

"A half-million people! They kept announcing Woodstock had become the second-largest city in New

York. They ran out of food, so the state began dropping boxes of bologna sandwiches.

"It was wild. For a while there was a rumor Johnny Carson was going to show up. In the middle of one night, the announcer said casually, 'Hey, there's some bad brown acid around. Be careful.' But no one was saying, 'Don't do that.' "

Drug dealers began to materialize, and the carefree spirit that had prevailed at first began to take on a harder, mercenary edge. For the four Buffalo guys, the drug scene was more than they'd bargained for. But then the rain stopped, the sun came out, and the musical magic still lingers in Tim Russert's memory.

"The Who played **Tommy**. Richie Havens came on. Sly and the Family Stone. We began to think we were part of something special, but it wasn't until Sunday morning, when we began to drive out of there after three days and listened to the radio, that we realized how big Woodstock really was."

Russert has a very close relationship with his college-age son, Luke. They're in constant touch by e-mail or cell phone, so, looking back, Russert can't imagine what his parents must have thought, knowing where he was, as they watched the televised reports of the nonstop chaos and in-your-face decadence that only escalated as the weekend progressed. When baby boomers became parents themselves, many had an entirely different perspective on the freedoms of the young.

Guthrie, of course, was not raised in a conventional Fifties family. His dad, Woody Guthrie, and Woody's friends—Pete Seeger and the Weavers, the folksingers blacklisted during the McCarthy era—were famously suspicious of big-government, authoritarian policies.

When he was subject to the draft after dropping out of college, Arlo says, "I wasn't an antiwar person, necessarily. I was just opposed to this one.

"I knew I wasn't going to Canada and I knew I wasn't going to Vietnam. I didn't know what was going to happen."

What happened is that he got drunk the night before his physical and psychological evaluation for the draft and spent most of his time at the induction office playing mind games with the examiners.

When he managed to turn his arrest for littering into a psycho-drama on war crimes, the sergeant on duty decided Guthrie was not fit for service.

He didn't have to fight a war he hated, but to this day, he says, "I'm a patriot at heart. I was a staunch American and I remain so to this day."

Guthrie has mixed memories of the time when music and drugs moved a generation in directions unimagined just a few years earlier.

"We were all going, 'Wow! This is different.' And some people got lost in that. Some people got killed in it. But there was a time when we were all helping each other discover a new world. We were able to move around, to see the world from a different perspective. It wasn't so much that it's good to get stoned. It was good to have another point of view. I would highly recommend it, but if you can do it by some other means, that would be terrific."

Guthrie also remembers when the drug culture

began to take a menacing new turn. "I remember hearing stories of people who were looking like hippies—disguised as hippies—but selling oregano instead of weed. All of a sudden it became a business. That was the end of it."

The end of one phase of the drug culture perhaps, but far from the end of drug taking. Guthrie believes, and statistics bear him out, that "there are more people smoking weed than ever before, and somewhere along the supply line is a big-time criminal. That big-time criminal is probably friends with someone in the government. I don't think anyone in their right mind would disagree with what I am saying."

Guthrie continues to tour, although "Alice's Restaurant" was his one big hit. In 1991 he bought the old church that was Alice's home on that eventful Thanksgiving in 1965. He has made it into the Guthrie Center, a nonprofit foundation involved in everything from meditation courses to raising money to find a cure for Huntington's disease, the condition that took Woody Guthrie's life.

Jann Wenner

Jann Wenner, who was a student at Berkeley when the Sixties music scene exploded, was a rock fan with entrepreneurial ambitions that he converted into a publishing empire. **Rolling Stone**, his signature publication, is now forty years old, and in its graphics and journalism, its early hallucinogenic haze has been replaced by a sophisticated corporate gloss.

Wenner and **Rolling Stone** provided the platform that elevated the gonzo journalism of Dr. Hunter S. Thompson to heights of fame and acclaim.

Hunter was a dazzling stylist, whatever the subject. He masked his wide-ranging intelligence and the softer side of his personality with his flamboyant ways and outrageous declarations.

I always looked forward to his political reporting, in which he got beneath the canned and homogenized structure of modern campaigns. And if you want to take a drug trip without actually ingesting any controlled substances, read Thompson's book **Fear and Loathing in Las Vegas,** based on his serial reports to **Rolling Stone.** It is a wild, mescaline-fueled evocation of that most unlikely city.

Thompson, for all of his over-the-top behavior and proclamations, could also be a polite and thoughtful companion in his private moments. My wife, Meredith, once shared a cross-country flight with him during the closing days of the Nixon administration. They had a very pleasant visit, and as the plane began its descent into Los Angeles, Thompson leaned across the seat almost apologetically and said to Meredith, "Look, I've only got one tab of acid, but I'd be willing to share it with you."

She politely declined.

Thompson's patron, Wenner, is not concerned about the role of drugs and their destructive effects in the Sixties. He calls drugs "the discovery of the young. You knew that taking LSD was like being admitted to a special club. The insight it gave you into people, places, stuff like that." Wenner says what he calls "the

Jann Wenner at the Rolling Stone party for Jimmy Carter
in New York City, 1976

Working on an interview with Bono in Wenner's
New York office in November 2005

chemical madness" played into the explosion of energy and rebellion of a generation that had already witnessed the assassination of John F. Kennedy and the civil rights uprising in the South, two events that cracked the mirror of America's narcissism.

Wenner finds the legacy of the drug culture mixed. Yes, it's been destructive to certain individuals, but by and large, he believes society has dealt with it remarkably well—right up to the heights of power. "Everybody, I mean everybody, in the White House has smoked pot. I mean, George W. Bush. If you look at the whole generation, very few people suffered; there were some notable casualties, but very few. And this whole war on drugs is a complete hypocrisy."

Wenner's benign view of recreational drug use is not unique among the Sixties generation. While the tragedies caused by addiction and overdoses are admitted and regretted, they are almost considered as acceptable—perhaps inevitable—collateral damage by substances that are so widely used because they appeal to so many people for so many reasons. But what almost never comes up in the white-bread discussion of drugs is their ongoing and devastating effect on the black family culture in the inner city and the role of illicit drugs in organized crime and the murderous street gangs in large cities.

And crystal meth, cheaply produced and widely available, has now become a major scourge across rural America. The war on drugs has been largely ineffective primarily because the appetite for drugs remains voracious. Drug use is not as openly celebrated as it was in the rock-and-roll culture of the Sixties, but marijuana, cocaine, methamphetamine, heroin, and prescription-drug abuse still plague a broad spectrum of American life, from Wall Street to Main Street, as the saying goes. It's affected everyone from the conservative commentator Rush Limbaugh to the liberal television and screenwriter Aaron Sorkin, from big-name athletes to factory workers and high school kids.

Kris Kristofferson

One of my favorite hippies—well, not exactly a hippie, more of a country music outlaw—to emerge from the Sixties is Kris Kristofferson, the singer-songwriter of such classics as "Me and Bobby McGee," "Sunday Mornin' Comin' Down," and "Help Me Make It Through the Night." I've always been drawn to his lyrics and intelligence, and intrigued by the lifestyle U-turn he experienced in his late twenties.

I first saw Kristofferson in person around 1971 at the Troubador on Santa Monica Boulevard in Hollywood, the now-legendary small club with the big roster of star performers, including Neil Young and Bob Dylan. Kristofferson was performing with his soon-to-be wife, Rita Coolidge, a beautiful, sultry singer who wore beaded buckskin sheaths and her long black hair in a single braid, reflecting her Native American ancestry.

When they came onstage for the late show, Kristofferson was, as I remember, waving a half-empty bottle of Jack Daniel's, swearing at the lighting director, and scowling at the audience. He then proceeded to give an absolutely electrifying performance, singing in his husky baritone about hard nights and lonely roads with such feeling that the whole club might as well have been a single back booth at some Nashville honky-tonk.

Just three years earlier, Kristoffer "Kris" Kristofferson had been a crew-cut helicopter pilot ferrying supplies to oil rigs in the Gulf of Mexico. Before that he'd been an Army pilot, a Golden Gloves boxing champion, a football star, a Rhodes scholar at Oxford University, and a candidate for a professorship in English literature at West Point.

When we met at the Mandarin Oriental Hotel in New York in 2007, he laughed when I brought up his colorful and checkered background and said, "Yeah—duty, honor, country. My dad was in World War II and Korea. He retired as a two-star general from the air force. I wasn't ready to believe what Joan Baez and everyone were saying.

"I wasn't part of the whole antiwar thing because I had buddies over there. I asked a couple of my friends that were over there, 'Should I go back in the Army and go to Vietnam?' One of them said, 'Are you out of your mind? This is the most screwed-up thing we've ever seen!' And this was a veteran of Korea. So in 1968 I wasn't into sex, drugs, and rock and roll; that would come later," he says. "'Straight Arrow' was my nickname."

In fact, he had been troubled about what to believe ever since the Warren Commission Report on the assassination of John F. Kennedy. He believes the Zapruder film of the shooting—the short home movie made by Abraham Zapruder as the Kennedy limousine passed through Dealey Plaza—gives the lie to the single-gunman theory. So when Lyndon Johnson shocked the nation by announcing that he wouldn't run for renomination or reelection in 1968, Kristofferson didn't buy the explanation that was given—that he had to devote all his time to dealing with the Vietnam War.

I asked him if he thought LBJ was worried that something would come out about the assassination. "I don't know," he answers. "Was he threatened? I wouldn't have been surprised to find out he was involved in the assassination of Kennedy, but I don't know."

After years of exhaustive research and investigative reporting, there is no credible evidence that Johnson had any role, in any way, in Kennedy's death. The notion is still nonetheless widespread, and for Kristofferson, the LBJ withdrawal, along with the other traumatic events of 1968—the Tet Offensive in Vietnam and the murders of Dr. King and Bobby Kennedy—was the turning point in his thinking.

That was when he started not believing anything he was hearing—a common condition among many young people in those years. They were buffeted on one side by the misleadingly reassuring reports about the war that America was manifestly not winning, by the resistance to civil rights, the murders of King and Kennedy, the harsh treatment of antiwar protestors, and the mainstream society's general reaction to long hair, sex, drugs, and rock and roll.

And they were buffeted on the other side by false prophets proclaiming sex, drugs, and rock and roll as answers to everything and insisting that all cops were pigs, that nothing the government or big business did could be honest or decent, and that no one over thirty could be trusted.

Kristofferson was not the only one who did, as he puts it, "a one-eighty in 1968. I completely turned around from what I had been. I had been living my life up to the expectation of family and friends. My parents were horrified. The professors who had steered me toward Oxford—just horrified."

While he was flying helicopters to oil rigs in the gulf, he was also working as a janitor in Nashville, trying to break in as a songwriter. He had gone there after deciding not to teach at West Point. When he began his one-eighty, as he puts it, he was listening to another young singer-songwriter who was destined to change forever what was possible in popular music.

Kristofferson says, "Bob Dylan—it wasn't just that he was writing stuff like Woody Guthrie. He was changing it. I was trying to write pop songs back in the Fifties, and they all sounded like all the others back then. But if you look at the Beatles before Dylan and after their exposure to him, it's a whole different ball game. It liberated me. It was like poetry. He elevated pop songs from 'That Doggie in the Window' to an art form. Something respectable."

Dylan is the high priest for many of the songwriters and singers of what can be called the Sixties sound. But when he was interviewed by Jann Wenner for **Rolling Stone**'s fortieth-anniversary issue, he was typically vague and indifferent about his role as his generation's oracle. Asked about his influence, Dylan responded, "Maybe just like the books say, that my stuff allowed people to write and perform stuff they

Kris Kristofferson,
a crew-cut helicopter
pilot before he
"did a one-eighty"
in 1968

Kris Kristofferson
in 2006, ready to
release his new album,
This Old Road

felt like singing, which hadn't been done before. But I don't think about that as much of an influence."

Wenner persisted, saying, "You just gave them the opportunity to open up their own thinking?"

But Dylan, the master deflector, was not about to be pinned down. "Yeah, but I never opened up my own thinking," he said. "My stuff was never about me, per se, so everybody who came after me who thought it was about me, per se, or them, per se, they took the wrong road."

Nonetheless, Kristofferson and an untold number of other young songwriters were inspired. "The first song I ever had cut in Nashville was called 'Vietnam Blues.' I never thought the barriers would come down as quickly or as completely as they did. Johnny Cash's show on television had country people, Dylan, Joni Mitchell, and James Taylor all mixed together."

Kristofferson never looked back. He became not just a major singer and songwriter but a film star as well—albeit an indifferent one. His heart always seemed to be on the road or with his buddies Johnny Cash, Waylon Jennings, and Willie Nelson. He had a long, well-publicized bout with drugs and booze, but now, at seventy-two, he seems to be happiest when he's with his eight children and third wife at their home on Maui.

"I didn't want to raise my kids in Malibu. Maui reminds me of growing up in the Rio Grande Valley with mostly healthy, brown-skinned people. I think it's been good for my kids. In some ways, they don't get the education they could back on the mainland, but so far they're doing okay."

Kristofferson hasn't retired his strong views on what

America should be about. He was furious with the attacks on John Kerry by the Swift Boat Veterans during the 2004 presidential election. He worries that America is becoming what he calls "the new-millennium Nazis. We grew up thinking the worst thing that could happen to another country is what Japan did to us at Pearl Harbor. But now we can bomb Baghdad flat."

He doesn't follow the contemporary music scene much anymore, but he is encouraged by his one-man tours where he just sits onstage with his acoustic guitar and plays his old standards. "I'll probably be writing songs when they throw dirt on me," he says, "but I've got enough that still mean something to me.

"My impression is that people are missing what we were trying to do back then, which was to write serious, meaningful songs." He had played to a sold-out audience at Carnegie Hall the night before we met, and he was greatly encouraged by the reaction, saying "I can only believe there's a hunger for the old, good stuff. Dylan, hell, he's hotter than ever."

As for the old Kristofferson lifestyle, Kris the dad says, "I think my kids are smarter than I was; maybe a couple will go too far in one direction, but they have pretty good values. I don't look to them to make the same dumb mistakes I did."

Then the old Rhodes scholar calls up a quote from the eighteenth-century English poet William Blake to describe his hope for the future. "'If the fool would persist in his folly, he would become wise.' Maybe the people who were antagonized by what they thought was the irresponsible left will now become wise because of the folly this country is currently involved in."

Berry Gordy

One of the most important transitional figures in the pop culture of the Sixties was Berry Gordy, the powerful and controversial founder of Motown Records, the Detroit-based music factory that was home to Smokey Robinson, Marvin Gaye, Stevie Wonder, Michael Jackson and the Jackson 5, and Diana Ross and the Supremes. Between 1960 and 1979, Motown produced more than one hundred top-ten hits.

Gordy didn't sport a big Afro, or wear a dashiki, or hold up a clenched fist, but he had real and meaningful financial and cultural black power that came from building a recording empire based on a marketing strategy that relied on emotions and sexual fantasies crossing racial lines instead of polarizing them.

Before Motown, the music business relegated most of the great black artists to second-class citizenship. They played in out-of-the-way clubs in black neighborhoods, recorded on little-known labels, and were featured on radio stations at the far end of the dial. Gordy and Motown changed the place of black music in America by dressing it up (critics would say whitewashing it) with simple, emotional lyrics and sweet harmonies performed by artists who were carefully groomed and coached to cross over to the white audience of record buyers and radio listeners, without losing standing with their black base. Equally important, he made a black-owned company into an American entertainment colossus.

The founding of Motown is now the stuff of leg-

Motown founder Berry Gordy playing the piano in 1964. Smokey Robinson is at the back of the room; Stevie Wonder is second from right.

Producer Berry Gordy in 2004, at the 17th Annual ASCAP Rhythm and Soul Music Awards

end. Gordy was the son of entrepreneurial parents who moved to Detroit from the South. His dad had a contracting business, a print shop, and a grocery store. His mother opened an insurance agency and was active in the Democratic Party.

Gordy was a familiar figure in the expanding black middle-class neighborhoods of Detroit—a cherubic hustler who was a door-to-door salesman, a boxer, a piano player in jazz clubs, and a factory worker on the Ford assembly lines. What he really wanted was to be rich, and he concluded that there would be big money in the music business.

He started Motown with a family loan of eight hundred dollars. He organized it along the lines of a Ford assembly line—crossed with one of the old Hollywood studios—hiring teams of songwriters, musicians, choreographers, wardrobe consultants, and charm-school coaches to work with artists he discovered and cultivated. He was a pop Pygmalion, the demanding impresario who knew exactly what sound he wanted—a sound that was unmistakably black, and yet not so black that it would turn away white audiences.

There was no shortage of talent in the greater Detroit area. Smokey Robinson's neighbor was Aretha Franklin, who went to another label, Atlantic Records. Gordy signed Florence Ballard and Mary Wilson, two young friends who had been singing together since the third grade. They became two thirds of the original Supremes. A young blind musician born Steveland Hardaway Junkins was the friend of a young man who had a brother in the Motown studio band. Steveland became a legendary star as Stevie Wonder. Joe Jackson came in with his singing sons and daughters, including ten-year-old Michael. Diana Ross, who became the Motown diva and Berry Gordy's lover, and who bore him a child, was raised in the nearby public housing projects.

Motown became the musical equivalent of Gordy's old employer, the Ford Motor Company, where the hits just rolled off the assembly line—"Baby Love," by the Supremes; "Dancing in the Street," by Martha and the Vandellas; "I Heard It Through the Grapevine," with Marvin Gaye; Stevie Wonder and "For Once in My Life"; Smokey Robinson's "The Tracks of My Tears," with the Miracles, and on and on. One critic likened the music to black cotton candy, a clever phrase but a misleading one. Cotton candy melts in your mouth, but the Motown hits are still around and fresh forty years later.

By 1968 Motown had five of the top ten hits on the pop charts. Berry Gordy, who once wrote a song with Jamie Bradford called "Money (That's What I Want)," moved to Hollywood to begin producing films, hoping to write a new chapter for Motown. He left behind some embittered artists who claimed he'd shortchanged them on royalties. He continually denied it, along with the persistent but unproven rumors that he was mobbed up and in debt to organized crime for the early financing of Motown.

He was upset when **Dreamgirls** was released in 2006. The Academy Award–nominated film is clearly based on the rise of the Supremes, and in it, Jamie Foxx plays a character very much like Berry Gordy. The Foxx character is Mob-connected, and when Gordy complained to his longtime friend David Geffen, the producer said, "It's a play made into a film. It's not you."

Gordy was not satisfied, and eventually Dreamworks and Paramount, the two studios that brought **Dreamgirls** to the screen, published an ad in **Daily Variety**, reiterating that the film was a work of fiction, adding, "For any confusion that has resulted from our fictional work . . . we apologize to Mr. Gordy and all of the incredible people who were part of that great legacy."

Gordy is defensive about the rumors because, despite the persistent gossip, he was never indicted or charged with any connection to organized crime. In fact, he says, federal investigators once told him they had looked into the allegations and concluded that there was nothing to them.

In Hollywood, Gordy was concentrating on making his lover, Diana Ross, a major movie star.

He produced and financed an elaborate but critically flawed movie called **Lady Sings the Blues**, in which Ross played the part of Billie Holiday, the great Forties blues singer bedeviled and finally brought down by drugs. Ross also starred with Michael Jackson in **The Wiz**, an all-black version of **The Wizard of Oz**. She became Gordy's greatest star, recording eighteen number one singles either as a soloist or as a member of the Supremes. Gordy has often said he still loves her, but Ross married someone else. She's divorced now and lives in New York, occasionally doing concerts or guest appearances.

Motown kept going for a few more years, powered by Michael Jackson and his talented family. When the

Jacksons left in 1975, Motown's glory years were already fading fast. Gordy sold the record label to MCA for sixty-one million dollars in 1988, but he kept the publishing rights from the original hits.

America's musical tastes were changing fast, and by 1970, just two years after Berry Gordy left Detroit for Hollywood, the most popular artists were B. B. King (not one of his recording stars); Black Sabbath; Simon and Garfunkel; Neil Young; the Beatles; the Kinks; Joni Mitchell; and the Who. Many of them gratefully acknowledged that they and their music had been influenced by the Motown sound. In fact, the Beatles had recorded a song co-written by Gordy—"Money (That's What I Want)"—on their second LP, which was released on November 22, 1963, the day JFK was killed.

When we met in 2007 at his large mansion in the Los Angeles neighborhood of Bel Air—a very pricey gated community hidden in the hills next to the UCLA campus—Berry Gordy was hospitable but cautious as I tried to plumb his thoughts on the transition from the dominance of Motown to the new artists on the charts. We sat in his well-appointed library as one assistant videotaped our interview and another monitored the time. His celebrity was on display in silver-framed photographs with Muhammad Ali, Sugar Ray Robinson, President Bill Clinton, Clint Eastwood, and other movers and shakers in the world of entertainment and politics. Incongruously, there is also a framed photograph and letter from Doris Day, the quintessential Fifties sugary blond singer and film star who recorded such hits as "Que Será, Será (Whatever Will Be, Will Be)." Gordy proudly admits he's a fan and counts her as a good friend. They met after he sent her a fan letter, telling her how much he admired her singing style.

Looking back on 1968 and the loss of Dr. King and Bobby Kennedy, Gordy says it was the year "when the bad guys were cutting off our dreams." He says, "I think we lost our innocence" at that time. But, he insists, although the world was going sour, the fundamental Motown message through its songs and artists remained essentially the same, concentrating on the universal experiences of love and relationships. And no less important for Gordy the businessman, that was still the way to make money—which, as his own song guilelessly and joyfully proclaimed, was what he wanted.

When I asked about the challenges of establishing a black-owned business with black stars in the Sixties, Gordy explains the dilemma he constantly faced. "We were in a general-market business. Being a black man in a general-market business, white people didn't want me in there, and black people didn't want me in there. So I was walking a thin line. I was always having to defend myself. 'You're not black enough!' Well, I'm black, and my mama's black. But I don't do black music. I do music with black stars. I don't do black films; I do films with black stars. I wanted **all** people to understand my music and love my music."

Every Friday, at the peak of Motown's popularity and success, Gordy would hold a meeting with everyone on his assembly line of hits—the songwriters, producers, and promoters—in order to review what they were going to do next. He says, "There was a Motown philosophy: There are no stupid ideas, nobody could be embarrassed. Everybody spoke up. We didn't let politics get in the way. It was about the best idea."

Gordy was less than pleased—and far from convinced—when the music began to change and take on more of an edge, advancing a social agenda. He recalls when Marvin Gaye, who was his number one artist at the time, came to him in 1971 with a song about police brutality called "What's Going On."

Mother, Mother, there's too many of you crying.
Brother, Brother, Brother,
there's far too many of you dying
You know, we've got to find a way
To bring some lovin' here today, hey.
Father, Father, we don't need to escalate.
You see, war is not the answer,
For only love can conquer hate. . . .

Picket lines—brother—and picket signs—brother.
Don't punish me with brutality
Now, what's goin' on? What's goin' on? Yeah.

Gordy was adamantly opposed to releasing the record. Gaye stood his ground and threatened to quit. Gordy now describes their showdown in polite terms: "I was not in favor of Marvin coming out and talking about police brutality and those types of things. My music was romantic. He was our biggest male pop star, and I didn't want him going from that to doing political-type songs and ruin his career. But I told him, 'If you really want to do it . . .' "

"What's Going On" was released in 1971 and became one of the biggest sellers in the Motown library. It is widely considered a soul classic. Gordy laughs now and says, "He was right."

Gordy also says he had no interest in the Sixties' most common denominators of sex, drugs, and rock and roll. That wasn't what he was selling. "Not at all," he says decisively. "Motown was not about that. Our bigger purpose was to make the world a better place. I must admit, I was a little more conservative than most people. I grew up in the inner city, but I was a good boy. I was hip, but I was also square in my crowd."

At the age of seventy-seven—and from all appearances in very good health and looking at least ten years younger—Gordy is working on his personal legacy. His conversation is laced with references to the freedom he gave his artists, his role as a teacher, almost a kind of philosopher-king of the entertainment world, the man who gave audiences everywhere messages of love and heartbreak delivered by black singers and musicians from the working-class neighborhoods of the Motor City.

The street-smart kid who was driven to build an entertainment empire with an eight-hundred-dollar loan from his family insists he's much more mellow nowadays. He's working on a secret health regimen that he promises will change the quality of life for seniors, just as Motown changed the sound of their music when they were young.

"I'm happy now. I'm enthusiastic. When I used to be portrayed differently than I was, it would really affect me. I would sue everybody. When they checked everything, they'd find nothing. So when people call to interview me, I say, 'For what? Are we dealing with the truth here?' Most of the time I am not interested, because I am happy with my life."

Woody Miller

Rock music and drugs, two very large components of the Sixties rebellion, had staying power, lasting far beyond the adolescence and early twenties of the Sixties generation. The hard-core hippie lifestyle, on the other hand, came and went swiftly for most participants. But not all. You can still see the old hippies along the Big Sur coast of California or in the backwoods of New England, with their graying ponytails, love beads, peasant shirts, and Birkenstock sandals, driving vintage cars or vans with Greenpeace bumper stickers and RALPH NADER FOR PRESIDENT decals. It's a vanishing population, now in its mid-Sixties, but it is still committed to enjoying—and perfecting—the lifestyle that took it out of the mainstream forty years ago.

Woody Miller of Franconia, New Hampshire, is a proudly unreconstructed Sixties hippie who remains deeply committed to the choices he made while growing up in a privileged family in Vermont. Miller, who is now fifty-nine, recently attracted a fair amount of attention because of the manner in which he raised a son who grew up to be one of the greatest competitive ski racers in the world.

Woody is the father of Bode Miller, the existential and nonconformist Olympian who offended legions of sports fans with his casual dismissal of his disappointing performance at the 2006 Winter Games in Turin, Italy. Despite predictions that Bode would dominate the slopes, he failed to win even one medal, much less a gold.

But then Bode was raised not to put too much stock in conventional expectations or rewards. Woody lived primitively in the woods in a rudimentary cabin and later in a commune on an island off the coast of Maine, and Bode grew up in that environment. Cruising the woods as a toddler, first in his father's backpack and then on his own as a free-spirited youngster, he was taught early on to question everything and follow his instincts instead of relying on others.

I first met Woody and his famous son at the 2002 Winter Olympics in Salt Lake City. As an avid skier and admirer of Bode's daredevil style, I was curious about his unusual upbringing, which by then was getting a good deal of attention. I found a confident young man, a little brash, who fully realized the magnitude of his skiing talents. He saw no reason to take even slightly less than what he deserved from ski sponsors and others. He was his own man and not just the creation of agents and image specialists. Woody's early mentoring had paid off.

When I was invited to join the Miller family at the base of Bode's first run, I had little trouble spotting Woody. "Ah," I thought, "this is what hippies look like forty years later." He is tall and athletically built, with long gray hair and a faded flannel-based wardrobe that is best described as functional. He is clearly proud of his son, but he's hardly the typical stage parent. He watched impassively and didn't join the crowd shouting encouragement as Bode made his first run.

We met again four years later at Turin, Italy. Bode had just finished his final event by missing a gate. He was zero for five in medals, a stunning reversal of predictions that he would be the Games' skiing superstar.

Bode didn't help matters when he told an interviewer that he'd had a good Olympic experience regardless, because he'd partied at the Olympic level.

When I arrived at Bode's recreational vehicle for an interview, Woody was standing outside. When I said something to the effect of "So sorry this didn't work out better, Woody," he just said, "Yeah, too bad. But can I ask you something? Why isn't the country paying more attention to global warming? I don't get it." Woody plainly thought the world had weightier matters to consider than his son's medal count.

I've had a hard time explaining this to my sports-fan friends who've grown accustomed to the stories of parents turning over their lives to athletically gifted offspring. The Millers, father and son, are determined to live their lives by their own navigational charts and not follow whatever course someone else lays out for them.

Woody has stayed true to many of the hippie beliefs he formed as a young man. He was into drugs, smoking a fair amount of dope and ingesting hallucinogens. He says now that one of his biggest disappointments is that marijuana was never legalized.

"I think if marijuana had been legalized, it would have led to a wider social enlightenment. I think people tend to get into mental ruts. Marijuana and LSD helped people become hippies, to see things in a different way. Now everyone's susceptible to **affluenza**—the ill effects of too much wealth and materialism. I don't think it was drugs that affected people the wrong way. I think society got corrupted by people wanting more material things."

Woody began his counterculture lifestyle by doing just that—walking away from the comforts and conventions of an upper-middle-class family. He was born the son of a prominent heart physician and christened John Airheart Wood Miller II. He discarded the other names and settled on Woody in about the fourth grade because, he explains, "It has a real iconic meaning to me. I think from an early age I wanted to live in the woods, to be a part of nature instead of part of a culture that separates itself from nature."

His dad had other plans. Dr. Miller, a past president of the American Medical Association, was the epitome of the medical establishment and he expected his three sons to become doctors, just as their grandfather had been. Woody enrolled in premed at the University of Vermont, but from the start he felt he was only going through the motions. "I guess I was more interested in helping the health of the planet than the health of human beings. My father argued that a medical education would also serve my interest in the environment, but I just wasn't very enthusiastic."

After completing his undergraduate studies, Woody spent a summer as an instructor at a New Hampshire tennis camp. It was a small camp, and everyone was having a good time and getting along

Woody Miller
playing
in a tennis
tournament
at the Burlington
Tennis Club
in 1968

Woody and his son Bode Miller in 2006,
after winning an open doubles tournament
in Lincoln, New Hampshire

well. In Woody's family, as he puts it, "feelings were pretty repressed, so the camp was a very opening experience for me." He began to see the world in a new way. He also met his future wife, Jo, the daughter of the camp's owners.

Despite his reservations about medical school, Woody decided to go back after a year at the Tamarack Tennis Camp. "I was very conflicted. You know, it's supposed to be such a noble profession, but I had a feeling I was getting sucked into something I didn't want to be. With my dad as a doctor, there was a big push to be a success and earn a lot of money. I definitely rejected that more than my siblings did. I went to a lot of peace marches and rallies for Native Americans.

"I'm also not that smart. I was feeling consumed by medical school. I had to get to school before it was light out and work all day. I hated it. I just wanted to be outside."

He quit and went back to Tamarack. The Selective Service soon came calling. He drew a low draft number and figured the only way out was to exacerbate an elbow injury he'd developed playing tennis. "I threw rocks and did anything I could to screw up my arm." It worked. He was declared ineligible for the draft, and now he could follow the hippie life that was beginning to take hold in the woods of New Hampshire.

"I sort of turned from getting an education to doing something for the environment and finding a way to live more simply." Woody and Jo got married and began building a cabin next to a mountain stream deep in the woods.

"My heroes," Woody says, "were Scott and Helen

Nearing. They wrote a book called **Living the Good Life,** about farming, maple sugaring, and building stone houses. The idea was to live a simple, good life and not get in your car every day and drive off to work.

"That's what Jo and I wanted to do with our children—to spend as much time with them as possible while they were growing up. We did that in a cabin that was originally about twelve-by-fifteen, without plumbing or electricity. All four kids were born there. It was pretty chilly in the winter.

"We carried the kids up and down the hill and we were working some. I think our income taxes showed we earned about five thousand dollars a year. Our next-door neighbor operated a sawmill, and if you helped him, you would get a thousand feet of lumber for about twenty-five dollars. I also worked as a landscaper and on the ski patrol at Mittersill. I did some maple sugaring, which wasn't very profitable, but it was lots of fun.

Woody and Jo homeschooled the four Miller children. Kyla came first, then Bode. When the next two were born, Kyla and Bode helped name them. It wasn't just an exercise in family togetherness; Woody had an ulterior motive. "It was part of an antiestablishment thing that we heard of. If you have enough names, it screws up the government computers. Besides, I had a lot of names, and I think names are power." So the last two children were named Genesis Wren Bungo Windrushing Turtleheart Miller and Nathaniel Kinsman Ever Chelone Skan Miller.

By 1978 the Millers had moved to a commune on an island off the Maine coast. Four couples shared shelter and child rearing and earned a small income by chopping firewood. Woody said they made the decision because "you can do more things if you do it cooperatively; if your goal is to live simply, you can do that easier if you cooperate with other people as opposed to doing it all yourself."

But the commune didn't last. The four couples simply couldn't get along, either with one another or with their own mates. He says, "It's hard enough getting along with your own husband or wife, much less four of them. All four couples that lived on the island have since broken up—gotten divorced."

Woody and Jo's marriage began to unwind. Money was tight, and Woody was barely making ends meet by working as a woodsman and helping out in the maple-sugar business. Jo didn't want him around, so he worked summers in Tennessee, trimming trees and clearing brush, but he was suffering from depression and type 1 diabetes.

While he was struggling with his demons, an unusual opportunity presented itself. His father, the stern and accomplished surgeon, had slowly succumbed to Alzheimer's disease, and Woody's mother and sister put him in a nursing home. Woody volunteered to take care of him. When the nurse handed over his dad to him, she said, "For all practical purposes, he is dead, you know."

Woody didn't think so. He took his father to the first cabin he had built in the woods. The old doctor was now in the hands of the hippie son he had failed to persuade to stick with medicine. If Woody had become a doctor, would he have given up four years of his life to care for his ailing dad? Woody's hippie beliefs about goodness and nature made him, in the end, a perfect caregiver. "Dad would spend his days listening to music in the cabin or walking outside. I could always keep track of him. It was like turning a horse out to pasture."

It was not easy. Woody had hooked up a water-powered turbine to provide some electricity, and it needed constant attention. There was firewood to cut, water to be heated on the stove, and the long trek into town for supplies. But as Woody says, "I like living off the grid."

Two days before Dr. Miller died, he said something Woody didn't expect to hear: "Thank God for Woody." That was when he knew it had all been worthwhile.

These days Woody is living in slightly better quarters in Franconia, working with the homeless, concentrating especially on those who are mentally ill. After his own struggles with depression, he feels a kinship with those who are struggling to keep it all together. He says, "A lot of homeless people, the mentally ill in particular, really want to be in the country, so I am working to develop some rural shelters. I'd like to combine it with my ideas about being green, making them energy-self-sufficient, and give the homeless some opportunities to do things."

Woody remains completely committed to the environmental movement. "It's a very big disappointment," he says, "that environmentalism got so marginalized as a bunch of kooks rather than something everyone should be worried about. Many of the things I read about global warming say, 'And you won't have to sacrifice anything.' But it **does** require sacrifice. History shows that people are capable of sacrificing far more than is required now. But we want to have it both ways. We want to do something, but we don't want to give up anything."

PART TWO

Aftershocks

Consequences, Intended and Otherwise

So powerful were, are, the energies let loose
in the Sixties there cannot now be,
and may never be, anything like a final
summing up. After all, what is the final
result of the Civil War? It is too soon to say.

—GEORGE WILL

Thank God the Sixties are still
controversial. It means nobody's lost yet.

—ARLO GUTHRIE

IN THE OPENING YEARS of the twenty-first century,
we're living with the residue of the Sixties in large ways
and small: we no longer have a military draft; there is a
substantial and growing black middle class; the Hispanic or Latino part of American culture is more
prominent every year; women are part of the professional ranks in ever increasing numbers; youth is now
a credential, not a disqualifier, in the entrepreneurial
world. The lifestyle differences between parents and
their children are not nearly as distinct as they were in
the Fifties; couples are getting married at an older age;
families are smaller.

The rise of the evangelical movement was a response to the "anything goes" spirit of the Sixties. The megachurches that are flourishing across the country, and not just in red-state America, have not totally rejected the Sixties, however; they've cleverly adopted the theatrics of a Sixties light show as they feature Chris-tian rock bands to keep the congregations engaged.

Drugs, recreational and hard-core, are a fixed part of the American landscape in a way they were not before the Sixties.

We're living longer and staying younger, and that combination is having a significant effect on how we organize and manage almost every aspect of American life. The entrepreneurial, break-the-old-rules spirit of the Sixties changed the economy, as talented young people were unwilling to stand in line, awaiting their turn in enterprises that were organized around patriarchal models, with all of the authority emanating from the top down through a rigid structure.

I was raised during a time when the young were expected to grow old fast, to adopt and imitate the manners and conventions of our elders if we wanted to succeed.

The Sixties changed those rules.

The continuing debate over the Sixties—what they meant, what they mean, who won, who lost—is a traveling road show for those of us who lived through them as well as for those who are coming late to our virtual reunion party. Everyone agrees the Sixties were consequential.

But where do we go from here and how do we get there?

How can we even begin to have that discussion if we still can't settle on a common set of terms or language for discussing the Sixties and the lingering aftershocks? That, I believe, is a place to begin.

A Dream Fulfilled and a Dream Deferred

My father blocked James Meredith at Ole Miss.
I taught at Lanier High. So we've come pretty far.

—OUIDA ATKINS

The lesson of Katrina is that racism is very tangible
today. I suppose every American can probably think to
themselves, "There's a Lower Ninth Ward somewhere
in my city." In their heart of hearts, they know it's
there. Refusing to recognize it is a form of racism.

—STAN SANDERS

We still have not had the national conversation
on race—or class and gender, for that matter.
We've tried to have it, but not in a meaningful way.

—DR. CLEVELAND SELLERS

IN 2007 RADIO TALK-SHOW HOST Don Imus ignited a firestorm of racial controversy with his remark that the black members of the Rutgers University women's basketball team were "nappy-headed hos." At first he thought everyone would understand that it was a joke. He made the remark in what was clearly intended to be a comic context. Besides, Imus has long been known as an equal opportunity offender with a heart that is at the very least gold plated if not actually made of gold. His jibes have been aimed at—and traded with—prominent politicians, journalists, and celebrities of all shades, as well as major business leaders.

And, as he correctly pointed out, it was exactly the kind of language that black rap stars use all the time in their hit records and concerts.

Within minutes of Imus having made the remark, two of my African-American friends, one a doctor, the other a Wall Streeter, sent me e-mails saying he had crossed the line. They were listening because they were fans of his show; but they were outraged by this remark and insisted that there was only one course of appropriate action: He had to be fired. African-American employees of NBC, led by the popular **Today** weatherman Al Roker, made the same case to their bosses and on their blogs.

Gwen Ifill, a prominent black journalist, wrote a strong **New York Times** op-ed citing Imus's past transgressions and chastising the many prominent journalists (I was one) and others who had appeared on his show over the years, arguing that their appearances had added to his credibility even as he was engaging in racist humor.

At the same time, Imus had his defenders on the Internet and on other talk shows, who praised his political interviews as some of the best on radio and television, and raised the double standard issue: hip-hop artists and black comedians, they said, used far more offensive and degrading language.

Al Sharpton was criticized for never having personally apologized for his role as an enabler and provocateur in the Tawana Brawley affair. Brawley was the young black teenager who falsely accused white policemen and a local assistant district attorney of raping her and then conspiring to cover it up. Her story was finally revealed as a hoax.

Many people who accepted all the arguments made in defense of Imus still felt that this time he had gone too far by ridiculing young women who were not in a position to fight back and whose accomplishments merited being praised rather than picked on. Imus apologized to the women on the air and traveled to

Rutgers to do so personally. He went on Al Sharpton's radio talk show to be pummeled by the host for his insensitivity.

Unlike many other controversies Imus attracted over the years, this one just wouldn't go away. He was fired by CBS, which carried his show on radio, and by MSNBC, which broadcast the show on cable. Imus was not happy. He knew he had said something stupid, and he had apologized. But those three carelessly spoken words—"nappy-headed hos"—will be with him forever, despite all his good works on behalf of kids with cancer, autism, and SIDS (sudden infant death syndrome).

When I told Imus that I hoped his unfortunate experience would at least lead to an elevated dialogue across racial lines, he laughed sardonically and said, "Yeah, call me at the ranch when that happens."

He has reason to be skeptical. As a society, we still resist putting all the pieces of the race problem on the table so they can be examined and discussed openly and honestly. I continue to be disappointed by the absence of effort and the entrenched interests on both sides of the racial divide that keep that dialogue from happening.

Almost forty-five years after Dr. King made his famous "I Have a Dream" speech in Washington, D.C., in 1963, the place of race in American life is still an unresolved issue. It is freighted with suspicion, weighted by myths, and bedeviled by anger, resentment, and bigotry.

This despite the fact that a great deal of progress has been made in race relations since the Sixties. Barack

Obama is a leading candidate for president of the United States. Stanley O'Neal, a black man, is CEO of Merrill Lynch, the American financial services company. Ken Chenault, another African-American, is the boss at American Express. Richard Parsons is the boss at Time Warner, the entertainment and Internet conglomerate. Colin Powell remains one of the most admired men in America. And the election of black mayors is now routine.

Oprah is one of the most powerful woman in America, along with Condoleezza Rice, the African-American secretary of state.

Black-owned entertainment companies are a major force in popular culture. More black coaches and executives are showing up in major college and professional athletic endeavors. Black anchors are a staple of local television news broadcasts. Television commercials regularly feature black professionals and middle-class nuclear families.

There are black big-city police chiefs and Deep South highway patrolmen. Vernon Jordan, former head of the Urban League and one of America's best-known establishment figures, black or white, tells the story of returning to Mississippi in the Nineties and seeing a black highway patrolman writing out a speeding ticket to give to a white woman. He says, "I almost cried, and I thought, 'If only Medgar could see this.' "

Medgar Evers was Jordan's friend and the head of the Mississippi chapter of the National Association for the Advancement of Colored People when he was murdered in 1963 for his civil rights activism.

Despite all the real progress, in too many areas,

often just beneath the surface, we remain a black-white society, divided by race in our neighborhoods and schools, and in our politics and culture, color is a powerful prism that still shapes—and too often still distorts—our view of each other.

Forty years ago, one of our most gifted and liberal writers, the late William Styron, was attacked by black authors, activists, and academics for having written a fine literary novel about the slave Nat Turner. **The Confessions of Nat Turner** won the 1968 Pulitzer Prize for fiction, but because Styron was white, he was deemed unqualified—and, by some, disqualified—to write in the voice of a black slave, just as Mark Twain had been attacked for his depiction of Jim, Huck Finn's black friend. If Styron and Twain were alive and wrote their novels today, they would likely be subject to even harsher treatment. As unfair and counterproductive as that may be, can you imagine the uproar in the South if a black writer attempted to approximate the voice of a white Confederate soldier?

The divisions are not just black-white. Within the racial communities they are also generational and cultural. Gwen Ifill was asked by her pastor to have a dialogue with young church members following the Imus affair. The young women in the group, all African-Americans, said they were accustomed to hearing the word "ho" in their neighborhoods. They didn't seem unduly bothered by the word or by the Imus incident. Ifill says the church elders were shocked by the young women's casual acceptance of such a derogatory description.

The generational divide is not confined to the

black community. Young people of all socioeconomic
and ethnic groups are coming of age exposed to language and humor that not so long ago was confined to
the locker room or the barroom.

The lines around what is permissible and acceptable grow fainter every year, and so does the opportunity to examine or question those lines.

A decade ago, I attempted to address some of these
issues in a documentary called **Why Can't We Live
Together?** It was set in Matteson, Illinois, a largely
middle-class suburb forty miles south of Chicago. As
black professionals from the city had started to move
into Matteson, the familiar pattern of white flight had
begun almost instantly.

Despite efforts on the part of a black and white
coalition to keep racial harmony in the city, white families defended their decision to move out by saying it
had nothing to do with racism. "I'm worried about
property values. My home is my biggest investment."
Or "I just don't think the schools are as good as they
once were."

The newly arrived black home owners were at
once hurt and defensive. One, a high-ranking federal
employee, said, in effect, "Good riddance." Another
refused to take calls from or exchange Christmas cards
with his former neighbor who had moved to the next
suburb in the interest, he said, "of property values."
The white man was plainly troubled by his black
friend's reaction, but he made no extra effort to heal
the wounds.

The changing complexion of the town was roiling
the community, yet the language was guarded and the

suspicions festered on all sides. The police chief spent a lot of time fighting off rumors that the increased black population had triggered a surge in crime.

When I gently pressed one white matron about what troubled her about having black neighbors in town, she hesitated and then said, "They're just so loud," referring to the gregarious black teenagers who walked by on their way home from school.

Another young white woman explained that she no longer frequented a shopping center in the community because she wasn't comfortable there anymore. When I told her we had checked and the crime rate had not gone up in that area, she was not dissuaded. She just didn't want to go to a place where there were so many black customers.

I tried to get at the stereotypes that bedevil both sides.

A black psychologist was taken aback when I asked about his son, his pride and joy. What would you do, I asked, if your son came home with a new girlfriend? She's a top student, very popular, cute, and she's white. He had not considered the reverse effect of black and white dating in his family, nor had he talked with his son about what to expect if he dated across racial lines.

I'm sure he had expected me to ask that question—what would you do if your white daughter came home with a black boyfriend?—of the white fireman who was part of our conversation. The fireman listened attentively as the psychologist, struggling with the ramifications of the scenario, said, "I love my son unconditionally, but I would have to tell him that in our society, biracial couples still have difficulties, and he should be aware of that."

Why, after all these years, do we still shy away from honest talk about the unasked questions when it comes to race? Why do so many elements of both the white and black cultures automatically assume the defensive as soon as sensitive subjects such as absentee black fathers or white flight are raised?

Vernon Jordan is someone with whom I can, and do, have completely candid conversations about race. He grew up in the Atlanta projects in what was effectively the black middle class. His dad had a steady job, and his mother had a successful catering business. Jordan won a scholarship to DePauw University in Indiana and earned a law degree at Howard University. After serving as executive director of the Urban League for nine years, he joined a prestigious Washington, D.C., law firm and a number of important corporate boards, including Xerox and J. C. Penney.

He is a close friend of President and Senator Clinton, and also of many Republican leaders, such as former secretary of state James A. Baker and former Wyoming senator Alan Simpson. At this stage in his life, Jordan is a significant establishment figure in the upper reaches of the political, legal, and financial worlds.

Nevertheless, as no one knows better than he does, when he walks into a room of strangers, he is first of all a black man. I was witness to that during an awkward moment in a Washington, D.C.–area golf club where Vernon was president. Three boisterous white men entered the locker room to get ready for their round of golf. Vernon, who is six-four and full-framed, boomed out, "Good morning, gentlemen."

One of them looked up and said, "Oh, hi, Bill."

Vernon quickly responded, "No, I'm Vernon. Vernon Jordan."

The white man was momentarily flustered, but Vernon brushed it off and said cheerily, "Have a good day out there."

Vernon and I got in our golf cart without saying anything about the incident and drove about thirty yards before Vernon suddenly stopped, gave me that big killer grin of his, and said, "You want to see Bill?" I said of course. Vernon pointed out a small, balding black man on the practice range. All black men do not look alike, but plainly, to some white men, they still do.

We both laughed, and then I said, "Vernon, how do you put up with this?"

He just shrugged and said good-naturedly, "I've been dealing with it all my life, and I decided a long time ago not to let it bother me anymore."

Barack Obama, in his best-selling book **The Audacity of Hope,** devotes a chapter to his personal experiences and his political analysis of race in our society. It is a thoughtful, evenhanded treatise on the familiar myths on both sides of the racial divide, the harsh truths about black poverty and the breakup of the black family, the dividends of affirmative action, the progress that has been made, and the gaps still to be closed.

He says, "To think clearly about race . . . requires us to see the world on a split screen—to maintain in our sights the kind of America we want while looking squarely at America as it is." He goes on to say, "Rightly or wrongly, white guilt has largely exhausted itself in America; even the most fair-minded of whites, those who would genuinely like to see racial inequality ended and poverty relieved, tend to push back against suggestions of racial victimization—or race-specific claims based on the history of race discrimination in the country."

Obama argues that we have to move beyond black-white-Latino divides and address the real issues that exacerbate them: education, employment, personal responsibility, and intolerance. He says that while his own rise to prominence is not evidence that we're living in a postracial society, neither should we ignore the real achievements that have been made.

On many meaningful fronts the quest for equality has been successful. But still, when it comes to talking to each other, we remain largely—to play on the famous formula of the 1968 Kerner Commission characterizing race in America—two societies, separate . . . and suspicious.

That became painfully clear again in 2005, when in the course of a few brutal days Mother Nature forced us all to confront the realities of race and poverty in America.

When Hurricane Katrina swept into New Orleans, she stripped away the protective cover of jazz, blues, funky bars, elegant restaurants, casinos, and the bawdy pleasures of Bourbon Street and exposed a desperately poor black underclass that had been ignored and forgotten. The world was stunned, and America was uncomfortable with the ugly truth about the racial divide and persistent poverty that belie the promise of America.

Having spent a good deal of my professional life in the poor black precincts of other American cities— Atlanta, Los Angeles, Philadelphia, New York, Chicago— I was not surprised by the reality Katrina brought home, nor was I surprised when it started a national dialogue of guilt, bewilderment, and blame. I just wondered how long that discussion would last and whether it would produce any useful results.

Not long, I discovered. And not many. Despite the intense coverage of the storm's almost equally devastating aftermath, the initial reaction of shock and shame in the rest of the country gradually faded as new stories filled the front pages and people returned to the regular rhythms of their daily lives.

With colleagues at NBC News, I set out to find a way to show that the conditions in the poor black neighborhoods of New Orleans were not unique to the Crescent City. I surveyed the national urban landscape and found that there were many choices, as the black underclass is a fixture in many cities, including New York, Philadelphia, Cleveland, Chicago, Detroit, Dallas, and Los Angeles, as well as throughout the Deep South.

For reasons of history and geography we decided to do our reporting in a state capital that had been ravaged by racial discord before it was visited by racial progress.

Jackson, the capital of Mississippi, is a city that had undergone some profound changes since the bad old days of violent racial conflict in the Sixties. Now it had a black mayor, a black editor of the daily newspaper, **The Clarion-Ledger,** a flourishing black professional class, and black neighborhoods of expensive homes on large, well-manicured grassy lots.

For all the changes, one immutable truth remained: Jackson is still a city divided by race.

There has been very little integration, and as the black majority began to make its presence felt in the city, whites quietly left for neighborhoods outside the city limits. There was also a degree of black flight, as well-to-do and socially prominent black families also started moving to outlying neighborhoods.

Jackson and so many other cities represent the unexpected consequences forty years after America began to address racial inequality with tough federal laws. This made it possible for black families and individuals of ambition and talent to move out of impoverished neighborhoods, into the opportunities of the white culture. Inevitably they left behind other black families not motivated or incapable of following them. As a result, the traditional black neighborhoods in many cities sank even deeper into the cycle of despair brought on by poverty, drugs, missing fathers, and an indifference to hard work and focus.

That is the unfortunate story of Georgetown, Jackson's largest black neighborhood, and the home of Lanier High School, the community's heart and pride.

Lanier proved to be an unlikely intersection for two Mississippi women, one black and one white, who came of age in different ways in the Sixties.

During the years of segregation, Lanier High School was Mississippi's best-known black high school, educating the children of black merchants, lawyers, physicians, and ministers, as well as the working-class residents of Georgetown. When the civil rights bill of 1964 provided new opportunities for the black professional and middle classes, many moved out of that neighborhood, leaving behind a more desperate community of residents slowly being sucked into a downward spiral.

The neighborhoods of small bungalows represent a checkerboard of the past and the present. In one home, you may find an elderly couple, retired on Social Security pensions, who bought their house in the Fifties on earnings from jobs in nearby factories. Next door is a single mother with four children by three different fathers, just getting by on a combination of wages from fast-food jobs and food stamps. Drugs are openly available on the streets, where young school-age boys hang out at midday.

At Lanier High School, a dedicated corps of administrators and teachers—including a few white men and women—struggle against stingy budgets, student absenteeism, and parental indifference to provide an education for those who do show up hoping to build a better life.

Charlene Stimley Priester and Ouida Barnett Atkins

Charlene Stimley Priester is the youngest child of one of Georgetown's best-known black families. Her mother and father, Charles and Bernice Stimley, were both graduates of Alcorn State University, a state-supported all-black college in Lorman, Mississippi. They both trained as teachers, but when they were unable to find work in Mississippi, they joined the great postwar migration to Chicago. Life in the Midwest was only marginally better, so they returned to Georgetown to help operate a grocery store. They prospered by neighborhood standards and raised four children, but they could not escape the random cruelties visited upon blacks in Mississippi in the Fifties and early Sixties.

Priester remembers that when she was about twelve, local white policemen came into the store, looking for her uncle, a quiet man well respected in the community. "They said he had laughed or smiled at a white woman while driving home," she remembers. "This was on the heels of the Emmett Till murder in Mississippi. If the police came and got you, you were guaranteed to be beaten, locked up, and maybe never heard from again.

"When they put my uncle in the police car, my mother knew what was going to happen, so she put me in her car, and off we went. She followed them right to the police station. The way you survived in Mississippi in those days was if you knew some white people, you got them involved to bring some balance to the craziness."

Her mother spotted a white man she knew and begged him to help. Priester remembers that the man told the police, "These are good black folks," and they let her uncle go.

Her mother's resourcefulness paid off that day, but for Priester and her siblings there were other rules of life. "There were certain places you did not go, not just here in Mississippi but throughout the country. All parents tried to tell their children about the places that were safe and those that weren't." If two major white schools were playing a big football game, the Stimley children were told to stay off the big streets because white rabble-rousers would drive through black neighborhoods, waving the Confederate flag and yelling racial epithets. "As a girl child," she says, "you had to be particularly careful."

Priester was a junior at Lanier High in 1968 when she heard that Dr. King had been murdered in Memphis. "I thought the world was coming to an end. I mean, literally. I knew how people felt when Hiroshima was bombed. The principal was worried about riots in the Georgetown streets, so he locked the school doors because he knew if the students got out and started rioting, they'd be shot or beaten.

"My mother came to school and took me home, but I was so angry. . . . I felt hopeless and helpless. I wanted to show the world how we felt about this."

It was that same year, 1968, that Priester heard Lanier High School would be legally desegregated the following year. "I didn't believe it would ever happen," she says, "because I didn't think the hatred that was overt in every part of Jackson society for so long would ever change. So when they said they would send white children to Lanier, I didn't believe it. And it didn't happen. They sent in a couple of white teachers, and that was it."

Whether the school was segregated or not, the Stimley offspring were already making their own ex-

Charlene Stimley
a few months
after her 1969
graduation from
Lanier High
School in Jackson,
Mississippi

Charlene Stimley Priester, now an attorney
at the Priester law firm, with her husband,
Judge Melvin Priester

ceptional ways with their Lanier education. Priester's older sister, Pernila, set the pace, enrolling at Harvard Law School. Frank Stimley joined his sister the next year, followed by Sherman, thus making the Stimley family the first ever to have three members enrolled at Harvard Law School at the same time. When her time came, Priester also went north, to Boston University. It was during college in Boston that Priester had her first true experience of being a minority. Everyone in her old school and neighborhood was black. Suddenly, she found herself on a mostly white campus in a Northern city with its own very old and complex patterns of racial and religious discrimination.

I ask how she managed to adapt. "The black students on campus all quickly bonded," she says, "but I also think in many ways, the white students were as curious about us as we were about them.

"I'd never had any white friends or much contact with whites, so it was a different environment . . . but in the dormitory, close living quarters generate friendships. It was not a bad situation for me at all at Boston University . . . but the city of Boston mirrors some of the same segregationist viewpoints as the Deep South.

"I think the first time I was ever called the N-word to my face was in South Boston. Someone just walked up to me on the street. We were down there on a school project, and I thought it was quite interesting that I had traveled two thousand miles to hear that."

Nonetheless, when her youngest son, Jonathan, graduated from a racially mixed public school in Jackson with statewide honors in science contests and voted by his class "most likely to succeed," his mother encouraged him to enroll at her alma mater. When they arrived in Boston in the fall of 2006, however, she was distressed to see only a hundred or so black freshmen in the incoming class of more than four thousand new students. She says that some of the same debates she heard in the Sixties and Seventies still are going on: "Should we have a difference in our admissions standards? Do we need a quota?"

Following the Stimley family's new tradition, after graduating from BU Charlene went to law school at the University of Texas in Austin. She married another lawyer, Mel Priester, and they set up a law practice in Jackson with her sister, Pernila. Priester's oldest son is a Stanford law graduate and a member of a prestigious firm in San Francisco.

Although the Priesters have often discussed the racial struggles of their childhood with their sons, Charlene worries that the latest generation is mostly oblivious to the real pain and sacrifices exacted by the separate-but-equal policy that the South adopted to masquerade the realities of pervasive bigotry.

"You have children who really don't have a clear idea of that struggle and their responsibility to keep trying to improve things. Everybody knew what was going on when I was a child, and where we came from; I think it's important to know where you came from so you can know where you're going. Yes, we have Martin Luther King Day, and we have Black History Month, but we don't have a clear picture of the struggle of African-Americans to show our children."

She also thinks the black power movement got a bad rap from the white establishment, encouraged in part by the FBI under J. Edgar Hoover, who was obsessed with the civil rights movement, constantly characterizing it as Communist-inspired.

Charlene says she got involved in black power at Boston University "a little bit . . . what the Panthers and the Muslims were talking about was 'buy black.' If you see a black store, go buy your groceries there. Keep the dollars in the community. Have educational programs for the children. But what the white society was told was that these groups were radical militants out to kill and maim."

Once she'd graduated from Boston University and Texas Law, she never hesitated about returning to Mississippi. "It's home for me. We had talked about building a family law firm. I always thought Mississippi would change only if people who cared wanted it to change. I knew my generation could really change some of the stuff. Have we overcome the problems of the Sixties? No. Has racism disappeared? No. But I think Mississippi has more African-Americans elected to office than any other state in the country."

Priester believes that black families trying to do the right thing are not getting enough credit. "I think we have in Mississippi, and throughout the country, more families trying to raise children, have a cohesive family unit, and provide nurturing than gets recognized. I think there are more good folks than bad folks.

"I think what happens is that the gap between those making money and those not has become so great it is more shocking to see those families in crisis." She sees big differences in the scale of the economy. "In my day, the cost of living was different. And you had people who were poor, but they had big gardens or a few chickens. That was how they fed their families. People didn't resort to crime for a quick fix.

"Also, now you have segments of the American middle class—whatever the color—who have no contact with the poor. They give to the United Way or to their church, but there's no one actually helping a poor family, as there was when we all lived close to each other."

She does not excuse the failure of government to help solve these problems in the past or exclude its role in addressing them today. "I think the government has not gone far enough to try to rectify the old race-based system that was put in place to deprive minorities of their fair share of opportunities. Not fair share, period, but fair share of opportunities. You cannot have forty years of social programs to try to even it up and then just say, 'Okay, that's enough. That's it.' "

However, she also strongly advocates personal responsibility, which she says is a learned trait. "Somebody says, 'It's up to you. You've got to do it.' But now there's been a breakdown, an assumption somehow has gotten into the system that 'this is a black child, so it's his fault if he doesn't learn.' "

Priester remembers that her teachers were stuck in the same place as the students, so they tried to bring everyone along. She was reminded of that during a conversation with Fred Banks, a black lawyer and former member of the Mississippi Supreme Court. "He said, 'You know, Charlene, we had the worst books because the best books went to the white schools. But no one said because the book was old and worn, you didn't have a responsibility to read it.' "

When she drove her oldest son, Mel Jr., to school on the morning of a test, before he could get out of the car, Priester would make him repeat after her: "I am a lean, mean, test-taking machine!" When he finished, she'd say, "I know, that's right. Now, go get me an A and bring it back here, baby." It never occurred to her that every mother in town, black and white, wasn't cheering on their children in the same way.

When Charlene Priester was growing up as a young black woman in Georgetown, Mississippi, Ouida Barnett Atkins was also coming of age in Carthage—only about one hundred miles distant but a world away from the neighborhood where the Stimley family was confronting racism and economic oppression every day.

Atkins's ancestors owned slaves and fought for the South at Vicksburg and Shiloh. Her father, born in 1898, heard those stories from his grandfather and father as a boy growing up in Carthage, where the family settled and prospered. He felt that Confederate heritage in every fiber of his being when he earned his law degree from Ole Miss.

Atkins's father became one of the most powerful lawyers in Mississippi and, eventually, the governor of the state. His name was Ross Barnett, and he is forever linked to one of the most violent and shameful episodes in the struggle for racial equality in the South.

Ross R. Barnett was governor in 1962 when James Meredith, a Mississippi black man and Air Force veteran, tried to enroll at Ole Miss. Meredith's efforts ac-

On the arm of her father, Governor Ross Barnett, Ouida Barnett Atkins is presented as a debutante in Jackson, Mississippi, 1953.

Despite Governor Barnett's opposition, on October 1, 1962, James Meredith became the first black student at the University of Mississippi. President Kennedy sent in federal troops and U.S. Marshals to quell ensuing riots.

An unexpected turn: Ouida Barnett Atkins with her students at Lanier High in 2003

tivated the state's racists from the Ku Klux Klan all the way to the State House. Ole Miss, after all, was more than just the state university. It was the citadel of white Southern tradition, passed along from generation to generation in the fraternity and sorority houses, at the football stadium on Saturday afternoons, and in the myriad social, political, and economic alliances that were formed on campus and lasted for a lifetime.

Atkins grew up in privileged circumstances. Like many white Southern children she had black play-mates, up to a certain age. When her father visited his tenant farms on Sundays, she'd spend the day with the black children of the sharecropper, playing with the new kittens, jumping into the hay in the barn, and wondering why, if they could have such a good time on Sundays, they couldn't be in school together Monday through Friday.

She remembers one night when she was about eight hearing her parents talk about whether the U.S. Supreme Court would rule that schools could no longer be segregated. "They were saying how terrible that would be, when I ran out into the hall and said, 'Oh, no. I think that would be fun.' They said to me, 'Get back in bed. You don't know what you're talking about.' "

Atkins finished her education in all-white schools, married, and moved to Louisiana while her father's power in the state grew steadily.

During his campaign for governor in 1959, he be-came increasingly outspoken on race and state's rights. He said God had made black people that color in order to punish them, and he attacked his opponent as a moderate on race, a political kiss of death in those times. He secured the backing of the White Citizens' Council, at best a marginally more refined version of the Klan.

When the U.S. Supreme Court ruled that James Meredith must be admitted to Ole Miss, Governor Barnett promised to defy the order, arguing that Mississippi law trumped the highest court in the land. It was a tense time, and this would be a historic test for the new president of the United States, John F. Kennedy, and the attorney general, his brother, Robert F. Kennedy.

Bobby Kennedy had more than a dozen telephone calls with Barnett, trying to find a way to enforce the law without violence. Barnett was a cagey negotiator, constantly playing for time and for a scenario that would serve his political interests. At one point he thought he had a deal that would allow him to save face: U.S. marshals would arrive on the campus with Meredith, and Barnett would confront them. The marshals would draw their guns, and Barnett would be forced to step aside.

However, when word of Meredith's registration got around the state, racist whites got their guns and headed for Oxford, the quiet little town that is home to the university, so any thought of marshals drawing their weapons on the governor was overtaken by events. A large mob, armed and dangerous, gathered, determined to keep Meredith from becoming a student.

Barnett had more telephone calls with the attorney general and with the president, pleading with them to understand his dilemma. Atkins believes her father genuinely wanted a chance to cool off the mob, but others saw him as a shrewd old trial lawyer still looking for an advantage.

By then Ouida Barnett had married and was living in Louisiana. She returned home now to help her father, moving into the governor's mansion. She remembers answering the phone and callers saying, "What do you think about us blowing up the bridges between Oxford and Jackson, or between Memphis and Oxford?" She'd respond, "No, don't do that. Please, stay home."

The U.S. marshals sneaked Meredith onto the campus and hid him there while they took up positions around the grounds. They were forced to take cover when shots were fired and rocks were thrown. A full-scale riot broke out, and before it was over, 2 protestors were dead; 79 others were wounded or injured; and 166 marshals were hurt, 30 of them with gunshot wounds. President Kennedy sent in the 82nd and 101st Airborne to restore order and to make sure James Meredith, an air force veteran, could register as a student at his home state's university.

The Meredith debacle was a serious blow to the reputation and career of Ross Barnett. He left office after one term, and when he tried to run again, he finished fourth in his party's primary.

Ouida Atkins and her husband went back to Louisiana. They divorced in 1974, but she remained in Louisiana until 1987, when she returned to Jackson for good. She moved into a quiet, all-white neighborhood just up the street from the writer Eudora Welty and led the genteel life of a woman from a white establishment family.

That life took an unexpected turn that still is playing out.

She had a call from the Lanier High School principal, asking if she could fill in as a substitute social studies teacher. Her only childhood memory of Lanier was driving by one day when someone asked, "What school is that?" and she answered, "Oh, that's the colored school."

When she agreed to become a substitute teacher at Lanier, her friends and family were stunned. "They thought I'd lost my mind. My family was nervous. The children got me a cell phone so I could call them in case of emergencies."

When she entered Lanier, she was startled to discover how little she knew of the black culture. "I really didn't know as much as I thought I did. I was very quiet, really kind of shy, and finally, one of the students said, 'You better speak up if you want to be heard here.' And I did, and that made all the difference in the world with them."

She says many of the students knew about her family background, but it didn't seem to bother them. "They'd say, 'My grandparents or my great-aunt knew your daddy.' Or they'd refer to the Ross Barnett Reservoir north of Jackson and wonder whether I owned it!"

It was such a markedly different world for Atkins that some days she'd wonder whether she could make it. But as she came to know the students and appreciate their potential, she took on a missionary role. "I grew up in the First Baptist Church, where I was always told, 'You should be a missionary, you should go to China or the Belgian Congo.' I always agonized over where I should go, but now I realize I was on a kind of mission at Lanier."

A major part of her mission was to encourage promising Lanier students to continue their education. "I'd say to students, 'You're smarter than you think you are. You can go to college.' They weren't hearing that at home. They'd say to me, 'You're the first person ever to tell me I'm smart enough to go college.' "

For many of the students, Atkins became a second mother. Some of them even begged her to adopt them, which shocked her at first, but when she began to understand the depth of despair in many of the black families, she understood. "What's distressing to me is that many of them sort of accept it as a way of life."

She is encouraged that during her eleven years at Lanier, both sides of the racial divide worked harder to provide more opportunities for those who wanted to escape the cycle of poverty, drugs, and violence. In 2006 alone, she had six former students graduating from Ole Miss and one at West Point. She also has one former student who is at the Harvard Law School.

She continues to volunteer at Lanier, and she sees herself as a kind of informal ambassador from the school and the surrounding neighborhood to the white establishment, including her own family. Her children—her son, Ab, and her daughter, Angelyn—had grave reservations about their mother going to Lanier in the first place, but now they, too, have a better understanding of a culture that was alien to them.

Ab says, "My impressions took a 180-degree turn when I visited her there. I was raised in Louisiana, so what I knew about Mississippi was based on just what I'd heard. So when I got to Lanier, I was absolutely shocked. The love and affection they showed not just my mom but me as well. It was an epiphany for me personally."

Angelyn also had reservations about her mother teaching at Lanier, but when it became clear that the students loved her and she loved them back, Angelyn became a convert. She admits she sees race in a different way as a result of her mother's experience.

Ab adds, "We're very proud of her—from her friends to our friends to our children—her grandchildren. It's all very, very honorable."

And what about Ross Barnett, her segregationist father, what would he think? Atkins smiles. "I can't decide if he would laugh or be horrified. A lot of people say, 'Oh, he's turning over in his grave.' But I really don't know." She still believes he became much more of a segregationist when he ran for governor, and she thinks the James Meredith riots might have been avoided if there had been time for a cooling-off period so emotions might have subsided and the confrontation could have been averted.

Using her own life as an example, she charts the changes from what she calls "the years of silence," when her generation of white Mississippians did what their parents told them to do. "My great-granddaddy fought in the Civil War," she says. "My father blocked

James Meredith at Ole Miss. I taught at Lanier High. So we've come pretty far."

Atkins was born a Mississippian, and she will die a daughter of that state. Her final resting place will be a tribute to her family roots, and her life will be a monument to the capacity for change and redemption.

"Joshua, my great-grandfather's personal valet [a black man], when he died, he asked to be buried in the family cemetery. They said to him, 'We can't do that. We'll bury you right outside the fence.' But then they had to enlarge the cemetery, so now Joshua's inside the fence—and I'm going to be by him, next to my father."

Stan Sanders

"Watts in 1965 was a riot, not a revolution."

When Ouida Barnett Atkins was growing up in white privilege in Mississippi, Stan Sanders was growing up in Watts, the sprawling black community in South Central Los Angeles that became an international symbol for urban racial rage when it exploded into six days of riots and fires in 1965 after a young Watts resident was beaten by police.

Before the riots, Watts was to Los Angeles what Georgetown was to Jackson, Mississippi—the city's largest and best-organized black working-class community. The Sanders family was typical of the residents who settled in Watts following World War II. Stan's mother and father migrated there from Texas in the late Forties, after his dad came home from the war. They were looking for work and hoping to escape the

Stan Sanders in the early Seventies, in a send-up of a popular Black Panther Party picture of Huey Newton

Stan Sanders today, a successful lawyer in Los Angeles

harsh racism of their native state. Stan's father went to work for the city of Los Angeles, hauling trash, and remained a city employee for forty years.

For a modern young man in California in the Fifties, Stan Sanders had an unusually close connection to slavery. His mother was forty-four when he was born. Her mother, Stan's grandmother, was born into slavery in 1857 on an eastern Kentucky tobacco plantation. She gave birth to Stan's mother forty-one years later. As a result, he says, the legacy of slavery was very real. "It shaped the ethos of our family. I can remember my mother singing lullabies sung to her by her mother—slave lullabies."

Sanders's older brother, Ed, personified the family's brief generational journey from its roots in slavery to the slow opening of opportunities for black families in urban America in the Fifties. His football prowess in Los Angeles earned him a scholarship at Idaho State. He joined a now-integrated Navy during the Korean War. He was a gifted boxer, so the Navy assigned him to its service boxing team, and he was soon the talk of the sport. In 1952 in Helsinki, Ed Sanders became the first African-American to win an Olympic gold medal in boxing. He defeated Ingemar Johansson of Sweden, who would later become the world heavyweight champion.

"It was huge," Sanders remembers. "Here we are, this Watts family, and my brother is representing America in boxing and getting all this acclaim. When he comes home, there's a big parade and headlines in the **Los Angeles Times,** sportswriters coming out to the house.

"Ed was—still is—my hero. He was athletic and

bright and so gentle. We all looked up to him. He was such a source of support for my parents. I don't think they were ever the same after he died."

Ed Sanders collapsed in the eleventh round of a professional fight in Boston in 1954 and died a few hours later. Doctors thought it likely that he had been injured in an earlier fight. The family was devastated. His youngest brother was only ten years old and would soon be following his path to athletics. First, he had to go to high school, and in Watts there were two choices for bright and ambitious young African-Americans: register at Jordan, the large public high school in the middle of the community, or arrange for a transfer to one of the better schools on the west side of Los Angeles. Stan was wary of going to school at Jordan; it had a well-deserved reputation as a tough place. But his parents insisted he go there, just as his brothers had. "The first week I came home with a black eye from a fight, and I said to my mother, 'See, this is what happens when you go to Jordan!' My mother said, 'Well, you're gonna have to learn to fight, because Monday you're going back. But you have to study, too. You have to do both.' "

Now, half a century later, he credits his mother with making the right call. "It was one of the most important decisions of my young life," he says. "Jordan toughened me for the real world. I went to school with kids from neighborhoods like mine—with fathers who worked and mothers who cared—but also with kids from the big nearby housing projects, kids who were always looking for a fight. I learned how to be tough and still do my studies."

When Stan Sanders returned to Jordan after his tough-love talk from his mother, he became a student leader, a star athlete in football and track, and a serious young man interested in the civil rights movement that was under way in the South. "I attended a United Nations model assembly in Northern California and heard this young preacher from Montgomery, Alabama, speak.

"It was Dr. Martin Luther King, and he had an electrifying effect on me. I went back to my high school and told the counselors I didn't want to be a doctor—which is what my parents wanted—I wanted to be a lawyer. I wanted to do something in the community."

Sanders's favorite teacher encouraged him to attend Morehouse, the all-black college in Atlanta, but his mother and father and the Jordan counselors had other ideas. "My parents said, 'We don't want to send you to a school in the South—in Atlanta. That's why we're in California.' The Jordan counselors were always trying to get Jordan students into schools that didn't have black students."

He was accepted at Whittier College, just forty miles down the road from Watts, in Orange County, but a world away from the life he'd been living. Whittier, Richard Nixon's alma mater, is a Quaker school in the middle of an all-white middle-class suburb. The location, the student population, and, most of all, the Quaker sensibilities of Whittier had a profound effect on Sanders's education outside the classroom. "I saw Whittier as a place where I could do just about anything I wanted to. I played football. I was student body president. I was in the top of my class academically. I could let it all hang out."

The Whittier administration had something else in mind for their star student: a Rhodes Scholarship, the first in the school's history. "I remember my political science professors coming to me at the beginning of my junior year and saying, 'We want to be sure you're taking the toughest classes, because you're going to be Whittier's first Rhodes scholar.'

"A year later, they came back to me with the application and told me to fill it out and then give it back so they could check it over. I didn't have any choice. That was Whittier for me. A series of green lights. It was a fantastic experience."

His growing fame as a scholar, star athlete, and student leader made him the toast of the black middle class in Los Angeles. He was invited to speak at service clubs and to meet prominent black judges. He was moving within many worlds. "I was really navigating. I had speech patterns for both worlds. When I was in Watts in the summer, I spoke one way. At Whittier College, as the student body president, I spoke another way. I remember someone coming to me and saying, 'How does it feel to be the first black Rhodes scholar in fifty-five years?' and I replied, 'Oh, I'm a Rhodes scholar who just happens to be black.' I didn't want the focus on race.

"We all did it, blacks who were achieving. Rafer Johnson did it. [Johnson, the Olympic decathlon champion, was also the student body president of UCLA and a member of a white fraternity]. We marginalized the race business because we wanted to focus on our skills."

When Sanders returned to his old neighborhood after completing his Rhodes Scholarship at Oxford, he was surprised by how much more outspoken the community had become about the conditions confronting urban blacks. President Lyndon Johnson had announced the Great Society with great fanfare, but the dollars from that panoply of federal programs designed to create jobs and end poverty were slow in trickling down at first.

August 11 was a hot, humid Wednesday night in the streets of Watts in 1965. The streets were full of local residents trying to find some relief. A black motorist was pulled over for drunk driving, and when the police tried to arrest him, his mother jumped on the back of one of the cops; his brother got involved in the melee as well. The officers arrested all of them and took them in for booking.

Word spread that there had been a police beating, and before long, the streets were filled with angry people throwing rocks at passing cars and store windows. The uprising spilled over into a second day, and the anger escalated. Stores were burned and looted. There were violent clashes with police on almost every corner.

Dr. King came to Watts to appeal for calm, but his pleas for nonviolence were shouted down. Stan Sanders remembers the Watts riots as a real turning point for the country. It was no longer just about protesting the separate water fountains, the back of the bus, and the all-white lunch counters. Now it was about de facto segregation, fair housing, poverty, and jobs, the issues that linked every part of America, and not just the South, to the blight of racism.

During these critical years for his country and his race, Stan Sanders was thousands of miles away amid the spires of Oxford. But he was watching closely and thinking deeply about his place as a black man in the new America to which he would soon be returning as a law student at Yale. He had always been aware of the civil rights movement in the South, but as a Californian, he had felt removed from it. Now he and other urban blacks wanted to take the struggle to a new level.

"The Vietnam War had not really kicked in yet; it was still on a low burner, but it was in the news enough for people to ask, 'Why are we squandering resources on Southeast Asia when there's such a critical need here?' Every black who had any sense was reconsidering what it meant to be black in America."

After almost a week of rioting and burning and looting—think about that for a moment: a vast area of Los Angeles looking like Baghdad for six days—the uprising ended. Thirty-four people died, and another thousand were injured. More than six hundred stores and buildings were destroyed, most of them white-owned. The National Guard was called in to seal off the area with armed troops.

I arrived in Los Angeles the following spring, and Watts was still smoldering emotionally, if not physically. Now suddenly aware of the conditions that had led to the blowup, city, state, and federal officials started rushing aid to the neighborhoods. White residents in other parts of Los Angeles who had never heard of Watts until the uprising formed groups to help build day care centers and support organizations to deal with the area's many needs.

The tensions wouldn't go away so easily, and in the spring of 1966 Watts went up a second time when police arrested a black motorist for running red lights. He said he was rushing to get his pregnant wife to a hospital.

During the arrest there was a struggle and the driver was fatally shot by police. This time the rioting went on for two days. Two people were killed and dozens were injured.

A flashy young black lawyer represented the dead man's family, and I came to know him well during the heated court proceedings and community rallies that followed. We stayed in touch over the years, and I was not surprised when, in 1995, he successfully defended O. J. Simpson. His name was Johnnie Cochran, and his specialty back in 1966—well before the glove that didn't fit—was defending black clients by attacking police practices.

I also met Stan Sanders in the summer of 1966 and spent many hours with him in his old neighborhoods. He was on a break from the Yale Law School and joining the efforts to help put his old home ground back together. He was tireless and quietly inspirational, a handsome and athletic man moving through his old neighborhoods, where the Sanders name had legendary standing.

When Stan Sanders graduated from Yale Law, he was, predictably, a hot prospect for all the big firms in Los Angeles. But he decided to go to work first for the Western Center on Law and Poverty, and then he ran the L.A. offices of the Lawyers' Committee on Civil Rights.

That turned out to be a discouraging experience in many ways. "I'd ask young lawyers in large firms to take a temporary leave to work on social issues, but there was so much competition to make partner, getting on with their life, having that first baby—you know, it's tough competing with the American dream. So it sputtered. Nothing really got started."

He tried private practice with a large firm that promised he could open a branch office in Watts, but again, his fellow lawyers had other priorities. So he moved on to representing black businesses and black athletes, but he felt guilty. "There was no trickle down to the working class. I was getting away from the baseline condition in the inner city."

For all of his successes at Whittier College, as a Rhodes scholar, as a Yale Law graduate, and as a practicing attorney, the Watts riots represented the reality of being black in urban America in the mid-Sixties. He could have walked away from that reality, but it stuck with him, and it frames his thinking today.

"I could have decided to go to Wall Street and do mergers and acquisitions or antitrust law, but it would have been totally irrelevant to the actions and passions of my time," he says.

When I first met Sanders in the aftermath of the riots, we both believed what had happened there would be such a wake-up call for the nation that it would force a resolution of the many racial issues that continued to divide the country more than a century after the end of the Civil War.

As we talk now, two men in our sixties, fathers and grandfathers, we agree that our optimism was only half justified. There has been so much progress; and there is still so much deep, dark despair. Sanders says bluntly, "The state of black men in America is in free fall. The whole prison system is a huge industry, largely devoted to warehousing black men.

"It is a total betrayal of the American dream and all that Dr. King fought for. I blame the way we reacted to the Watts riots. We didn't fight fire with fire. If low educational levels were a primary cause of poverty, why didn't we pour in massive amounts of educational aid? When I went there, Jordan High was a decent school. I visited recently, and now it's just a joke. There's no real teaching. Kids can't read. We kind of gave up."

It is a complaint I hear again and again across the country from black members of Sanders's generation. The combination of the dissolution of the black family structure in too many neighborhoods, the loss of parental involvement in the education of too many black children, and the indifference of the majority community adds up to warehousing, not educating.

Sanders is persuaded that black and white America needs a reality check on how long all of this will take. "When Lyndon Johnson started the Great Society program, everyone underestimated the needs. You have to have something that runs a long period of time, twenty to twenty-five years. Like what we've been doing in Iraq." Sanders sees President George W. Bush's plans for a long-term commitment to ensuring a functioning democratic Iraq as a contrast to what has not happened in the poorest black neighborhoods.

Referring to the old Great Society programs of the Lyndon Johnson years, he says, "When those programs faded away, a void developed—and that void was filled by a lot of self-defeating habits, one of which was drugs and the gangs that came with it. You cannot overestimate the role the crack-cocaine epidemic had on black America."

In fact, Watts and all of South Central Los Angeles is much more dangerous now than it was before and immediately after the 1965 riots. When Stan Sanders was attending Jordan High School, there were gangs but, as he says, "they only carried switchblade knives. Now it's gunfire." Heavily armed gangs—most of them involved in the big-money drug trade—are regularly involved in lethal firefights in which, all too often, innocent bystanders are the victims. In the Sixties no one anticipated that so many inner-city neighborhoods would end up living under siege by well-organized and utterly ruthless gangbangers.

Sanders's two sons, themselves fathers, are both successful Los Angeles lawyers. When he laments that too many black men are behind bars, they're likely to say, "Dad, they belong there. We don't want them out on the streets endangering our children—your grandchildren." Sanders chuckles as he says, "I think one of my sons may be a Republican; I'm not sure."

The Sanders sons grew up in upper-middle-class neighborhoods in Los Angeles, and though their father's early life seems a world away from their own experiences, they've also connected to Watts as supporters of a charter school and by working in the South Central district attorney's office. One of the sons writes regularly to a member of the extended family who is in prison.

Meanwhile, Sanders and many of his old friends from Watts still return to the community to worship on Sundays at the Grant AME Church. "We're the guys who think what happened in '65 was a riot, not a revolution," he says. "We're lawyers, doctors, very senior government managers now retired. We were the black middle class who, silently and with dignity, pulled ourselves up by our bootstraps.

"We made it, but the lesson of Katrina is that racism is very tangible today. I suppose every American can probably think to themselves, 'There's a Lower Ninth Ward [the poor black neighborhood in New Orleans destroyed by the flood] somewhere in my city.' In their heart of hearts, they know it's there. Refusing to recognize it is a form of racism."

Dr. Shelby Steele

At about the same time Stan Sanders was beginning to make his mark as a black man in South Central Los Angeles, Shelby Steele was coming of age in the Midwest.

Steele has established himself as one of America's leading black critics of what he describes as the vacuum of moral authority generated by white ambivalence on race. That ambivalence, twinned with the power of prominent blacks such as Jesse Jackson and Al Sharpton to "shame, silence, and muscle concessions from the larger society," has led to what Steele describes as a cancer of moral relativism. Steele, a fellow at Stanford University's Hoover Institution, is a persistent and articulate critic of what he considers to be the "black victim syndrome," in which standards are lowered for the black community because of their history as victims.

Back in 1968, Shelby Steele hardly imagined that he was on the first steps of a road that would make him a prominent, politically incorrect, contrarian intellectual. He was a senior at Coe College in Cedar Rapids, Iowa, one of about sixty black students on campus and president of the local SNCC chapter, which by then had become an unapologetically militant black power organization headed by Stokely Carmichael.

The four years at Coe represented a dramatic change for Steele, a young man who had grown up with a black truck-driver father and a white social-worker mother. They were active in mainstream civil rights activities in the Chicago area, and although they were decidedly lower-income, they embraced middle-class values. He remembers that all his friends at home had a father, that every family went to church on Sunday, and that Dr. King was giving voice to their hopes for better lives for their children.

At Coe, a small liberal arts college in a small city famous as the home of Quaker Oats, Steele received financial assistance. He made many friends in the mostly white student body. He remembers it as a good time. "Honestly, I had no trouble making friends with people of other races. Sometimes we black students would sit around and complain about the white majority, but then we'd all just go out and have fun."

As a freshman, Steele was president of the campus chapter of SCOPE, the student branch of Dr. King's Southern Christian Leadership Conference. "Our philosophy," he says, "was very integrationist; we were trying hard to reach across racial boundaries. It was that classic civil rights movement."

But in the mid-Sixties, that movement was undergoing some profound changes away from Dr. King's nonviolent philosophy. Militants were beginning to move in on established organizations such as SNCC.

"By the time I was a senior, I was something of a black nationalist," Steele says, "and the politics of race had changed into this anti-white militancy. That was a big transition for black America—the idea that we weren't going to focus on integration. We were expected to be militant toward America, and hostile.

"Up to that point, the theory of the civil rights movement was to show yourself to be a better human being than those who hate you. In the late Sixties, the opposite was true. You didn't try to be better . . . you tried to be just like them and fight them openly. Show your anger and hostility for what you had suffered for being black."

In his provocative book **White Guilt: How Blacks and Whites Together Destroyed the Promise of the Civil Rights Era,** Steele describes a seminal moment for him. He went to hear Dick Gregory, a hugely gifted and successful comedian who had shattered the color line in entertainment by directly addressing race. By 1967, Gregory's initially light and humorous approach had taken a new turn. He was still very funny, but his humor had a hard new edge. Now Gregory was even willing to risk his lucrative nightclub career to spread the message of black power. Steele recalls Gregory's mantra, "Raise your consciousness," suggesting that for blacks to accept responsibility on the white man's terms was just another form of oppression. Steele now argues that this demand that there be a redistribution of responsibility for black advancement from black America to white America, from the black "victims" to the white "guilty," was a tragic turning point in the long struggle for better lives for black Americans.

He remembers wondering at the time whether his father would buy Gregory's argument. "I could not imagine it," he concludes. "Responsibility was his great faith; he would never see the logic in thinking of it as something that 'blamed the victim.' " His son, however, embraced it. "I was convinced we were in a new era of civil rights."

His parents were not prepared for this radical change from taking charge of your own life to blaming others. "They were shocked. Most people of their generation were absolutely shocked by it. I remember talking to my father about 'blackness,' and he had absolutely no idea what that was—even though he had been born black in the South in 1900."

Black pride, black power, black nationalism, black studies—none of these was part of the consciousness of the general population of black Americans born before World War II. They were, for the most part, the "go along, get along" generation, accommodating to the formal and informal rules of a dominant white society. They did not expect to advance on the color of their skin. They would have to find other means.

The blackness Steele was describing to his father, he now believes, was a politicized form of identity. "It has no real life beyond politics. Then it was a huge, sweeping change, and my parents knew it was inevitable . . . but I don't think it ever sat very comfortably with them."

By 1968 Steele was writing student editorials castigating whites for supporting Dr. King, insisting that simply asking for equality was all Uncle Tom stuff. "We were going to demand it now." Steele sees the passage of the civil rights legislation as a huge change. "We had won an enormous victory. Freedom! It came as a shock. It also came to us as a shame because we realized how far behind we were" in the fundamental rights of voting, access to public facilities, and education.

But Steele has now concluded that "that freedom is just the absence of restraint; it doesn't give you anything." He believes that civil rights legislation, still widely regarded as a benchmark of racial justice, didn't really change anything. "We didn't know what to do," he says. "We didn't have experience with freedom, didn't have the values for it. Still don't in many ways.

"The more it shamed us, the blacker we became. We were not going ahead on what King was talking about . . . economic development and education, those sorts of things. We were going ahead on the basis of our identity, our blackness, and we were going to see what society was going to give us for that. They gave us a few things. Not much. Just enough to keep up the illusion."

Even while he embraced black power as a student, Steele was beginning to have doubts. "There was a part of me that never quite believed," he says. Now he calls the black power movement "fool's gold"—a form of delusion about the power of pride and pigmentation alone, absent the authority that comes only with broad financial and educational success. He says simply, "we got terribly lost during that period and we have never fully recovered from it.

"In the civil rights movement, we had fought against anyone asking for anything in the name of their race . . . that's white supremacy. We wanted to be treated as human beings and as individuals. Well, in the late Sixties, black power comes out, and we treat our race the same way the Ku Klux Klan treated whiteness." In other words, skin color trumped all.

Steele's own education continued when he graduated from Coe and moved to East St. Louis, Illinois, to teach poor children as part of a Great Society program. East St. Louis was a hard-core place with none of the middle-class values of his childhood. It remains today one of the poorest and most desperate neighborhoods in urban America. He was not prepared for what he found there. "Families were shattered . . . illegitimacy was extremely high. There was gang violence . . . drug dealing. I was shocked, and I learned a lot there.

"We were suddenly in a situation where the government was giving us a lot of money for being black . . . and I was sort of teaching it at that point. We took it as our due . . . in the name of race and militancy, we taught black separatism." For all the federal money that was poured into East St. Louis, the situation today is as grim as it was when Steele was teaching there. Black power was well financed, but as a means of getting people ahead, it was bankrupt.

At the same time, Steele was personally hedging his bets, worried that his blackness was not enough. He attended night classes at Southern Illinois University and earned a master's degree. "In my family, education was an absolute. I accepted I had to make up for lost ground."

From there he went to the University of Utah to get a Ph.D. in literature, which got him a teaching job at San Jose State University. "Now," he says, "I was an adult in the real world. I had a family. I had a job. One day I was late for class. I had a pile of papers to grade. I had four classes to teach, and when I got on the bus, there was this young black kid. In the middle of the day, doing absolutely nothing. But he had all the emblems of black power—the big Afro, the pick stuck in his hair, the whole regalia. And doing nothing.

"That moment began to turn me around. I thought about the civil rights legislation passed in 1964 and how to use it. At Utah I was placed in segregated housing, so I took the case to court and won. It occurred to me I was now living in a society that didn't hate me . . . that was itself trying to transform and grow." The rule of law, the great binding force in this nation of so many competing and conflicting interests, was finally beginning to be felt in the areas of race.

His critics, black and white, argue that Steele's view of a racially tolerant America is colored by his privileged status as a highly educated black man with conservative views who moves through a rarified environment inaccessible to working-class or even middle-class blacks. But Steele insists that the "enormous moral evolution" of white America from the Sixties to the present is one of the great untold stories of our times.

"White people," he says, "are different human beings today. They do not want to be seen as racist." He uses as an example the well-publicized racial rant of actor Michael Richards—Kramer from **Seinfeld**—in a Los Angeles nightclub. "In one slip of the tongue," Steele says, "the man is ruined. White America punishes its own in a profound way. They banish them, and there's no redemption.

"America has always been grappling with the perniciousness of racial oppression. Always. It's not new. You can go all the way back to Thomas Jefferson struggling with this problem."

Steele takes direct aim at his critics, whom he calls "these yammering blacks out there—the Jesse Jacksons, the Al Sharptons, the Dick Gregorys." He claims "racism is valuable to blacks now because it keeps whites owing us. In other words, racism is the single greatest source of power blacks in America have today." Although he doesn't quite say it, Steele believes white America is being conned into believing it is a racist society. "Because," he says, "the more you think that, the more you're gonna be open to our demands.

"It all began in 1968. White America lost its moral authority. That's the price it paid for being good, for acknowledging it was wrong. Whites could be stigmatized, and they've been living in terror ever since. The worst thing that can happen to a white person is to be labeled a racist."

Steele recalls a white woman who worked at a YMCA that he attended as a child. Steele spoke in the patois of the black community, and this woman took it upon herself to correct him. "She'd do it right in front of everyone," he says. "She'd say, 'You have to put a **g** on the **-ing.** You just can't leave it hanging with the **n.**' She would tell me to learn proper English or it would hurt me later in life."

"God bless that woman. She didn't have to do that. She cared about me. She had the authority to say assimilation is necessary if you're going to be successful. No white woman would do that now." He also says, "Nobody now stands up to blacks, and so white Americans have lost their moral authority." But he admits that when he was going through his own black power phase, he would have called the YMCA grammarian a racist.

Black power advocates, he says, began to see "whites who insisted on traditional values as racist whites, sexist whites, warmongering whites. Relativism became a virtue, and that's when the culture war began." It was what the writer Tom Wolfe so perfectly captured in his account of Leonard Bernstein and other New York liberal swells entertaining Black Panthers in Bernstein's apartment. In his book **Radical Chic & Mau-Mauing the Flak Catchers,** Wolfe described the Panthers' rant against all whites and Bernstein's obsequious response, "I can dig."

The phrase "radical chic" stuck as a sneering description of those who wanted to identify with militant causes without leaving the comfort of their luxurious homes or comfortable lives.

Steele has as little patience for those he considers white enablers as he does for black leaders who exploit the notions of a racist society. "I haven't had a frank conversation about race with a white person since I was a kid," he says.

When I ask him to elaborate, he says that if the subject is race, conversations are rarely going to be honest. He asks rhetorically, "What white person is going to speak honestly to blacks after what happened to Imus?" If they honestly think Imus was punished too harshly, they'll worry their opinions will mark them as racist. If whites ask how black rappers and black comedians can use those phrases—"nappy-headed" and "hos"—without punishment, won't they be accused of another kind of racism, a failure to understand the black culture?

To Steele, these all add up to what he calls "powerful taboos" that eliminate the opportunity for examining the complex issue of race on its merits and within the framework of moral authority. When race is the subject, everyone gets into a defensive crouch, and, in Steele's experience, whites lose confidence in their ability to deal with the issue. That, in turn, he believes only "perpetuates racism."

As for his own life, Steele looks back and concludes, "I spent '68 losing myself in blackness. I thought in 1968 there was going to be a revolution. . . . America was going to be overthrown. It really looked that way." By the Seventies, he was changing, launched on what he now calls a long journey of overcoming all the illusions of his life in the Sixties—the illusions of black power growing out of black skin alone.

Steele says that when he meets with an all-black group, with no whites in the room, 80 percent of the people agree with the ideas and values he promotes. Outside that room, however, Steele sees black America wearing black-militant masks and chips on their shoulders. "And if you **don't** wear that mask," he says, "then you're an 'Uncle Tom.' "

He cites Colin Powell and Condoleezza Rice, America's first and only black secretaries of state. Steele says black manipulators hate them because they don't wear the mask—because "they're not trying to manipulate white guilt."

He is also an admirer of Bill Cosby's exhortations to young urban blacks to spend more time on the books and less time on the streets. Cosby deplores the growing trend in many inner-city neighborhoods to mock students who do well in their studies or those who disdain the hip-hop style in favor of wardrobes more likely to help them get jobs in the mainstream economy.

Cosby has said to black parents, "Straighten up your house. Straighten up your apartment. Straighten up your child. We don't need another federal commission to tell us what's wrong. We need parents overseeing homework, parents sending their children off to school well fed, well rested, and ready to learn." Steele calls Cosby "a great man for having the courage to do that," but he says the famous entertainer is getting too little support. In an interview on CNN, Cosby said that the poet Maya Angelou told him, "Bill, you're a nice man but you have a big mouth."

Personally, I was surprised by the reaction of a prominent black businessman when I praised Cosby's statements. My friend, a product of exactly the kind of upbringing Cosby is talking about, said, "I wish Bill wouldn't do that. We have enough trouble without him going public."

While Steele gives Bill Cosby high marks, he is not much impressed with Barack Obama on the issue of race. Steele worries, "He's really more old than new. He's not really challenging any of the taboos. To whites he sells himself as a redemption for all they've done right. He sells himself to black America as a chance to gain real power." Steele told me, "Senator Obama is not the kind of figure to open up a real, honest debate about the issues of race."

The day after Steele offered this opinion on Obama, I picked up an edition of the **Chicago Sun-Times** that had a picture of Senator Obama's wife, Michelle, with the bold headline IS SHE BLACK ENOUGH?

That provocative question—just the kind Steele deplores—did not in fact reflect the tone of the insightful profile of Ms. Obama written by Mary Mitchell, one of the paper's black reporters. Billed as a "sister-to-sister talk," the story was an instructive lesson in the racial balancing act the Obamas are expected to maintain as they make their way through the heady experience of a presidential campaign.

Below the headline, Mitchell posed her own, more useful question: How do the Obamas convince white voters that a black man can represent all Americans while assuring black voters they've not forgotten where they come from? Mitchell said the question reflects the black community's long battle with internal class divisions and the fears of low-income and working-class blacks that successful blacks are too quick to deny that racism still exists.

Michelle Obama, who grew up in a one-bedroom home in Chicago's mostly black South Shore community and went on to get degrees from Princeton and Harvard law, responded, "I think race is a reality of our society . . . we've made great strides but we've got a lot of work to do."

However, those questions—what is black and who is black enough?—trouble her because she's been hearing them since she was a child, when she was criticized for talking "too proper" or attending certain schools.

"I did exactly what leaders in my community told me to do. They said do your best in school, work hard, study, get into the best schools . . . and when you do that, baby, bring that education back and work in your community."

She did just that, yet now that she's campaigning beside her husband in the most serious presidential campaign by a black candidate in American history, they still face the question of whether they are black enough. "The thing I worry most about," Ms. Obama is quoted as saying, is, "What does it say to our children? If I'm not black enough and Barack is not black enough, who are **they** [the Obama children] supposed to be in this world?"

It is the kind of honest, first-person testimony that Shelby Steele would like to hear more of in the long-running dialogue that will continue in America about race and its place in establishing standards of achievement, behavior, and opportunity.

He recognizes that he has few public followers in

the black community, but he isn't bothered. "It's been good for me," he says, "because it's made me think more carefully. I think of my life as a journey, and I want to learn more."

Dr. Cleveland Sellers

About the time Shelby Steele was growing up in the Midwest, Cleveland Sellers was growing up in the South, where he became a wounded veteran of the early days of the civil rights movement. He was one of thirty people shot by South Carolina state police (three were killed) during a campus protest in 1968 at South Carolina State College, an all-black school in Orangeburg.

It was a violent night, too little remembered or remarked upon in the general history of the time but never forgotten by those who were there, including Sellers, who now teaches African-American studies at the University of South Carolina.

Cleveland Sellers grew up in South Carolina and began to participate in sit-ins in 1960, while he was still in high school. "I was one of those students that grew up knowing we had to avenge the murder of Emmett Till. We had long discussions at school about it. We would be the generation that would step into the pages of history and create change not just because society had allowed this to happen but because a judicial system appeared to actually condone the murder of Emmett Till."

By the time he enrolled at Howard University in

Cleveland Sellers (third from left), program director for the Student Nonviolent Coordinating Committee, along with Martin Luther King Jr. (center) and Stokely Carmichael (second from right in foreground), confronted by police in Memphis in 1966

Shelby Steele in Paris, 1970

Dr. Shelby Steele, research fellow at the Hoover Institution at Stanford University

Washington, D.C., in the fall of 1962, Sellers was a committed civil rights activist, so he was surprised when he discovered that his fellow students—many of them middle-class blacks from the North—didn't share his passion. "It was a very rude awakening," he says. "I couldn't find students ready to participate in sit-ins and freedom rides to protest segregation and the absence of the right to vote. That disheartened me tremendously."

Sellers became involved in a low-key campus organization loosely affiliated with Dr. King's crusade. He was asked to help organize the now-famous March on Washington in 1963. By the morning of the march, only a few participants had trickled in, and Sellers was worried it would fail. But then busload after busload of civil rights activists from around the country began to appear, and the march took on historic dimensions, capped by Dr. King's classic oration, "I Have a Dream."

"There was euphoria after the speech," Sellers remembers, "with the joining of labor, the religious community, and civil rights groups. There seemed to be a coalition building. But then a month later, the church bombing in Birmingham made us reassess. I was very hurt spiritually, politically, and intellectually. I realized I had to do more."

He dropped out of Howard and joined the Mississippi Summer Project in 1964, the year when civil rights workers James Chaney, a young black man, and Michael Schwerner and Andrew Goodman, two white students from the North, were murdered and buried near Philadelphia, Mississippi.

Sellers became part of a group that tried to find the missing young men. "We didn't want to alert anyone to the fact we were there. We'd go out at night in an old truck with no lights and search ravines and old houses, looking for their bodies. I wasn't frightened. We had a commitment to our fellow organizers, and we liked to think they'd be doing the same if we were missing."

During that summer, confronted with regular bombings and beatings, Sellers also began to explore the subtle but important differences between nonviolence as an organizational tactic and the need for self-defense. More than once he was summoned to a local black funeral home to gauge whether a person had died as the result of an accident or foul play.

He helped organize freedom schools as an alternative to community protests. "We tried to teach young African-Americans basic math and writing skills; we tried to introduce them to Negro history. It was twenty-four/seven. There was always something to do."

Sellers became formally involved with SNCC just as it was evolving from the leadership of John Lewis and Julian Bond to the more militant approach of Stokely Carmichael. He was there in 1966 when Stokely Carmichael told a rally in Greenwood, Mississippi, that it was time for black people to recognize their heritage and build a sense of community, shouting out, "Black power, black power," to the cheers of the crowd.

Sellers still blames the press for misrepresenting the context of Carmichael's speech and thereby making it more threatening to the white population. He recognizes that the phrase "black power" and the SNCC tactics under Carmichael did represent a break with Dr. King's style and approach. "We didn't believe in a central, charismatic leader as being the way to go. You had to decentralize the leadership . . . and grow leadership in the local community, even if they had only a fourth-grade education. We were opposed to the middle-class status quo idea."

By 1967 Sellers was a SNCC program director in Atlanta. It was there that he received his draft notice. At the appointed day and time he stood on the steps of the induction center and, surrounded by Carmichael and other SNCC leaders, announced that he would refuse to report, citing what he called America's racist and imperialist foreign policy. After making his statement, he turned and walked away.

Those were trying times for Sellers, and by 1968 he was worn out and decided to return to South Carolina, where he got involved with a local black power organization that was trying to reform traditionally black institutions—to make them, in effect, more black in their thinking and policies. As Sellers says, "This was about reform, not direct action. I had my share of direct action by 1968."

Little did he know what lay ahead.

In short order, he was shot and wounded by South Carolina state troopers during a student protest on the campus of South Carolina State College. What came to be known as the Orangeburg Massacre began with a black student sit-in at an all-white bowling alley. It spilled out into the parking lot and turned violent when students and local police began to clash.

The students retreated to their campus, but their

anger festered for two days. Then, on February 8, 1968, they built a large bonfire, and when state troopers arrived with a fire truck, the students began to taunt them. The demonstrators began to throw things at the troopers. One of the cops pulled out his gun and fired warning shots into the air, and that, in turn, prompted other troopers to pull their weapons and begin shooting into the crowd.

Sellers was asleep in a campus dorm at the time, but he was quickly summoned to help. As soon as he arrived, he was shot in the shoulder. It was mayhem. Wounded students were dragged away to the college infirmary, and others were loaded into cars and rushed to the local hospital.

Sellers was reluctant to go to the hospital. He knew law en-forcement officers would be there, and he strongly suspected he'd been fingered by FBI spies as a black power rabble-rouser. Sure enough, shortly after his hospital treatment, Sellers was arrested and shipped off to the state's Central Correctional Institution. Bail was set at fifty thousand dollars.

Eventually, the celebrated civil rights lawyer William Kunstler and a team of attorneys got Sellers out of jail, but a few weeks later he was back behind bars, this time in Georgia, for having refused to answer his induction notice the year before.

He was tried, convicted, and sentenced to five years in a federal prison. He spent the next four months being moved from jail to jail, he says, to disorient him and make it harder for him to communicate with his lawyers. "During that time," Sellers remembers, "I would tell my mind—focus, focus, focus. Just work on knowing who you are . . . and that you have to stay alive and healthy."

By late summer 1968, his case had reached the U.S. Supreme Court, and Justice Hugo Black, a one-time member of the Ku Klux Klan turned judicial liberal, ruled that the lower courts had been wrong in determining that Sellers was a flight risk. Bail was reduced to five thousand dollars, the case was remanded, and Sellers was never reprosecuted on the draft charges.

But by 1970 he was back in the dock, this time charged with participating in the Orangeburg riot, inciting the riot, and conspiring to incite others to riot. He was convicted of one count and sent away for one year of hard labor.

When he was released, it was time to move on. He returned to Howard University to finish first his undergraduate degree and then his master's in education. He went on to get a doctorate in education from the University of North Carolina in Greensboro, and today he heads the African-American studies program at the University of South Carolina.

Sellers looks back on those years in the civil rights movement—the accomplishments, the shooting, the jail time, the long, dangerous nights—with great pride. "That was an experience I wouldn't have had under any other circumstances . . . I wouldn't give that up for anything. I have no regrets.

"I think we've been tremendously successful. Did we complete the job? Absolutely not. But the movement was run and organized by ordinary people who were fighting for basic justice and equal rights and peace. I think as long as those things are denied, there will always be people willing to stand up. You don't have to have a Ph.D. in theology to make a difference."

Like many veterans of the civil rights movement, Sellers is troubled by several developments within the African-American community in recent years. "One is the eradication of . . . values. We see an erosion of the old commitment to community and Judeo-Christian values. We see the terrible scourge of drugs.

"It's not just an issue of race. It's an issue of being poor and not having any mechanism for changing one's status. We went to a high-tech economy. We had an erosion in affirmative action. We saw an outsourcing of manufacturing and textiles in the South. You had a shift in the economy, and it wasn't a shift that benefited poor people.

"We haven't confronted the demons of the past," he says. "You have to get to the point where people actually recognize the pain and suffering." He'd like something similar to the Marshall Plan that America financed to help rebuild Europe after World War II.

Sellers envisions a massive government investment in America's social infrastructure, particularly in the areas of education and health care, that could help make the African-American community whole again. "I am not a fan of paying anyone compensation, but I do think apologies are a first step," he says.

"You cannot overcome in the short haul. We still have not had the national conversation on race—or class and gender, for that matter. We've tried to have it, but not in a meaningful way.

"Today where do you get that? Who provides that? I think we've not had a real values discussion.

Conservatives have taken that discussion . . . away from the rest of us. The only people who can discuss values are the conservatives, and they're not discussing values as much as behavior, what they consider to be appropriate."

That was a recurring complaint I encountered while working on this book, the failure to communicate. It is a multiracial issue not made any easier by the instant polarization that takes place as soon as race is introduced into a conversation.

Try it sometime with a mix of black and white co-workers. Instantly, stereotypes, defenses, slights, distortions, and suspicions tend to frame the discussion. People of goodwill on all sides of the racial divide start forward and then back off because it is so uncomfortable and—black or white—they have been so conditioned not to get at the essential questions for fear of playing the race card.

I dislike the idea of all-black dorms or fraternities on college campuses as much as I dislike the social and racial discrimination in all-white fraternities and sororities. I dislike it, but I think I get it. It's a comfort zone, and it's a statement about black pride. But what it is not is a preparation for living in a world where assimilation is now much more highly valued than is separation.

Assimilation does not require the surrender of ethnic pride or cultural distinctions. It is about values that transcend racial distinctions. It is about common goals, standards, conduct, tolerance, and empathy. It is about challenging hypocrisy and dishonesty.

As a society, we're still inclined to cling to our old

racial and cultural landscapes, fenced in by insecurities, biases, ignorance of others, and intellectual laziness. The danger is that the American landscape then breaks up along the fault lines of anxieties that only continue to develop and deepen.

Too many individuals and organizations are ready to help that destructive, divisive process along because of their own narrow views or for their own power. They do not have the common welfare, as Thomas Jefferson described it, in mind. The laws are now in place, thanks largely to the Sixties; the opportunities are manifest for a profound change in racial dialogue, attitudes, and how we live our lives.

It is hard, sometimes uncomfortable work to talk about these matters and confront them. Consider affirmative action, the beneficial if controversial program for advancing the chances of African-American students to get a college degree.

It has been praised by senior military, corporate, and academic leaders as an important instrument in expanding the universe of educated Americans and advancing racial diversity. It is attacked mostly from the right as a quota system that rewards color, not merit or need.

Although it is imperfect, I believe that affirmative action, a concept first introduced by President Kennedy in 1961 in an effort to relieve institutionalized racism, has worked, especially for the generation of African-Americans who were the first to take advantage of it.

I also believe it is time for a reexamination of the terms of the almost exclusively racial basis that was applied in the past. There should be a place for a color-blind combination of need and merit. The tensions surrounding affirmative action could be reduced by a more systematic measure of its success, which in turn may lead to a sunset provision, a goal of phasing out the program based on its success.

Most of all, everyone has to face the hard truth behind the need for color-blind affirmative action: the failures of public education at the elementary and secondary levels for all students of all races. If the majority community doesn't want to do the hard work of improving public education for everyone, and if the minority community wants to abandon the importance of education, we're trapped in a self-defeating spiral in which the exceptional cases need the lifeline of affirmative action.

In the difficult but necessary days of the civil rights movement, the matter of racial equality and the place of race in our culture took a prominent place on the national agenda. Dr. King forced the land of Jefferson and Lincoln to confront its shameful racial record. The very considerable progress that has been made over the last forty years began with the vision, the courage, and the moral commitment of those in the movement, black and white together.

When President Lyndon Johnson signed the 1964 civil rights bill into law, knowing full well the serious political consequences for his party in his home state of Texas and throughout the South, he surprised almost everyone by looking into the network cameras with that homely, earnest expression that he adopted on such occasions and said, "We shall overcome."

"We Shall Overcome" was the anthem of the civil rights movement, a soulful and moving promise by marchers on the dusty roads of Alabama, in rural and big-city churches, on city streets, and wherever the cause of racial equality was raised. To hear those evocative words uttered sincerely by an old-fashioned white political boss from deep in the heart of Texas was a startling and promising moment.

More than forty years later it remains a promise unfulfilled.

The Reagan Revolution and the Democrats' Identity Crisis

The Republicans made a living off the excesses of the Sixties until the 2006 election.

—President Bill Clinton

The Sixties are a sign of what elite opinion can mean. There was an animus toward the military in the Sixties that was palpable, a moral revulsion among the elites toward the war. Yet when they got a candidate who represented the essential nature of that, he won one state.

—Karl Rove

Is this what the political activists on the left had in mind in 1968 for the next forty years: six years of Richard Nixon as president; two years of Gerald Ford as president; eight years of Ronald Reagan as president; one term as president for George H. W. Bush; and two terms, eight years, for his son, George W. Bush?

When Lyndon Johnson battered Barry Goldwater in the 1964 presidential election, it appeared that the wounds inflicted on the Republican Party by the conservative takeover would require several election cycles to heal. But as a consequence of a combination of events—Vietnam, the growing militancy of the civil rights movement, the rise of feminism, and the beginning of the counterculture—the Democratic Party suddenly found itself divided in such spectacular fashion that just four years later the Republicans were able to recapture the White House. The GOP, led by Richard Nixon, even annexed the once solidly Democratic South and the working-class Democrats who were outraged by the long-haired, flag-burning, free love advocates who seemed to be hijacking their party.

The Republicans thus were the beneficiaries of what historian Alan Brinkley called a "counterrevolution." It was a revolt against the cultural revolution that was playing out nightly on the news—a revolt against the so-called counterculture itself. In 1964, Johnson scored the biggest landslide in American history; Pat Brown, the Democrat who beat Nixon for the job, was governor of California; and the South was solidly Democratic. In 1968, Richard Nixon was elected president; Ronald Reagan was governor; and the South was, in effect, filing for re-registration in the GOP.

President Bill Clinton and Speaker Newt Gingrich

Watching all of this from opposite ends of the political spectrum were two political prodigies in and of the American South. By the end of the twentieth century, these two men, William Jefferson Clinton of Arkansas and Newton Leroy Gingrich of Georgia, would be protagonists in a fierce and sometimes sensational struggle for control of the political soul of the country.

For the baby boomers, it would almost come to seem as if Clinton and Gingrich were the captains of two different political teams, one determined to extend the social activism and cultural changes of the Sixties, the other with a game plan to check those changes or even roll them back. Clinton's colorful mother, Virginia, had three husbands and a taste for racetracks. At one point, young Billy had to confront an alcoholic and abusive stepdad to stop him beating his mother. Newt, whose stern stepfather was a career military man, was whip-smart, always chatty and very ambitious.

Gingrich became interested in Republican Party politics early on, and after getting a Ph.D. at Tulane University, he began teaching at a small Georgia college while planning to run for the U.S. Congress. He failed in his first two runs as a Rockefeller Republican and then took a hard turn to the right and won the election. He also divorced his first wife, who was seven years his senior; they had met when she was his high school teacher.

When they were both in power in Washington, with Clinton as president and Gingrich as speaker of the House of Representatives, I used to say, not entirely facetiously, "I think they were separated at birth. Two bright, prematurely gray, gabby Southern boys from dysfunctional families, they both avoided military service, discovered politics at an early age, became powerful and influential and got into trouble over women and ethics." Clinton and Gingrich may often disagree, but they're seldom in doubt, and as they were contesting for America's political soul in the closing days of the twentieth century, so are they still at it in the opening decade of the twenty-first.

Although their differences have been on display for many years now, often at a high decibel level, they have a grudging respect for each other's political instincts.

William Jefferson Clinton, born in the summer of 1946, was the first baby boomer to be elected president. Covering his 1992 campaign against the incumbent president, George H. W. Bush—who had been an international hero just a year earlier with his success against Saddam Hussein in Operation Desert Storm—was like watching a dazzling new high-wire aerialist in the circus. Clinton had all the moves—and he needed them, to deal with claims of infidelity, rumors of financial scandals, charges about avoiding the draft, and questions about his lack of foreign policy experience.

He also had unsolicited help from Ross Perot, an energetic billionaire with a colorful backstory and the ability to turn a phrase. He ran as a third-party candidate, participated in the televised presidential debates alongside Bush and Clinton, and ended up garnering an astonishing 19 percent of the vote. Perot's drain on Bush's conservative base was critical to Clinton's 6 percent margin of victory.

Clinton's campaign, masterminded by political strategist James Carville, the "Ragin' Cajun," took the fight directly to the incumbent over his failure to deal with a short, sharp recession that hit just before the election. In a war room that the Clinton campaign established to map the daily offensive, the mantras were "It's the economy, stupid" and "Speed kills," referring respectively to the importance of not being deflected away from the economy to more "interesting" issues and to the campaign's determination to respond to every attack on Clinton quickly and offensively (a lesson that a recent Democratic presidential candidate clearly hadn't learned well enough).

The campaign had a Sixties feel, with a charismatic, saxophone-playing Rhodes scholar out in front of an organization headed by men and women in their

thirties and forties who had been through the wilderness years of presidents Reagan and Bush 41. Led by
Clinton, they were determined to move the Democratic Party back from the romantic left to the practical
center.

Clinton teetered on the high wire a couple of
times, but as the campaign moved along, he found his
balance, especially in the televised debates and through
his pledges to bring fresh talent to a White House that
had been in the hands of older preboomer Republicans
for twelve straight years. His impressive mastery of the
issues and the ease with which he appeared on the campaign trail and on television were reassuring to those
who worried he might be too young and too inexperienced. He was teamed with another baby boomer, the
earnest and savvy Al Gore of Tennessee, an energetic
campaigner who had served in Vietnam and voted for
Desert Storm when many other Democrats had not.

When the Clinton-Gore ticket won, the first of
their generation to occupy the top offices in America,
no one knew quite what to expect. **USA Today**
summed up the prospects this way:

When the 46-year-old Clinton takes the oath
today, he ushers into the Oval Office a huge,
influential caste of his peers: baby boomers,
those 77 million men and women born from
1946 through 1964.

"It's deeply troubling to a lot of the older
baby boomers, that they're finally older than
a president," jokes political analyst Charles
Cook. . . .

Still, the inauguration of Clinton and Vice President Al Gore, 44, has loosed a sort of youthful exuberance in the electorate. For baby boomers, it's the exciting—and sobering—experience of seeing one of their own assume the nation's highest office.

The Clinton and Gore families traveled to their inauguration in Washington on a bus from the new president's home in Little Rock. I joined the final leg of their journey at Thomas Jefferson's home Monticello in Charlottesville, Virginia, to interview them. I listened while Gore briefed Clinton on the deteriorating situation in Bosnia, where a badly fractured country was in a murderous rage. Could the United States stand by and allow genocide? Gore talked about American-led air strikes, but Clinton was noncommittal. The rest of the conversation was mostly about the upcoming inaugural events.

Then the new president and Hillary moved to the back of the bus for some private time. I could see them holding hands and laughing, and I could only imagine what they must have been thinking just hours before they were to become the most powerful couple in the world, two masters of the political realm, bright and ambitious, children of the Sixties now charged with running America during the last decade of the twentieth century.

I got off the bus in Washington a bit shaken by the realization that the four of them were all younger than I and that while they were understandably eager for their new roles, they seemed not quite ready.

When they moved into the White House, they brought with them many of their Sixties instincts—a big public spending bill and a complicated energy tax—but Clinton was determined to move his party more to the center, the "Third Way," as it came to be known, a strategy also later adopted by the British prime minister, Tony Blair.

After initial resistance within his ranks, President Clinton decided to adopt the more pragmatic economic policies of Robert Rubin, his economic adviser and, after 1995, his highly regarded secretary of the Treasury.

With important help from Gore, Clinton also pushed through the North American Free Trade Agreement (NAFTA), despite strong opposition from his party's labor allies. He persuaded Congress to pass the Brady Act and the assault weapons ban, the first major gun control laws passed by Congress since it had banned the importation of small, cheap handguns ("Saturday night specials") following the assassinations of Dr. King and Robert Kennedy.

Helped by the astonishing expansion of the information age—personal computers, cell phones, the Internet—the economy boomed, which made it much easier for Clinton to balance the federal budget, something neither of his Republican predecessors had been able to do.

In other areas, the youthful administration struggled. Clinton promised a cabinet that "looked like America"—a Sixties echo effect—but initially had trouble finding a woman to fill the post of attorney general. His pledge to end discrimination against gays in the military ended with the "Don't ask, don't tell" policy, a compromise that infuriated many of his liberal supporters.

Hillary's attempt to overhaul America's health care policy got off to a controversial start when she assembled a task force of advisers and did almost all of the planning behind closed doors, refusing to spend much time with the traditional health care community, including the American Medical Association and corporate experts on employee health plans.

The result was a massive plan, more than a thousand pages long, outlining a complicated, sweeping reorganization that instantly became the target of a well-financed conservative media campaign. One TV ad featured a mythical couple puzzling over the proposal and worrying that their health care would get worse, not better. The late Senator Daniel Patrick Moynihan, who later endorsed her as his Senate successor, said, "Anyone who thinks the [Clinton health care plan] as presently written can work in the real world . . . isn't living in it."

The Hillary plan died aborning.

Through those first two Clinton White House years, Gingrich was on C-Span regularly, attacking the president and First Lady as elite holdovers from the Sixties who didn't understand or care about middle-class values such as lower taxes, school prayer, and welfare reform. They were, he said, "counterculture McGoverniks."

For his part, Clinton played the wide-open game, relying on his exceptional oratorical skills, finely tuned political instincts, and a bottomless appetite for the contest morning, noon, and night. He just loved politics, and it showed in every large and small occasion. He entered every room determined to win every occupant to his side, and he was reluctant to leave until he had done so. He was the Elvis of the new generation, a rock-and-roll politician with all the new moves.

Gingrich coached that the best defense was a good offense, and he had a minutely detailed playbook that included words for Republicans to use to describe Sixties-era Democrats. The words "liberal" and "failure" were seldom separated in the Gingrich patois. At the beginning, he also had the advantage of a disciplined group of followers who took orders and carried them out.

Barack Obama, who has been described as a postgenerational candidate, delivered a stinging critique of the Sixties in an interview with **New York** magazine in 2006: "To some degree . . . we have seen the psychodrama of the baby boom generation play out over the last forty years. When you watch Clinton versus Gingrich, or Gore versus Bush, or Kerry versus Bush, you feel like these are fights that were taking place back in dorm rooms in the Sixties.

"Vietnam, civil rights, the sexual revolution, the role of government—all that stuff has just been playing itself out, and I think people sort of feel like, 'Okay, let's not relitigate the Sixties forty years later.'"

When I asked President Clinton about Senator Obama's observation, he smiled tightly, waved his hand, and, mindful of his wife's presidential campaign, said, "Oh, that's just a cheap political shot." Clinton leaned forward and said that as president, he had had to engage Gingrich to defend what he, Clinton, was trying to do. As a student of politics since he was in junior high, Clinton credits Gingrich for his masterstroke marketing idea of a "Contract with America."

For the 1994 midterm elections, Gingrich produced a printed handbook that he held up at every opportunity and that he called a "contract," a user-friendly political document that synthesized the conservative message into a Republican Party manifesto and led a band of conservative ideologues to a stunning takeover of the U.S. House of Representatives. Gingrich became the Speaker, third in line for the presidency.

Congressional Republicans failed to enact much of the Contract with America, and Speaker Gingrich overplayed his hand when he shut down the government because the president wouldn't make a budget deal on Gingrich's terms. The Speaker gave the president a big opening by saying he had acted in part because he felt snubbed by Clinton on an Air Force One flight to the funeral of the martyred Israeli leader Yitzhak Rabin when he was made to disembark, along with other congressional guests, from the plane's rear ramp. The White House neatly trumped the charge by releasing photos of the president socializing with the Speaker and other VIPs on the flight.

Clinton, however, had his own, more damaging experience with the government shutdown. That was when a young intern from California, Monica Lewinsky, delivered a pizza to the President's office. Their subsequent relationship would set the stage for the next showdown between the two protagonists.

Gingrich led the House drive to impeach Clinton

for lying under oath during the special prosecutor's investigation, but Clinton's team held off conviction in the Senate trial. Gingrich's claim to a higher standard of behavior collapsed when he was fined three hundred thousand dollars by the House for ethics violations and it was disclosed that he was having an affair with a House staff member. He was able to hold off a coup attempt by young House Republicans, but he resigned from Congress after the 1998 elections.

Clinton left office in 2000 with an approval rating of over 60 percent. Defying his Sixties stereotype, he had signed into law the most significant welfare reform bill in forty years and added federal money for police on the streets. But he marred his departure with a number of controversial presidential pardons, including one for Marc Rich, a fugitive American financier who had fled the country rather than face criminal tax evasion charges involving allegations that he had cheated the U.S. government out of millions in tax revenues.

Clinton and Gingrich, two aging former boy wonders, have carried their different impressions of the Sixties and their different visions of America's future into the twenty-first century. Clinton has become an authority on new approaches to third-world poverty and global warming. Gingrich is determined to change the approach to health care in America and to promote the use of the new information technology for medical record keeping and online health advice, including wellness programs—and, in effect, comparative shopping for physicians and treatments.

Clinton is eager to talk about the Sixties when we meet for an interview in a mid-Manhattan law office where he is scheduled to raise money for his wife's presidential campaign. He has the appearance and carriage of a senior statesman, with tailored suits, an imposing helmet of carefully coiffed silver hair, and a physique now kept trim after the reality check of a heart bypass operation.

In such settings, Clinton and Gingrich are alike in another way: They're always armed with their talking points, and they're always ready to engage and be engaged.

I ask how the beliefs he formed in the Sixties were affected by his eight years in the Oval Office. How many of those beliefs were still intact when he left the White House?

He answers after a short pause. "All of them were still there." He cites the beneficial effects of the civil rights movement, even though his party had paid a penalty in votes in the South; the rise in equality for women; the beneficial effect of President Johnson's war on poverty; and the opportunity for personal discovery that the Sixties had encouraged.

Clinton acknowledges that his party had initially failed to appreciate the pressures on the middle class that came out of the Sixties. These were the working-class families of the Fifties that finally had a little financial security and wanted to hang on to it. In the Sixties, he says, "We assumed the strength of the economy for the middle class was permanent, and we wanted to do something about the poor. But in the Seventies, the middle-class squeeze set in, and you began to have this division in the country, the alienation against affirmative action and all that."

Vietnam, which he says began with noble objectives, was enormously consequential on two fronts. The burden on the economy of trying to have both guns and butter settled heavily on the middle class. As for national security, "it broke up the consensus Democrats owned . . . the kind of liberal interventions that had been popular since the end of World War II, with the Marshall Plan, NATO, the UN, and all that.

"Vietnam was a conflict seen through a Cold War lens, and it didn't play out that way." In other words, as a result, Clinton says, in his party, "it remains in the back of our collective consciousness and makes us a little warier than we might otherwise be about the use of force and a little warier than we might otherwise be about being attacked as weak."

When Clinton first took office, the military establishment was wary of him. He'd dodged the draft, and national security had not been a priority in his campaign. As commander in chief, he had an awkward saluting style getting on and off Marine One, the presidential helicopter.

He inherited from his predecessor a substantial U.S. military presence in Somalia, the beleaguered East African nation. His plans for what to do next were ill formed until one of the warring militias managed to bring down a Black Hawk helicopter and dragged the dead bodies of the crew through the streets of Mogadishu. It was a signal to the world that the American superpower could be humiliated by ragtag insurgents in third-world capitals. Within less than a week, Clinton withdrew American forces from the country.

As president, Clinton authorized force to stop the

ethnic cleansing in Bosnia and Kosovo. His friend and later UN ambassador Richard Holbrooke—a tough-minded diplomat and foreign-service veteran of Vietnam—hammered together the Dayton Peace Accords, which brought peace to a place where genocide had become routine.

But Clinton did not intervene in Africa—in Uganda, the Congo, or especially Rwanda—where millions died in tribal genocides. What would have been the reaction of the student activists in the Sixties to such horrors? After he left office, Clinton talked with David Remnick, editor of **The New Yorker,** about Rwanda. "Whatever happened, I have to take responsibility for it," he said. "We never even had a staff meeting on it. But I don't blame anybody that works for me. That was my fault. I should have been alert and alive to it. And that's why I went there and apologized in '98. We just blew it."

Given his experience in office, as Democrats view the war in Iraq as a latter-day Vietnam, Clinton warns that they should not be "Pavlovian" in rejecting the use of military force. As much as he disagrees with the policies that followed the initial decision to launch the war in Iraq, he says, "Our party ought to acknowledge that our kids have done a good enough job in Iraq that the carnage is less than it would have been [if civil war had broken out under Saddam's rule]." He uses the civil war in Bosnia, with its staggering death toll and refugee crisis, as an example of how much worse it could be in Iraq.

Clinton, who supported the Bush administration's decision to go to war in Iraq and then criticized its execution, worries that the Democrats will be inclined post-Iraq to become isolationist or to say, in effect, that we don't need a military.

He believes the vast majority of the American people understand the need to stay tough on the issue of terrorism by combining military might with other means, such as international cooperation on intelligence and money tracking. Clinton points out that even countries criticizing U.S. policies in Iraq are working with America in other ways to deal with international terrorism, and that the Democrats should encourage more of that.

He personally welcomes the heightened public interest in national security issues, saying, "I think this may be the first election in my lifetime in which there are votes on the question of what the rest of the world thinks of us. I hope America will demand and really get a **sophisticated** discussion on what kind of military we need in the twenty-first century.

"In 1960 Kennedy and Nixon got into a macho fight over those islands in Asia—Quemoy and Matsu— but it was a fairly infantile discussion. Now we have a chance to talk about what we learned in Iraq and Afghanistan, what we should and shouldn't do, when to intervene and when not to. And that's a victory for what we were talking about in the Sixties."

On domestic matters, Clinton has heard the arguments from the left in his party that he sold out core principles for political gain. When he changed the rules for welfare, making work a requirement for eligibility, he thought the reaction on his left was "emotional . . . on the part of people in the Congress and in various liberal groups who thought the way to victory . . . was to reclaim the rhetorical legitimacy of traditional liberalism.

"When I said work was the best social program, that sounded like conservative rhetoric to them. But Franklin Roosevelt, John Kennedy, Lyndon Johnson, and Jimmy Carter had said the same thing. The fact is, we moved one hundred times as many people out of poverty during my terms than in the previous twelve years.

"Interestingly, I think grassroots Democrats agreed with me, but I think a lot of the intelligentsia of the party still talk as if I sold out by moving to the center on welfare reform."

Clinton considers the debate within the party on economic expansion and job creation a more worthy discussion. "Once the Republicans took the Congress in '94, we had to ask, 'Is it better for America to expand trade relations?' and run the risk of alienating the labor base. I thought the answer was yes, and by my second term, we had rising wages for the first time since '73.

"So that economic debate was worthy and legitimate, but when I talked about expanding the middle class, that sounded like conservative rhetoric to many on the left."

The former president regularly attacks the Republicans for what he sees as a stacking of the deck in favor of the wealthy, a class he admits he's now a part of as a result of lucrative speaking, consulting, and author fees. For the Republicans to get away from the "party of the rich" reputation, Clinton believes they'll emphasize solutions, not ideology, in 2008.

"Americans want to get back to goal setting and solutions," he says, "so they [Republicans] will say, 'If you don't like our fact-free concentration of wealth and power, we're back into finding solutions.' They'll tell voters, 'You want someone tough enough and realistic enough to do it, someone who understands the world is not perfectible.'" In other words, he expects the GOP to reactivate the message that has worked so well for so long: "Liberals are starry-eyed. They can't get things done. We can." Going on in his version of the Republican line, Clinton imagines them saying, "Now, those Democrats are good-hearted, but they're misguided. They'll always go a step too far." Clinton also believes the GOP will attempt to put the Democrats back in a cultural box, attacking language in films and song lyrics, the idea that Democrats are out of sync with real American family values.

He cites a Southern Republican official who, in early 2007, was sizing up the prospects for his party. According to Clinton, the Republican official said the GOP's problem was not with its field of candidates. It was that "we don't have our enemies yet. We need an enemy to win."

The Sixties Democrats became that enemy in the South with their ambivalence about military action twinned with their antigun, prochoice, affirmative action positions. Clinton thinks that created a schism in the two parties in the Sixties, one that was much more the result of culture and psychology than it was of economics, and that erasing that dividing line remains a major challenge for his party.

To that end, Clinton thinks the Democrats have been unfairly stuck with a hippie image. "I think it's important not to read the whole generation in terms of what its most famous, outspoken, or highly publicized members thought." Without a trace of irony, the man who has been mocked for saying he didn't inhale observes, "The Sixties gave us the illusion of free love and a lot of drug abuse, but I was mostly on the sidelines for that, and I thought a lot of it was self-indulgent."

For Clinton's critics on the right, his own behavior with Monica Lewinsky in the White House and his lying under oath during the investigation will always be emblematic of what they see as the situational ethics that emerged during the Sixties.

On the weekend he testified before Special Prosecutor Ken Starr and confessed to Hillary and the nation that he had lied about the relationship, I was with California friends who were adamant that he was being persecuted for excusable indiscretions. "It was just sex," they argued. "Who cares?"

I countered that a lot of people cared and that Clinton should acknowledge that and apologize. Yes, I agreed that Ken Starr was guilty of what I thought was sexual McCarthyism, a witch hunt similar to the Communist scares of the Fifties, but the nature of the Clinton–Lewinsky relationship and the length of it personally offended Americans who otherwise supported the president's policies.

My friends thought the greater blame lay with the media for making such a circus out of the case. The evening ended with too much wine and too little resolution.

Newt Gingrich, Clinton believes, was a master at exploiting those images and, as he puts it, "the Republicans made a living off the excesses of the Sixties until the elections of 2006." Clinton is persuaded that every development of the Sixties—political activism, sweeping social change, and the creation of a more diverse society—had positive aspects. At the same time, he is aware that they had what he calls "the seeds of their own destruction" because they became targets for cultural conservatives.

When I remind Clinton that many denizens of the student-hippie culture of the Sixties—who were so disdainful of material goods and the free market—are now among the wealthiest people in the world, worrying about their second homes, private schools, and private jets, he says he is not surprised by the accumulation of wealth. "It was always an energetic generation," he says, "the best educated in history. Some thought we were lazy because of a relatively small number of highly self-indulgent figures, but this was never credible."

For Clinton, the real test of his generation will be how it responds now to its wealth. "I don't think," he says, "we've done that in an appropriate way yet." Clinton, who moves easily in the jet stream of his wealthy friends, has established the William J. Clinton Foundation, dedicated to the relief of poverty and disease in third-world countries, especially Africa. His annual Clinton Global Initiative seminars in New York are a combination of town hall and evangelistic tent meetings as he brings together everyone from Rupert Murdoch to old lefties to address issues of poverty, climate change, health issues, nutrition, and third-world development.

He isn't satisfied that his generation is spending enough of its money on good causes yet, but he believes the progress is encouraging. In September 2007 he published a book on philanthropy called **Giving: How Each of Us Can Change the World**. He says, "When it comes to our money, we like to keep score. That grows out of the Sixties. We want to make an impact. The number of foundations in America doubled in the last decade of the twentieth century. But we need to do more."

As a coda to our conversation, he says, "You know, the rhetoric of my administration was remarkably free of the Sixties. I was trying to move us beyond that." Then he smiles and shakes his head, half in admiration, half in frustration, and says, "Newt built a movement out of a **caricature** of the Sixties."

Newt Gingrich, however, does not see what he has to say about the Sixties as a "caricature," and he is not about to abandon his familiar criticisms of the Sixties for the foreseeable future. He does recognize, however, that the sad state of his own party in the third presidential election cycle of the twenty-first century is not helpful to his continuing crusade against the Sixties residue.

For inspiration about today, Gingrich looked to the spring 2007 election in France, in which Nicolas Sarkozy, a law-and-order conservative, won by running against the lingering Sixties attitudes in his country's

Bill Clinton with his Oxford
roommates, Strobe Talbott (left)
and Frank Aller, in the late Sixties

Newt Gingrich (second row,
wearing glasses) in his high-
school yearbook photo with
the Beta Kappa Hi-Y boys

Newt Gingrich
today

politics. Sarkozy's significant victory against an experienced and attractive Socialist candidate was built around older French voters receptive to his message that it was time to return to traditional French morals and values, that it was time for the French to go back to work.

Moreover, Gingrich, as if he'd been listening to Clinton predict a solutions-based campaign in 2008, tells me, "My party—the right—is tactically much worse off than the left because we have a president who fundamentally doesn't know what's going on. That's a huge problem."

This is the same Newt Gingrich who was effusive in his praise of President Bush when he appeared on the deck the USS **Abraham Lincoln** on May 1, 2003, in a flight suit with a large banner behind him that read MISSION ACCOMPLISHED. Baghdad had just fallen to U.S. forces, and the nightmares to come in Iraq were not yet on anyone's screen.

Commenting on the president's aircraft carrier speech, Gingrich said at the time, "He has grown into a leader who is becoming one of the great articulators of freedom, justice . . . and safety in a way that that really rivals President Reagan, President Roosevelt, President Wilson, President Lincoln."

Four years later Gingrich believes government is broken, citing in interview after interview the calamity of Hurricane Katrina, the failure of the administration to fix immigration, and the absence of a health care plan. He thinks the problem for his party is understanding fundamental change. Then, in a remarkable condemnation of his Republican brothers and sisters, the former professor tells me, "Most of our problems require applied intelligence, and we have a party that doesn't believe in books and applied thought.

"The ideology of the Democrats blocks them from making the changes, even though they understand the need. In my party, they can do it, but they don't understand the need to make the necessary changes."

So, typically, Gingrich is on a personal crusade to advance the ideals that brought him to such prominence in the first place. He has a website called Newt.org—Winning the Future, a veritable L. L. Bean catalog of Newt-think on presidential politics, national security, health care, immigration, the economy, and the environment. One day when I looked at the website, it read in one corner: "Video—Border security World War II–style." Just below that, "Buy Newt's NEW book, **Pearl Harbor,** today!" Off to the side, a schedule of his upcoming speaking engagements. Below, his newspaper and radio commentaries, ready to be printed. The text of his commencement address at the College of William & Mary. Papers on markets versus government; building a new congressional majority. One-stop shopping at Newt's convenient corner shop on the Internet.

A centerpiece of his personal crusade is health care. He founded the Center for Health Transformation, a think tank in Washington, D.C., and his theories are often the subject of his speeches. Simply put, he wants more personal, family, and community responsibility in a healthier lifestyle that will, he says, save enough money to finance health insurance for all. He also wants uniform pricing procedures for Medicare and other government health services from state to state.

Gingrich preaches that the current health care system must be totally overhauled to deal with the advances in medical science that are coming at warp speed. Like his nemesis Bill Clinton, Gingrich is never short of an impressive set of statistics. He says that four to seven times as much medical scientific knowledge will be gained in the next twenty-five years as was gained in the last twenty-five.

These are the issues he believes his party should be discussing if they want to win. The Democrats, he is persuaded, will still be dealing with what he calls "the collective weight of the Sixties." He sees it pulling Hillary to the left, "when she knows better, into isolationism."

Gingrich was in high school in the Sixties when the civil rights movement was roiling all around him, and it made a lasting impression on him. "The general effect was all positive, but it left too much of that community without real economic opportunity—and when I hear Julian Bond and the others now, they're still trapped in the glorious memories instead of doing something about the current problems."

In his various appearances, Gingrich is increasingly agnostic about party labels. During our talk, his sharpest comments were reserved for Republicans. He thinks they've fallen prey to one of the outgrowths of the Sixties, that what was necessary in politics was to master a technique: a get-out-the-vote drive, a fund-raising scheme, a use of power simply for the sake of power.

As an example, he cites congressional redistricting,

a passion of one of Gingrich's most ruthless acolytes, the disgraced former Texas congressman Tom DeLay. As a result of redistricting, Gingrich says, "We've made incumbents too powerful. They don't have to work hard anymore."

This is the same Newt Gingrich who told a group of College Young Republicans in 1978 that they must seize the party from their elders, who had failed them. Gingrich said, "You're fighting a war. It is a war for power." When Gingrich got that power, he elevated the likes of Tom DeLay, who were all about preserving their power.

He has not lost hope, however. "America remains," he says, "a remarkably hardworking and religious country. It does not embrace hard-left values. We have an astonishing ability to change when we want to. Look at the advances in technology. That didn't come out of a commune or from students occupying a dean's office."

Returning to the theme of solutions, Gingrich praises New York City mayor Michael Bloomberg, a former Democrat turned Republican turned independent. Bloomberg, a billionaire businessman, low-key and utterly results-oriented, is "implausible and successful because he delivers."

As we have seen, when Gingrich was successfully conducting his revolution in the early Nineties for the Republican takeover of the House of Representatives, he handed out to his colleagues a list of words to use to describe Democrats: decay, failure, collapse, defeat, crisis, destructive, endanger, coercion, antifamily, antiflag. He cleverly invoked that glossary of despair to promote the Republicans as the party of hope.

Now he says of the Republicans in Washington, "Our party is so exhausted trying to run the old order, it can't come up with a new order."

As a result, he believes that Hillary Clinton, a woman he once called derisively a "McGovernik," will be nominated and could be elected president in 2008.

Senator George McGovern and Senator Gary Hart

George McGovern, after all these years, remains an enthusiastic and, when given the chance, outspoken student on the state of national politics. He carried only Massachusetts and the District of Columbia when he lost the presidential election to Richard Nixon in 1972. Two years later, Nixon was forced to resign in disgrace and McGovern's lopsided loss didn't seem so ignominious. McGovern at least still had his honor.

In 1972, McGovern, a prairie populist from South Dakota with a Ph.D. in history, positioned himself as the heir to the legacy of his friend the late Robert F. Kennedy. But McGovern had none of Bobby's star-power charisma, combativeness, and instinct for counterpunching. McGovern did inherit some of RFK's organization, but he was plainly not a prince in Camelot.

McGovern's opposition to the war in Vietnam was the central theme of his campaign, and as a result, his candidacy attracted the most strident of the anti-war protestors, many of them with their own agend

George McGovern
with President Kennedy
in the Oval Office
in 1961

Senator McGovern
with his family in
front of their home
in Chevy Chase,
Maryland, in 1958

Bill Clinton and George McGovern at the
dedication of the George and Eleanor McGovern
Library and Center for Leadership and Public
Service in October 2006

Conservatives quickly tagged McGovern as soft on national security issues and Communism. His campaign, perhaps as an overreaction to the antimilitary leanings of his anti–Vietnam War constituency, even failed to honor his heroic service in World War II, where he won a Distinguished Flying Cross as a B-24 pilot in Europe.

Robert Novak, the conservative columnist, labeled the McGovern campaign "acid, amnesty and abortion" for its perceived tolerance of the drug culture, its antiwar stance, and its support for the right to choose—an issue that was just beginning to emerge as an important matter to many American women. In his 2007 book, **The Prince of Darkness,** Novak said he first heard that phrase from Missouri senator Tom Eagleton, who was afraid McGovern was too liberal for the general election.

Eagleton was subsequently chosen as McGovern's running mate and then was forced to withdraw because he'd failed to disclose he'd undergone shock treatments for depression.

The McGovern campaign was disorganized from the beginning. The 1972 convention in Miami Beach was a raucous series of clashes between the old Democratic Party and the new delegates, who had been chosen with an emphasis on their ethnic and gender diversity. McGovern had successful business executives and prominent Democratic office holders as his delegates, but overall the convention had a hippie, antiestablishment tone.

McGovern, now in his mideighties, stays active in the political dialogue of the day, appearing on cable news shows, writing an occasional column or small book on issues that interest him, and lecturing at the new McGovern Library on the campus of his alma mater, Dakota Wesleyan University in Mitchell, South Dakota.

When Senator McGovern and I talked in 2007 about his 1972 presidential campaign and the legacy of the Sixties on American life, he was true to his beliefs and also honest about his own shortcomings as a match for the Nixon juggernaut.

When I ask about the atmospherics of the McGovern-for-president campaign, the hippie qualities that provided such a stark contrast to the blue suits and serious shoes of the Nixon crowd, McGovern says: "We should have been more sensitive to the effect of the new lifestyle—the long hair, the introduction of pot, the beads—on the working class. I was worried about it at the time, but I should have addressed it more directly." McGovern adds, "Bill Clinton did that twenty years later, but I think he probably went too far in his concessions to the so-called right."

About the lasting effects of the Sixties, McGovern says he thinks the Sixties rebellion against the established order was helpful, since it forced his own generation, the World War II generation, to take another look at the status quo. And so, he says, "I more or less went along with it politically, if not culturally."

Going forward, he says, "we've got to speak strongly and clearly on moral values, on the family and the founding ideals of this country."

McGovern does worry about the Democrats trying too hard to address the so-called strength question:

Do they have what it takes to be strong in a dangerous world? Does strength mean throwing your Army into the middle of the Arabian Desert, or into the Southeast Asian jungles back in the Sixties and Seventies? That's actually a sign of weakness.

"Strength," he goes on, "is a good health care program for our people; a good job for everyone who wants to work; confidence in our government and in our leadership. I'd like to see the Democrats talk more about that kind of strength."

He worries that there's a blurring between the two parties at a time when the American people want clear choices. "I think they're looking for more fundamental change in the direction of the country. If I were running," he says, "I would come out with a comprehensive health care plan for every American, a single-payer plan that would be an extension of Medicare." In a small shot at Hillary Clinton, he adds, "I wouldn't come up with a fancy two- or three-thousand-page plan; I'd just extend Medicare to all Americans in stages from birth on.

"That," he says, "is the kind of bold idea the country wants to hear now. Why should you and I get our medical bills paid because we're sixty-five, when our kids and grandchildren have more immediate needs?"

McGovern has no illusions about some enduring divisions in the country. "I think," he says, that many Americans believe "that those who agree with us [around the world] are right and those who disagree are wrong. Republicans tap into that force better than Democrats do. They say it with more bite than we do. They have more of an emotional commitment to anyone we see as a potential threat—Communists, terrorists."

Of the Democratic Party, he says, "I think we've lost our nerve. I guess because we got knocked off so many times in advocating progressive, forward-looking programs, we think, 'Let's make peace with the middle of the road.' There's nothing wrong with the middle of the road, but everyone who stands there gets hit; who is going to move us ahead?"

McGovern concludes by telling me, "My time has come and gone, but if I were a little younger I'd be out there running again on these big issues."

Gary Hart, McGovern's 1972 campaign manager, now a former U.S. senator, shares many of McGovern's analyses of their party in the Sixties and its faults today, and he's even more critical of the McGovern campaign they ran together in 1972.

In 1968, Gary Hart was a young lawyer with a wife and two small children in Denver when he got involved with Bobby Kennedy's presidential campaign in Colorado. He joined the effort to reform the party's delegate selection after witnessing the debacle of the Chicago convention, where most delegates were selected and controlled by party bosses. The Kennedy and McCarthy supporters charged that the party bosses had "stolen" the nomination for Hubert H. Humphrey. "I tried to stir up interest in changing the rules for 1972," Hart says. "It was clear that the deck was stacked and the rules were rigged . . . even though Kennedy won primaries in '68, the delegations from those states were committed to Humphrey."

After the 1968 convention, the McGovern-Fraser

Gary Hart (center) shortly after his 1974
election to the U.S. Senate, leaving for
Washington, D.C., with his wife, Lee

Commission reformed the party's rules so that the majority of delegates were elected through direct primaries, and it was mandated that each state's delegation contain a certain proportion of women and minorities.

Although Hart wasn't formally part of the McGovern-Fraser Commission, he defends its members against critics who claim that the imposition of de facto "quotas" destroyed the party by fracturing it into too many constituencies. "If we had not made those changes," he says, "1972 would have been worse than 1968. The party would have blown apart."

If there had not been some changes in the delegate selection process there would have been trouble, but no good deed goes unpunished. The inclusion of more ethnic minorities, more activist women, and more young people immediately made the party more liberal, and that brought its own set of consequences in the general election.

Hart's early writings on the need for reforms prompted McGovern to invite Hart to help on his presidential campaign. McGovern and Hart shared a political philosophy and common roots in heartland Christianity. McGovern's father was a Methodist minister, and McGovern brought to politics a certain ministerial style. Hart's parents were members of the Church of the Nazarene, a conservative offshoot of the Methodists that forbade social activities such as dancing and attending movies.

When it came to running a national presidential campaign against incumbent Richard Nixon, the McGovern-Hart team needed much more than a shared faith. Hart has no illusions about the deficiencies of the campaign staff and organization.

"Those of us in our thirties," he says, "weren't economists or defense experts. We were totally weak on substance. We could organize a circus in the Sahara, but no one had any new economic ideas. The liberal wing of the Democratic Party had gone bankrupt by the early Seventies."

The New Deal begun by President Roosevelt in the Great Depression; the New Frontier of John F. Kennedy, Hart's first political hero; and the ambitious Great Society social agenda of Lyndon Johnson in the Sixties—all of that was gone. Hart believes it began to disappear with the assassination of JFK. "Suddenly, things turned ugly," he says. "All that hope about the 'best and brightest,' going to the moon, the call to service—everything seemed to go to hell. The world of 1968 was a much different place than it was eight years earlier, when he was elected."

There were other cultural and economic shifts as well. The middle- and working-class families were on their feet and looking for less rather than more government in their lives. Hart credits the Republicans, particularly their conservative wing, with exploiting this by never giving up the drive for a smaller government.

"They formed think tanks, published magazines, held seminars, exchanged ideas, and all the while, the New Deal was running out of steam," Hart declares. "And all of a sudden, there were Ronald Reagan and people wanting easier answers—cut taxes, face down the Soviets, be strong—and the people went for it."

Hart believed he could move the country back to

the left as a presidential candidate, first in 1984 and then as a front-runner among Democrats for the nomination in 1988. But he was spectacularly forced from the race when he was caught entertaining a young woman named Donna Rice in his home after assuring reporters that his days as a womanizer were over and, literally, daring them to prove they weren't.

Hart now lives in a suburb of Denver with his wife, Lee; they have been married for forty-four years. He practices law and writes on public issues, concentrating on national-security matters, an interest he first developed in the Senate when the Cold War was winding down. He co-chaired, with former New Hampshire senator Warren Rudman, the Commission on National Security/21st Century, which was charged with studying terrorist threats to the United States. Their report, calling for a cabinet-level agency to deal with the threat of terrorism, was issued in February 2001, just seven months before the attacks of 9/11. It was a blueprint of what was to come, but when it was released it received little public or press attention.

Hart remains an active student of Democratic Party politics, an outsider now, frustrated by the consequences of past failures. He says, "I think the Democrats still have not fully recovered from the losses in 1968 and 1972. The party hasn't come out of the wilderness, not nearly enough."

Hart recognizes the inherent problems of steering the Democrats in a new direction. "We're a coalition party. There's no coalescence, however. No dominant leader. But the Republicans all sing out of the same hymnbook."

He sees other problems for the Democrats in how they handle ethnic constituencies. "We always suffer from our successes," he says. "The more we do for people, the better off they are, they turn Republican. Take middle-class black Americans. They're now saying, 'Wait a minute. The Democratic Party is a bunch of overlords. They help us, but they want to dominate us. I want freedom. I've got income, and I am not marching to that tune anymore.'"

Hart has long believed his party spends too much time worrying about how to regain the South and too little time planning how to win the interior West. His home state of Colorado, as well as Nevada, Montana, Arizona, and Wyoming, are undergoing significant changes in their population profiles, economies, and cultures.

The longtime Colorado resident is persuaded that a Democratic presidential candidate can successfully campaign in those states by spending less time on social issues and more time on the concerns of western voters, such as the prudent use of natural resources, gun-control laws that reflect regional sensibilities, and immigration laws that recognize the burdens on local institutions.

As someone who got involved in national politics in protest against the policies of the Vietnam War, the former senator recognized early in his own public career the importance of his generation's developing a new national-security strategy.

"No one," he complains, "wants to take the time to study military history or learn from it." So in addition to his work on the bipartisan commission studying terrorism, Hart has continued his interest in the broader subject of twenty-first-century national security challenges and prospective approaches.

In **The Shield and the Cloak,** a book he wrote in England while a visiting fellow at Cambridge University, he lays out what he thinks is a new approach to the vexing problems of stateless warfare. He writes, "In many ways, America's security will depend on our ability to create hope among the hopeless." Global poverty, Hart believes, is the next great challenge for the national security of the industrialized world.

The former senator and youthful campaign organizer is now almost seventy years old, a tireless blogger and lecturer but a marginal player in the scrum of his party's presidential politics. Still, he retains his intellectual zest for the issues of the day, and he believes that national security is **the** issue.

"In large ways and small," he writes, "the issue of national sovereignty will dominate the international and domestic political debates in the coming decades. Do we ignore the problem? Do we seek to solve it ourselves? Or do we create institutions with others and give them sufficient authority to act?'"

Hart, who so admired John F. Kennedy's personal style and politics that he often mimicked, consciously or unconsciously, JFK's mannerisms, believes the Democrats of the twenty-first century should take a page from the New Frontier's "soft and hard" mix of foreign policy and national security.

Kennedy championed Western alliances and reorganized the U.S. military to deal more effectively with the growing threat of insurgencies. He created the Peace

Corps to offer developing nations a helping hand that wasn't carrying a military weapon. In a speech at the University of Washington in his first year in office, JFK said, "Diplomacy and defense are not substitutes for one another." Quoting Winston Churchill, he added, "How many wars have been averted by patience and persisting goodwill? How many wars have been precipitated by firebrands?"

That is the John F. Kennedy whom Hart so admires; but it was the same JFK who two years later said he believed if Vietnam fell to Communism it would create a domino effect through Southeast Asia.

Karl Rove and
Vice President Dick Cheney

When the historian Alan Brinkley described the Sixties as a counterrevolution rather than a revolution, he also could have been describing the reaction of two men who had grown up in the American West and were destined to play hugely important roles in promoting the so-called counterrevolution in the use of conservative political power at the turn of the century: Karl Rove and Dick Cheney. They are two of the most influential, powerful, and controversial figures in modern politics.

In 1968, Karl Rove was a high school junior in Salt Lake City and, by his own description, "a complete nerd." He even wore a plastic pen protector in his shirt pocket, carried a briefcase, and padded about in

Hush Puppies instead of the sandals that had already swept his generation. His classmates were almost all members of the Church of Jesus Christ of Latter-day Saints. "I was definitely uncool," he says.

But however "uncool" he may have been sartorially, Rove knew how to organize campaigns and get out the vote by the time he was seventeen. That's how he managed to get himself elected president of the Olympus High School student senate.

His favorite teacher was Eldon B. Tolman, a bow-tied civics instructor, liberal Democrat, and big supporter of Lyndon B. Johnson, then in the last throes of his presidency. Rove remembers Tolman saying, "You may get an A in the course only by the proper conclusion of the exams and the work—and only if you get involved in a political campaign."

For his part, Rove says he was interested in Nelson Rockefeller, the moderate Republican governor of New York, because he had been promoting at one point the idea of a volunteer army. When Richard Nixon defeated Rockefeller for the GOP nomination, Rove turned his loyalties to Nixon.

For a young political junkie, Eldon B. Tolman and Salt Lake City were a perfect mix in 1968. Tolman wanted his students to see the political process up close, and since Utah was then a swing state with a Democrat as governor, Salt Lake City became a major stop on the way to the nomination for the candidates of both parties.

Like a former high school basketball player recalling every shot in long-ago games, Rove excitedly describes Tolman taking the class to the Mormon Tabernacle to hear Richard Nixon, Nelson Rockefeller, Ronald Reagan, and Hubert Humphrey. It was in Salt Lake City that Humphrey belatedly jump-started his campaign by breaking with LBJ on the issue of a bombing halt.

Rove also remembers Robert F. Kennedy well and says, "I thought he was a remarkable and charismatic individual. Kennedy was one Democrat I could have been enthusiastic about in 1968. He talked about responsibility, about the devolution of power, of pushing things from the federal government back down to the states and individual."

But it was George Wallace, the demagogic governor of Alabama, running as an independent, who made the strongest impression on Rove. "I was fifty feet away from the stage when he spoke to the packed auditorium. It's the first time I felt real fear in a large body of people. Wallace encouraged hecklers and protestors. In his talk, he'd say, 'Lie down in front of my limousine, and it will be the last time you try that.'"

Rove remembers, "I thought he was a gifted demagogue; he was a calculated bully who was attempting to play off people's worst fears and prejudices. It was all a deliberate and calculated game."

After high school, Rove became a foot soldier in the GOP's drive to recapture the country, interning with the Utah Republican Party while attending the University of Utah and traveling to Illinois in a vain attempt to help Republican senator Ralph Tyler Smith hang on to his seat.

In June 1971, Rove began an odyssey that eventually led to an office in the White House, where his patron and client, George W. Bush, called him simply

"the Architect," for the way he constructed two winning presidential campaigns. He's also been called
"Bush's Brain," for his supposedly Svengali-like control
over the president. At least until the 2006 congressional elections, even his fiercest critics acknowledged
his mastery of the game.

In 1971 Rove became executive director of the
College Republicans, the incubator of future movers
and shakers in the GOP, a little-known but perfect position from which to build a national network of con-
tacts and sources. Members of the College Republicans
were hard-core conservatives, the antihippies who
found sanctuary in the GOP from the long-haired,
free-loving, flag-burning crowd.

In Richard Nixon's 1972 reelection campaign
Rove worked with Donald Segretti, the young California lawyer who was later convicted as a Watergate con-
spirator for his dirty tricks against the Democrats. The
following year Rove was accused of endorsing similar
techniques in campaigns. It arose as he was running in
a contentious campaign for national chairman of the
College Republicans. One of his principal allies was
the late Lee Atwater, the young Southerner who rose to
controversial fame as the architect of another Bush
campaign, the election of George H. W. Bush as the
forty-first president of the United States.

Rove won a contested election as college chairman with the help of the elder Bush, who was then
the GOP national chairman, a thankless job while the
Watergate scandal was unfolding. Rove and Atwater
were eager young acolytes in the Bush inner circle,
and when the candidate's son George W. came home

during a break in his studies at Harvard Business School, Rove was asked to pick him up at the airport. For Karl Rove and George W. Bush, it was political love at first sight.

Just five years after leaving Salt Lake City, the scrawny nerd from Olympus High was on a power trip that would eventually lead to 1600 Pennsylvania Avenue.

He was also on a trip through various institutions of higher learning. He dropped out of the University of Utah and enrolled part-time at the University of Maryland. He also attended George Mason University and the University of Texas, but he never managed to get a college degree.

But no one, friend or foe, underestimates Rove's intellect and grasp of American politics, especially the ultimate test: how to get elected. Through his direct-mail and campaign consulting firm, he's helped elect governors, congressmen, senators, state supreme court justices, and, of course, a president. Through it all, he's maintained a take-no-prisoners style to advance the deeply conservative beliefs he holds so dear.

When we met in his ground-floor office in the West Wing of the White House shortly after he'd lost the portfolio as the president's domestic policy adviser in a staff shakeup, he was, as he has always been in our meetings, cordial, professorial, and as eager to talk quail hunting as he was to talk politics.

In the 2004 election, we had bet a box of shotgun shells on voter turnout. I thought it would go over 110 million, and he thought it wouldn't. The fact that a larger turnout would mean more voters energized to vote against the president gave him, so to speak, a very real dog in that hunt. Roughly 122 million Americans went to the polls, and the president won a three-million-vote plurality. I won the bet but gave him a pass on paying off. I thought that Karl Rove sending me shotgun shells could just be too difficult to explain.

When I ask Rove if he thinks the Democrats have recovered from 1968, he answers emphatically, "No." He elaborates: "The Democratic Party split in the Sixties. The Harry Truman wing, robustly anti-Communist, using America's great power in pursuit of our goals in the world and recognizing that it was in our interest to expand the realm of freedom, was overwhelmed by the isolationist left.

"It's funny, you look back on 1968 and think everybody was against the war—and two of the candidates were not [Nixon and Alabama governor George Wallace]. And they got nearly sixty percent of the vote.

"The Sixties are a sign of what elite opinion can mean. There was an animus toward the military in the Sixties that was palpable, a moral revulsion among the elites toward the war. Yet when they got a candidate [George McGovern in 1972] who represented the essential nature of that, he won one state."

Rove thinks the culture of the left was as destructive to the Democrats as their position on the war. He says the classic FDR coalition of urban ethnics, white Southerners, labor, and the civil rights movement blew up over culture and issues; he cites the expansion of the welfare programs during the LBJ years as an example of how the Democrats lost their way. The working- and middle-class elements of the old FDR coalition were not enthusiastic about bank-rolling programs that looked to them as being light on individual responsibility and heavy on white guilt.

"Today," Rove says, "the great social experiment of our time is welfare reform." He goes on to describe in detail a meeting President Bush had in Charlotte, North Carolina, with welfare mothers who were grateful and proud to be in work-training programs and teaching their children about individual responsibility.

"You think back about the cultural dependency we were building in the Sixties," Rove says, "for good reason and with a good heart but in a wrongheaded way, with unintended consequences. We thought about the welfare class as a **class** that was dependent on us without thinking of them as human beings who could function on their own.

"Suddenly, these people were saying, 'Hey, wait a minute. I'm a human being, too. Give me a system that will support me for taking responsibility, not tie me to a life of dependency.'"

Warming to the subject, Rove continues his attack on the Sixties culture. "Then young people said either 'I'm gonna drop out' or 'I'm gonna get a gray flannel suit and go to work for a big company with a good pension at the end of my life.' Now, when I was teaching in the Nineties, everyone wanted to start their own business. And those who wanted to go to work at, say, Microsoft wanted to make big money so they could start their own business later."

Rove, like most conservatives, worries that the Sixties culture continues to flourish in the academic world among what he and others call "the elites." "The elites still share the same attitudes that were formed in the Six-ties . . . particularly in higher education or the media or in the popular culture. So, yeah, culture matters, and there was a weird culture that intruded during the Six-ties . . . and it was an aberration for the vast majority of the people in this country."

Rove rejects the idea that what many conservatives saw as the tyranny of the left in the academy and media in the Sixties has been replaced by the tyranny of the right in the twenty-first century on cable news, on talk radio, and in the blogosphere.

"Look," he says, "the range of choices of where you can get information means the idea of an overwhelm-ing, dominant culture, imposed on the people, is now gone . . . because we're now in a country so diverse in media streams."

But could there be a dominant opinion on some-thing that is a widely shared consensus? "Yes, I hope so, because we're about a consensus on some fundamental questions. There's a reason the Declaration of Indepen-dence has been sort of the essential charter of people's emotions. The American Dream, while it changes over time—nonetheless, there still is a consistency in the be-lief there is such a thing. You don't hear about a Pak-istani Dream or a French Dream or an Italian Dream, but the phrase 'the American Dream' conjures up some-thing concrete and real across the board."

My reference to Kevin Phillips's book **American Theocracy**, in which Phillips argues at length that the Republican Party has been taken hostage by the evan-gelical Christian movement, with the result that it now applies ever narrower litmus tests for ideological purity, sets Rove off. "Don't waste your time!" he fairly shouts. "Anyone who thinks Southern Baptists and Missouri Synod Lutherans are the moral equivalent of the Taliban . . . is a nut. He's been drinking some very funny swamp water."

Rove says of Phillips, "He's a smart guy, but this is an embarrassment. His 1968 book [**The Emerging Republican Majority**] was brilliant, but this thing is just plain nutty. He really does believe the social and religious conservatives have moved in on the GOP with the precision of a Prussian drill team.

"The religious conservatives, the social conservatives . . . maybe you don't see a lot of them in the media business, but a lot of them are normal people. I see what is happening today as a reaction to what happened in the Sixties, when it was . . . 'If it feels good, do it. If you've got a problem, blame someone else.'

"I think my generation," he goes on, "awakened at some point in their lives and said, 'The materialism of the Sixties and the self-fulfillment of the Sixties, what was that all about?' I think what is happening is that people are starting to drink again from the wellspring of faith. They're trying to figure out 'Why am I here, what is expected of me, what is important in life, and how can I have an intimate relationship with God that is supportive of my family and my values?'"

When I suggest that the political debates on evolution versus creationism and the Republican Party's handling of the Terry Schiavo case in Florida had a polarizing effect because of the threats of retribution against those who didn't walk the GOP line, he strongly disagrees. First he says, "They're easily caricatured in the public arena. I think the Schiavo case became a cause célèbre for social conservatives because of the deep moral questions that are there. Are we, as a society, going to be too eager to rush to conclusions and questions involving the disabled?" He insists the Schiavo situation lacked clarity and presented a gray area that concerned advocates of the disabled. He argues that a prominent liberal Democrat, Senator Tom Harkin, was on their side in the Schiavo case, but the media ignored his role.

Does Rove worry that the success of Republicans at election time will generate the same hubris that so undermined the Democrats in the Sixties and Seventies? "Absolutely," he answers, "The thinking of the Democrats became ossified and led them to believe they were entitled to their power, that they had no responsibility and all they had to do was be there."

How do you guard against that in the Republican Party? I ask. Rove answers, "The country expects you to take on big projects, identify the challenges facing the country, to offer answers and keep on thinking. We know what the challenges are: public education, the tax system, litigation system, economic underpinnings, cultural values."

Rove is a long way from the civics class of Eldon B. Tolman, but he's kept track of some of his classmates. "The biker in my graduating class—in a leather jacket, boots with chains on them, smoked cigarettes behind the shop class, and necked with his girlfriend in the alley—he's now a banker. The ski bum who used to take off in his Volkswagen bug at the earliest possibility every day to ski at the local resorts wound up as the police chief of Alta, Utah."

Rove left the White House and the side of George W. Bush in the summer of 2007. He spent the first weekend following the announcement of his departure appearing on all the Washington Sunday morning talk shows declaring that Hillary Clinton was a fatally flawed candidate and that he thought it would be tough, but that the Republicans would win in 2008. He didn't disclose his own plans, but it's difficult to imagine Rove has left the political arena for long.

Rove's ideological soul mate, Vice President Dick Cheney, was a doctoral candidate in political science at the University of Wisconsin in 1968, urgently trying to make up for lost time after a lot of hell-raising and drinking in his early undergraduate years. He had tried three times to get a Yale education and failed.

Cheney grew up in Casper, Wyoming, where he was senior class president, homecoming king, cocaptain on the football team, and sweetheart of the brainy and popular Lynne Vincent, the state baton-twirling champion and homecoming queen. When he went off to Yale with a football teammate on a scholarship following high school graduation in 1959, it must have been a proud moment for the town.

However, Cheney and his friend were not prepared for the big leap from the cowboy culture to the Ivy League. His teammate dropped out after a year in New Haven, and Cheney lost his scholarship because

White House Deputy Chief of Staff Karl Rove,
"the Architect," with President Bush in July 2005

Dick Cheney
in 1964, in his junior
yearbook photo at the
University of Wyoming

President George W. Bush and Vice President Dick
Cheney talk together in the Oval Office before their
morning intelligence briefing, March 1, 2002

Dick Cheney and
Lynne Vincent, the
soon-to-be Mrs.
Lynne V. Cheney,
pictured on a
motorcycle in Casper,
Wyoming, in the
early Sixties

of his poor academic performance. He was told he could return and try again with student loans.

With help from his family and Lynne's encouragement he went back to New Haven, but turned in another substandard performance. One of his Yale classmates remembered Cheney as a hard-partying guy who rarely drew a sober breath.

As I had understood the story over the years, that was the end of the Yale experience for Cheney, but the vice president told his biographer Stephen Hayes that he made one more try, paying his own way in the spring of 1962. But his heart still wasn't in it and his poor grades sent him away for the final time, out on his third strike.

Shortly, he was back in Wyoming, an Ivy League failure. He went to work on construction crews erecting power line towers and became a Saturday night regular in the bars of the hard-drinking state. In the spring of 1963, in Rock Springs, a tough little town in the state's oil patch, he was arrested a second time for driving while intoxicated and thrown in jail. He was behind bars on the weekend when his former Yale classmates were graduating and his Casper High School classmates were getting their degrees from the University of Wyoming and other institutions in the region. It was a sobering moment, and it may have saved his life. When he got out of jail, he moved out into the country and teamed up with a reclusive World War II veteran, working hard all day at erecting the transmission towers, camping out at night, and venturing into town only to buy supplies and take a weekly shower.

He enrolled at the University of Wyoming that fall,

"paying my own way, which focused my attention," he recalls. Lynne was already on the campus, getting a master's degree in English literature, and she was relieved to know he was finally getting serious about his education.

Cheney worked part-time and pursued a degree in political science full-time. He liked the academic life so much this time around that he got a master's degree and made plans for a Ph.D.

In 1968, Dick and Lynne married and headed for the bare-bones life of graduate students at the University of Wisconsin, in Madison. While the liberal Wisconsin student body took to the streets in regular antiwar protests, the Cheneys were focused on finishing their graduate work.

"We were in student housing," he says, "trying to make it as poverty-stricken graduate students. We had one child, Liz . . . and so we were starting a family in the midst of all this chaos. People were leading normal lives despite . . . all the demonstrations, National Guard callouts, and tear gas on the campus."

He says he didn't have time for campus politics. "I was an adult, twenty-seven in 1968. I had already blown a great opportunity at Yale to get a first-class education. I was making up for lost time. . . working my butt off. At night I'd be in the computer center, doing my computer runs with my punch cards."

It was the same computer center blown up by radicals two years later, in 1970, killing a researcher. Nothing quite so violent happened while the Cheneys were on campus, but the vice president does remember Lynne having trouble getting to class because protestors were throwing around animal blood and entrails as a part of their political theater of the day.

He was determined to finish his Ph.D. and teach political science at the college level, but an unlikely opportunity developed. The liberal Maryland senator Joe Tydings was on campus to recruit volunteers for his friend Bobby Kennedy's presidential campaign and to find a prospect for a Washington fellowship sponsored by his late grandfather, Joseph E. Davies, a former U.S. ambassador to the Soviet Union.

The Wisconsin political science department had recommended Cheney as a promising choice, so one night, after rallying Bobby Kennedy volunteers, Tydings met Cheney for a beer. Obviously, Tydings was impressed, as he selected the earnest young man as his congressional fellow for the American Political Science Association.

Tydings, a Kennedy family friend and a well-known eastern seaboard liberal, in effect arranged passage for Cheney to the nation's capital and set him on the path that led to one of the most powerful and controversial vice presidencies in American history.

Cheney remembers that Tydings never inquired about his political affiliation, but if he had, he would have discovered a young westerner with Fifties values who was not deeply engaged by the politics of the day. Cheney's parents were FDR Democrats, but he was less interested in partisan politics than in how government, particularly Congress, functioned.

Cheney had worked for Warren Knowles, Wisconsin's moderate Republican governor, as a student, and he recalls Wisconsin congressman Melvin Laird warning Knowles not to get too deeply involved in supporting the Vietnam War.

Still, Cheney says he "basically supported the war" even after hearing Laird's cautionary note. He also addresses the long-festering question of why he didn't serve in the military during Vietnam when, as he once put it, he had other priorities. "The basic sequence is that I had deferments as an undergraduate. I was 1-A when I got out of college in the early Sixties, but the draft calls [in Wyoming] were minimal, and by the time I got to Wisconsin, I was twenty-six and married and no longer eligible. It wasn't a major problem in my eyes; the war wasn't something that touched me personally, obviously."

As he put it in 1989, "I had other priorities in the Sixties than military service." Altogether, Cheney received five student deferments, leading his political critics to label him a "chicken hawk" for avoiding military service personally and then aggressively promoting military action while secretary of defense and vice president

Cheney, typically, doesn't respond to that criticism, but he does believe the place of Vietnam for his generation has been distorted. "If you look back . . . it's as though Vietnam and campus unrest were the center of the universe. It was a wild time; there was a lot of stuff happening; but Vietnam was just a piece of it. There were roughly thirteen million my age in this country, and something like three million served in the military.

"If you were in the kind of situation Lynne and I were in—we had worked hard to get to graduate school, to get teaching or research assistanceships, starting a family—that was the center of our lives. There was other stuff going on you were aware of periodically, but that wasn't something you spent much of your time on."

Vietnam, however, would be a part of Cheney's life in ways he could not have imagined then or when he first went to Washington to become one of his generation's most skilled players of the inside game of American power politics.

His first assignment was in the office of a bright, young, moderate Wisconsin Republican congressman, Bill Steiger, who gave him substantive assignments well beyond the normal intern fare. Cheney, who was just a dissertation short of his Ph.D., liked the work, but he still planned to finish his doctorate and return to academia.

However, he attracted the attention of an ambitious and abrasive young Republican congressman from the Chicago suburbs named Donald Rumsfeld. Rumsfeld had been picked by President Nixon to run the Office of Economic Opportunity, a federal anti-poverty program left over from LBJ's war on poverty.

Ever the student of government operations, Cheney sent Rumsfeld an unsolicited lengthy memo on the challenges ahead. He didn't know what to expect because Rumsfeld had earlier rejected him after a short interview for an intern position in his congressional office.

This time Rumsfeld was impressed and brought the young man wearing cowboy boots onto his team. It was the beginning of a long, very close political and personal relationship that took the two men to the pinnacles of power and into a war that will forever determine their place in history.

Cheney worked closely with Rumsfeld at OEO, a well-intentioned program that infuriated some Republican governors who complained that Democratic congressmen and mayors were using the federal money simply to secure their constituent base.

OEO was a walk in the park compared to the next assignment President Nixon gave to Rumsfeld and his efficient and quiet aide from Wyoming. As bizarre as it sounds now, Nixon in 1971 tried to head off the possible damaging political effects of inflation by subjecting the American economy to rigid price and wage controls that would be regulated by a new Cost of Living Council.

It was a bureaucratic, political, and economic horror show featuring long, detailed government regulations on which wages could be raised and in what circumstances, and what prices on what products were subject to government regulation. Rumsfeld, who made no secret of his disdain for the federal government trying to manage the economy, relied on Cheney as a general relies on a colonel to keep the troops in line and the plans on track during combat. Cheney by all accounts did his job well.

When Nixon was reelected in 1972, Rumsfeld went to Brussels as the U.S. ambassador to NATO and Cheney took a consulting job in Washington, where Lynne was teaching English literature at George Washington University.

The next two years will forever be recorded as a great test of the resiliency of the American political sys-

tem because of Watergate—the great and dangerous
unraveling of a presidency, the paranoia and self-
inflicted wounds of Richard Nixon, his closest aides
going to jail for their blind and felonious allegiance,
and, finally, his inevitable resignation.

The new president, Gerald Ford, was a well-liked
man of the House of Representatives whose personal
integrity and decency had led to his confirmation as
Nixon's vice president. Ford summoned Rumsfeld
back from Brussels to be his new White House chief of
staff. Rumsfeld brought Cheney with him, still the
general and the colonel.

A little more than a year later, Rumsfeld moved
across the Potomac to become secretary of defense, and
Cheney became the youngest White House chief of staff
in history, the man who saw the president first in the
morning and last at night. I was the White House correspondent for NBC News at the time and I remember
being impressed by Cheney's quiet, self-effacing style,
especially after the brusque self-importance of Alexander
Haig, who had served Nixon, and the aggressive style
Rumsfeld was perfecting.

I was surprised that Cheney was only thirty-four
years old. He looked older and carried himself with
the confidence of someone ten years his senior. He
was affable but not gregarious. He had an easy relationship with the press corps, but he didn't try to be
one of the boys.

Cheney and I were almost exactly the same age, and
we shared remarkably similar life stories—Wyoming
and South Dakota, working-class families, high school
stars who stumbled badly in the first pass at college, both

married to bright, independent women we'd known as teenagers. We were two recovering college dropouts who managed to get to the White House in reasonably good time. He wasn't particularly ideological and in my experience then he rarely made the usual "liberal media" kind of complaints I'd hear from other White House aides.

One night the Cheneys invited Meredith and me, and CBS correspondent Bob Schieffer and his wife, Pat, to join them in the president's box at the Kennedy Center. It's the kind of an occasion at which a White House official will generally try to sell a journalist on a story favorable to the president or complain about some real or imagined slight.

There was none of that with Cheney. We simply watched the performance, exchanged some small talk at intermission, and then said good night at the end. It was all perfectly pleasant, but Schieffer and I were a little disappointed we didn't get **something** useful out of the night.

That was the Cheney style. He could be mischievous—he helped with some silly White House press corps pranks—but he was mostly content to be in the background, quietly juggling all the demands that come to the most powerful office in the world. As my friend Bob Schieffer says, "He was the best staff man I ever worked around—and when I needed to know something, he was the best guy to ask."

When Gerald Ford lost to Jimmy Carter in the 1976 presidential election, the Cheneys returned to Wyoming to begin two new phases of their lives, one exhilarating, the other terrifying.

Cheney was elected as Wyoming's lone representative in the House of Representatives as a Republican but not before suffering a heart attack at the age of thirty-seven. It was the beginning of thirty years of heart problems, including four heart attacks of varying degrees, bypass surgery, and an implanted cardiovascular stent.

Cheney went on to become a five-term congressman from Wyoming and a rising star in the GOP ranks from the moment he arrived. His original mentor, Wisconsin congressman Bill Steiger, was scheduled to guide Cheney through his rookie season, but Steiger died of a heart attack at the age of forty just as Cheney's term began.

How Steiger, a Republican moderate, might have influenced his old intern is hard to say, but on his own, and reflecting the political roots of his home state, Cheney became a reliable conservative vote on almost every issue. His voting record was so conservative, and so at odds with his reputation as a pragmatic sort, that it surprised a lot of longtime Washington observers when George W. Bush chose Cheney—who had even voted against making Martin Luther King Jr.'s birthday a national holiday—as his running mate.

The University of Wisconsin political-science wonk was becoming a hard-line party man and a force to be reckoned with in House Republican ranks. Cheney told me, as he has others, that he liked the House—the chamber of the people—with its style more spirited than the Senate.

In 1989, when George H. W. Bush's first choice for secretary of defense, Senator John Tower of Texas, failed to win confirmation, the president unexpectedly turned to Cheney for the job. Ironically, Bush was in-fluenced in his choice by his national security advisor, Brent Scowcroft, who had worked closely with Cheney in the Ford administration. That long and close rela-tionship was severed when Scowcroft became an early and prophetic critic of the Iraq War.

Cheney had a busy first two years on the job. In late 1989 he supervised the American military operation to remove Panamanian military strongman Manuel Nor-iega from power after Noriega overthrew the democrati-cally elected government in the country whose canal was vital to U.S. interests.

Less than a year later Cheney was planning a major war against Iraq: Operation Desert Storm. From the moment Saddam Hussein invaded neighboring Kuwait, Cheney took a hard line. In the early stages of the invasion his boss, the first President Bush, publicly said he was not contemplating military action. The chairman of the Joint Chiefs, Colin Powell, suggested a more balanced approach: Begin to prepare for possi-ble military action, but continue to put pressure on Saddam through sanctions.

Cheney thought force was inevitable. He arranged to be the Bush official who made the case to the Saudi royal family, persuading King Fahd to accept American troops' being based in Saudi Arabia, the home of Mecca.

In the Pentagon, Cheney ran a tight ship. He fired the Air Force chief of staff on the eve of the war for bragging to reporters how the Air Force bombing cam-paign would devastate Iraq.

He even sternly reminded his superstar chairman

of the Joint Chiefs of Staff, Colin Powell, to confine his remarks in White House discussions to military matters and to stay out of political discussions about whether to go to war. General Powell learned that even his legendary charm had its limits around his taciturn boss from Wyoming.

I remember seeing Defense Secretary Cheney in Saudi Arabia shortly before the first air and then ground combat began. We exchanged casual waves across a tarmac. I was struck by the fact that this man, a year younger than I, still dressed in his Casper, Wyoming, cowboy boots, was about to preside over a major war and it didn't seem to faze him. He had a commanding presence. He was no longer a staff man.

The success of that war, the sometimes strained relationship he had with General Powell, and his introduction to the neocon academic and Pentagon adviser Paul Wolfowitz, would provide a framework for another war in Cheney's future.

When Bill Clinton was elected president, Cheney went to Houston to become the CEO of Halliburton, the giant global oil services company and military contractor. He maintained his ties to the Republican Party establishment and was a natural choice to head George W. Bush's search committee for a running mate in 2000.

He assembled a detailed portfolio on the personal strengths and weaknesses of a wide range of candidates, including popular Republican governors Frank Keating of Oklahoma and Tom Ridge of Pennsylvania. But George W. Bush kept coming back to one name: Richard Bruce Cheney of Texas and Wyoming, a former White House chief of staff, a former well-regarded congressman and a former secretary of defense in his father's administration.

The choice of Cheney as a running mate was praised by the mainstream political pundit class as a shrewd move. Cheney would bring heft to a national security team that also included a familiar name from his past: Donald Rumsfeld. Colin Powell, with whom he had a mixed relationship, would be secretary of state.

Cheney's role as the vicar of the Bush administration's national-security policies before and after the 9/11 attacks has been well documented. From the moment he moved into the White House bunker on the morning of the attacks, he has been a central and controversial figure in determining when and how to respond, what to expect once war began, and what should be done—or not done—next.

Among his friends and longtime Washington observers there is almost universal agreement that Cheney changed after the attacks. He became more militant and less inclined to listen to other points of view, less politic and more willful, more dour and less affable.

And he gave the speculators a good deal to consider. His declarations that the United States would be received as "liberators" in Baghdad and that the insurgency was in the "last throes" when plainly it wasn't, combined with his stubborn conviction that he was right when even his longtime friends and mentors had grave doubts, prompted a new question in Washington: "Whatever happened to the Dick Cheney I used to know?"

It was asked publicly by Brent Scowcroft, the national-security authority who had known him since the Ford administration. Scowcroft became estranged from Cheney and persona non grata in the Bush White House for his public warnings that a preemptive war against Iraq would be a mistake.

Other longtime friends, such as James Baker, the former secretary of state, and former Wyoming senator Alan Simpson, stay in close touch with Cheney, but they, too, have confided to friends that he has changed.

When I interview him in his office in the northwest corner of the White House, the vice president is friendly and cooperative but typically not chatty. I ask about the changes he has been part of in Washington. He traces the evolution of the modern Republican Party from his days in the Ford administration to the presidency of George W. Bush. "We became Reagan Republicans in relatively short order. In 1976 I worked hard to beat Ronald Reagan [helping Ford turn back Reagan's challenge for the Republican presidential nomination], and by 1980 I was running [for Congress] as a Reagan Republican."

Cheney credits Ronald Reagan's success for ending the moderate-conservative split within the GOP just as the Democrats were entering what the vice president calls a "weak phase" as a result of Vietnam and the McGovern candidacy.

Cheney made these observations a few months before the congressional elections of 2006, when his administration suffered a stinging defeat in both the House and Senate. At the time he didn't see that coming, but he was aware of the perils of modern political cycles. He conceded that there possibly were lessons for the Republicans in the experiences of the Democrats in the Sixties. "There are periods, I suppose, when you have to go out and get the party revived. The big question in the 2008 election is whether it will regenerate both parties or one party will emerge from the process. I don't think the outcome is foreordained by any means."

He has not given up on a fundamental tenet of the Bush administration: Damn the torpedoes, full speed ahead. "Close elections don't mean you trim your sails in terms of your agenda," he says. It was that attitude that surprised many of his old friends following the 2004 presidential election, when the war in Iraq was getting worse, not better, and when the country's patience with political polarization was running thin.

It was a trend that exploded in the administration's face in 2006, a development that might have been averted if the president and vice president had shown a greater inclination to reach across party lines and listen to other ideas. Allies and friends from the vice president's past suggested just such a scenario in informal settings, but they were routinely turned back.

Outside the arena of electoral politics, Dick Cheney is surrounded by the contradictions in the conservative culture of the post-Sixties world. His wife, Lynne, is smart, tough, independent, and accomplished. His daughter Liz is a mother and formerly a high-level State Department employee, and his daughter Mary, an executive at AOL, is an outspoken lesbian who elected to have a child and raise him with her female partner.

Cheney acknowledges that the public acceptance

of Mary's lifestyle was likely an outgrowth of the expanded tolerance on race and homosexuality that came out of the Sixties. Living, as he does, with three strong, accomplished women, Cheney recognizes the importance of gender equality; he thinks the opportunities his daughters have had are "great."

That part of Cheney does not go unnoticed by the press and his liberal opponents. The conservative movement is unapologetically critical of gay rights, yet Cheney, a prominent conservative, is proudly supportive of his daughter's life and choices. When others point out the contradictions between his embrace of Mary's life-style and conservative criticism—as Wolf Blitzer did in a CNN interview—Cheney snaps that the question is "out of bounds" without explaining why.

He also doesn't share the concern of many conservatives that for all of their political gains, they can't compete with the liberal domination of popular culture and that this will eventually realign the country again along liberal lines. "I don't think so," he says. "There are so many more media outlets . . . the Internet, it's phenomenal. The variety of political views that get expressed . . . we used to be dominated by the major networks and **The New York Times** and **The Washington Post** in terms of national political dialogue. That is no longer the case. It's now a far more diverse field."

That doesn't mean the vice president is happy with the press coverage that the administration, or he personally, receives. "I think the press overdoes the cynicism. I think there's a tendency to think if you're a politician, you're suspect and your motives are suspect."

In the spring of 2007, **The Washington Post** ran a series on the vice president's staying power in the administration, through his detailed knowledge of the system and his tireless efforts to protect his friends and interests against federal regulation, operating constantly behind several screens of secrecy. The series prompted the venerable **Washington Post** political columnist David Broder, known for his evenhanded treatment of politicians in both parties, to write about his own deep disappointment in Cheney, a man he originally thought was perfect for the job of advising a neophyte president.

Broder said the extent of Cheney's influence and his ability to bend the decision-making process to his own ends and purposes, often overriding cabinet officers, had resulted in what Broder said was the "wreckage of foreign policy, national security policy, budget policy, energy policy, and environmental policy under Cheney's direction and on Cheney's watch."

When friends of Cheney have referred to other criticism of him from credible sources, he's been known to wave it off with the line "Aw, it's just the same old shit." Friends say he was more than a little miffed when he and Lynne gave $7 million to charity, after some Halliburton stock options kicked in, and the mainstream press skipped over the donation to emphasize instead his tax refund.

He says the kind of guilt-by-association coverage on the part of the press began with Watergate, and it has not abated. As a result, he feels, it's more difficult to attract good people to national service at the highest levels. "I think it frightens a lot of people . . . there are some very talented people who would like to serve, but they see how others get treated and say, 'Not for me.'"

On national security matters in the post-Sixties world, Cheney told me, "The Vietnam legacy still affects debate about the use of military force anywhere in the world. You've got a whole generation of academics who came of age during the Vietnam period . . . who, when we talk about Iraq, they draw on the analogies to Vietnam.

"Johnny Apple [the late R. W. Apple of **The New York Times**] sort of made his bones in Vietnam, and when we marched into Iraq, I remember a front-page story he did . . . using the language reminiscent of Vietnam, 'quagmire,' to describe what was going on in Iraq. So it clearly still affects our judgments, and it was, from a historic perspective, clearly a traumatic event for the nation."

He then recalls his days as defense secretary during Operation Desert Storm when "guys, Vietnam vets, would come up to me and thank me for what we did in the Gulf because it wasn't the American military that had been defeated in Vietnam. We restored their confidence in themselves because of what we were able to do and the way the nation treated those who served."

However, by 2007, among the most persistent critics of Bush administration policies in Iraq were Republican senator Chuck Hagel of Nebraska, a twice-wounded Vietnam veteran, and Pennsylvania Democratic congressman John Murtha. Murtha, a Marine in Vietnam, a stalwart supporter of the military, had been close with Cheney during their years in the House together and when Cheney was secretary of defense.

When I ask Cheney what the positive effects of the Sixties were, he immediately cites the advances in civil rights and race relations as well as the progress for women, but then he ticks off the downside: "You had Tet—that was Vietnam; and Johnson's resignation/retirement, which was Vietnam-related; you had the King assassination; you had the Kennedy assassination; you had riots in the cities. Those were wild times. There was a lot of stuff happening. And Vietnam was just a piece of it."

He does not have the same dark view of what many of his conservative soul mates consider to be a terrible hangover from the Sixties: moral decay in the culture. Cheney is much less alarmist in his reaction. "I think there's been a certain amount of decay . . . I guess. The drug culture, which became a significant problem."

Did he ever smoke pot, or even see it very much? "I was never around it. No one offered me any. Casper, Wyoming, when I was growing up, somehow it hadn't reached there yet."

As most westerners are, he is troubled by the latest evolution of the drug culture, the rapid rise of the use of meth, a cheap, highly destructive drug that is a scourge of the Rocky Mountain and Midwestern states. One of his Wyoming friends has a family member in jail for murdering her own infant in a meth rage.

Cheney confesses he feels a certain nostalgia for the way society used to work when, as he puts it, "maybe there was more of a national consensus." He smiles and cocks his head as he goes on, "I suppose if you're a conservative, like me, it's attractive to think about that time."

That time, of course, is also when Cheney was a hard-drinking college dropout, when homosexuality and race were easy targets for bigots, and when women such as his wife, Lynne, were routinely denied opportunities and appropriate compensation to match their skills.

As he leaves the room after the interview, I ask how he personally has changed since the Sixties. "Oh," he says, "I guess I'm a lot more conservative now."

Pat Buchanan and
Senator Hillary Clinton

Pat Buchanan's conservative credentials have never been in doubt, but he is troubled by the lasting impact of the policies of President George W. Bush, Vice President Cheney, Karl Rove, and company in the name of conservatism. He is a forceful and articulate critic of the rise of the neocons and their decision to invade Iraq.

Buchanan worries that a combination of neocon recklessness and the spreading influence of a liberal popular culture will undo all the considerable gains the right has made in American politics since 1964, that **annus horribilis** when their reigning champion, Barry Goldwater, was flattened by Lyndon Johnson.

Through it all, however, Buchanan has retained his robust Irish humor, often breaking into a raucous laugh after getting off a tough verbal shot against the network news or the latest liberal pronouncement. It is that ability to mix it up with good humor that has made Buchanan enduringly popular even with liberal observers.

One of his unlikely occasional companions, when I knew him in Washington, was Dr. Hunter S. Thompson, the pill-popping, invective-spewing, hilarious godfather of gonzo journalism. Thompson would blow into Washington on assignment for **Rolling Stone** magazine, call up Buchanan, and off they'd go on a beer-drinking all-nighter, arguing their respective views of the world in long verbal jousts that seldom were resolved.

Buchanan recounts those occasions happily, saying, "I don't know how he did it. He must have had a case of beer, and yet he was swimming laps in the pool at my house." Thompson liked to call Buchanan the "best right-wing propagandist since Goebbels," a description Buchanan often repeats with a big guffaw.

In the post-Nixon era, Buchanan started writing a newspaper column and became the right-wing commentator always available on call. He is a familiar fixture on radio and television, always outfitted in his Catholic-schoolboy blue suit with red tie, his short, thinning hair neatly combed, shoes shined, ready for battle. In books, speeches, columns, and commentary, he regularly and passionately rails against affirmative action; homosexuality, which he believes is immoral; gun control laws; and feminism.

Typically, he has an in-your-face summary of feminism. "The real liberators of American women," he says, "were not the feminist noisemakers; they were the automobiles, the supermarket, the shopping center, the dishwasher, the washer-dryer, the freezer." In recent years, his greatest anger has been about illegal immigration, which he claims is destroying the white ethnic majority in America. If it is allowed to continue, he believes, it will lead to the death of Western civilization.

Buchanan, who has run for president three times, two of them as a Republican, is contemptuous of the neoconservative ideology that powers the administration of George W. Bush. He was an outspoken opponent of the plan to go to war against Iraq from the beginning, and he accurately describes the 2006 midterm elections as a "referendum on the neocons."

"Those guys who think this is a long, enduring Republican ascendancy in the presidential arena are mistaken," he says. He cites the diminishing margins of victory for the Republicans in 1988, the losses in 1992 and 1996, the narrow victories in 2000 and 2004, and the losses of 2006 as evidence that the conservative tide has begun to recede.

Buchanan believes strongly that it's about more than what he calls the misguided war in Iraq. "It's immigration and trade—those issues are breaking up the Republican Party. [John] McCain is closer on immigration to Ted Kennedy than he is to most Republicans. [Rudolph] Giuliani has been pro–gun control, pro–immigration amnesty, progay. [Mitt] Romney is doing a one-eighty on the positions that got him elected governor of Massachusetts. Now he's a hawk on guns, immigration, abortion."

As for Hillary Clinton, Buchanan gives her good grades for her Senate record, but he shares the conventional wisdom that she has too many negatives to win the White House. He thinks Barack Obama is just too new. But Buchanan would not be surprised if the voters in 2008 decide it is time to clean out this generation of Republicans and just start over.

When I ask him what good, in his judgment, came out of the movement in the Sixties, he is startled. "Seriously?" he says. "I don't think much. The good parts of the civil rights movement were over by '63, '64, '65. The riots that followed made people say, 'I'm just getting tired of this.' The student radicals were always despised. They were considered overprivileged brats who had privileges none of the working class had."

His wife, Shelley—they have no children—is not a fan of feminism. "She's not proabortion at all. No one in my family is. I think clearly there are women who feel the idea of equal opportunity for women is a good thing . . . but if you talk about abortion and the breakdown of the family, I think the feeling on our side of the fence is that the Sixties were a disaster."

Pat Buchanan plans to continue sounding the trumpets for what he considers the true conservative roots of his party, speaking out and writing on what he sees as the destructive effects of unbridled illegal immigration and the failure of Republicans in power to stay true to their catechism of a smaller government, fiscal responsibility, limited foreign-policy adventures, and no compromises on resisting abortion and homosexual rights.

"The moral, cultural, and social revolution of the Sixties, by and large, that revolution has succeeded [in the popular arena]. We crushed it politically in '72, '80, '84, and '88, but it has stayed alive in the popular arena, and what stays alive there eventually succeeds in politics."

When Buchanan raised the cultural issues in a fiery speech at the 1992 Republican National Convention, he described a "religious war going on . . . for the soul of America. The agenda of Clinton would impose . . . abortion on demand, a litmus test for the Supreme Court, homosexual rights, discrimination against religious schools . . . that's change . . . but it is not the kind of change America wants . . . not the kind of change we can tolerate in a nation we still call God's country."

It was a strident declaration, and some moderate Republicans cringed, thinking it was sending a "my way or the highway" message to American voters just when they were wondering whether they wanted to extend twelve years of Republican rule. Buchanan has not tempered his beliefs, but at the age of seventy he has no plans to run as a presidential candidate again.

The best-known woman in American politics, the most credible female candidate for the American presidency in the history of the republic, is a product of the white-bread suburbs of the Fifties, the Goldwater movement of the early Sixties, the antiwar movement of the late Sixties, the Watergate investigations of the Seventies, the higher profile of professional women in the Eighties, her husband's two terms as president in the Nineties, and her own election as a senator from New York at the beginning of the twenty-first century.

Hillary Rodham Clinton has been on a long, exhilarating, and very bumpy ride since she left home in 1965 to attend Wellesley College, carrying her own considerable ambition and the hopes of her mother with her.

Dorothy Rodham, the wife of a staunchly conservative Republican businessman in the Chicago suburbs, read Betty Friedan's **The Feminine Mystique** and became more determined than ever that her daughter would have the opportunities for higher education and a career that she had been denied. She sent her to college, saying, "I want you to go places I didn't go; I want you to have chances I didn't have; I want you to see the world."

As Clinton fondly recalls, "It wasn't 'Woe is me.' It was more like 'I've had my life, and I didn't get to do the things I wish I could have, and I am investing a lot in you so you can do that.'" She left for Wellesley College, thinking, "There was this sense that we not only had to live our lives but, to a certain extent, fulfill the hopes of our mothers. I felt that very strongly. The more I learned about my mother's life as I got older, and how difficult it had been for her, I felt a real obligation."

Seldom have a mother's hopes and wishes been so famously fulfilled. After graduating from Wellesley with honors in political science, Hillary Rodham went to Yale Law School and became a member of the legal staff of the House Judiciary Committee's Nixon impeachment inquiry.

She married Bill Clinton, a law school classmate, and moved with him to Arkansas, where they became the ultimate power couple as he was elected governor four times and she was a partner in the most successful law firm in the state.

She had initially refused to take her husband's name, but she added it after it became a minor campaign issue and he lost his first reelection campaign. It was as Hillary Rodham Clinton that she moved back into the governor's mansion with him after he made a successful comeback.

Next stop, the White House, where she became one of the most powerful first ladies in American history—and one of the most controversial.

She had trouble defending a quick $100,000 profit in the commodities market while Bill was governor of Arkansas. Her Little Rock law partner Vince Foster, a deputy White House counsel, committed suicide in the midst of an investigation of Whitewater and the so-called Travelgate, a Clinton effort to re-organize the White House travel office.

She became a lightning rod for conservative criticism for her magisterial role in attempting to overhaul American health care. Those early days made her a favorite target not just of conservative political opponents but also of the growing ranks of conservative commentators on radio and television.

She was portrayed as pushy and presumptuous, very liberal, and personally cold. She was not a first lady in the Barbara Bush or Nancy Reagan tradition. She wore pantsuits and led women on a pilgrimage to the largest-ever international women's conference, in China, where she reminded the international community that "women's rights are human rights." She went to India and the third world to draw attention to women and girls who led lives of subjugation and poverty because of their gender.

As first lady, she also was deeply involved in the establishment of a federal program to provide health care coverage to poor, uninsured children, and in legislation overhauling the nation's adoption and foster care laws.

During the Clintons' first term, my wife, Meredith, and I were honored by an organization promoting day care for children in the workplace. The organizers invited Hillary to speak.

She arrived without an entourage and spoke eloquently without notes on the difficult choices working mothers have to make because of the absence of a strong day care commitment in the corporate world. Republicans as well as Democrats left the evening remarking on her impressive performance.

Not for the first time, I was struck by the difference in her image in small gatherings—warm and engaging—and her image in a big hall or on television, where she came off as hard-charging and formidable. And, of course, she suffered the humiliation of her husband's affair with Monica Lewinsky after initially blaming the allegations on a "vast right-wing conspiracy."

Still, Hillary—her first name became her primary identification for friends and foes alike—never was able to shake a high negative rating as a first lady, a problem that continues into her presidential campaign.

When the Clintons left the White House and Hillary decided to run for the U.S. Senate from New York—a state where she had never lived—I was aware of a substantial number of accomplished women who

Hillary Rodham Clinton's parents, Dorothy Howell and Hugh Rodham Jr. Dorothy was determined that Hillary would see the world: "I want you to go places I didn't go; I want you to have chances I didn't have."

Hillary Clinton in 1969, during her student days at Wellesley College

Senator Hillary Clinton in 2004

were sympathetic to her political ideology but opposed to her candidacy. They thought she was too opportunistic, coming into their state and expecting a free ride to the Senate nomination because of her celebrity.

Before the campaign was over, many of those same skeptical women were on her side, impressed by her personal and professional conduct. She won impressively, even carrying the traditionally Republican upstate counties.

Once in the Senate, she proved herself to be a collegial, and increasingly influential, member of the club, earning the respect of colleagues on both sides of the political aisle, including some who started out as bitter foes.

She was now able to run for the presidency as the best-positioned woman candidate for that office in American history. Wherever presidential politics were discussed, the only real question quickly became "Can she be elected?"

Democrats who acknowledged her skills as a politician worried that if she got the nomination, she would be a drag on their party's best chance to reclaim the White House, not because she was a woman but because the voting public was so divided on her politics and character.

As a candidate she continued to get high marks for her intelligence and her command of the issues, but her negatives in the areas of trust and personal comfort remained high.

Few Americans, men or women, have advanced through life with so many people looking on and commenting on what they see—or what they think they see.

The senator is aware of the changes from those long-ago Wellesley days in the late Sixties to the demands of running for president in 2008. "Obviously, I am a different person, you know, maybe not a different person as much as a person who has lived a lot longer and had a lot more experience, so I have to leave it to others to judge how I'm different. I just feel like I'm the same person but with more real-life experience."

A lasting part of that real-life experience was her defiant appearance on **60 Minutes** during the Gennifer Flowers crisis in her husband's first campaign for the presidency. "I'm not sitting here, some little woman standing by my man like Tammy Wynette," she said. "I'm sitting here because I love him and respect him and I honor what he's been through and what we've been through together."

In one heated moment, she managed to insult a popular country-and-western star personally and come off as an elitist modern woman who had no time for ordinary wives who stand by their men whatever the circumstances.

She says she learned a lot from that moment and personally apologized to Ms. Wynette. But she went into the White House as the unapologetic embodiment of her husband's campaign mantra: "Elect one, get one free."

Now, fifteen years later, she is in a historic race for the presidential nomination of her party against Senator Barack Obama of Illinois, a black man with little national experience but a winning style and a compelling message of moving the country beyond politics as usual. Gender and race have found their way into the highest levels of American politics in a new fashion in the third presidential election of a new century.

In her accomplishments, travails, and controversies, Hillary Rodham Clinton is, in many ways, the personification of ideals and realities of the women's movement in which she grew up. She is at once admired and reviled for her beliefs, capabilities, and ambitions.

She is also unwavering in her determination to lead the life she chooses, not one that is chosen for her.

In that sense, Hillary is very much a product of the Sixties. In her autobiography, **Living History,** Senator Clinton wrote about the transforming effect of that time: "I was born an American in the middle of the twentieth century, a fortunate time and place. I was free to make choices unavailable to past generations of women in my own country and inconceivable to many women in the world today. . . . My mother and grandmothers could never have lived my life; my father and grandfathers could never have imagined it. But they bestowed on me the promise of America, which made my life and my choices possible."

No one knows better how the left, in the Sixties, opened the door for the right wing in American politics. When I ask her, "Did enough people on the left say, 'Hey, wait a minute; this is going too far'?" I was thinking of the conspicuous flag burning, the idolization of Ho Chi Minh in some quarters, and the dismissive attitude toward anything resembling the establishment. She answered, "I think a lot of people did just that through their own behavior, but as so often happens, the good was overlooked, and the problems were exploited for crass political purposes."

Senator Clinton had her first brush with national fame when she was selected as the student commencement speaker at Wellesley College in 1969. Her class had lived through the riotous Chicago convention, through assassinations, spreading antiwar protests, the rise of the counterculture, and demands for greater student authority on campus. The president of Wellesley introduced her as the president of college government, an honors graduate in political science, and someone who "is cheerful, good-humored, and good company."

She spoke following the official commencement address delivered by U.S. senator Edward Brooke, a dashing and eloquent moderate Republican who also happened to be the first black senator since Reconstruction. She began by dismissing Brooke's gentle reminders of the social progress America had made in recent years and his appeal to the class to be empathetic to the continuing effort.

Abandoning her prepared text, she responded, "Part of the problem with empathy with professed goals is that empathy doesn't do us anything." Going on, she said, "We're not interested in social reconstruction; it's in human reconstruction. How can we talk about percentages and trends?"

Reminding her audience that she had canvassed her classmates for ideas and themes for the speech, she praised Wellesley faintly. "Luckily, when we questioned the meaning of a liberal arts education, there were enough people with imagination to respond to that questioning. So we have made **some** progress."

Later in the speech, ratcheting up her Sixties rhetoric, Hillary said, "There are some things we feel, feelings that our prevailing, acquisitive, and competitive corporate life, including, tragically, the universities, is not a way of life for us. We're searching for a more immediate, ecstatic, and penetrating mode of living."

When I ask her about the difference in her thinking then and now, the senator uncharacteristically wanders through her answer, trying to find a safe intersection. "Oh, that was a long time ago," she begins. "You know, I believed what I said then. I thought it was an expression of a kind of youthful hopefulness, investing in trying to make our country and world a better place. To a great extent, I still do today. I may not express it in the same way, but it's what I get up every day and try to do."

As for the political climate in America, she understands that America has historically tilted toward the conservative side, with intermittent periods of what she calls "progressive energy." She also believes that modern conservatives such as Karl Rove are "obsessed" with defeating her.

She prefers the godfather of the modern conservative movement, Ronald Reagan. He was, she says, "a child of the Depression, so he understood it [economic pressures on the working and middle class]. When he had those big tax cuts and they went too far, he oversaw the largest tax increase. He could call the Soviet Union the Evil Empire and then negotiate arms-control agree-

ments. He played the balance and the music beauti-
fully."

In 1969, who would have imagined that the
Hillary Rodham on the Wellesley commencement
stage would find herself thirty-eight years later paying
tribute to Ronald Reagan?

It was Senator Clinton who originally said to me
of the Sixties, "Have you cracked the code yet?" referring to the complex legacy of that time, filled as it is
with so many contradictions, interpretations, romantic
notions, myths, and harsh realities. When we meet in
her Senate office, I turn the question around. "What,"
I asked, "do you think is the code?"

She laughs and answers, "I've thought a lot about
it, and it's always struck me as curious that the Greatest Generation produced the Sixties generation. What
were the sort of unmet aspirations, dreams, the frustrations that our parents had that led us to a period of ferment and rebellion and questioning of authority?"

Many on the left, I point out, say the Vietnam War
was the catalyst for the rebellion. She thinks that's an
overstatement. "I think it was on the way to happening
before Vietnam took off. You'd have to ask if the rebellion would have happened without civil rights, without
Vietnam, without the women's movement. I think the
answer is no." Going on, she says, "I was obsessed with
Vietnam, but a lot of kids I went to high school with
were not. And they went through the same questioning
and challenging and wondering what their future
would be like."

She acknowledges that perceptions are as important as reality in politics. "I think a lot of the New Right

[her phrase] energy comes from the freedoms and activism of the Sixties. Some people did take that all to excess, as people do . . . but because the baby boomer numbers were so large, if you had 10 percent of the people who went to excess, that's a lot of people. Everyone could see the lessons of drugs, sex, and rock and roll taking you to a place that wasn't healthy. It was self-destructive, or whatever."

Warming to her subject, she goes on, "But the larger message of the Sixties was really liberating. African-Americans, by God, you could stand up and demand your rights like Dr. King inspired you to do. Women, you don't have to stay two steps behind. Choose your own life, make your own decisions. I think that was great for America."

Second Thoughts
and the Long View

For those who went through the Sixties fully immersed in the currents running left, right, and in the middle of those high-water times, the passage of four decades has brought some personal perspective and some thoughts on the future.

Dolores Huerta, who was a seminal figure in the organization of what were then called "Chicano" farmworkers, has not given up her place in the fight for what she considers to be economic justice.

She also wants everyone to know the Sixties did not arrive overnight.

She sees the early part of the twenty-first century as being like the 1950s, before the explosion of social activism in the Sixties. "People think of the Sixties as a full-grown movement, all at once. It wasn't," she says. "There was a buildup to the movement."

The question now is, what happens next? And what lessons can be learned from the Sixties?

Sam Brown

Sam Brown, the McCarthy campaign organizer, and his wife, Alison, have remained true to their Democratic Party roots, but their involvement now is mostly confined to election years, when they campaign for congressional candidates and others who share their political sensibilities. They were true children of the Sixties when Sam ran the Mobe, the Mobilization Against the War in Vietnam, and organized students for Senator McCarthy's presidential campaign.

In his post-McCarthy campaign days, Brown moved to Colorado and was elected state treasurer in 1974 on a slate that also included the election of Sixties children Tim Wirth and Gary Hart to Congress and Richard Lamm to the Colorado governor's office.

In 1977, President Jimmy Carter appointed Brown head of ACTION, the federal umbrella for programs such as the Peace Corps, VISTA (its domestic equivalent), the foster grandparents program, and other efforts to provide social services in a new form. Since then Brown has been active in what could be called socially responsible investments: building low-cost, energy-efficient housing in Aspen for those who couldn't afford the resort's trophy home prices; representing well-known American brands such as Nike and Polo in negotiating agreements that focused on the elimination of sweatshops; and managing portfolios of investments that reflect his personal ethos.

The Browns were back on the campaign trail in 2004 and 2006, volunteering full-time for John Kerry's presidential campaign and working for candidates in races attracting little national attention. "I was amazed by the people I saw," Brown says. For Brown, the election of 2006 seemed to kindle a revival of the spirit of John F. Kennedy's famous inaugural exhortation to "ask what you can do for your country."

Brown saw a combination of public dissatisfaction with the direction of the country and a revived Democratic Party that provided opportunities missing on his side of the political spectrum for a while. As he put it, "If you offer people real opportunities and fire their imagination, it's always amazing to me how many people will respond."

When national security remains such a major consideration for voters, Brown says bluntly, "Our party doesn't yet know how to think about war and military use. I think so much of the debate still is constrained by how people [in the Democratic Party] were shaped by Vietnam."

He believes the debate on the war in Iraq would be much different if there were still a draft, which he favors renewing. "Personally," he says, "I don't think we'd have this war if the people who have the power and the resources in the country were subject to a draft."

He also believes the Democrats have to acknowledge—and not be afraid to criticize—the cultural changes in music lyrics, in the language and tone of movies, in the nature of video games, and in personal behavior. He thinks the Democrats lost their bearings during the debate over explicit rap-song lyrics in the Nineties. "We couldn't even talk about it," he says, "and when Tipper Gore tried, she was demonized for being prudish and wanting to diminish civil rights.

That's nonsense. We didn't take a stand. We're the party that says it's for women's rights, and yet when we hear these misogynistic lyrics that are so awful about women . . . we don't take a stand. This stuff really matters. People care about this stuff."

Jeremy Larner

Jeremy Larner came to Senator Eugene McCarthy's presidential campaign in 1968 as a speechwriter, fresh from the world of magazine journalism. We first met in 1967, when he was with **The Atlantic** magazine and we were both covering the court-martial of an Air Force Academy graduate who came back from Vietnam and refused to train other pilots for duty there. He collected his **Atlantic** pieces into an insightful book, **Nobody Knows: Reflections on the McCarthy Campaign of 1968.**

We stayed in touch, and before long he was writing the screenplay for Robert Redford's film **The Candidate**. **The Candidate** won Larner the 1972 Oscar for best original screenplay.

Today Jeremy Larner lives outside San Francisco and remains active in social causes and screenwriting. Like so many in McCarthy's campaign, he was ultimately disappointed by the senator's failure to truly transform the Democratic Party—although he gives him great credit for initially demonstrating that a majority of the American people were moving toward opposition to the war.

He thought there was a real opening for McCarthy

to take the debate to a higher level following the death of Robert Kennedy, but instead, McCarthy retreated into himself. In Larner's words, "He stood all summer, passive and self-absorbed, in the winding down of his campaign."

Larner now believes the greatest after-effects of the Sixties were cultural rather than political. He laments that "The basic attitudes [of the Sixties] you can buy or sell. . . . it's rebellion as a T-shirt."

The Candidate angered the liberal establishment with its portrayal of a liberal, antiestablishment candidate who steadily succumbs to compromise and makes deals throughout his campaign to win a Senate seat from California. Larner believes that "what happened to Redford [in the movie] doesn't have to happen; you can be . . . wiser. There is something about being a principled person that makes politics very hard. You have to have a real skill for it, but it is possible."

He isn't entirely joking when he says of the Sixties, "The only thing that lasted was that boys and girls could stay in the same dormitories."

Larner's famous last line in **The Candidate** comes when Redford realizes he's been elected to the U.S. Senate and asks plaintively, "What do we do now?"

That's a question Larner believes has to be asked not by a fictional politician on a big screen but by those who went through the Sixties and strayed from their idealism.

Carl Pope

Carl Pope knows exactly what to do now: Make sure that another generation gap doesn't develop. "Our generation," he says, "which was so alienated from the older generation—and them from us—has a real opportunity to pass along all we've learned to those now beginning to take their place in society. That should be our next movement."

Pope has been watching the baby boomers coddle their children in myriad ways—all but doing their homework for them, hiring tutors for their college SAT exams, financing their indulgences well past their teens into their twenties. "And these kids," he says, "are entering a world in which their economic opportunities will not be as great as their parents'. Housing costs so much more; so do education and health. How are they going to cope?"

Pope thinks that it is in confronting this conundrum that his generation has an opportunity for a new social compact with the young, the kind of compact he would like to have had when he was their age and first confronting the new problems of his time.

Pope, the diminutive longtime executive director of the Sierra Club, America's best-known member-based environmental organization, is a true representative of the social-movement zeitgeist of the Sixties. A public school graduate, he entered Harvard in 1963. By then Harvard and the other Ivies were expanding their reach into the middle and working classes of America, and Pope remembers that the traditional prep school crowd was, in his judgment, "marginalized . . . they were there, and they hung with each other, but the rest of us didn't pay that much attention or take them too seriously."

It's not hard to imagine Carl Pope as a different kind of student—a bright, articulate liberal activist, doing well in the classroom and in the center of whatever campus debates were taking place. The civil rights movement was his first calling. He went south to work with the Student Nonviolent Coordinating Committee in Arkansas during the second Freedom Summer in 1965.

But when he returned to work in the movement that fall, he was fired by Stokely Carmichael, the militant black power advocate who had seized control of SNCC. Pope still is angry about his dismissal. "I was actually fired for being white. That was their philosophy. So the civil rights movement was closed off to me."

Pope shifted his attention to the Students for a Democratic Society (SDS), which had been founded in Ann Arbor, Michigan, in 1960. In those days, SDS comprised four distinct groups, not always working in sync.

"One group," Pope says, "was associated with the traditional Communist Party. One with the Mao Tse-tung branch of the party. Another larger group was not very ideological; they were mainly focused on the war. And I was a member of a smaller group—not Marxists, but with a broader agenda than the war."

The Maoists, the progressive labor types, he remembers, moved into working-class neighborhoods and went so far as to tell everyone to get married because that was the working-class way. But according to Pope, that branch of the SDS started attracting the radical set, and before long, they wanted to start blowing things up.

In retrospect, Pope sees the contradictions in the leadership ethos of the movement. "We had no mentors," he says. "I had never met anyone older than me from whom I had learned anything. That was not an unusual attitude for baby boomers. They had been raised in the comforts of the Fifties, and when they decided to break with their elders, they did so with breathtaking hubris, few regrets, and some very consequential lapses in judgment.

"Obviously, I'd learned things . . . from people who were older than I was, but I hadn't learned anything about how to change society from anybody older. . . . Oh, I suppose, literally speaking, that is not true. I met Michael Harrington [the author of the influential book on poverty **The Other America**] once. So there was Michael Harrington, there was Dr. King in an indirect way. . . . [Although] the relationship between SCLC and SNCC was not a mentoring one.

"But in the whole Vietnam stuff, you know, there were a lot of professors at Harvard who shared our view of the war, but they were not providing movement leadership. There was a big teach-in at Harvard, and Stanley Hoffman, who was one of my professors, spoke. Stanley provided a very helpful perspective on how to understand the historic moment. But when we went out to the next meeting to decide what to do, there was nobody there over twenty-two."

As Pope says now, "So on the one hand, we got to

exercise leadership . . . but it also meant we weren't very effective at the time." It's not that there were no grown-ups around, but many of them simply abdicated their roles as mentors in a misguided attempt to win favor with even the most irresponsible of the student activists.

The author and commentator Roger Rosenblatt, a card-carrying liberal of the FDR school, was a junior faculty member at Harvard in 1969, when the campus erupted in a series of protests that steadily escalated in violence. The climax came when the local SDS chapter stormed University Hall, forcibly removed the Harvard deans and administrators who had offices there, and generally trashed the place.

Police were called in to clear out the protestors, and the large-scale bust touched off a contentious debate within the faculty about what to do with the offenders, most of whom were lightly punished, if at all. Rosenblatt was in the middle of the debate as someone who had standing with the university's elders but also with the students.

What he went through, he has described in a small, fine book called **Coming Apart: A Memoir of the Harvard Wars of 1969.** The failure of many faculty members and the inability of the institution to uphold certain standards of behavior so unnerved him that he decided to abandon his plans to become a university professor.

Almost forty years later, Rosenblatt can barely contain his contempt for those who buckled in the face of contemptuous behavior. As he told me, "The students had the advantage of being young. They could be

Carl Pope (left) by the Stanislaus River in California, 1969

irritating. They could be dangerous. But they were educable.

"My fellow faculty members . . . had seen enough to know how to behave in a situation in which important things are in peril. The students were in peril. As a parent, one of the worst things you can do is side with a child when you know he's wrong."

Carl Pope had graduated from Harvard by the time of the University Hall takeover, and he'd already begun to have his own reservations about the realities of the student activist culture, most of which was centered on the war. "There was an op-ed in **The New York Times** about how the youth were going to save America from the war. I thought, 'This is bizarre. I am young. I can't get a piece in **The New York Times**. Why am I supposed to save America from the war? Why aren't **you** guys saving America from the war?' There was this tremendous sense that the generation ahead of us had abdicated. I think they believed in social action. They just wanted someone else to do it. They were not unsupportive; they just wanted someone else to lead. And so the movement was led by kids, who are impulsive—not very strategic. It's ultimately unstable and volatile." Most of his fellow activists, he says, expected immediate results, but he was more pragmatic. He remembers an episode that summed up the shortcomings of the movement.

Defense Secretary Robert McNamara visited Harvard in 1967 for a closed, off-the-record forum on the war, and the SDS decided that if McNamara wouldn't debate his policies publicly, the group would physically prevent him from leaving the campus.

McNamara declined the invitation, so about a thousand students filled the space around Quincy House (where the forum was being held), surrounding McNamara's limousine.

When the official visit was over, McNamara could have slipped away through the basement, but he chose to confront the protestors. He was escorted to his limousine by a small posse of Harvard conservatives. As the crowd closed in on him, yelling, "Debate the war, debate the war!" McNamara got testy and challenged the crowd, "Okay, let's debate the war. Who wants to debate?"

Still incredulous at the memory, Pope says, "And we didn't have anyone to debate him." So McNamara's car began to drive away. Pope quickly organized a lie-in, positioning students in front of the car so it couldn't move. **That** they knew how to do. McNamara got out and left through the basement.

Pope sees this as a seminal moment. "We had no adult leadership. That in turn allowed the radicals to take over the antiwar movement in 1968." The domino effect, in Pope's judgment, was that the war became the issue, not broader social change. "You didn't have people who'd read thoughtfully about social change. You just had people who didn't want to get drafted."

Even after he left Harvard, Pope continued to find an older generation that was right-thinking, well intentioned, and, essentially, timid and adrift.

"Later, I came to California working on environmental stuff—this would now have been the Seventies, but it's still my generation, and I would meet people who had been sub–cabinet officials. Okay? These were people who had been movers and shakers, and I was still a puppy. And they would look to me for guidance. . . .

"It was extremely disconcerting. They were the silent generation. They had been through McCarthyism, and I think they were deeply scarred by McCarthyism. They had learned not to stick their necks out. These people were socially engaged, but they were not willing to lead. They wanted to follow. Forty-five-year-olds wanted to follow twenty-eight-year-olds. It was bizarre."

After a time in India as a Peace Corps worker, Pope returned to the United States thinking he would go to graduate school, but an interim position with Zero Population Growth changed those plans. "I was twenty-five and running an office with three employees, lobbying on Capitol Hill, testifying before Congress. I was having a helluva good time, so I didn't want to go to graduate school."

After a couple of years, he decided to try living on the West Coast, and the Sierra Club was a perfect fit. The timing was fortuitous. President Nixon had created the Environmental Protection Agency, establishing enforceable federal standards for clean water, air, and other natural resources, including endangered species. It was a historic step forward, a critical element in raising the public consciousness about the environment.

Those were glory days for Pope, combining, as they did, the challenge of overdue reforms and the opportunity to get it right substantively and politically. "The environmental movement was bipartisan and diverse, with organized labor providing much of the funding for the first Earth Day in 1970," he says.

Now, however, Pope believes the movement has been fragmented, and he traces the problem to a three-step evolution. He says the other side was caught off guard when a wave of environmental protection legislation was enacted in the early Seventies—and by Nixon, of all people. But by 1975 the business community had regrouped and was mobilizing scientific challenges and legal roadblocks to the actual implementation of the stealth legislation.

In response, environmental organizations had to shift from community organizing to technical expertise. As a result, according to Pope, most of the environmental community became a technocracy concentrated on defending the science behind the environmental movement. But in Pope's view, the Reagan-led reorganization of the Republican Party as a singular, ideologically coherent power in the Eighties and Nineties—combined with the big financial stakes involved in the environmental issues—completely changed the playing field. It was the environmental movement's turn to be caught off guard, still heavily invested in scientific expertise when politics had once again become the currency of the debate.

"When environmentalism was whether you were going to set aside land in the Olympic Peninsula, most congressmen had zero risk. When the issue is the amount of carbon dioxide industry is allowed to emit, the financial stakes are huge." That changed the game plan significantly, and Pope believes the environmental movement still hasn't changed its strategy effectively enough.

The young Sixties activist is now an elder-statesman strategist as he lays out the realities and figures out the responses. "Our base is bigger than ever . . . our strength has increased, but the stakes have gotten so much bigger, so rapidly, we're now outgunned. We have three imperatives going forward. One, we have to rebuild power before we can influence policy. Two, we have to intensify public sentiment rather than mobilizing environmental expertise. And three, we need to engage new constituencies rather than just mobilize our base."

He also worries that the movement has become too institutionalized, especially with its emphasis on expertise and issues. He keeps returning to the need to return to "people power."

"The average American neighborhood doesn't have someone who's the go-to person on the environment— who talks it up to their neighbors. Because, of course, Americans don't know their neighbors anymore."

Pope has no doubt that the environmental movement is one of the great legacies of the Sixties. "It is clearly hardwired to the Sixties idea that we're one country. And, of course, it was the Sixties generation that had the greatest influence on the movement."

Yet, always the student, Pope sees the contradictions. Referring to Ruth Benedict's classic book **Patterns of Culture**, in which she said there are basically two sides to human culture—Dionysian and Apollonian—Pope sees the Sixties as Dionysian. "It was about freedom, and it was about liberation—sex, drugs, and rock and roll, having a good time. It was kind of reckless."

But the environmental movement, he says, "is quite Apollonian. It's about control. It's about restraint. It's fundamentally a conservative movement in the traditional, old-fashioned sense. You're conserving things. You're trying not to turn people loose. So in that sense, the environmental movement is not like the Sixties."

Ed Crane

Ed Crane was a student at Berkeley at the height of the Free Speech Movement, when Mario Savio was a deity on campus. But Ed Crane was not impressed. "They were just unsavory people. It was the **filthy**-speech movement. And it was not a question of **what** you could say. It was a question of **where** you could speak. The Berkeley administration handled that very badly, the police were called, and it was a mess."

Crane, who was president of the UC Berkeley chapter of the Sigma Chi fraternity, strongly opposed the war in Vietnam, but he refused to get involved in the student protests, he says, "because they were as much anti-American as they were antiwar."

Crane, who is now president of the Cato Institute, a libertarian think tank in Washington, has an idea for rejuvenating American politics: Strike all the election laws restricting campaign contributions from the books. He says, "The reason there's not a true national third party is because of those laws. Without them you'd have a Libertarian Party, small but not radical, that combines support for dynamic market capitalism, free speech, and civil liberties, and a less grandiose foreign policy. You'd have a Green Party much more progressive than the Democratic Party on issues such as the environment.

"Without these restrictions, anyone along the political spectrum with good ideas could get ten people in a room who would say, 'I'll give you two hundred and fifty thousand dollars, full disclosure, because I agree with you.' Then you'd have some real competition. As it is now, it's just embarrassing. We go around the world promoting democracy, and we have basically a 99 percent rate of reelecting people who are in office"—because they have access to the money available under the current rules.

What kind of message, Crane wonders, does that send to third-world countries that see more money being spent on a campaign for some local political office in America than they can afford for their school lunch or children's health programs?

When he left Berkeley in 1967, he went on to get an MBA at USC and then became a money manager. He also became involved in the Libertarian movement, and by 1970 he was actively working to build it into a national party.

The Libertarian Party was able to get on the ballot in all fifty states for the 1980 election, a Herculean effort, given the tight hold that Democrats and Republicans have on the election process. But Crane realized the renegade party's future was limited. First there was the Libertarian platform, which even he admits appeals primarily to the fringe element, with its heavy emphasis on a society free of government programs, including the subsidies that both major parties use to keep con-

Ed Crane
in 1969, a money
manager at the
Alliance Capital
Management
Corporation

Ed Crane, founder
and president of the
Cato Institute, at a
celebration of the
organization's
twenty-fifth
anniversary in 2002

stituents loyal. Crane likens the 1974 federal election laws, which restrict campaign contributions to one thousand dollars, to Wal-Mart saying anyone can advertise against it but can spend only a thousand dollars doing so. "No third party can survive with these restrictions," he says.

Crane cites the 1968 campaign for the Democratic presidential nomination as a case in point. "McCarthy got six-figure contributions from wealthy liberals, including Stuart Mott, the General Motors heir. Everyone knew, and no one said anything about it.

"McCarthy told me if the '74 restrictions had been in place, he would not have run against LBJ. So what does that tell us? I like to remind my liberal friends who are big campaign finance reform advocates, 'You ought to think about that.'"

Despite his revulsion for much of the counterculture movement of the Sixties, Crane welcomes many of the changes the decade brought. "It was an important period in American history. Take women's rights. When I was a young money manager, my secretaries were so smart. Today they'd be doctors, lawyers, or business leaders.

"Big business back then was centralized and controlled from the top down. But the Sixties forced a management revolution that led to much more innovation and the explosion of economic growth."

As he sees it, the success of the civil rights movement forced the country to deal with the terrible consequences of racial discrimination to the individual, but the programs that came out of President Johnson's

Great Society introduced the concept of victimhood to black neighborhoods. He says, "If you were black, you came to believe society owed you all these things, and if you didn't have them, it wasn't your fault.

"White Americans foisted on black Americans the idea of dependency. We're beginning to move away from that now, with the reforms in the welfare programs. More and more black Americans are asking how they can help solve the problems that are endemic to their society."

Crane blames the Great Society culture for another problem that extends well beyond racial lines. "We're still living with these massive government programs, such as Medicare, with their massive unfunded liabilities, and the baby boomers getting ready to retire. It's going to be a mess."

As a libertarian, Crane also believes strongly in the decriminalization of drugs. He sees the current laws as an unwarranted restriction on individual liberty. Forty years after he graduated from Berkeley, with short hair and as a card-carrying Greek-letter fraternity member, Ed Crane figures he remains a contrarian child of the Sixties. After all, when the movement was calling for the young to take control of America's institutions, he was a young money manager controlling a quarter-billion dollars in assets. As a Libertarian, he was writing newspaper commentaries and appearing on television criticizing big government. He was promoting drug legalization and criticizing the military. He says now of his life, "I guess it was a Sixties kind of a deal."

Dolores Huerta

Dolores Huerta grew up in Stockton, California, where her mother, a successful middle-class businesswoman, owned and operated a restaurant and hotel. Huerta, who was born in 1930, was a Girl Scout and drum majorette before getting a teaching certificate from a local community college. Her classroom, filled with the children of poor migrant workers, became her conversion chamber; she began the life of a community organizer and social activist that would define her forever.

In the Fifties and Sixties, she was a seminal force in organizing California's large Latino population in the agriculturally rich San Joaquin Valley, where immigrant farmworkers toiled and lived in third-world conditions. One of her fellow organizers was the young Cesar Chavez.

She remembers going door-to-door to register voters and seeing homes "with dirt floors, cardboard crates for furniture, and yet you knew how hard these people were working—you saw the injustice of working so hard and yet hardly having enough to eat. At the time we started organizing, the wage was seventy to ninety cents an hour; there was no unemployment insurance, so at the end of the season, the workers would have to follow the crops and travel, taking their kids with them. There were no bathrooms in the fields, no water breaks . . . they worked from sunup to sundown."

In 1962, Huerta and Chavez, the teacher and the farmworker, took their organizational skills to the next level with the formation of the National Farm Workers

Association, a fledgling union that found its national voice when it joined Filipino grape workers in a walk-out and boycott of the Schenley wine company. Five thousand grape pickers walked off the job, and within a year Schenley had signed the first-ever collective bargaining agreement with farmworkers.

It was just the beginning. The NFWA, by then known as the United Farm Workers of America, or UFW, organized a nationwide consumer boycott of California table grapes in 1967 that quickly became a divisive issue between Democrats who supported it, and Republicans who adamantly opposed it (including the members of the California Republican delegation flying to the 1968 Miami convention who decided to do so conspicuously).

In 1970 grape growers agreed to recognize the union and sign contracts that covered about twenty thousand workers. By then Chavez and Huerta were two of the best-known labor activists in America. Their profiles were raised considerably after Bobby Kennedy took them into his inner circle when he ran for president in 1968.

Huerta was onstage with Kennedy the night he gave his victory speech at the Ambassador Hotel in Los Angeles. She remembers being worried for his safety. "During this time we had so much violence around us. Cesar was always getting these death threats. I was very worried Bobby didn't have enough protection around him. On the way out, he wasn't supposed to go through the kitchen. He was supposed to go into a room where we had mariachi bands and all the people who had worked for him. But he went through the kitchen.

"It was an incredible, irreversible loss. People had faith in him. He was connected to poor people. He was a real leader, and he wasn't afraid. I think he would have made life better for all people, not just farmworkers."

It was never the same for Huerta or Chavez after Kennedy's death, although they continued their work in the California farmlands and across the country. Chavez remained the soft-spoken, almost mystical figure who subjected himself to lengthy fasts in Gandhi-like fashion to make his point. Huerta was the fiery, often belligerent organizer who fought with anyone—ally or supporter, it made little difference—if they didn't see the world her way.

As she raced from meeting to meeting, negotiation to negotiation, protest to protest, her eleven children by two husbands frequently had to be left in the care of others. She was at once divisive and effective, referred to as the Madonna of the Fields by her supporters and as the Dragon Lady by the growers.

She had a subsistence income, and one of her sons, a farmworkers' lawyer, told the **Los Angeles Times,** "She sort of belonged to the farmworker movement and it was our job to support her."

In 1988, San Francisco police roughed Huerta up during a protest against then–Vice President George H. W. Bush, and her spleen was ruptured. The city paid her over $800,000 and changed its crowd-control tactics as a result.

She's now in her late seventies, but her fires have not been banked. She continues to roam the country, rallying workers and sympathetic audiences to the cause of labor justice and the plight of immigrants. It's a different time, however, and she laments, "Young people today have no memory of the issues we fought for and take for granted. It's up to the people in the movement to remind them."

She misses the camaraderie and sacrifices of the Sixties, when "you had people who were committed—who dropped out of school and organized full-time for almost no money. The movement became a lifestyle. People didn't mind not having material goods; that was a kind of badge of honor."

Her big issue these days is what she calls "corporate greed" and, as she sees it, the failures of the news media to deal with economic injustice. "Could we imagine in 1968," she asks, "the kinds of salaries corporate officers now receive? The wage gap between workers and the CEOs?"

Warming to her subject, she says that when she talks to college students, she tells them to read the business pages if they really want to know about crime in America. She insists that the haves as well as the have-nots are misinformed and being taught to hate blacks and immigrants.

She travels constantly, across America and to places such as Venezuela, where she admires that country's anti-American president, Hugo Chávez, for his use of oil revenues for social purposes, such as schools, housing, and job training, overlooking his well-documented record of using violence to suppress political opposition.

Huerta is encouraged because the American left is making a comeback politically. She thinks the right has overplayed its favorite themes. "I think," she says, "the attacks on immigrants, gays, on women's reproductive

Dolores Huerta, vice president of United Farm Workers of America, during a grape pickers' strike in 1968

Dolores Huerta in 2003, as a member of the University of California Board of Regents, appointed by Governor Gray Davis

rights are distractions from the real issues . . . the economy and the income gaps."

Now, she believes, there's something to build on, a residual effect of the Sixties. "Now we have an environmental movement. We have a full-blown women's movement all across the country." She is encouraged that some of the elders of the civil rights movement— Andrew Young, John Lewis, Harry Belafonte, and others—are beginning to discuss how to pass the baton to a new generation.

"Change comes from the bottom up, not from the top. We've got to organize. As long as I have energy and my health, I will spread the word." She concedes that the Sixties seem like a "thousand years ago," and, she believes, so many of the gains of that time have been eroded. But now, she says, "it's been a big wake-up call . . . people are starting to open their eyes again."

Referring again to what happened in Venezuela, where Chávez overthrew the oligarchy in an election, Huerta says, "I think we're going to have in our country a nonviolent electoral revolution."

Maybe not a revolution, but both parties recognize that 2008 is destined to be a year of realignment. The Democrats, in the words of author Norman Mailer, "have been on their hands and knees since 1968, and they're now attempting to pick themselves off the floor." In 2006, as the war in Iraq dragged on at an ever higher cost in American lives and dollars, the Democrats were the beneficiaries as the leading critics of the war, helped in part by the presence of James

Webb, a Democratic senator and a decorated Vietnam veteran who took the lead in attacking the Bush war policies.

They also welcomed an antiabortion advocate, freshman senator Bob Casey of Pennsylvania, into their ranks. And they took notice when middle-of-the-road Democrats, male and female, with no ideological ties to the Sixties were elected governor in states such as Montana, Wyoming, and Arizona. They capitalized on the heightened public concern about global warming, a crusade long and prominently led by one of their own, former vice president Al Gore.

The journalist Jeff Greenfield believes that if Robert Kennedy had lived, he would have turned the Democratic Party away from the path of Sixties political correctness much earlier. Kennedy was already talking about solving many of the great social ills in the country from the ground up, instead of from the top down.

Greenfield asks aloud, "When **Roe v. Wade** came along, do you think Bobby Kennedy, a strong Roman Catholic, father of eleven children, would have allowed choice to be one of the litmus tests of the Democratic Party? You're either for choice or you're not welcome?" Greenfield doesn't think so.

The Sixties realigned both political parties, and the great questions for 2008 will be "Is this the end of the Sixties for the Democrats? And will the Republicans find a new champion who can keep the conservative base and still appeal to the ever growing numbers of independent voters?"

Going into what both parties consider to be a

transformational election year, Democrats have been the beneficiaries of public fatigue with the ideological certainty of the administration of George W. Bush.

Mr. Bush bet his presidency on his war plans for Iraq, and when one premise after another collapsed, at an ever higher cost in American lives, a large majority of voters lost their patience and turned away.

As 2008 arrives, the Democrats have an opportunity to move beyond the culture of self-destruction that grew out of the internecine battles that have wracked the party since 1968.

To do that, they must become more than the sum of their many parts, and party leaders have to acknowledge the centrist instincts of the country, especially in red states such as Kansas, Arizona, Montana, and Wyoming where Democratic governors have been so successful.

Republicans have the tricky challenge of balancing the narrow interests of their hard-core conservative base against the new realities of an electorate that is much more tempered, and temperate, in its political ideology. The Republican checkerboard of red states combined with impressive get-out-the-vote efforts in the so-called battleground states can still win elections. But when it comes to governing, the GOP remains hostage to the most conservative elements of its base and unable to strike the kinds of compromises that have always moved the country forward.

Both parties are guilty of creating high walls for admission at the national level. If you're Republican, all ye who enter here must be absolutely, unconditionally antiabortion, anti–gay rights, progun, antitax, and antienvironment, whatever the consequences. Democrats must be unquestioningly prochoice, pro–gay rights, antigun, protax, and proenvironment, come what may.

It is not just coincidental that an ever larger number of young voters consider the Internet their political system, and that with every modern election cycle, the universe of voters who consider themselves independent and unattached to either party continues to expand. They're interested in answers for **their** lives, not in the feuds of forty years ago.

For them, the Sixties? Wasn't that when Mom and Dad wore those weird outfits, when the Beatles were still a group and you had to use pay phones?

The War
Without End

It took ten or fifteen years before people
were proud of serving in Vietnam.

—GENERAL WAYNE A. DOWNING,
U.S. ARMY (RET.)

[The World War II veterans] got the parades, the good
war, that we didn't. But then we all became friends
because we had all endured combat, and that trumps
other differences. It crossed party lines.

—FORMER U.S. SENATOR BOB KERREY

Those of us who were in Vietnam know it's the same
damn scenario. For a time we thought we were never
going to get out of Vietnam; now I don't know
if we'll ever get out of Iraq.

—RON ARMELLA

In THE COURSE of writing this book, I was startled by the number of people I encountered who said, "I didn't know anyone who went to Vietnam." Or they would say, "I think a kid in my high school class went; I don't know if he came back." It is one more manifestation of the generation gap that appeared in America in the Sixties. The parents of the baby boom generation had experienced World War II as a unifying experience. Everyone, in and out of uniform, had a role. But Vietnam was the war that deeply divided a generation. Moreover, the nature of the resistance to Vietnam—which included burning the American flag, cheering on North Vietnamese leader Ho Chi Minh, welcoming an enemy victory, and disparaging military service—was taken (and in most cases meant) as an insult to the patriotism of the World War II generation.

Forty years later, Vietnam—as a war, as a political issue, and as a deeply significant personal experience for many—continues to occupy a central role in our collective memory. I continue to encounter Vietnam veterans in two distinctly different spheres: the public arena, where their service is now a badge of distinction, and the working-class arena, where Vietnam is a common bond that is only occasionally mentioned and remains all but invisible to those who do not share it.

I find that it usually comes up in unexpected ways. A few years ago an affable driver, a white-haired man about my age, picked me up at an airport in Florida, and I commented on the heat and humidity. He said, "Yeah, you're right, but after Vietnam, I've never complained about the heat. God, **that** was hot." Only when I pressed him did he volunteer that he'd been in combat there for a year. "It was tough," he said. "I was lucky to get back." That was as much as he wanted to say, except that he had liked my book about those who had served in World War II.

I reminded him of a story in that book about a family friend, Gordon Larson, a World War II Marine who watched his brother die during a firefight with the Japanese. Gordon had a long, difficult war, and after he got back, he said to me, "If I went into a bar and they were talking about combat, I walked out. I knew if they were talking about it, they hadn't been there."

The Vietnam vet just nodded and drove on.

David Cadwell

When we lived in a leafy corner of northwest Connecticut, I had a friend, David Cadwell, who ran a small country café alongside a covered bridge on the

Housatonic River. A teddy bear of a man, with a thick beard and curly hair, David had an ever-present twinkle in his eyes and a corny joke always at the ready.

We talked sports and local politics, reviewed David Letterman's latest opening monologues, and jointly decided whether I should have the French toast for breakfast. We did not talk about Vietnam because I had no idea he was connected to the war until he spoke at the local Memorial Day services the year after the terrorist attacks of 9/11.

His Memorial Day remarks were called "The Worst Day of My Life," and they recounted the time his company in the 1st Cavalry Division spotted what they thought were some North Vietnamese.

In an interview, he elaborated. "Captain Johnny Ward grabs his rifle, and off he runs," Cadwell remembers. "And it's like, holy crap, I've got to try to keep up with him. I'm trying to catch up, and everyone's on the move—rat-tat-tat, not a lot of fire, but a little back and forth.

"Meanwhile, our artillery officer is doing his job. We're gonna put artillery on the other side of them. Somebody goofed somewhere. The rounds hit us.

"The only other medic was killed. Captain Ward— God, this drove me crazy—he never wore a helmet. He'd always wear a little boonie cap—and literally, the top of his head was taken off by our rounds. But he was alive, and the lieutenant was seriously hurt.

"I was scared to death. I cannot tell you how inadequate I feel that I couldn't save these guys. And oh, God, the blood—the worst part was the blood. You can't say, 'I'm gonna grab a shower now.' It was days, weeks later till we came in and I had to wear the same uniform with all the blood."

Dave Cadwell's journey to that gruesome scene in a Vietnam jungle began in Southern California, where he grew up, the son of an Allstate Insurance executive and a stay-at-home mom. He graduated from high school in 1968 with no particular thoughts about Vietnam—or about much else, for that matter. He enrolled in a local community college and, by his own description, was "just floundering" when his draft notice arrived.

"It was like 'Okay, buddy, it's your time.' I just sort of got sucked up into the system. I was nineteen years old, and what did I know? I didn't really have anything physical that was going to get me out of it. I'm not politically put together, and there's no way in hell I'm off to Canada.

"I just knew I couldn't be counted on to shoot anyone, so I entered as a conscientious objector who was willing to serve. They made me a medic, which was fine. You basically have two sorts of personalities when someone gets hurt. One goes, 'Ew, I don't want to do that,' and the other goes, 'What can I do?' I'm more of a 'What can I do?' kinda guy.

"Quite frankly, I thought they'd put me in a hospital or something like that. Surprise, surprise, I'm with the First Cav, the infantry, and off you go. I never took any heat from the guys for being a CO. I'd always say, 'Hey, since I don't carry a rifle or ammo, I can carry more stuff to look after you guys.' "

As for the politics of Vietnam, Cadwell wasn't

Army medic Dave Cadwell
(second from right) with his
platoon in Vietnam

Dave Cadwell in Vietnam.
"The worst part was the blood."

Today, Cadwell is an
emergency medical technician

paying much attention. "I thought, 'There must be a reason for this, or we wouldn't be doing it.' " He was more troubled by what he was seeing firsthand in the jungle.

"It was '70 to '71, so Vietnamization was under way; we were turning it over to the South Vietnamese. So we didn't go on search-and-destroy missions. We went on search-and-**avoid** missions.

"There were the exceptions. We'd put unearthly firepower on a target and—it just broke my heart— you'd go up and discover a couple of bodies, no weapons or anything. And you'd realize these guys were probably just kidnapped from the village to carry rice, and the guys with the guns are gone."

Even so, Cadwell volunteered for another six months when his year tour was up. He was assigned to a field hospital a safe distance from the combat zones. "We had our own PX, a swimming pool, the Bob Hope show came through. It was terrific, a very **M∗A∗S∗H**-like experience."

Cadwell was not unaware that he had been inhabiting two different worlds in Vietnam. "They served four hot meals a day at the hospital, and one day I'm standing in line with my tray, and the guy in front of me is hollering, 'What? No Jell-O today?'

"He was screwed because he didn't get his Jell-O that day. That was Vietnam to him. And I'm thinking, 'A few weeks ago I was carrying all my food, water, medic supplies on patrol, and this guy is pissed off because he doesn't have his Jell-O?' "

As a medic, Cadwell said, he saw death so routinely that he became emotionally oblivious to it. When he came home and went to funerals, he was not affected by the sight of the dead; he had learned to block it out.

Years after he was back, he rediscovered his emotions. He was working as a volunteer emergency medical technician for the local fire department. One day they were called to a ski hill where a young girl had been killed in a freak accident on the slope.

"What really affected me was a dear friend that I've worked with for years in the ambulance, a manly man—after the rescue helicopter left, he went to pieces. Loudly weeping, broke down. And it struck me: 'What's the matter with you, Dave? Why aren't you weeping right alongside him?' It really struck me that I got desensitized by Vietnam. It certainly numbed me, because I had seen death before.

"And I saw how random and arbitrary it could be. It really wasn't until we actually had a meeting and they brought in a grief expert and everything to get you through these things that I actually broke down." Once again Cadwell was able to grieve over death. Vietnam had drained that from him, but thirty years after he returned, the death of a child rekindled his heart.

General Colin Powell

General Colin L. Powell, USA (Ret.), is one of the few people in America—indeed in the world—who literally needs no introduction. He combines being one of the most famous with being one of the most admired men in the country. The former chairman of the Joint

Chiefs of Staff and secretary of state was born in Harlem in 1937 and was in his midtwenties when the Sixties began. Now, four decades later, he describes the late Sixties and early Seventies as the "scariest time" of his adult life. As America was buffeted by the assassinations of Dr. King and Robert Kennedy, racial confrontations and riots, the drug culture, the sexual revolution, the dissolution of the culture, and the disillusion of Watergate, it sometimes seemed as if the country were self-destructing. Adding to the tension, Powell remembers, was a concern well beyond the American borders. As he puts it, "A Soviet Union that says, 'We told you. **We're** winning.'"

But Powell says America found its footing again thanks to Gerald Ford, "a plainspoken guy from the Midwest who makes a few bold decisions: the pardon of Nixon to get that behind us, and the Helsinki Accords, which force the Russians to acknowledge human rights."

As Powell describes it, Jerry Ford pulled the country out of a dive, Jimmy Carter managed to muddle through, the country was getting better day by day, and then . . . "Out of the West comes Ronald Reagan, riding on a horse and saying, 'It's morning in America again! We can do anything! We're strong!' From my angle, as a soldier," Powell says admiringly, "it was the most remarkable thing."

By the time Reagan left office in 1989, with the Soviet empire collapsing, Powell believes the Sixties were effectively over. This was especially true for the military, which had been put back together thanks to the all-volunteer military and the stewardship of Defense Secretary Caspar Weinberger, who was a tenacious promoter of military budgets and military pride.

Powell also credits those of his fellow young officers who elected to stay in uniform while others were bailing out during the Nixon and Carter years. "I am proud," he says, "very proud, of those of us who stayed. A lot of my fellow black officers left in those days; they started getting pulled out by corporate America. People started asking me, 'Gee, why don't you leave? You were a White House Fellow, got a graduate degree in business administration.' There were opportunities, but I was a professional soldier. Professional soldiers stay."

Powell has no illusions about the price of the Sixties for the American military and for the country. The consequences of war and the attitudes of so many at home, he believes, were deeply painful. "We lost a generation of young men; either they were killed, or they weren't coming back for a third tour or making the Army their profession. So we were told, 'No draft—it's all volunteer. You guys are on your own. Make it work.'" And Colin Powell, America's best-known former soldier, believes they made it work spectacularly well. "There aren't antimilitary attitudes out there. Most people have enormous respect for the military. There are divisions between those who go and those who can elect not to go, but there's no animosity."

The more important question for Powell is "Will Iraq create a problem where you can't get enough volunteers? Kids are taking a second look. Their parents are taking a second look. There are too many multiple amputees walking around out there right now."

Minutes after a helicopter crash in Vietnam in 1968. Colin Powell, in the right-hand corner, with his face bruised, keeps an eye on the circling helicopters

Retired general Colin Powell enjoying a favorite pastime in November 2006: tinkering with old Volvos

Beyond the effect of the Sixties on the military, he worries about the Sixties' influence on the popular culture. "It's a helluva lot better than it was in the Sixties, but it is still being cheapened . . . particularly in the black community. Bill Cosby is right in his criticisms, but he goes too far. My kids and grandkids are black, and they're fine. But among the inner-city black kids, the culture's being diluted by bad language and comedy appealing to the most base instincts."

He describes watching television with his grandkids. "We'd channel surf, and you'd never know what was going to come up. And to think you're gonna protect them from this? It's almost comical."

Not surprisingly, when Powell's son Michael, the father of those grandchildren, was chairman of the Federal Communications Commission, he cracked down on indecent material on the public airwaves, levying substantial fines against networks and individual television and radio stations. His most famous reprimand went to CBS for telecasting Janet Jackson's infamous "wardrobe malfunction" during the Super Bowl half-time show.

Where race is concerned, however, Powell knows personally the gains that have been made. He tells the story of coming home from Vietnam in 1964 and not being able to get a hamburger at a popular place in Columbus, Georgia. Yet, he says, "We freed **white America** more than we freed black America with the passage of the Civil Rights Act that year. White Americans were stuck with racism, and they had to be freed by the federal government." Powell's provocative point is that morally, economically, politically, and culturally the 1964 Civil Rights Act lifted the entire country, not just the black population.

"Things are a helluva lot better. There is no place a black American with means can't go and live. There are a few, you know, stupid golf clubs that won't let me in, but I don't care . . . but nobody really cares if there are these crazy old white men who want to sit around playing golf without any black guys around."

Powell wasn't happy when Tiger Woods seemed to be backing away from descriptions of himself as a black man. Woods's father and mentor, Earl, was an American black man, but Tiger's mother was born in Thailand, so he referred to himself as "Cablinasian," referring to his black, Chinese, Thai, Caucasian, and American Indian heritage.

Powell says, "Tell you what—if Tiger goes around to the back of the clubhouse at Augusta [home of the Masters Tournament], he'll know what black is."

Powell wants to use his considerable influence to be a leader in America on his terms: "I want to be an American who is black and can speak to the whole population. I don't want to be a 'black leader,' but now that I've made it, I want to continue to be black. I don't want anyone to think anything else, because too many guys died and worked like the devil, and they could have been chairman of the Joint Chiefs, but they never got there because of the way the country used to be.

"What kills me is when I run into black Americans who are not taking advantage. I tell this story. I went to a Congressional Gold Medal ceremony. They were giving it to Rosa Parks, and I had to leave there for a high school commencement speech in the District. Two blocks from the Capitol, I see a gang of boys hanging out on the street, whispering and passing stuff from hand to hand. They were dealing—right there in broad daylight."

When he got to the high school, he congratulated the graduating seniors and then described what he had just witnessed: first the Rosa Parks ceremony and then the street-corner drug deals. He told the graduates, "That's not why Rosa Parks refused to give up her seat on the bus. It's not why we fought. It's not why we struggled . . . so some goddamned kid can stick his nose out and think it's cool because he's wearing baggy pants and a shirt with a basketball number on it. He can't speak the King's English. That's not why we made all these sacrifices."

Powell continues his public life, sitting on the Board of Overseers of the International Rescue Committee, a global refugee assistance organization; America's Promise, his national mentoring program; and the Colin Powell Center for Policy Studies at his alma mater, the City College of New York.

The City College program bearing his name— that alone is a commentary on the sweeping changes of the last forty years in America. A black man who rose from the streets of the Bronx to become, in many polls, the most respected public figure in America returned to campus to establish a studies program that serves, among others, émigrés from the old Soviet empire that Powell spent so much of his military career worrying about.

When he convenes a meeting of his center's trustees on campus, City College students gather to watch his famous and powerful friends arrive. The students' quiet reverence for their famous alum is another measure of the changes since the Sixties.

Here he is, a career military man, a retired chairman of the Joint Chiefs of Staff who presided over one war—Desert Storm—and as secretary of state helped justify another war—Iraq—with his appearance at the United Nations.

In the Sixties that résumé would have touched off campuswide demonstrations.

General Wayne Downing

While Colin Powell was coming of age in the Bronx, one of his military contemporaries was growing up in America's heartland without a father in a family with a record of military sacrifice.

Wayne Downing's dad was killed in combat in the closing months of World War II in Germany. "My memory of World War II," Downing told me before he died of complications from cancer in the summer of 2007, "is that the only man in my family was my grandfather. My father, uncle, and all my cousins were serving. We were a very patriotic family."

Downing, a high school wrestling star in Peoria, Illinois, was admitted to the U.S. Military Academy at West Point, the first member of his family to attend college. He graduated as a second lieutenant in 1962 and shipped out to Okinawa for two years with the 173rd Airborne Brigade, which became the first American combat unit assigned to Vietnam.

His outfit was based at Bien Hoa Air Base, nineteen miles north of Saigon, and Downing quickly learned what turned out to be the enduring truth of that war: The Vietcong were tenacious fighters, and they wanted to win more than the South Vietnamese did. When his first year in Vietnam was up, Downing returned to the United States to be an instructor in counterinsurgency, and by 1968 he was enrolled in the Infantry Officer Advanced Course at Fort Benning.

The class was comprised of young captains, all of whom had served in Vietnam. Downing admits they were a cocky group. "Whenever anyone cut class or fell asleep during class, we'd say, 'What are they going to do? Send me back to Vietnam?'"

The class also had a fatalistic attitude because the war was changing, and not for the better. At home the antiwar movement was spreading and becoming more raucous.

From inside Fort Benning, Downing heard the news of violent protests, Dr. King's assassination, then Robert Kennedy's murder, and wondered, "What the hell is going on?"

He says now, "In the advanced course, we had a large contingent of allied officers from Vietnam, Laos, Iran, Africa. So here they are in the United States, and Dr. King, our civil rights leader, is assassinated. I couldn't make sense of it myself. How could they?

"I didn't feel very comfortable with my explanation to them, which was 'We're still a very violent society. Our westward expansion put a certain character in the American people.' I'm afraid we're still a savage people. Look at the death penalty."

When Bobby Kennedy was shot to death by young Jordanian émigré Sirhan Sirhan, a Jordanian officer training with Downing didn't show up for classes for a week. "First he was afraid he'd be held accountable, and then he was ashamed," Downing remembers. "When he did return, we all tried to make him feel welcome."

The outside world was penetrating Fort Benning in other ways as well. "We had a classmate, Joe Dieduardo, who received notice that one of his best buddies, a black infantry captain, had been killed in Vietnam a few days before King's assassination. So Joe flew to San Francisco to meet the body and escort it home to Baltimore. Joe takes his friend's body to a funeral home in a black section of Baltimore, and when King is killed, Baltimore goes up in a riot.

"Joe is the only white guy around, so the funeral home folks hide him for three or four days—and then finally smuggle him to the airport in a hearse so he can get back to Benning. When he arrives, Joe, a Vietnam vet, says, 'You'll never believe where I've been.' "

There was a bizarre disconnect between Downing's Fort Benning world and the world just outside the base.

"The protests forced the military to turn inward. We had more of the Foreign Legion mentality. Here I was, a professional soldier, and I felt totally underappreciated. It was devastating."

Army efforts to turn public opinion around were often anachronistic, a throwback to World War II's heavy-handed propaganda efforts to keep the American public cheering on the men in uniform. Downing laughs when he remembers the Fort Benning premiere of John Wayne's big Vietnam movie, **The Green Berets**.

"We'd been drinking heavily at a cocktail party before the movie, and when it began to roll, we were hooting and hollering. It was terrible. It had nothing to do with Vietnam. It was stupid . . . jingoistic, very Hollywood."

When it came time to return to Vietnam, Downing was pessimistic about his chances of surviving. "In my heart of hearts, I really didn't think I was coming back. I drank too much, and I partied too hard. I wouldn't buy any new civilian clothes. There was nothing of permanence I would buy. I thought I'd be wasting money.

"I was married, and I had two children at the time. I later divorced, not because of Vietnam, but you have to think about the stress military service puts on families. You have mixed loyalties. Do you owe allegiance to your family or to the Army?

"I bought as much insurance as I could afford, but I never thought about getting out. I was a professional soldier. I had taken an oath. I owed the Army my allegiance."

When Downing returned to Vietnam with the 25th Infantry in 1968, he faced a much tougher enemy, and the men in his command were much greener than those who had served under him in the first tour. "In 1965 I was with a professional unit. They had been together for two or three years, and most of them were veterans of Korea or even World War II. They had tremendous experience.

"When I went back, it was with all draftees. They

Major Wayne Downing (at top) in Vietnam in 1968, checking on a wounded squad member

Downing as a student at Tulane University in 1974, after serving two tours of duty in Vietnam

Four-star General Wayne Downing

were fairly slovenly. It was a struggle to get them to cut their hair. They wore peace symbols around their necks or on their helmets. But once you got past their cosmetics, they were very good soldiers.

"I remember one machine gunner named Fudo. He wore an enormous peace symbol around his neck, probably two inches in diameter. I viewed it as some kind of an antiwar statement, but one day a North Vietnamese unit tried to attack us, and Fudo's unit made the initial contact. When I got to him, Fudo was standing up in a rice paddy like John Wayne, shooting these North Vietnamese, while that peace medal banged up and down on his chest.

"Another guy was a Korean-American, a tremendous young kid who became a talented medic. When he first got to Vietnam, he was a pacifist, but after he'd been there six weeks, he was carrying a rifle, a pistol, and a big knife. He'd figured out the North Vietnamese were trying to kill him, and he didn't appreciate it."

It was a very challenging second tour for Downing. The enemy was better organized, and it now had access to heavier, much more sophisticated weapons. "Our younger kids," he says, "didn't realize you had to be careful not to offend the host population. We'd get into these big knock-down, drag-out fights, slugging it out, and the ordinary people were taking heavy casualties. That probably created more Vietcong than anything."

Downing didn't talk to the draftees about their feelings on the war. He knew they wanted to do their year and go home, a system he believes destroyed unit cohesion. "People were always coming and going," he says, "but the morale of the troops was pretty good. They wanted to survive. They wanted their leaders to be competent. If they were, the soldiers would do what you wanted. I had no discipline problems."

Downing returned to the United States in 1969, when the Army sent him to graduate school at Tulane. "It was amazing . . . going to class with the protestors and getting to know them personally. I began to recognize what was driving them and what they didn't understand.

"Many of them were dodging the draft by going on to graduate school. Going to class with them, working on projects with them, socializing after class and on weekends, I got to know them and their families, and they got to know me.

"I began to understand their frustrations with the war for the first time, their personal fears of getting drafted into a war they didn't understand and didn't support. It was clear to me why we were in Vietnam but not to them. The national leadership was not able to send a message the general public understood, and of course, the professors were largely antiwar, and that affected the students, even in the business and engineering schools.

"My classmates got to know me because I let my hair grow and I had a big mustache. Many of them were surprised I was an Army officer; I didn't fit their stereotype of a 'baby killer.' I can't tell you how many people would tell me they thought I was open and considerate to their views. In turn, I was able to give them my views on Vietnam. I'm not sure I changed many minds, but I gave them the other side, which they respected.

"There were patriotic acts at Tulane. The football team assembled at the flagpole in the center of the campus to keep a radical student group from lowering the flag and burning it. I applauded that."

Downing continued his military service, and before he retired as a four-star general he had earned two Silver Stars, two Distinguished Service Medals, and the Purple Heart. He left active duty after serving as commander in chief of United States Special Operations, the force of highly trained special warriors from all the services who carried out the most dangerous missions.

After 9/11 Downing was a special consultant in the Bush administration on terrorism before he came to NBC News as a commentator on military tactics and strategy. When we went to Iraq together, I'd catch him looking longingly at the men and officers going out on patrol. Until the day he died I always thought he was Ranger-ready to get back in uniform if called to duty.

During our many conversations about his career he made it clear he was impressed with the quality of the draftee Army he served with in Vietnam. "I found them to be great soldiers, and I was amazed at what they could do when it was demanded of them. I saw nineteen- and twenty-year-olds take over units in the heat of battle when all the officers and NCOs were killed or wounded.

"The all-volunteer force presents less of a leadership challenge, but the overall quality is not as high. Thus far, mainstream America understands and supports the troops, and one of the reasons for that is that National Guard and Reserve outfits, representing every community in America, especially in the Midwest, are fighting in Iraq and Afghanistan. I'm not sure what happens when the big fights are over. Will people still volunteer for the military? I'm not sure the public would support another draft."

Downing was a professional soldier for half a century, a warrior's warrior, and in his time he witnessed a lot of change in public attitudes. "It took ten or fifteen years," he says, "before people were proud of serving in Vietnam. I knew things were changing sometime around 1985, when I was in a Washington bar and I heard some guys bragging to some girls that they had been in Vietnam. I knew then that the tide had changed."

Senator John McCain

John McCain didn't get back to America until 1973, and by then the country had changed profoundly. He was last aware of the day-to-day life at home in 1967, just before he took off one fateful Thursday morning, October 26, for what should have been a routine bombing raid on Hanoi. McCain was making a final turn over the North Vietnamese capital in his A-4 Skyhawk Navy jet fighter when he took a hit from an enemy missile.

He catapulted from the cockpit, badly injured, and his parachute dropped him in a lake in the heart of the enemy capital. He nearly drowned before angry

North Vietnamese civilians pulled him from the water and held him for the authorities.

During our visit to Hanoi, James Webb and I visited the park and saw the lakeside plaque describing McCain's unexpected arrival almost forty years earlier. He was North Vietnam's most famous prisoner of war because his father, Admiral John S. McCain Jr., was commander of all American forces in the Pacific.

Webb and I also toured the infamous "Hanoi Hilton," the prison where McCain spent five and a half years as a POW. He has written eloquently and emotionally on the difficulty of staying alive through illness and malnutrition and of staying true to his military code of conduct, his country, and his fellow prisoners during long weeks and months of torture on his already broken body.

At the prison now, the emphasis is on what the North Vietnamese describe as their mistreatment at the hands of the French before the United States became involved. The prison's posted explanation of America's role is comically self-righteous: "Though having committed untold crimes on our people . . . American pilots suffered no revenge once they were captured and detained. Instead, they were well treated with adequate food, clothing and shelter according to the provisions of the Paris peace agreement."

The display of staged photographs is so clumsy it is laughable. An American is shown standing in front of a table laden with fresh fruit. The caption reads, "Plenty of fruit; it's as if we're in California."

There are pictures of Ping-Pong matches, basketball games, and weight lifting. One photograph is of a

Christmas tree with the caption "Time flies. Here's another Christmas again. It's hard to believe one's soul is being taken care of in this Communist land."

Nearby is a display of McCain's flight suit, boots, and helmet, with the date, October 26, 1967. He arrived in Hanoi just in time to miss all of 1968. And also all of 1969 through 1972, until he was released in 1973.

McCain remembers that the North Vietnamese were selective about what news from America they let get through to the American POWs. "The deaths of Dr. King . . . Bobby Kennedy . . . the riots in Washington and all over the country, but not Neil Armstrong's landing on the moon. The guards shot off their guns in celebration of the Tet Offensive, and they started to celebrate Khe Sanh [another big battle], but after a while they were quiet, when the U.S. started winning. But in prison we really didn't appreciate how big the changes were, because in '67 things were going all right with the war."

When McCain was eventually released and sent to the Philippines to prepare for his trip home, he was presented with large binders filled with news clips of what had happened while he was away. "I was really taken aback. I was so intensely curious that I would read until my eyes hurt. I'd go to sleep, wake up, and read some more. When I got back, I went to the National War College and spent that year reading and studying about Vietnam and trying to figure out what happened. I went all the way to Bernard Fall's book about Vietnam, **A Street Without Joy.**"

McCain says he was not angry with the antiwar

Lieutenant Commander John S. McCain III with his father, Vice Admiral John S. McCain Jr., at the U.S. Naval Auxiliary Air Station, March 1966

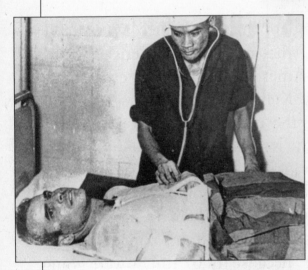

Photograph of John McCain in Hanoi hospital, November 1967

Senator John McCain today

people, as a lot of veterans were, because "everyone has the right to protest the policies of our government. . . . Nor did I blame the protestors for the lack of support for the war. I blame the lack of support on those who failed to tell the American people exactly what was going on. That led to cynicism."

His service in Vietnam and his years as a prisoner, McCain says, made him more aware of his own failings and frailties, and that in turn made him understanding of other points of view. "Because I had my own failings, if someone was wrong or I disagreed with them, it put me in a mood to heal those differences rather than take sides. I found out I wasn't as tough, as strong, as confident as I thought I was. I failed, and when you fail, you realize you're human, and that gives you more tolerance in your disagreements with others."

Those who have been on the receiving end of McCain's fiery temper in political disputes may question his depth of tolerance for other points of view, but he cites as an example his relationship with David Ifshin, a prominent antiwar protestor with whom he became close friends. McCain says, "He died of cancer. I saw him the day before he died. I spoke to his family, and I treasure his friendship to this day."

It was an unlikely friendship. Ifshin made a trip to Hanoi in 1970 and broadcast a condemnation of the American war effort that was piped into McCain's cell. When McCain returned to America, the two men met at a forum on the war and quickly formed a strong personal bond even though they continued to see the world through different political prisms.

By then Ifshin had become a Democrat who was

conservative on military matters. His conversion came when he was living on a kibbutz in Israel during the 1973 Yom Kippur War. Israel was in peril in the opening days after the surprise attack by Egypt and Jordan, but relief came in the form of a massive U.S. military airlift ordered by President Nixon. Ifshin began to see the value of military power and the reality of a dangerous world.

He later said, "I have agonized every day of my life for my conduct in Vietnam." He became an energetic advocate for the Institute for Democracy in Vietnam and a strong voice within Democratic circles for active national security policies.

Ifshin worked in the Clinton White House and died of cancer in 1996 at the age of forty-seven. At his funeral, McCain said, "Some may think David and I became friends because David's political views became more compatible with my own. That is not really true. My regard for David is more personal than political affinity. We remained partisans in different camps.

"Most of the important and lasting friendships I have made in my life," he continued, "were formed in the shared experience of war. David and I did not fight a war together, but neither did we fight a war against each other. We chose instead to make peace together.

"I learned about courage, honor and kindness from all my friendships. From David I learned to look for the virtue in others, and I also learned the futility of looking back in anger. I am a better man for the experience."

McCain has no illusions that all the wounds from Vietnam have been healed. Referring to the 2004 presidential election, he says, "Four or five weeks were spent on a conflict that took place thirty-seven years ago, a conflict in which we could not change one thing while we're in another war. All those arguments, 'You were for the Vietnam War, you were against the war,' you'd think we'd be talking about terrorism and the war in Iraq. Instead, it was the Swift Boat ads and John Kerry at his convention with his Vietnam crew."

When will that political debate end in the political arena? I ask him.

"Tom," he replies, "I think maybe our generation has to die off."

Now, of course, the question is what the lasting effect of the war in Iraq will be, a conflict McCain has outspokenly supported for its goals if not for the manner in which it is being fought.

He appears to be paying a political price for his Iraq stance. McCain's campaign for the 2008 Republican presidential nomination all but unraveled in the summer of 2007, with the resignation of key aides, fund-raising problems, and low standings in the polls.

On other matters, he says he remains an optimist. "You've got to be optimistic . . . we've made great strides as far as tolerance and women's rights. I think the Sixties probably broadened our society and our views. I think there was a swing toward liberalism, and then the pendulum swung back with Reagan. But I don't view him as a particularly right-wing ideologue. He was everybody's hero and loved. I still think there's a great center in America, and it doesn't budge a helluva lot."

John McCain doesn't spend a lot of time looking back. It's not in his nature and, understandably, too many of the memories are too painful. While his country was being rocked by momentous political, cultural, and generational changes from 1967 to 1973, he was struggling to stay alive in a bare-walled North Vietnamese prison laced with cruelty.

When he emerged, he noticed all of the differences at home and took particular notice of one. "I was glad about the miniskirts."

Senator Bob Kerrey

Bob Kerrey was a quintessential Midwesterner when he was accepted to the U.S. Navy officer-training program following his graduation with a B.S. in pharmacy from the University of Nebraska. While in training, he volunteered for an elite corps, the SEALs, a Navy version of the Special Forces operating at sea, in the air, and on land. The few who actually make it through the SEALs' legendarily brutal physical training regimen emerge as warriors of the highest order.

The Bob Kerrey who went to Vietnam as a Navy SEAL in 1969 was a much different young man than the one who three years earlier had expected to spend his life filling prescriptions in a Midwestern drugstore.

He had been in-country less than two months when he had a heroic, fateful experience on a small island off the Vietnam coast. Leading a nighttime assault on a Vietcong cell, he took a direct hit from a grenade but somehow managed to stay conscious and direct the rest of the operation in the midst of a ferocious firefight. The VC were subdued, and in his Medal of Honor citation, Kerrey is credited with valorous action under fire that resulted in the capture of enemy combatants who later provided valuable intelligence.

Kerrey was evacuated to a naval hospital in Philadelphia to begin a long year of operations on his terribly damaged right leg, which had to be amputated just below the knee. When he was released, he caught a military flight to Offutt Air Force Base, about fifty miles from his hometown of Lincoln, Nebraska, and decided to hitchhike the rest of the way home.

"Ironically, I got picked up by some Midwesterners returning from the Mobilization Against the War demonstration in Washington that year. I was in uniform and still in a great deal of pain as I sat in the backseat of their car, so I don't remember much except that they treated me well."

Both Kerrey and his fellow Nebraskan, Senator Chuck Hagel, another Vietnam veteran, say they didn't encounter in the Midwest the personal attacks that many Vietnam vets experienced in other parts of the country. Kerrey's most memorable confrontation came with another Vietnam veteran, an Army infantryman, Doug Schmitz, who had been badly wounded in Vietnam. Schmitz came into a restaurant Kerrey had opened with his brother-in-law in Omaha, and they quickly got into an argument over Vietnam.

"By then I hated the war," Kerrey says. "I had voted for Nixon in '68 because I thought he was going to end it, but it was still going on, and I thought it was just a waste." Schmitz pushed back hard, saying that

Bob Kerrey, U.S. Navy SEAL, receiving
the Congressional Medal of Honor
from President Nixon in 1970

Bob Kerrey today,
with his son Henry

veterans were proud of their service, that it was the decision makers who were at fault, not the people who fought the war.

Kerrey and Schmitz became friends when Kerrey decided Schmitz had a point. Several years later, I had dinner with the two of them in a popular fish restaurant in the heart of South Omaha, the city's largest working-class neighborhood. They had separate lives, but that night they were just two veterans out for dinner with a buddy.

As before when socializing with Vietnam vets, I felt just outside a common bond. It was such a searing experience, in combat and in the pitched debate at home, that they subconsciously become members of a special club. Later, when Kerrey got to the Senate, he said the first of the Vietnam vets to arrive in Congress had a kind of a chip on their shoulder against the World War II guys. "They got the parades, the good war, that we didn't. But then we all became friends because we had all endured combat, and that trumps other differences. It crossed party lines."

Like so many others, Kerrey got involved in politics because of the influence of Allard Lowenstein, the Pied Piper of his generation. Lowenstein came to the University of Nebraska in 1971, to speak against the Nixon presidency, and Kerrey was so taken with his message that he began to seriously think about public service.

There were other factors influencing Kerrey's growing interest in public service. As an entrepreneur he was frustrated with the red tape that small businesses were required to navigate.

Finally, in 1982, Kerrey decided to take on the well-entrenched Republican governor, Charles Thone. It was far from being a sure thing. By then Kerrey was divorced, so he was now single in a family-oriented state, a novice Democrat running against a well-known incumbent in a conservative state where registered Republicans outnumbered Democrats by a margin of 6 percent.

Not for the first time, Bob Kerrey defied the odds and won. On his inauguration day, old members of his Vietnam SEAL team parachuted onto the front lawn of the Nebraska governor's mansion and sauntered inside for a beer-and-pizza party the new governor had organized in their honor.

Kerrey brought a rock-star quality to the staid state of Nebraska. In one well-publicized incident, he went to the airport to officially welcome film star Debra Winger to Nebraska, where she would be filming **Terms of Endearment.** Handing her a spray of flowers, he said, "I'm an officer but not a gentleman."

Winger, well known for her rebellious ways, apparently took him at his word. Before too long, they were romantically linked, and it was a sign of the changing social mores in Nebraska that there were few critics of their living arrangements, which included overnight stays in the mansion.

Kerrey's successful management of the governor's office and his puckish charm no doubt helped. When pressed by reporters about his relationship with the glamorous actress, he responded, "What can I say? She swept me off my foot," an endearing reference to his war wound. The romance didn't last, but the friendship endures.

Despite his popularity, Kerrey was restless as governor, and after one term, he unexpectedly quit and moved to Santa Barbara to teach a course on Vietnam at the University of California, Santa Barbara. By 1988 he was back in Nebraska, preparing to run for the U.S. Senate. He won easily against a Republican who had been appointed to fill out the term of a popular incumbent who had died in office.

In the Senate, Kerrey quickly became a player as a member of the Senate Committee on Intelligence and the bipartisan national commission to reform Social Security, an ambitious effort that failed despite its high-profile membership.

Kerrey was a founding member of the Coalition of New Democrats, a group of senators determined to steer their party back to the middle and toward the new issues of international trade, technology, new applications of military use, and social reform. The group included his fellow Vietnam veteran Chuck Robb of Virginia, John Breaux of Louisiana, John Edwards of North Carolina, and Evan Bayh of Indiana, all of them from traditionally conservative states.

Even as a senator, Kerrey maintained his reputation for going through life by what he liked to call "jungle rules"—a carryover from his Navy SEAL days, when life in the bush was kill or be killed. Senate protocol wasn't always his strongest trait.

Referring to Senator Rick Santorum of Pennsylvania, an outspoken colleague given to lecturing everyone on the superiority of his political ideology, Kerrey said, "Santorum? Isn't that Latin for 'asshole'?"

In 1992 Kerrey made a hastily arranged, quixotic

run for the Democratic presidential nomination. He faded fast. Critics and even friends saw it as one more manifestation of his quirky, restless style. They were not surprised when he retired from the Senate at the end of his second term in 2000.

They **were** surprised when he accepted the presidency of New York City's New School, a liberal university in Greenwich Village formed in 1919 by, among others, the historian Charles Beard, the philosopher John Dewey, and the economist Thorstein Veblen. They wanted, the founders said, an institution where progressive thinkers could express their ideas without censure and where a spirited dialogue could take place between the public and the intellectuals.

"Spirited" would be a polite way of describing the tone of the debate between Kerrey and New School students in his first year over his support for the war to remove Saddam Hussein from power in Iraq. Kerrey held his own and used the raucous occasion to say it was in the tradition of the school's history of open debate.

He had a chance to renew that argument in the spring of 2006, when he invited his friend John McCain to give the New School commencement address to the graduating class. McCain, an outspoken supporter of the Iraq War—although critical of its execution—defended his position, but the New School graduates were not interested. He was booed, walked out on, and lectured by a student speaker who declared, "I am young . . . [but] I do know preemptive war is dangerous and wrong."

It was a scene reminiscent of the late Sixties on

college campuses, but it was confined to Madison Square Garden, where the ceremonies were held, and it didn't shut down or destroy any parts of the institution. Kerrey's defense of his choice of McCain as a speaker was vigorous, and although he appeared not to change any minds, the students didn't occupy his office or protest until he resigned.

Though Kerrey had initially supported the Iraq War, he was appalled by the absence of a realistic plan for postcombat Iraq and by the failure of senior Bush administration officials to accept responsibility for developments such as the abuses at the Abu Ghraib prison.

The old Navy SEAL, however, strongly believes a consequence of the Sixties is that his party is still hostage to an unrealistic attitude about the use of military force. He believes that is a hangover from Vietnam, strengthened by an Iraq War gone seriously off the tracks.

When the Nobel laureate Shirin Ebadi, an Iranian lawyer and human rights activist, delivered a well-received commencement address at the New School in 2007, she declared, "Democracy cannot be imposed by military force," a not unreasonable judgment in view of what had happened in Iraq.

Kerrey praised her courage and most of what she had to say, but he was troubled by the disconnect between democracy and military force. He said it is a commonly heard criticism of U.S. involvement in Iraq, and then, in an op-ed written for **The Wall Street Journal,** he proceeded to challenge the premise.

He began by citing the influence of military force in creating democracies in Japan, Germany, and Bosnia.

He also defended the case for war against Saddam Hussein largely along the lines cited by the Bush administration, saying Iraq was a larger national security risk after 9/11 than it was before.

Kerrey said he was troubled the most by critics of the war who were not normally on the side of dictatorships, the same critics who were in favor of military action to prevent genocide in Darfur or who "argued yesterday for military intervention in Bosnia, Somalia and Rwanda."

To his fellow Democrats, Kerrey offered this message: "The war to overthrow Saddam Hussein is over. What remains is a war to overthrow the government of Iraq.

"Those who argue that radical Islamic terrorism has arrived in Iraq because of the U.S.-led invasion are right. But they are right because radical Islam opposes democracy in Iraq. If our purpose had been to substitute a dictator who was more cooperative and supportive of the West, these groups wouldn't have lasted a week."

Kerrey concluded his provocative message with a call to Congress to build a bipartisan strategy to deal with the long-term threat of terrorism, arguing that it would not be enough simply to withdraw from Iraq. Wherever terrorists find sanctuary, he wrote, "we cannot afford to allow diplomatic or political excuses to prevent us from using military force to eliminate them." It was a message from the unconventional warrior and the politician who refuses to bend to the conventions of his party.

He also disagrees about Iraq with his friend and

former colleague Bill Bradley, the ex-senator from New Jersey, another Democrat who thinks their party has to change to succeed in the future. In interviews publicizing his 2007 book **The New American Story**, Bradley repeatedly called the Iraq War "the worst foreign policy mistake of my lifetime. It dwarfs Vietnam." He calls it an "oil war" that is leading America "down a dangerous path toward empire." Bradley doesn't discount the need for a strong military or the use of military force, but he counsels his party to work harder to pursue diplomacy first. "After Iraq," he wrote, "our threat to intervene anywhere in the world will be much less credible; we have revealed the limitations of our power."

When I asked Kerrey about Bradley's judgment—that the Iraq mistake dwarfs Vietnam—he disagreed. Although it is too early to know, he believes Iraq won't hang over U.S. foreign policy as Vietnam did. As an example, he cites Cambodia, where the Khmer Rouge, led by Pol Pot, unleashed an Asian holocaust of historic proportions. "We didn't do anything on Cambodia." In Kerrey's view, the opposition at home to the war in Vietnam and the opposition to the war in Iraq were significantly different. "In Vietnam," he says, "we had Americans hoping for Ho Chi Minh to win. I don't think anyone wants al-Qaeda to win. No one is burning the American flag [here] over Iraq."

Senator Chuck Hagel

Republican senator Chuck Hagel arrived in Vietnam in December 1967. By the time he left a year later, he had been wounded twice, once while rescuing his brother Tom from a burning armored personnel carrier. He was returning a favor, since Tom had already saved his life when they were both wounded by shrapnel from a land mine while on patrol.

The Hagel brothers were both in the same Army squad, fighting through the Mekong Delta during some of the bloodiest times of the war. Between them, they received five Purple Hearts.

There were four Hagel boys, and they had a rough childhood. Their father, Charles, an itinerant manager of lumberyards, was an abusive alcoholic who often had to be retrieved from local bars by their mother.

It all came to an end on Christmas Eve 1962, when Charles was again drinking heavily and abusing the kids. He finally went to bed, and on Christmas morning they found him there, dead at the age of thirty-nine.

While their mother held the family together, the Hagel sons were typical small-town-Nebraska boys, active in sports and school activities. Chuck was the star. He played football and was elected homecoming king. He bounced around several small Nebraska colleges, playing football and having a good time, until the draft caught up with him. He performed well in basic training, and the Army was prepared to send him to Germany to train other recruits. That would have been a good job in a safe place, but Chuck Hagel asked for an assignment to Vietnam.

It was there that his life almost came to an end twice, and it was there that he formed a closer but complicated bond with his brother Tom, with whom he served in the same infantry squad. Having saved each

Chuck Hagel, infantry squad
leader with the U.S. Army's
9th Infantry Division

In 1968, Chuck Hagel (right) and his brother Tom
served in the same Army squad in Vietnam.
Each saved the other's life in combat.

other on the battlefield and survived too many firefights to remember, they came home to a different America and took distinctly different directions.

After they returned home, Tom suffered bouts of post-traumatic stress disorder. He was in a rage about the war, which he saw as a monumental waste of young lives. Chuck defended the mission in Vietnam, although he conceded to his brother that big mistakes had been made. Back home in Columbus, their differences were so great that their arguments often erupted into fistfights. Finally their mother cracked down, saying, "No more."

Chuck, who was interested in Republican Party politics, went back to college, got involved in radio broadcasting in Omaha, and met local GOP officials. By 1971 he was working for a Nebraska congressman in Washington and taking an interest in an exciting new form of telecommunications—the cellular phone.

When Ronald Reagan moved into the White House, Chuck Hagel was named deputy director of the Veterans Administration. Before long, however, Hagel was forced out when he took on his boss, who dismissed the effects of the herbicide Agent Orange on those serving in Vietnam.

Back in private life, Hagel studied the possibilities of the new telecommunications industry; he invested his life savings in a start-up cell-phone company and hit the lottery. He became wealthy, so wealthy that he could do what he wanted, and what he wanted to do was be a U.S. senator.

In 1996 Hagel won the seat. In Washington he was quickly identified as a newcomer to watch. He compiled a solidly conservative voting record and began to impress foreign policy wonks. By 2000 he was attracting enough attention that he made it to George W. Bush's short list of vice presidential prospects.

When I talked to Chuck Hagel in July 2000 about his chances to be Governor Bush's running mate, it was clear that he wanted the post but that he thought the search had already moved on. "I think they have someone else in mind," he told me, then paused and added, "You may want to look at Cheney."

I was startled. After all, Dick Cheney was the man running the search. But I alerted my colleagues in Washington, and Lisa Myers nailed the story with Pete Williams, our Justice Department correspondent and Cheney's former press secretary. They discovered that Cheney was changing his voter registration from his new home in Texas back to his home state of Wyoming, a sure sign that something was up, since the president and vice president can't share the same state.

When Cheney was confirmed, I was interviewing Bush at his ranch in Texas, and he said with a twinkle, "NBC did a nifty piece of work on the Cheney story." I didn't share my source with him.

Hagel didn't get to be vice president, but if he had, would the decision to go to war in Iraq have been altered? After all, Hagel, the Vietnam hawk, had done what his brother called "a one-eighty" on Vietnam and war generally, after they made a joint trip back to their old battlegrounds.

With his brother Tom, the senator returned to Vietnam on a journey that was reported by Myra Mac-Pherson. She wrote, "Tom is overcome by emotion standing by a river where many friends lay dying so many years ago, a river that flowed red with blood—'like Campbell's soup,' Tom says."

Chuck, she said, remained characteristically cool, but Tom was encouraged that his brother had finally begun to see things as he did: that the Vietnam War had been a tragic mistake. Senator Hagel—who announced in late summer 2007 that after two terms in the Senate he would not seek re-election in 2008—later told me that his change in thinking was completed when he read the tape-recorded conversations between President Johnson and his close friend and Senate ally Richard Russell of Georgia. That was when he decided that the public had been purposely misled regarding the purposes of the war and the chances of its success. As early as May 1964, Johnson was on the phone to Russell, seeking his counsel on Vietnam. Russell responded in blunt language:

> Frankly, Mr. President . . . it's the damn worst mess I ever saw. . . . I don't see how we're ever going to get out of it without fighting a major war with the Chinese and all of them down there in those rice paddies and jungles. . . . I just don't know what to do.

Johnson responded:

> That's the way I've been feeling for six months.

Russell came back with the heart of the problem:

> Our position is deteriorating. And it looks like the more that we try to do for them, the

less they are willing to do for themselves. It's just a sad situation.

Johnson:

How important is it to us?

Russell:

It isn't important a damn bit, with all these new missile systems.

Russell was telling his friend that a ground war in Asia was, as so many predicted, a losing proposition for the United States.

After that sobering assessment, Johnson nonetheless returned to his great political fear:

Well, they'd [the Republicans] impeach a president that would run out, wouldn't they?

Despite Russell's assurances that they wouldn't, Johnson was not mollified.

Johnson was elected in a landslide against Barry Goldwater in November of that year and continued to escalate America's involvement in Vietnam until early 1968, when the political pressures from his own party, not an impeachment organized by the Republicans, drove him from office.

When Chuck Hagel read these accounts of great private doubts by two of the most powerful men in Washington about the chances of success in a war in which, four years later, he and his brother fought, he began to form new standards for his personal judgments on when war is necessary and wise.

Dr. Charles Desmond

Two other Vietnam veterans, one black and one white, one in the Army, the other a Marine, both decorated for valor in heavy fighting, returned to America to distinctly different lives as a result of the war.

Charles Desmond, an African American, one of ten children raised in a mill town north of Boston, describes his childhood as one of "subsistence—living on my dad's meager paycheck, week to week."

There were only a few black families in Desmond's hometown, so, he says, "I didn't have a clue about the civil rights movement. We were sort of tokens in our community—not a threat to anyone. We just sort of went along anonymously without a lot of racial stress."

Desmond didn't think much about the wider world beyond his neighborhood, or much about his future, either. He expected just to get a menial job and go through life as his father had. "I didn't even know there was a public system of higher education in Massachusetts," he says, which is all the more remarkable considering where he would eventually wind up.

However, one of his older brothers, who had been in the Army, did know about college, and he encouraged Desmond to take the SAT exams to see if he could get in somewhere. Desmond, to his surprise, did well enough to be accepted at Boston University.

When he arrived on the BU campus in 1965, he was startled to find a lively culture that centered on ideas and movements, particularly the civil rights movement. He began to see that there was a world beyond the confines of being the son of a man who collected and sold junk for a living.

But Charlie Desmond preferred the life of pool halls around campus, the vocabulary that went with them, and especially the money game. He was a hustler, a pool shark, good enough at nine ball to make as much as a thousand dollars a week at a time when gasoline was thirty cents a gallon and a hamburger with fries went for fifty cents.

When I ask him if he made a lot of his money off wealthy prep school classmates, he laughs and says, "Yes, but they knew what was going on. They wanted to learn to play pool, and I taught them—for a price. Besides, it was their parents' money."

The classroom couldn't compete with the pool hall, and before long, a dean said, "Hey, Charlie, you need to take some time off to decide what you want to do with your life."

Shortly after he dropped out, the draft board came calling. Until then he hadn't thought much about Vietnam. It never occurred to him to try to avoid the draft. "I came from a very patriotic family," he said. "I just didn't feel I had an option to leave the country."

Desmond went into the Army in March 1967, and when basic training ended, he was shipped out to Vietnam as an infantry squad leader. He was impressed by the absence of racial tension when he got into combat. "Race is not a relevant factor when you're fighting for survival. When someone next to you helps determine whether you live or die, a different race or culture is not the issue."

Fighting north of Da Nang, near the DMZ, he

Charles Desmond in 1951, the youngest of ten children

Charles Desmond and his sister Nathalie in 1965

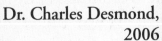

Dr. Charles Desmond, 2006

was in heavy combat for much of his tour, and he performed so well that he won the Silver Star, the Army's second-highest award for valor. He also remembers that he was in the biggest battle he'd seen in Vietnam, on April 4, 1968, when he heard that Dr. King had been assassinated back home.

"I was just devastated," he said. "We heard there were race riots back in the United States, and the military worried about how the black soldiers would react in Vietnam." Desmond was not surprised when there were no problems in his unit. The code of mutual survival held.

Desmond had a life-changing conversation with himself while hunkered down in a rice paddy during a major battle. "It was just hell on earth—that day. One of the worst things I could possibly imagine. Death and dying all around. I'm not a very religious person, but I sort of said, 'If I survive this, I'm going to turn my life around.' If you don't make the right choices in your life, other people make them for you, and they may not be in your best interest."

After a year in Vietnam, Desmond was back in the United States in the spring of 1969, walking through the San Francisco airport, wearing his uniform, when he received his welcome home: "This young woman, she must have been my age or a little younger, looked at me with rage in her face and said, 'Baby killer!'" Desmond was all the more determined to get on with his new life.

Four days after leaving Vietnam, he was back home in Massachusetts. He remembered his rice-paddy pledge. "I knew I was not the person I was when I left home. I was very, very focused."

So focused that he enrolled at Northeastern University and spent much more time in the classroom than in the pool hall. He graduated with honors and was awarded a prestigious Fulbright fellowship to study in Germany.

When he returned, he was hired by the University of Massachusetts at Boston to run the campus Upward Bound program, designed to help poor students with backgrounds similar to his navigate what, for them, was the difficult terrain of higher education. He stayed for thirty-one years, rising through the ranks to become the associate chancellor of the university. "I spent most of my career working with students who had questions like 'How do you get your life focused? I don't have enough money to pay my bills—what do I do now?' Those kinds of questions. I could help because I'd been through that."

What would have happened if he hadn't gone to Vietnam at all? "I certainly don't think I would have done what I've been able to in my life. My dad was an alcoholic, and I probably would have gotten into drinking and Lord knows what else."

Instead, Desmond became a prominent educator and a family man. He's been married to Phyllis for almost thirty years, and they have three children of exceptional accomplishment. One is an honors graduate in economics from the University of Chicago, another is getting a master's degree in architecture at MIT, and the third, a graduate of the University of Virginia, teaches second grade in Harlem.

Ron Armella

Ron Armella, another Vietnam vet, sums up his feelings about Iraq more bluntly: "Those of us who were in Vietnam know it's the same damn scenario. For a time we thought we were never going to get out of Vietnam; now I don't know if we'll ever get out of Iraq. It is such a parallel."

Armella lives in the mountains near Elgin, Arizona, spending his days in a form of self-imposed isolation, as far away from other people as he can get.

Armella, who graduated from high school in 1965, was raised in a working-class family outside Buffalo, New York, where he was an affable but aimless jock, uncertain about what he'd do with his life.

He tried business college for a while, but it didn't work out, so when his draft notice arrived he wasn't surprised. Armella decided he'd choose the Marines rather than be drafted by the Army. He did so well in basic training that he was selected for Officer Candidate School, a highly unusual honor for someone with no college education.

Looking back, Armella is self-deprecating. "I was a pretty tough kid—a high school football star. I wasn't too bright, but I was strong. I was just twenty years old, pimply-faced, and all these college grads were twenty-three or twenty-four. Pretty traumatic, when you think about it—being thrown into something like that at an early age."

He cannot believe now how naive he was about the politics of Vietnam. "We were fighting Communism! How stupid was that? Were the Vietnamese going to jump in their little rafts and invade America? But I was gung ho, a Marine's Marine. I didn't question the politics of it until later, after I'd seen the horror. Then my politics changed."

The horror came quickly enough once Armella got to Vietnam. He arrived in August 1968, a second lieutenant with the 9th Marines. "We were ground pounders. We'd put on our heavy packs and march up and down the mountains. It was the combat of combats.

"It wasn't glamorous, like I figured it would be back at officer training. Once you got into the shit, you realized you'd made a big mistake. We had the dumbest tactics in the world against the guerrillas, just like now in Iraq."

Armella describes his feelings during days of heavy fighting as "just numbness. I was walking around in this little fog." The personal fog got worse when he was transferred to another outfit and met another young officer, Bobby Muller, a man he calls, to this day, "my comrade in arms."

Armella took over Muller's platoon when his friend made the fateful decision to command a South Vietnamese outfit against a strong enemy force. Muller led from the front during a fierce firefight, and Armella says that when the South Vietnamese didn't back him up, "Bobby just became target practice for the enemy. He was really shot up. It was the most traumatic moment of my life."

Muller was transported to a hospital ship offshore, and Armella managed to get a chopper flight out to visit him. He's never forgotten what he saw in the ship's hold.

"One whole level of the ship was filled with these guys—spinal cord injuries. Bobby had a bullet hole through his spine, and with the rest of the wounded, he was strapped onto a gurney that rotated. It would turn these guys over every few hours for circulation. They were like chickens on a rotisserie. It was horrible."

Yet when he got back to the base Armella volunteered for duty that was even more dangerous. He went into a Marine reconnaissance outfit, which meant penetrating deep into enemy territory with a six-man team, armed only with light weapons and dressed in camouflage without flak jackets and helmets.

"You quickly got into what we called 'the shit,' " he remembers. "You'd be way out there where no other Marines had been, laying in the elephant grass, hearing things, but you couldn't see anyone.

"We were there to observe, not to engage the enemy, but there were times when we had to throw grenades, open fire, and jump on the evacuation helicopters with guns blazing."

What was most frustrating to Armella was the constant "two steps forward, three back" pace of the war. "You'd secure a village, leave, and then the Vietcong would move right back in. A few weeks later, you'd be back, trying to take the same village, saying, 'Wait a minute. I've seen this before.' "

Despite the frustration and danger, Armella remained gung ho while in Vietnam. "I've got this photo of me standing there, totally camouflaged, with my M-16 rifle, and on the stock I had in big letters, 'Fuck

First Lieutenant Ron Armella,
leaving Quang Tri for a recon patrol
near Khe Sanh, Vietnam, 1969

Ron Armella today, retired and living the "good life"—"smokin' Cubans and driving my Corvette."

Communism.' " As he recalls the story, he adds, "Give me a break. It was futile, but they made you believe it. Even as an officer, you really didn't think for yourself."

Toward the end of his tour, Armella developed the paranoia I heard about from so many Vietnam vets. "Everybody had their calendar. 'I'm sixty days and a wake-up.' Then, with around thirty days to go, you really got scared because guys were getting blown up a week before they were to go home. Then, for me that last day, it was the most terrifying day of my life. 'Please, just get me through this day and get me out of here.' "

Yet on the flight home, Armella was surprised that the exhilaration he felt was mixed with numbness. To this day he can't remember much about the flight home. "It was like a dream world," he says. "Like it didn't really happen—and neither did Vietnam.

"At that early age, when you're so impressionable, your first major experience turns out to be so horrifying, so traumatic."

It wasn't helped by the unwelcoming conditions at home for Vietnam vets. Armella understood the new rules, so he didn't tell anyone he had been a combat Marine in Vietnam. He just went home to Jamestown, New York, grew his hair long, collected unemployment, and began to hang out with what he calls "hippie types and the group they called Vietnam Veterans Against the War.

"For a long time I didn't realize how much I'd changed until my mother said to me one day, 'You know, once you got out of Vietnam, I didn't even know who you were. You were a different person.' "

His buddy Bobby Muller was active in the organization, and they reunited, but it wasn't a heroes' welcome back home. Armella remembers pushing Muller's wheelchair along in a big antiwar protest in New York. "We were all in our fatigues. I had this big ol' white man's Afro haircut—and the people along the streets were booing and throwing eggs at us, calling us names."

The antiwar movement couldn't rid Armella of his demons, and he became a serious dropout from society. "I was fed up," he says, "so I went to Europe and bummed around there for a year or so just to get out of America.

"When I came back, I worked odd jobs and went to college every now and then just to collect the GI Bill money. For a long time, I had a motorcycle, a backpack, and a pup tent. I just wandered around the country until I got to Arizona, where it is a lot warmer." Armella finally ran out of the GI Bill money and decided he had to try something a little more permanent, so he got a job with the U.S. Postal Service. "I was a mailman for a couple of years. Then I got a promotion to postmaster for about eight years. But I couldn't get over this antisocial feeling, so after becoming eligible for a pension, I just quit.

"I went for psychiatric counseling a little while after I got out of Vietnam, but the VA shrink just looked at me and said something like 'Well, kid, what's wrong with you?' So I didn't go back.

"But then after the post office job ended, a buddy suggested I go back for a reevaluation, so I did and filed a claim. Now, between my post office retirement and my disability check, I'm doing okay.

Now, at last, Ron Armella seems to have found some peace in his life. He is married for the second time, has a small home in the mountains, dogs that he can take for a walk in the woods, and enough retirement and disability money to pay the bills. It's all he asks for at this stage of his life, almost forty years after returning from Vietnam. The future seems much brighter than the past.

When the Iraq War started, it brought back more difficult memories for Armella. "Most of us who had been in Vietnam knew that it was going to be the same damn scenario. Every time there's a new war, you have these—I don't know, flashbacks, bad memories. I could have been a fan of George Bush during Vietnam, but now I know better. His administration has just been stupid."

Armella looks at his own past with a sense of bewilderment. "There I was, a successful officer in combat, and then I come home to trauma after trauma. From Marine officer to just another hobo in the unemployment line. It was surreal.

"I got out when I was twenty-four, so it was like I had lived my whole life in just a few years."

While we were talking, he paused for a moment and then said, "You know, I went through a lot, but now, in hindsight, I'm proud of what I did."

When I ask if he ever goes to reunions with buddies from his old outfit, he says, matter-of-factly, "No, most of them were killed."

Ambassador Richard Holbrooke and Peter Davis

Two civilians who had memorable experiences in Vietnam have their own unique take on the lessons of that war and what it may mean to our future.

One is Richard Holbrooke, the **über**-diplomat of Democratic administrations. He has served as the U.S. ambassador to the United Nations for President Clinton; as the chief negotiator of the Dayton Accords, which brought a hard-earned peace to Bosnia; as the U.S. ambassador to Germany; and as assistant secretary of state for European and Canadian affairs.

During President Carter's administration, Holbrooke was assistant secretary of state for East Asian and Pacific affairs. He's a member of the board of the Council on Foreign Relations and chairman of the executive committee of the Asia Society. He writes a monthly column for **The Washington Post** and is vice chair of a large investment bank.

Before all of that, Holbrooke was a junior foreign service officer in Vietnam from 1963 to 1966 working in the provinces for the Agency for International Development—AID—and as a staff assistant for U.S. ambassadors Maxwell Taylor and Henry Cabot Lodge. From 1966 to 1968 he was Vietnam specialist on the White House staff of President Lyndon Johnson. In 1968 Holbrooke went to Paris as a member of the American delegation to the Vietnam negotiations.

Forty years later he is well known in diplomatic and New York social circles for his brash, blunt, and ambitious style. He is equally well known for his intelligence, his wide range of friends, and his physical and intellectual energy in pursuing his interests in foreign affairs and national security matters.

In his current role as a ubiquitous commentator on foreign policy, Holbrooke has taken a high-profile position as a critic of the Iraq War. He believes it is a much worse war than Vietnam.

Holbrooke supported the original congressional resolution authorizing President Bush to wage war against Iraq, and he, too, thought Saddam was a menace who had weapons of mass destruction. But he insists he couldn't imagine the administration would have no plans for what would happen once the so-called major combat phase was over.

He told me, "I never thought I would say anything was worse than Vietnam, but we're now in a war where the solutions are far more complicated—with the Shia, the Sunnis, the Kurds, and Iran.

"In Vietnam there were only two sides. You had a fixed enemy with a fixed ideology. You could negotiate."

He thinks the legacy of Vietnam, the lasting, bitter aftertaste, was not just the war but all that it brought with it: the hippie celebration of the Summer of Love with all the emphasis on smoking dope, rampant sex, and anti-American attitudes.

"It was all a mix," he says, "a shaping of our lives."

Holbrooke, who personally experienced the cost of Vietnam to Democrats as an active party member, told me, "Time after time we thought we had turned the corner on Vietnam. It never happened.

"Now I think we have. Vietnam has been replaced by Iraq. It seems possible to me that Iraq may make Vietnam ancient history. We're finally moving into a new era."

When I asked Holbrooke, the student of national security and diplomacy, what he thought the lasting effect of Iraq would be on the ability of future presidents to go to war, he said, "American foreign policy is always on a pendulum between overinvolvement and neglect. My concern is that we'll hunker down and say, 'No more foreign adventures' when clearly there are times the U.S. has to get involved abroad."

He is dismissive of those who say that, in the aftermath of Iraq, the War Powers Act must be tightened so Congress has more control over when and how the United States goes to war. "That's a legislative technicality," he says. "If a president decides to go to war it won't make any difference."

Holbrooke sees very dark days ahead. He told me, "The next president will inherit the worst opening scenario in history—two wars [Iraq and Afghanistan] plus Iran, the rise of China and India, and the continuing problems in Africa."

If that is true, the end of the Vietnam syndrome has not come cheaply.

Peter Davis will forever be connected to Vietnam through his documentary **Hearts and Minds,** which was the Motion Picture Academy's controversial choice for the Oscar for best documentary in 1975. When Davis and his producer, Bert Schneider, accepted the gold stat-

uette, Davis thanked his family and friends and reminded his two small sons at home that it was past their
bedtime.

And Schneider, who had initiated the project, read
a statement from the Vietcong representing the provisional government of Vietnam, extending peaceful
greetings to the people of the United States.

First there was a silence, then scattered applause
and some hissing. A short while later Frank Sinatra
took the microphone and, reading notes scribbled
backstage by Bob Hope, insisted that the Schneider
statement did not represent the views of the Academy.

Davis, who can still be called boyishly handsome at
age seventy, seemed an unlikely person to be involved in
such contentious circumstances. He has the cheerful
demeanor of everyone's favorite neighbor, but, in fact,
he had been there before in a situation weighted with
significance and freighted with controversy.

He was a boy wonder producer at CBS when he
made **The Selling of the Pentagon**, a tough-minded
and revealing look at how the American military markets itself with millions in taxpayer money. Davis refused to edit out a section with Walter Cronkite, then
the face of CBS News, narrating what Davis described
as a piece of military propaganda. Members of the defense establishment and high-ranking officials of the
Nixon administration tried but failed to get the film
killed, and Davis's reputation was burnished within the
creative community, if not the CBS corporate offices.

When Schneider approached him about directing
a film dealing with how the United States got involved
in Vietnam, Davis was intrigued. As he has said, it

wasn't that he wanted to know why the three million people who had filled the streets as protestors were against the war. He wanted to know why the other 197 million people in the country at the time were **not** against it.

Before taking on the marketing of the American military he had made noteworthy documentaries on hunger in America, the heritage of slavery, and the Free Speech Movement, all important subjects but not on a level with the question of a nation's decision to wage war in a distant country.

"My early work . . . was largely about racial problems in America. I thought that was the most crushing and crucial problem we had. Vietnam was the most crushing and crucial foreign problem we had. What I thought I could do," he says, "is enact a kind of psychological inquiry that had three questions in it: Why did we go to Vietnam? What was it we did there? And what did it do to us? The film doesn't ask those questions, nor does it answer them, but every sequence revolves around one or more of those questions."

He began his research by examining the domino theory, the premise for the war that had been articulated by President Kennedy: If Vietnam fell to Communism all of South Asia would follow, one country after another. In fact, his research took him in an entirely different direction.

"The Vietnamese hated China. Thailand didn't like the Vietnamese and didn't want to adopt their form of government. We didn't take that into consideration."

On the first day he actually spent in Vietnam, Davis had a thought that would frame his entire film. He was taken to a village that had been bombed by American forces. There was a large crater, maybe twenty or thirty feet across, and in the crater he could see the wreckage of a child's bicycle, a broken doll, shards of pottery.

He thought about how a correspondent from CBS, where he used to work, would use the crater as a stand-up location for a report on the damage to the village. "He would be interpreting the war for you. You are not in the war. You are with him, in his pressed fatigues."

Davis decided to make a film that would take the viewers **into** the war. He filmed in a brothel with American soldiers casually abusing the Vietnamese prostitutes. There's a scene of a Vietnamese carpenter making coffins for his own children. An American lieutenant, permanently confined to a wheelchair, talks about his loss of faith in his country.

There on the screen is ramrod-straight General William Westmoreland, back home in South Carolina, after serving as commander of American forces in Vietnam, saying that part of the problem was that "the Oriental doesn't value life as much as the Westerner does."

When the film was rereleased in 2004, admiring audiences emerged to say, "That's just like Iraq," or to mutter, "Now we have our own quagmire." As Davis describes it, "From Saigon to Baghdad."

After the conspicuous success of **Hearts and Minds,** Davis continued to make documentaries and we stayed in touch intermittently. When he heard I was writing a book about the aftereffects of the Sixties, he sent a long, thoughtful e-mail setting down some of his reflections.

With his usual deft touch, he praised my work on

what I called "the Greatest Generation," the men and women who came of age in the Great Depression, fought in World War II, and came home to build modern America, but he had a caveat.

"As great as the greatest generation was," he wrote, "and as deserving of canonization as they are, they did not give us the social or cultural advances of the Sixties"—from the civil rights movement to the women's movement. "What they gave us," he said, "was Vietnam."

Moreover, they didn't give the Vietnam veterans what they themselves had benefited from, he argued, "the GI Bill of Rights. So I don't believe the Sixties were the greatest generation's finest hour."

We had a friendly exchange on his declarations, some of which I had already acknowledged in print and lectures. I said I believed it was a great, but not a perfect, generation, and that it is worth remembering that the congressional charge against the war was led by World War II veterans, including senators McCarthy, McGovern, Hatfield, Church, Nelson, Fulbright, Proxmire, and others.

Then Davis shared with me the insight of his friend Jacqueline Kennedy Onassis. Jackie, who said so little publicly, was privately a perceptive and articulate student of her times and the events that defined them. Davis remembers her saying, "The awful ruin of the Sixties was that such overwhelming hopes were raised and then they were so cruelly dashed."

Davis argued, mildly, he says, citing the civil rights movement, the Voting Rights Act, and so forth. As he rightly observes, anyone could see how the murder of her husband, the mournful transition from Camelot to LBJ, the subsequent assassination of her brother-in-law Bobby, would cast a shadow on the decade for her.

It was not just those god-awful personal experiences, however, that led to her judgment about the Sixties. Davis said that three weeks after their initial conversation, she returned to the subject, this time raising it in the context of Vietnam.

He recalls her saying, "The problem with Vietnam is that we had three consecutive presidents who all believed their manhood had to be proven in the terrible assertion of military power."

One of those presidents, of course, was her late husband, the original proponent of the domino theory.

Davis gave me permission to print an account of his conversation with Jackie because he believes her judgment on Vietnam is an important and revealing part of her considerable legacy.

I Am Woman

I am woman, hear me roar
In numbers too big to ignore

—HELEN REDDY
AND RAY BURTON

As young parents of three girls, living in California during the late Sixties and early Seventies, Meredith and I couldn't help but be aware of the rising level of dialogue, debate, commentary, and proclamations about the place of women in society and about how to raise females in light of this raised consciousness. It made the new experience of parenthood more interesting, and we knew that our daughters would be coming of age in a world very different from the one in which we were raised. But, like most parents, we were not prepared to accept every polemic on how to raise women.

Some of the ideas we did find intriguing, even if they later turned out to be laughable. Sometime in the early Seventies, gender-free toys were briefly a popular idea. So at Christmas on the California beach in 1972, we downplayed the dolls with frilly dresses and loaded up Santa's sack with toy trucks and earth movers for our three daughters.

The last I saw of the trucks, they were rusting and abandoned in the surf, but the dolls found good homes in the bedrooms of their caring surrogate parents. What were we thinking? The place of women doesn't depend on their affection for the toys of boys; it is much more complex than that.

Our daughters were coming of age during a rising consciousness about gender equality. Throughout their school years—from kindergarten through graduate school, 1972 to 1992—women were starting to take their places in areas traditionally reserved mostly for men. They were changing the face of law, medicine, business, education, politics, and the military. What did not change is that boys and men continued to dominate the leadership positions of all the important institutions of American life. In our family, Meredith and the girls have lived where my career took them, leaving behind their own friends and plans.

One of our daughters is now a physician; another is a vice president of a major entertainment company; and the third is a clinical therapist. They place no limits on their ambitions, but for them, those ambitions also have had to fit within the context of having children. For all the gains made by women, and the recognition within society of how important that is to a healthy body politic, we have not satisfactorily resolved the workplace consequences of having children.

I often cite Meredith as someone who managed gracefully to have it all. She stopped working when we began to have children and stayed home until they were all in school. Then she eased back into the workplace, first as a teacher and then as an entrepreneurial toy store owner and author of children's books. She went on a corporate board, was elected an officer of a major international environmental organization, and became passionate about horseback riding at the age of fifty. Of course, I think of her as exceptional, but she is not the exception in her generation of women, who seized the long-overdue chance to soar high above the nest of home and homemaking. By the time she was sixty Meredith had a complete set of experiences—motherhood, career, and active outside interests.

She is the first to acknowledge that her choices were made much easier by the security of our marriage and the financial dividends that came with my job. She had choices not available to, say, a single mom in a company where maternity leave was a benefit but also a penalty, or a wife whose family depended on two incomes to survive.

For most women the struggle to find a balance between work and family is a conundrum without a perfect solution. Maternity leave and day care centers are welcome and important steps, but they fail to address the larger issue of balancing the role of the mother and the father in child care and in the workplace, particularly at a time when the middle-class standard of living is becoming harder and harder to achieve.

The late Ann Richards, the silver-haired, tart-tongued governor of Texas, summed it up nicely when she observed, "They blame the low-income women for ruining the country because they're staying home with their children and not going to work. They blame the middle-income women for ruining the country because they go out to work and do not stay at home to take care of their children."

It led to what came to be called "the mommy wars," in which women were put in the uncomfortable position of arguing with one another over the choices they made, trying to justify their very personal choices about work and child rearing, to one another.

When Barbara Bush was invited to give the 1990 commencement address at Wellesley College, fully a quarter of the graduating seniors signed a petition protesting her appearance. They said, "Barbara Bush has gained recognition through the achievements of her husband. . . . Wellesley teaches us that we will be rewarded on the basis of our own merit, not that of a spouse."

Mrs. Bush gave her speech, despite the protest. She spoke to the graduates as a woman who was just twenty years old when she married George H. W. Bush immediately following his service in World War II.

Early in their marriage, they endured the heartache of losing a daughter to leukemia, but they had five other children—four boys and a daughter. Barbara was a stay-at-home mom while her husband pursued a career in the Texas oil business and worked his way up through the ranks of the Republican Party.

She had been witness to some profound shifts in attitudes about marriage, child rearing, and families by the time she appeared at the Wellesley graduation and said:

> We are in a transitional period right now, fascinating and exhilarating times, learning to adjust to changes and the choices we, men and women, are facing. As an example, I remember what a friend said on hearing her husband complain to his buddies that he had

to babysit. Quickly setting him straight, my friend told her husband that when it's your own kids, it's **not** called babysitting.

Maybe we should adjust faster; maybe we should adjust slower. But whatever the era, whatever the times, one thing will never change: Fathers and mothers, if you have children, they must come first. You must read to your children, hug your children, and you must love your children. Your success as a family, our success as a society, depends not on what happens in the White House but on what happens inside your house.

For over fifty years, it was said that the winner of Wellesley's annual hoop race would be the first to get married. Now they say the winner will be the first to become a CEO. Both of those stereotypes show too little tolerance for those who want to know where the mermaids stand. So I want to offer you today a new legend: The winner of the hoop race will be the first to realize her dream—not society's dreams—her own personal dream.

And who knows? Somewhere out in this audience may even be someone who will one day follow in my footsteps and preside over the White House as the president's spouse. And I wish him well.

In my experience, women with whom I work are not at war with one another or their individual decisions on the issue of whether to stay on the job or have babies. Among our daughters and the women I know in the workplace, the discussions are much more about being supportive of one another than about being critical or divisive.

One of the residues of the Sixties is the rise of a new category of womanhood: the single mom. A combination of rising divorce rates and a significant increase in children born out of wedlock has created the culture of the single mom. Google the phrase, and your computer will pop up almost three and a half **million** entries for single moms.

By the age of forty, one-third of all the boomer women who married early were divorced. Not all of them remained single, of course; the multimarriage household has also become a fixed part of the culture.

For those middle-class and working-class women who didn't remarry, getting out of a bad marriage was simply a transition to a difficult life, especially if there were children involved, since the kids almost always wound up with Mom for most, if not all, of the time. That created a large class of women who were a combination of breadwinner, mother-father, transportation chief, cook, housekeeper—and completely exhausted.

Sociologists wonder how these changes—divorces, multi-marriages, and single moms—will play out in ten or fifteen years, when the boomers start to reach their elder years. Will children pay as much attention to the stepdad or stepmom when one of the partners dies? Will single moms have an even more difficult time when their children move away?

No doubt women have many more choices as a result of the Sixties; but they're still in second place to men when it comes to the range of those choices—and their consequences.

Jane Pauley

Jane Pauley was, in her own way, a child of the Sixties who, through a combination of timing, talent, and good fortune, managed, as she says, to have it all. Career, marriage, children, wealth, manageable fame, recovery from a debilitating struggle with a bipolar condition, and, in her fifties, still more choices to come.

She became widely known for her role on **Today,** where, over the years, she established herself as the daughter every older couple wanted to have and every woman her age wanted as a good friend. She was just so darned nice and at ease with her fame. There were no "diva" whispers when it came to Jane Pauley, class of 1968 at Warren Central High School in Indianapolis.

When she set out on her television career, almost by accident, she had no idea any of this would happen: sharing her kids with one of the most coveted jobs in television, a cultural icon for a husband, and her own standing as a role model for an untold number of women her age, many of whom would write to ask, "Do you know how lucky you are?"

Yes, she did realize how lucky she was, but it wasn't quite as one-dimensional as it may have looked from the outside.

Pauley was raised in a white-bread, socially conservative neighborhood in Indianapolis, the heart of America's heartland. She and her sister, Ann, who is three years older, were bright, beautiful, and accomplished, the pride of their parents, neither of whom had gone to college.

Jane was a champion extemporaneous speaker in high school and the governor of Indiana Girls State, the American Legion program designed to introduce young leaders to the idea of public service during their teenage years. When she graduated from high school in 1968 and enrolled at Indiana University, she had no idea what she wanted for a career, but television news coverage of the civil rights movement and urban riots steered her toward majoring in political science.

After college, Pauley decided there might be a future for her in television news. More women were showing up on the local channels but not yet as anchors. She figured that with her interest in politics and the skills she had developed as a schoolgirl orator, she might be able to make something of this broadcast journalism business.

Her ambitions were modest. "I had no network aspirations," she says. "I didn't look at television and think, 'Wow, look—women are doing things they couldn't do before.'"

She had no grand plan for her life—not even any specific thoughts about marriage or a family. She represented the first wave of young women to emerge from college without the unspoken burden of "When are you going to get married?" Her sister, Ann, had graduated three years earlier and married right away before setting off on a successful business career. That marriage didn't last, but her second has, for over thirty-five years.

But for Jane, "It just wasn't on my mind; I had other options and figured I always would."

Her immediate future was anchoring the weekend news on the NBC affiliate in Indianapolis, WISH-T; it was a good job but not a great job. Then, unexpectedly, Pauley was "discovered" by Chicago television executives.

The ratings of the longtime king of local news in Chicago, Floyd Kalber, had slipped. Kalber was a prototype of the traditional local news anchor: a no-nonsense white male in his fifties, handsome and perfectly groomed. He was a World War II veteran who had started his career in Omaha, where he often contributed stories to **The Huntley-Brinkley Report**. By the early Seventies, he was under assault by the local ABC affiliate, which had adopted what came to be known as the happy-talk format. It was no longer just the news. There were a lot of belly laughs and sappy asides from the anchor.

Apparently, this was a welcome relief for viewers worn out by protests, the continuing war in Vietnam, and Watergate. It was an approach that transformed local news shows, which, until then, had serious journalistic formats modeled after **The Huntley-Brinkley Report** and **The CBS Evening News with Walter Cronkite.**

Local station managers began to hire polling firms and consultants to find their own new happy formula to appeal to changing viewer tastes. Not surprisingly, women began to show up in viewer preferences.

The NBC managers in Chicago found Pauley in Indianapolis and placed her at Floyd Kalber's side in

HOOSIER GIRLS' STATE, INC.

INDIANA UNIVERSITY

American Legion Auxiliary

Department of Indiana

Jane Pauley at Indiana University

Jane Pauley with her husband, Garry Trudeau

the WMAQ newsroom. Chicago's tough corps of television writers erupted in indignation. How could this twenty-four-year-old weekend anchor from Indianapolis possibly sit next to Kalber in one of the legendary cities in the world of hard-boiled journalism, the city of Studs Terkel, Mike Royko, and Ben Hecht of the **Trib, The News**, and the **Sun-Times**?

One critic said cruelly that she had the "IQ of a cantaloupe." Welcome to Chicago, Jane.

There was an unexpected dividend to all the negative publicity. When Jane Pauley made her debut in the fall of 1975, her name recognition was off the charts, and the curiosity quotient was just as high. "The overnight reviews from my debut were very, very good," she remembers.

But it didn't last. By the following spring, the ratings were back down, and Pauley was removed as a co-anchor. She faced an uncertain future. I remember meeting her about that time, and I was impressed by her poise and maturity. It was all a facade, she now says.

"Professionally, I looked poised, but I wasn't mature for my age. I was a girl, emotionally very, very young. I was less prepared than many women my age to become an independent woman. . . . My life was rather painfully empty at that point. My life was not governed by the feminist movement."

She didn't know it at the time, but she was about to get another lucky break. Barbara Walters had left the **Today** show for ABC News, and her **Today** partner, Jim Hartz, although talented, was not considered strong enough to carry the show on his own.

So the search was on for a new team, and I was chosen to be the male and, in effect, chief correspondent. But who would be the woman? The estimable Cassie Mackin had a weeklong tryout, but as skilled she was as a political reporter, she wasn't very comfortable doing two hours of live television every morning.

Jane Pauley's Midwestern wholesomeness and her experience as an extemporaneous speaking champion, as well as her experience on the air, were a perfect combination for a morning audience looking for someone fresh and new. She catapulted from failure in the Chicago ratings to one of the best and most important jobs in television news.

She had no illusions about her good fortune. Her first morning, she said to the **Today** audience, "Maybe you're wondering how I got here. Maybe I am, too." We have often laughed about how we were on the television equivalent of a life raft, two novices cast adrift in increasingly stormy seas with fresh challenges coming from ABC's **Good Morning America** and with a serious erosion in NBC's prime-time audience.

I honestly think there were plans to fire us when **Today**'s ratings slipped into second place during our first couple of years on the air together, but there was so much chaos in the rest of the network that no executive was around long enough to get rid of us.

By the time the front office had stabilized and the prime-time programming had recovered, we had found an easy rhythm working together. A new executive producer, Steve Friedman, had installed a new **Today** staff and a much more contemporary format suited to our talents. We were back in first place, and Jane Pauley was no longer the unknown from Indianapolis. She was a star, and she was marrying Garry Trudeau, the publicity-shy genius behind **Doonesbury,** the comic strip of their generation. They had a very private life together and let their work on television and in the daily **Doonesbury** strip speak for them.

Besides, she knew the limits of fame: It doesn't make you smarter or better at what you do. "I saw some female colleagues who didn't have much more experience than I did, but they were trying to pretend otherwise. They'd gotten their jobs through a form of affirmative action because everyone was trying to get women on the air."

When I left **Today** after five years for the **Nightly News,** to be replaced by Bryant Gumbel, she understandably thought her contributions should be recognized with a new title: cohost, an equal to Bryant, who had spent most of his career in sports.

"I made the case," she says, "that my seniority, my experience, and the viewer's attitudes made me unofficially the cohost—and we'd arrived at a point where it didn't look good for the woman to be consistently the junior partner.

"I made a strong case, but in my heart of hearts, I knew there was something else—Bryant was the first African-American. That trumped. I didn't win, but I fought the fight and made the case."

Besides, Jane and Garry wanted to start a family, and she knew "I couldn't be pounding on the desk, saying, 'Send me, send me' to the next big story if I had kids at home. I didn't want to be that kind of mother."

In a short span of time, they had three children. In her first pregnancy, she was carrying twins, a boy and a girl, and although she didn't advertise the fact, the irrepressible weatherman Willard Scott rarely missed an opportunity to make some reference to the pending arrival of a pair of babies for Miss Jane, as he called her in his Virginia-gentleman manner.

Nonetheless, when the babies arrived and she returned to the air after a short maternity leave, she was determined not to make her personal life her professional life. "I deliberately kept it generic," she says, "occasionally referring to 'my daughter' or 'my son,' but never by name.

"I think I may have helped other women my age when I showed up on the air looking tired and distracted. They could say, 'Jane must have been up with the babies.' They could identify with that."

She knew it was good for everyone in the family that she was a working mother who understood the demands and the limits of that title. She consciously referred to her high-paying **Today** position as a job, not a career, because "I thought the expression 'career' exaggerated my devotion to my job. In fact, I was deeply ambivalent about my job because it competed with my children.

"Still, I knew I had a great job with lots of flexibility and a big paycheck. Sometimes I felt I was letting the network down by not being more aggressive, which would have meant more travel, but in a way neither I nor my bosses understood at the time, the audience approved of my approach. They understood I wasn't putting my kids on magazine covers or on a red carpet at a premiere."

Pauley had a strong sense of what was appropriate

as both a real and a symbolic mother. "I didn't want a reputation that exceeded the reality," she says. "When I was nominated for the 'mother of the year,' I turned it down. For God's sake, I had a nanny trained in England; if I can't do this effortlessly, who can?

"My life was my life. When I was at work, I always felt like I should have been at home. And when I was home, I knew I should have been plotting to get the interview with Gorbachev, which went to Bryant. But I didn't do that, and I have no regrets."

She also had a husband who relished his responsibility as a parent and was openly promoting the feminist cause in his daily comic strip. He was officially a member of the National Women's Political Caucus, and his cartoon character Joanie Caucus spoke for an untold number of women.

Pauley says, "I was lucky. As a young woman, I came of age when currents of opportunity were opening up for women as they never had before. I got in on that, and I learned along the way that, as I have said, 'You can have it all. You just can't have it all at the same time.' "

Jane Pauley was part of the vanguard of women of her generation and slightly older who did get opportunities at the network level denied them just a few years earlier. There is not a city in the country without a woman anchor or coanchor of the local news.

The most powerful woman in television, and one of the most influential in America, is also a member of that generation. Oprah Winfrey, through her daily television show, magazine, film and stage production companies, and social interests, moves the market in the direction she wants it to go. Not even the most starry-eyed optimists of the Sixties could have anticipated that an African-American woman would achieve such an exalted status by the turn of the century.

Anne Taylor Fleming

A California friend, Anne Taylor Fleming, had an altogether different experience in trying to combine a career with motherhood. She, too, was a journalist when in 1994 she published a book called **Motherhood Deferred**, a moving, poignant account of her attempt to become pregnant in her late thirties after initially resisting, as a determined feminist, the idea of motherhood.

She was a true child of the Sixties, a bright and sassy sprite who had grown up on the liberal west side of Los Angeles. Anne Taylor was sixteen years old when she caught the eye of Karl Fleming, then thirty-eight, on a tennis court at the home of mutual friends. Fleming was a dashing reporter of the old school who had gained considerable fame as **Newsweek**'s go-to correspondent on some of the most important civil rights stories in his native South during the early Sixties. He had been seriously injured by rioters while covering "Little Watts," the uprising in South Central Los Angeles that was triggered by the shooting of a black motorist following the much larger riots there in the fall of 1965.

Fleming was also married and the father of four sons when he encountered Anne Taylor. He walked

The writer Anne Taylor Fleming
as a California college girl
in the tumultuous summer of 1968

Anne Taylor Fleming in 2006, at the home
in California where she's lived with her husband,
journalist Karl Fleming, for thirty-five years

away a changed man. Two years later, when he was forty and she was eighteen, as she has described it, Fleming was destined to have his "California experience, and I was it." He proclaimed his love for her, and they began an affair that took them from Malibu to the new, avant-garde University of California at Santa Cruz, where she was a student at the campus nestled in the redwood trees of the coastal hills and valleys.

Their affair, as you might expect, caused more than a little buzz among their friends. It was none of my business, but I did not approve. "What the hell is going on here?" I thought. "Has Karl flipped out? Who is this child?" I suspect most of his friends chalked it up to a midlife crisis for this Southern boy who had been raised in an orphanage and dropped out of college to become a liberal, hard-drinking reporter.

In **Motherhood Deferred,** written when she was in her forties, Taylor Fleming described their unhinged sexual encounters as a "complicated trans-generational dance . . . he smothering me with his sexual and profes-sional expertise. In truth nothing had prepared many of us young women for this. We hadn't heard anything at all about sex growing up, most of us. . . .

"There was no pause button. From one injunction we had switched abruptly to another: Don't do it / Do it." No one mentioned the biological clock, the wind-ing down of the fertility prospects, as the twenties give way to the thirties and then the forties. "It was scary and thrilling, liberating and nerve racking all at the same time," she wrote.

Karl and Anne Taylor Fleming became a new form of the Sixties couple as they tooled around town on his motorcycle or in a red convertible: the bright and sexy ingenue and the graying, crew-cut old boy who had made a big U-turn in his life.

Taylor Fleming, it turned out, was mature beyond her years, and they both knew exactly what they were doing. They were falling deeply in love, and in 1972 they had a flower-child-marries-Southern-romantic wedding. She was twenty-two and he was forty-four. They've been married ever since, and we've been close friends all these years.

From the start she enjoyed an easy, strong relationship with Karl's sons and had no thought of children of her own. When Karl first raised the possibility of children, in the early years of their marriage, she has written, "I couldn't imagine it, I didn't even feel the connection between love making and baby making, so methodically had I put contraception—and ambition—between my womb and pregnancy."

She demurred, but by the time she was in her middle thirties, she changed her mind. Getting pregnant, however, was not so easy at that age. They explored other options made possible by the new science of out-of-body pregnancy procedures: in vitro fertilization; gamete intrafallopian transfer; zygote intrafallopian transfer; intrauterine insemination.

During one procedure, she let her mind drift back to another time. "From a record player down the hall Janis Joplin wailed about freedom. Armed with my contraceptives and my fledgling feminism, I was on the cusp of a fabulous journey. My sisters and I were the golden girls of the brave new world . . . the old male-female roles were falling and the world was ours to conquer. I wanted in that world, I wanted to matter.

"Babies didn't cross my mind then and not for a long, long time after."

Twenty years later, she was driving home from a session at a fertility clinic, and she was hoping against hope that this time the injection of her husband's sperm in clinical conditions would take. It was what she described as a "stunning reversal—from all that sex to no sex, a lifetime of trying to hold motherhood at bay" to now trying desperately to have a baby.

On the freeway, she has written, she was "tempted to roll down the window and shout, 'Hey, hey, Gloria [Steinem], Germaine [Greer], Kate [Millett]! Tell us, how does it feel to have ended up without babies, children, flesh of your flesh?'

"'Did you mean to thumb your noses at motherhood, or is that what we heard or intuited for our own needs? Simone de Beauvoir and Virginia Woolf, can you wade in here, too, please, share any regrets, my barren heroines from the great beyond. . . .' "

Taylor Fleming concludes in **Motherhood Deferred** that she's on her own, a self-described agnostic midlife feminist sending up silent prayers to the fertility gods on high. She also sends up apologies to the mothers of yore, the station-wagon moms with their postpartum pounds who felt denigrated in the liberationist heyday by the young, lean liberationists such as herself.

Anne Taylor Fleming is now in her late fifties and spending more time on novels than commentary. She never did get pregnant, and for a long time the absence of a child of her own was an agony. But as time went on, she came to terms with her choices as a young woman at the beginning of something so revolutionary as the liberation of women and the sexual freedom that came with it, however uneven the experience may have been. She says, "It was absolutely joyous to be a young woman in the early Seventies. I've had to look that in the face and ask, 'Was it worth it?' Of course it was."

As for the hopes and expectations then and the reality now, she is not surprised that the record is at once encouraging and disappointing.

She laments the paucity of strong female voices in the op-ed sections of the country's major newspapers, **The New York Times, The Washington Post,** and the **Los Angeles Times.** "Those pages are decidedly male," she says, "and that's disturbing."

What she does find encouraging is the effect of the women's movement on fatherhood. Men who grew up with the women's movement arrived at marriage and parenthood with different expectations for their role. "Modern fathers are much more at ease being close, intimate, with their children. That change is vastly for the better."

What surprises Anne Taylor Fleming now is how much of the conversation with younger women revolves around money—acquisitiveness, as she describes it. "It makes them more conforming," she says, "less willing to take risks. Those are the demands of this expensive middle-class lifestyle we've created.

"I wish life could be more joyous for those women, as it was for me when I was part of something larger than myself." Her own experience has left her with wisdom and insights she is eager to share with young women in a simple, straightforward fashion. "I always put fertility on the table. I try to do that without scaring anyone. I do tell them, 'You're making choices if you're not making them. So pay attention.'"

Linda Greenhouse

Another woman who made her way into the almost exclusively male world of big-time journalism is Linda Greenhouse, who won a Pulitzer Prize in 1998 for her coverage of the U.S. Supreme Court for **The New York Times.** She graduated from Radcliffe in 1968 and returned to her alma mater in 2006 to accept the Radcliffe Institute Medal and reflect on her passage.

When she heard I was gathering stories for this book, she eagerly sent me her speech, acknowledging that it had gotten her in trouble with her **Times** editors when she first delivered it. I could see why, since she abandoned her journalistic neutrality to be sharply critical of the administration of President George W. Bush, which, as she put it, "turned its energy and attention away from upholding the rule of law . . . creating law-free zones at Guantánamo Bay, Abu Ghraib, Haditha and other places around the world." She also raised what she called "the sustained assault on women's reproductive freedom and the hijacking of public policy by religious fundamentalism."

Greenhouse made those observations after describing an emotional moment at a Simon and Garfunkel reunion concert. When they began singing "America"—about two kids riding a Greyhound bus through the night, counting the cars on the New Jersey Turnpike, "they've all come to look for America"—Greenhouse began to cry.

She told the class of 2006 that for all of the tumult and agony of 1968, her generation was united in the belief that when it came time for them to run the country, "our generation would do a better job." Her emotional moment at the concert, she said, came because "we were not doing a better job . . . our generation had not proved to be the solution. We were the problem."

It was then that she ticked off what she saw as the deficiencies of the Bush administration and the political climate of the opening days of the twenty-first century. She was not without hope, however, as she recounted for the new graduates conversations she'd been having with her eighty-six-year-old mother, who believed that the old days were the best and that everything today is going downhill.

Greenhouse presented her contrarian view, beginning with her difficulty getting a job in journalism in 1968 when she graduated, because there were so few openings for women. By the time of her 2006 speech, when Greenhouse was a major byline reporter for **The New York Times,** another Radcliffe graduate, Jill Abramson, was managing editor at the paper, yet another Radcliffe alumna was foreign editor, and other women held senior positions in virtually every section of the most influential newspaper in the world. As Greenhouse put it, "It's impossible to look at the trajectory of these recent decades and not feel at least some optimism."

She has no illusions that the progress came simply as the result of goodwill. She cited the class action sex-discrimination suit filed by the women employees of **The New York Times** as an important footnote because "the progress I described didn't come without the guts and hard work of many people."

Greenhouse also shared with the graduates an anecdote that, in its cast of characters, setting, and central idea, said volumes about the changes since 1968, as well as the work still to be done.

The year was 1993, and the setting was Harvard. The occasion was the twenty-fifth anniversary of the Harvard-Radcliffe class of 1968. The principal commencement speaker and honorary-degree recipient was Colin Powell, then still in uniform as the chairman of the Joint Chiefs of Staff. He had just worked out with the administration of President Bill Clinton the new "Don't ask, don't tell" policy for gays in the military.

It was a controversial compromise, and as Greenhouse recounted it, it started a sudden round of telephone calls from classmates, some of whom she didn't know, saying that as gay men or lesbians, they couldn't possibly attend a ceremony honoring someone involved in the new policy.

Greenhouse said the issue injected real energy—and uncertainty—into what otherwise would have been the usual sedate kind of reunion week, until the luncheon at which Powell was to speak. One of her classmates, wearing a top hat, tails, earrings, and buttons denouncing the policy, went up to General Powell and said, "I look forward to the day this issue no longer divides us."

Powell, with four stars on his shoulders and an array of medals across his Army uniform front, surprised the young man by embracing him with both arms, saying, "So do I, and I hope that day comes sooner rather than later."

When word of that encounter spread, Greenhouse said, "the anger went out of the air. When General Powell arose to make his speech, some in the audience stood in silent protest. He acknowledged them respectfully."

It didn't change the policy, but for the rest of the class, Greenhouse believes it created a sense of community "across a barrier that in the so-called good old days, we would not even have acknowledged. Back in college, I wasn't aware of knowing anyone who was gay, and I doubt it would have been the subject of a conversation."

Greenhouse concluded her remarks with a short lesson on the meaning of community and how she has come to identify her place in her own community. "I could choose from," she said, "woman, American, Caucasian, Jew, wife, mother, daughter, sister, straight, journalist, temporarily able-bodied, pushing sixty, Democrat, Radcliffe graduate (as I call myself), Harvard graduate (as the post-Radcliffe world would call me).

"I suppose if I had to boil down my side of the argument with my mother to one thought, it would be that in my lifetime, I have seen the fences around nearly all these definitions lowered, with a corresponding increase in the opportunities to make and maintain connections across barriers that not so long ago were nearly impermeable."

For her conclusion, Greenhouse returned to the Simon and Garfunkel concert, saying, "If I had been able to think through this . . . at the concert, maybe I could have stopped crying by the time they stopped singing.

" 'All your dreams are on their way,' they sing in their great 'Bridge over Troubled Water,' 'See how they shine. If you need a friend, I'm sailing right behind.' "

Dorothy Rabinowitz

Another prominent woman who is a journalist, and also a Pulitzer Prize winner, is intellectually furious about much of what goes on in the name of the women's movement. She is Dorothy Rabinowitz, the tiny, tenacious cultural columnist for **The Wall Street Journal.**

Rabinowitz, now in her Sixties, grew up in an FDR family in a working-class section of Queens. Her father was a grocer who lost his father to the Nazis during World War II; and her mother, she says, had a "rapier, assaultive" wit. So does her daughter, a quality that wins her personal admirers across the political spectrum, from neocons to Frank Rich, the relentless critic of President George W. Bush in **The New York Times,** who calls her "lively, incisive and witty."

An example: Even though the last Democrat Rabinowitz voted for was Lyndon Johnson, she admired many of the qualities of Howard Dean in 2004. "He connects one thought to another," she was quoted as saying. "He is absolutely jargon-free."

Then she added, "I thought everything he said was absurd, but not the kind of absurdity that's deep and corrosive. There's a kind of sexy core to him, even in his little, short-armed way." And do you wonder why she was voted class cynic in high school?

Now she's ensconced in the quiet, richly paneled editorial offices of **The Wall Street Journal,** the high church of conservative commentary in American journalism. We met in a conference room with a panoramic view of New York harbor, just a few hundred yards south of Ground Zero, where the twin towers of the World Trade Center once stood.

Rabinowitz, just five feet tall, is stylishly turned out in a smart salmon-colored jacket and black slacks. She carries herself with a kind of casual confidence that conveys the message "I know who I am, and I will tell you what I think." In our meeting, there is little small talk and no attempt at the contrived courtesies journalists often encounter when interviewing a subject they'll be writing about.

As she stares out the window, responding to my questions, she unleashes a quiver of Rabinowitzian arrows at what she thinks are the excesses and exaggerations of the Sixties in general and the woman's movement in particular.

"For an intellectual, the Sixties were the end of all standards, all history. The most infuriating part of it was the denigration of all that came before.

"It was the seed of a culture of no authority.

"Before the Sixties, most parents had respect.

"I had to listen to so much foolishness about women; I don't remember little girls being too intimidated in class to raise their hands.

"Can you imagine me walking around saying my voice was stifled because I was a woman?"

For Rabinowitz, the most outrageous recent example of what she considers to be a gender tyranny was the removal of Harvard president Larry Summers. Summers, a blunt intellectual, had already stirred up resentment in the Harvard family by asking tough questions about the African Studies program. Then, in a public meeting, Summers had raised the question of why there were not more women in math and science. According to news reports, he said, "Hypotheses were that faculty positions at elite universities required more time and energy than married women with children were willing to accept and that innate sexual differences might leave women less capable of success at the most advanced levels of mathematics and science and that discrimination may also play a role . . ."

Rabinowitz, barely containing her fury at the reaction to what she called "a genuine intellectual question," ticks off the consequences: "Got rid of the president of Harvard because he dared to suggest there may be something factual, something worth talking about. It became an outpouring of madness . . . driven by people who knew how to exploit the feminist theme for professional advancement. People started calling for the hiring of more women. Nothing about credentials."

For Rabinowitz, the Duke lacrosse case was an example of Sixties political correctness out of control. White members of the team were accused of rape by a black exotic dancer they had hired.

It was a sensational story: privileged white males at a distinguished Southern university, a poor black woman, a crusading district attorney. More than eighty Duke faculty members immediately signed an ad demanding that the university deal with what faculty members called "abhorrent sexual assault . . . and violent racism."

The ad ran as serious questions were being raised about the credibility of the woman's charges. A year later, after a long, traumatic public ordeal for the players and their families, all the charges were dropped. The dancer's constantly changing story was freighted with contradictory claims and memory lapses. There was no physical evidence linking the players to an assault on her.

The district attorney resigned, and he was barred from practicing law in North Carolina.

Rabinowitz concluded in **The Wall Street Journal** that the Duke case "was not simply a riveting drama . . . it was in its searing way an educational event . . . about a university world, reflective of many others, where faculty ideologues pursued the agendas unchecked and unabashed."

She mocks aging flower children. "They were part of a generation who thought they ended a war, had saved the world. It had discovered sex. No one had sex before the Sixties. No one!" she says with a hearty laugh, and not for the first time alludes to her own romantic youth. (She's often quoted as saying, "If they'd had AIDS in the early Sixties, we'd all be dead.") "All that faded after a while," she says, "but the English professors got tenure, and they're still here.

"Thomas Mann, William Faulkner, these are dead white males they're not going to teach. If the students know Edith Wharton, it is because they watch public television. Otherwise, it is the assignment of an overarching theme—victimization.

"So you come out with a deeply culturally uneducated population whose parents have paid—what?—thirty-eight thousand dollars a semester . . . for a child to be uneducated in anything but . . . victimization, American colonialism, imperial expansion, and a deeply dyed view that if there's something wrong in the world, America is at the root of it."

She's at once angry and puzzled. "Americans," she says, "are marinated in virtue. How can we have all this loathing? America is the freest, most generous nation in history. And to be **condemned**?" She shakes her head in disgust.

Dr. Ruth Simmons

Although not directly, Ruth Simmons disagrees with Dorothy Rabinowitz that there is some kind of ideological tyranny on campuses. "Faculties," she says, "are different in their diversity from what we find in society at large. They've traditionally been at odds with the status quo, not just in this country but at great universities like Oxford.

"As university professors, we stand apart. It is probably true that a lot of people in universities are much more left-leaning than the mainstream, but I don't find that surprising."

How Ruth Simmons came to be the first black president of an Ivy League university is a transformational story of scholarship, grit, ambition, and the opportunities for women and blacks that grew out of the Sixties.

Simmons, now a handsome matronly woman, was one of twelve children of a poor tenant farmer and his wife in Grapeland, Texas, part of the Cotton Belt of the Southwest. When she was seven, her family moved to Houston, where her parents both found work and where she found books.

For her, learning was a daily joy, and books were a way of life she embraced so enthusiastically that before long, teachers in her all-black school adopted her as a special project. This one, they seemed to be saying, will not be denied her chance at a life well beyond the confines of the Houston ghetto.

When Simmons graduated from high school in 1963, she was awarded a scholarship to Dillard University in New Orleans, a small, historically black liberal arts college. She quickly became an active participant in the civil rights movement and styled her hair in what she now says was "a very large Afro." She was, she says, on a journey of discovery during a time of great tensions, excitement, and hope for young blacks in the South. She wanted to be part of the new movement for civil rights, but she kept it from her parents because, as she says, "my mother and father believed segregation would be with us forever. The average black family felt

Dorothy Rabinowitz with her dog, Simon, in 2001

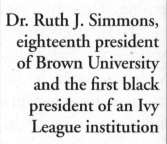

Ruth Simmons's high school graduation photo, 1963

Dr. Ruth J. Simmons, eighteenth president of Brown University and the first black president of an Ivy League institution

they had to accept things as they were and protect their children."

So Simmons didn't tell her parents that while she was doing well in her studies, she also admired black power advocates Stokely Carmichael and H. Rap Brown. She saw Carmichael and Brown as leaders whom her generation of black brothers and sisters could count on to challenge the expectation that they would remain silent, just as their parents had. As Simmons describes it, "There was nothing more painful or embarrassing for my generation than to see the traditions of 'step and fetch it' go unchallenged."

Ruth Simmons developed a love for the romance languages, particularly French, and by the time she graduated, she had won a Fulbright fellowship to do graduate work at Wellesley College and in France.

She was in Spain on a camping trip with her fellow scholarship students from France during the first week of April 1968 when one of them went to a nearby village for supplies. He quickly returned to awaken everyone with shocking news: Dr. King had been shot to death.

Simmons and her friends rushed to the village, where they found the locals all gathered in the town square, reading the news and weeping. Simmons was the only black American there, and the universality of mourning over King's death was very comforting. "Seeing those Spaniards and how they reacted, I realized for the first time the magnitude of his contributions and vision. It was otherworldly."

She returned to America to begin graduate work in romance languages at Harvard and to get married.

(She was divorced in 1983.) It was the beginning of a long odyssey through the ranks of American academia and opportunities that, just a few years earlier, would have been denied a woman of color, no matter how many degrees she had.

While continuing her graduate studies, Simmons taught at George Washington University in Washington, D.C., and worked as an admissions officer at Radcliffe. In the Seventies, she was a professor of French and an assistant dean of the college of liberal arts at the University of New Orleans and a visiting professor at Cal State Northridge, part of California's highly regarded state college system.

By the Eighties, she was on her way to bigger and more prestigious posts: associate dean of the graduate school at the University of Southern California; assistant dean of the faculty and acting director of Afro-American studies at Princeton; provost at Spelman College in Atlanta; and back to Princeton as vice provost.

In July 1995 she broke a significant color barrier, becoming the first black woman to become president of Smith College, one of the so-called Seven Sisters—the Ivy League for women before gender integration at Harvard, Yale, Princeton, and the others.

Six years later, she was named president of Brown University, the first black woman to hold that title at one of the traditional Ivies. Looking back on her life from that elevated position, Simmons says in her matter-of-fact way, "I'm still surprised to be president of Brown, because it hasn't been so long since I couldn't go into Woolworth's and have lunch."

What surprises her most of all, now that she's the personification of the new higher-education establishment, is that this outsider made it inside. "I was always the person who raised objections; I was very critical of the university structure, coming up through it. I made up my mind early to have a university life, but I was determined to be an agitator for change.

"What happened is that the academy changed around me." Why? I ask her. "Because the face of the world is changing, the face of our country is changing, and it is not possible for the academy or other institutions to stay the same."

When I ask if any of these changes worries her, she refers to her old neighborhood in Houston as an example. "When I go home, the neighborhood still is black, still homogeneous, people still agree on what life is all about. All of them root for the same teams.

"When you live in a more complex environment—where people disagree about everything, politics, lifestyle, religion—it is much harder, much more challenging. Is it better? I can't tell you, but it is what we have, because it is the reality of a flat world in which everyone is moving across all the old lines."

She also thinks race remains a central component of that challenge. Like so many of her generation, she says, "We don't ever face up to it. Instead, we whisper about it in corners."

Ruth Simmons, who found her way out of the confines of racial discrimination and low expectations through education at a time when the country was becoming a more tolerant society, believes the classroom remains America's best hope. But she has no illusions about the difficulty of getting there.

"Take a kid who's in a family with no dad and a young mother. Just getting to school every day is an ordeal. Walking the streets can be dangerous, and once they get to school, more danger. Also, will they be hungry? Will they be able to do any work?

"It is an enormous burden for a poor kid to go to school every day. The crushing effect of poverty is something this country still doesn't get. When we continue to abandon the public schools, we make the situation worse. If it's bad today, if we continue to abandon public schools, then what?

"It is a miracle when anyone escapes all of that."

Ruth Simmons, the president of Brown University, who began life as a bookish little girl in a large family in an all-black neighborhood in South Texas, remains an optimist. "There's good news and bad news," she says, "but the important thing is that there is steady progress—and I am an example of that."

Dr. Susan Miller

Dr. Susan Miller, a primary care specialist, grew up in San Luis Obispo, California, and she remembers to this day her male sixth-grade teacher mocking her essay stating that she wanted to be a doctor when she grew up. "He said, essentially, 'Come back when you graduate from high school; you'll find out about boys, and you'll want to get married.'"

When Miller was admitted to UCLA Medical School, she wrote the teacher, asking, "Do you remember me? I just want you to know I was admitted to medical school and I hope you understand how important it is that teachers not discourage their students. I hope you won't say something like that again."

She admits the letter was probably a bit over the top, but it also reflects the kind of determination it took for a woman to pursue a medical education, even by 1972. She recalls meeting women her age who were nurses who said to her, "You know, I wanted to go to medical school, but my parents told me I couldn't."

Her decision to become a doctor, Miller says, was entirely her own, and she received no encouragement from any teacher or counselor, so she knew it would be hard. "I got straight As because I knew I would have to be better than men to get into medical school. I knew I would be bucking the tide," she says, "but I grew up in a family where that quality was admired."

When Miller was attending UCLA Medical School, it was undergoing a historic shift. "When I entered UCLA [in 1973], the graduating medical school class was just four percent women. My freshman class was seventeen percent. When I was a senior, fully a third of the incoming freshmen were women."

The school had a hard time adapting to the changes. Miller says, "The doctors' lounges were just for the men; we had to change in the nurses' rooms. When you're on call and have to stay at the hospital, the rooms they had were just for men, so suddenly, we had to find ways to share the bunks."

During her senior year at UCLA, Miller married a

Susan Miller's self-described "semi-hippie
wedding" in November 1976

Stanford medical school graduate, Kenneth Kendler, and they set off on the next phase of their medical education that would allow them to live together.

It wasn't easy. He was going into psychiatry, and she was interested in family medicine. Medical schools had not yet developed the computer models they now have that make a residency "match" for married couples. Years later, when our daughter Jennifer and her husband, Alan, met at Dartmouth Medical School, the medical school network of computers cranked out a number of choices for them so that when they left and she wanted a residency in emergency medicine and Alan wanted radiology, they were able to settle on the University of New Mexico together. It was one more manifestation of the changes in American medicine: Every year brings more and more husband-and-wife teams into the field. But Miller and Kendler had to make their own way.

He found a position at Yale, the top tier in his field. She got into family medicine at the nearby University of Connecticut, which was not her first choice, but it was a decision that worked for her husband, who was already a rising star in psychiatry. Miller says it was the beginning of a pattern in their lives in which she characterizes her part as "the trailing spouse."

She was pregnant with their first child when he was recruited by Mount Sinai in New York City. Of course they would go, but for Miller that meant "I trailed along. I was on the 'mommy track.' I couldn't work full-time, and besides, New York didn't have family medicine, as it was being developed.

"I wound up at a wonderful place—the Ossining

Open Door clinic, a free clinic that was an offshoot of the Sixties. I also had a second child, so I began to think, 'I'll be on the mommy track for five years, and then I'll go gung ho into my career when they're in kindergarten.' Except kids don't stop needing you when they're in school or even in high school."

Besides, Kendler's star was still rising, and he was now interested in the genetics of behavior. He was invited to work with the renowned geneticist Dr. Lyndon Eaves in Richmond, Virginia. Miller felt at the time that it was a temporary postdoctoral assignment after which they would move back to California. Instead, Kendler and Eaves became an internationally known team—one in psychiatry, the other in genetics—and together they built the Virginia Institute for Psychiatry and Behavioral Genetics.

The trailing spouse accepted her role and set out to make the best of it. She started a family medicine practice with another doctor, a woman, and as they expanded, they decided they were happier with the female physicians they were interviewing, so they hired only women.

"Once there were three women in the practice, the guys wouldn't even come to be interviewed, so we said, 'Fine.' I made it a home for women so they could practice and also have families. We made decisions by consensus. We had beautiful soft colors in the office, not the usual formal male stuff. For twenty years I was the founding mother of this business for which I had no training. At one point we had seven partners, and they were all women.

"What did we sacrifice? I made half as much as

other family practitioners. We never earned as much as the guys in the community. It was a struggle to pay the overhead and keep the place running. But we could control our own lives. You may not make as much money, but you could go home when your kids were sick. You don't have to ask permission of anyone."

But it was still a balancing act. Juggling her roles at home and work, Miller sometimes felt like "half a mother and half a doctor. I was never baking cookies or going to the PTA meetings, and I wasn't a full doctor because I wasn't working sixty to eighty hours a week, like my male colleagues."

When her husband was invited to spend a year at his alma mater, Stanford, Miller was ready for a break and eager to return to Northern California. But again, she went as the spouse. When they returned to Virginia, she decided to give up the daily practice of medicine and accepted a fellowship at Virginia Commonwealth University in patient safety.

She's encouraged that in medicine these days, the trailing spouse is sometimes now the husband. Still, female physicians who want to have children face tough choices just when their careers are in the liftoff stage. Miller thinks that dilemma in medicine and elsewhere is a result of shortsighted attitudes on the part of the women's movement in the early stages.

"Why didn't the movement say about women, 'The most important thing that happens in society is that we perpetuate ourselves'? Otherwise, it comes to a halt if we don't have kids, raise them properly, educate them, and keep the family intact. That's critical to a healthy society, and we allowed it to be denigrated. We should have insisted women be compensated for that role, but we don't pay for it, we don't support it, and we don't recognize it.

"We used to say we also needed a men's movement so they can take paternity leave and stay home with the kids. So we can be equal. We can take turns. But the men's movement, you know, that never happened."

Like a Rolling Stone

I can't get no satisfaction.

—MICK JAGGER

I miss the immediacy and the
energy of the Sixties, even though
these days are better for me
personally than they ever were.

—JAMES TAYLOR

ONE WARM JUNE MORNING IN OMAHA IN 1964, I was driving to work, a twenty-four-year-old trying to grow up fast so I could realize my ambition of becoming a network news correspondent. At a four-way stop at one of Omaha's main intersections, I spotted a long black limousine headed in the opposite direction. We didn't see many stretch limos in Omaha in those days, so I wondered who might be inside. As the light changed, four of the shaggiest heads I had ever seen leaned out the windows and looked around.

This was my first glimpse of the Rolling Stones, a group I was barely aware of as part of the new British sound that was invading America, led by four mop tops called the Beatles. The next day an Omaha cop told me, wide-eyed in amazement, "Those Rolling Stones? They walked through some puddles to get into the auditorium, and these teenage girls scooped up the water and drank it!"

I didn't know what to think then, but now I realize that it was a small ripple of the tsunami of change in popular musical sounds, lyrics, and tastes that was about to break over an unsuspecting America. The Sixties were going to be about peace, love, rage, war, violence, rejection, confusion, and rock and roll in all of its many forms.

James Taylor

Close your eyes for a moment and think: "The Sixties."

The soundtrack of your mind is a rich mix of the voices of Bob Dylan, the Beatles, Joni Mitchell, Carole King, Crosby, Stills and Nash, Neil Young, and Paul Simon and James Taylor, those ageless troubadours who can still bring their audiences to tears with their sweet melodies and lyrics that linger as the chronicles of our lives and times.

Taylor says in his modest way, "I'm someone whose experiences, lived out on paper and in song, somehow supplied people with a language that was helpful to them." Or, as one writer described him, "He's a soul-baring icon of the early Seventies."

This gentle, tall, and handsome man, who walks onstage with his guitar in hand looking as if he's a little surprised to be there, has been Sweet Baby James to his large universe of fans since he first appeared at the Newport Folk Festival in 1969. Kris Kristofferson, who was also there as a promising newcomer, remembers, "James was the one everyone was talking about; we knew he was gonna be a big star."

For all of the serenity of his public appearances and his smooth country-road sound, Taylor's private life was a long journey of turbulence and painful recoveries. He has had to deal with the severe depression for which he was institutionalized, with heroin addiction, and with two troubled marriages. One of his brothers died from alcohol poisoning. His relationship with his father, the dean of the medical school at the University of North Carolina, was problematic at best.

He has seen fire and rain; now he is seeing the best years of his life. He's almost eligible for Social Security and Medicare, but he's working hard at his music with new albums and a concert tour sold out in the United States and the United Kingdom.

We've known each other a bit for twenty-five years, and when he talked to me from his home in Lenox, in the Berkshires of western Massachusetts, I was not surprised when he immediately brought up the war in Iraq, American foreign policy, and climate change. His artistry and his political interests are still the twin motors of his intellectual life.

Personally, he's settled in as the father of preschool twin sons with his third wife, Kim, an executive with the Boston Symphony Orchestra. His albums continue to sell well. His latest collection of Christmas songs sold more than two million copies.

When he was a favored child of the Sixties, this was not what he expected in the twenty-first century. "I miss the immediacy and the energy of the Sixties," he says, "even though these days are better for me personally than they ever were."

At the time when he was making his way into American musical folklore, did he fully appreciate the historic proportions of what was going on? "No," he says, "I was just concentrating on my music and career. Looking back, I know it was a time of great promise. A huge percentage of people were coming of age knowing not only could we effect change, but we could change the way we wanted to, not the way our parents wanted. There was a lot of folly of youth, but it allowed people to be creative. There were huge leaps of faith."

In the music business in the Sixties, all of the planets were in alignment for a cosmic shift in acceptance and distribution. A new generation wanted its own songs, a huge generation roiled by war, assassination, racial uprisings, a sexual revolution, and the need to have some personal connection to this world breaking apart in so many new ways.

Bob Dylan and the Beatles led the way, inspired as they were by the lyrics and music of America's great rhythm-and-blues artists, who had been telling their personal stories in song to largely black audiences for some time.

In those days radio stations were still owned by individuals or small companies, and the new music of the Sixties became their oxygen. They had their own play lists and local disc jockeys who took pride in "breaking" a new single by being the first to get it on the air in their communities.

Jonathan Schwartz, now the erudite host of a public and satellite radio program devoted to the Frank Sinatra school of music, recalls working Saturday nights at New York's WNEW-FM, a citadel of Sixties rock radio. He said it was an amazing time to be there, with new albums coming in every week from the likes of the

Sweet Baby James in 1969

James Taylor in 2006

Rolling Stones, Joni Mitchell, Neil Young, and Led Zeppelin. He remembers that the station didn't hesitate to play Arlo Guthrie's "Alice's Restaurant" even though it was eighteen minutes, twenty seconds long.

Schwartz is saddened by what has happened to radio in the era of big group ownership. Local radio today is really a distant satellite signal pumped through local call letters, chopped up into short generic bites. Pure satellite radio is a growing force, though it, too, relies on targeting specific demographics.

It's all part of a pattern for Taylor, one that surprises him some. "All the things we considered to be revolutionary were co-opted by the big corporations— our music, our radio, the record companies, our dress." What he finds a little ironic is that many of these corporations are now run by people who came right out of the Sixties movement. As he says, "There were a lot out there who were more than flower children." Taylor has his own checklist of what brought on the Sixties and the consequences of that time. "Number one," he says, "was Vietnam. The cynical manipulation of the truth and the people to whom you owed the truth.

"Number two, the pity and the shame of Watergate," which deepened the cynicism of citizens about what their government was telling them and what it represented.

"Number three, the assassinations of John Kennedy, Martin Luther King, and Bobby Kennedy," those cold-blooded murders of leaders who had stood for something that young people wanted to be part of.

"Number four, the constant threat of nuclear annihilation. A whole generation grew up with that during the Cold War—and believed it might happen because it had been witness to other wars that were a complete failure of diplomacy."

For Taylor, number five still is in play: "The erosion of concern for the big issues and the sacrifice of personal freedom and proportion for conventional matters. Ten years after the Sixties, everyone who was there was worrying about mortgages and a thousand little weights that had been added to their lives.

"They succumbed to the markets that were manufacturing trouble for them: 'You must have this or that, or you will be leading a vacuous life.'"

Taylor, a longtime environmentalist and board member of the Natural Resources Defense Council, is encouraged by the recent public awakening to the dangers of global warming. "I'd like people to make the health of our planet an appropriate forum to rebuild our global responsibility."

He has credibility on these issues because they've been a part of his life as long as his music has been a part of our lives. It is his music, however, that will forever draw us to him. In the fall of 2006, I went to the Beacon Theatre in New York to hear him live again, and I was not disappointed.

As he walked onstage with that familiar, loping gait, I thought back to 1972, when I was covering a "McGovern for President" concert in Los Angeles. Taylor was onstage in a surprise duet with his wife—sexy, sultry Carly Simon. They were, as man and wife, the first couple of pop music at the time, and their performance that night was at once sensuous and showstopping, two performers at the top of their game, physically and vocally intertwined. The marriage didn't last, but the image lingers.

What also lingers is the memory of the headliner of the concert, Barbra Streisand. Even in those days her public appearances were rare, and her devoted fans went wild as she appeared. The cheering grew even louder when she performed a sight gag, making a motion as if she were doing a line of cocaine. Streisand, a health fanatic, was not a druggie, but she knew the culture of her fans.

Gary Hart, McGovern's campaign manager, cornered me after the show and asked whether I thought that gesture would hurt the campaign. I said it depended on if it got out. As I recall, it didn't. Today it would be almost instantaneously available all around the planet on YouTube, transmitted via cell phone from the audience.

At the Beacon Theatre thirty-four years later, James Taylor was still in fine voice and form, revealing his self-deprecating sense of humor with a large display of black-and-white photos from his long career. He made gentle digs at the Bush administration, but mostly it was about the music.

I looked around the auditorium and spotted a very conservative friend who said he loved the James Taylor sound, if not the politics. Another fan was there with his metal walker, making his way slowly down the aisle to his seat. Most of the crowd were aging baby boomers, some of whom had brought their teenage children to complete the arc between then and now.

I remembered what Taylor had once told me: "It's important not to take yourself seriously but to always take the audience seriously." He also said, "It's hard to know exactly what's going on some nights, but in these appearances, I happen to be the center of something."

When he sang "Fire and Rain," he took us all with him on his long, eventful journey.

I've seen fire and I've seen rain
I've seen sunny days that I thought would never end.
I've seen lonely times when I could not find a friend
But I always thought I'd see you again.

Sweet Baby James is fifty-nine years old. He was able to kick his heroin habit before, as he puts it, "I damaged myself and others." He's past his old bouts with debilitating depression, and he's still packing them in at concert halls and on iTunes.

As his brother, Livingston, once put it, "How tough is James Taylor? Tough enough to make a career out of being sensitive."

Paul Simon

When I met Paul Simon in his spacious office in the Brill Building, the venerable unofficial headquarters of American pop music on Broadway in midtown Manhattan, he was just putting aside his guitar. He's still playing after all these years.

Surrounded by walls adorned with gold records and other plaques testifying to his enduring success, he says, "When I was coming of age, all the smart people wanted to get into rock and roll—John Lennon, Neil Young,

Mick [Jagger], [James] Taylor. Now all the smart people want to make films or go to Silicon Valley. It's not the same."

Referring to the musical revolution that came with the Sixties, he says, "You know, the guitar became the instrument. Before that, it was the piano. But with Dylan, McCartney, Lennon, and all those guys raised on rhythm and blues, the guitar was it. Now it's all technical stuff."

Forty years of performing and writing some of the most popular songs in the world have made Simon rich for generations of his family to come. Yet he's not a show-off rich man or a conspicuous consumer, like Elvis or Sinatra.

Yes, he flies in private jets and keeps a spacious apartment in Manhattan, a large home in the Connecticut suburbs, and an estate on the ocean in the Hamptons, but he keeps it all off the public radar. In fact, he finds the attitude about wealth one of the striking differences between the Sixties and today. "We couldn't imagine," he says, "being an advocate for greed or the yuppie lifestyle. We were anticorporation."

That was a common strain within the musical community of the Sixties. Neil Young, one of the founding members of the Sixties sound, won't allow any of his music to be licensed by Madison Avenue to sell commercial products, a growing trend in American advertising. He wants to stay true to the ethos of his time, telling **Rolling Stone**, "If the Sixties were overrated, then I don't know what you would say about some of the . . . other generations. Compared to what?

Paul Simon in the late Sixties, around the time he and Art Garfunkel recorded tracks for The Graduate, including "Mrs. Robinson"

Paul Simon in 2006

Generation X? Where's their mark? They didn't leave one. They left an X."

Simon, who campaigned for Eugene McCarthy in 1968 and George McGovern in 1972, has used the power of his fame and his bank account to perform benefit concerts for the homeless, for health care for the inner city, for autism, and for environmental causes. He is a serious student of music as a force in culture, and he seems dismayed that, as he puts it, "music is not the language of this generation." Except, of course, as it is loaded into an iPod.

By now the broad strokes of Simon's life are well known. His childhood in the Forest Hills section of Queens, the school play with his friend Art Garfunkel ("the best singer in our neighborhood"), their stop-and-go-and-stop partnership and friendship, the soundtrack for the breakthrough film **The Graduate**, one hit album after another, the introduction of African and Brazilian music to Simon's repertoire, three marriages, and a secure place in the Rock and Roll Hall of Fame.

First there was "Hey, Schoolgirl" in 1956, recorded for a small label right here in the Brill Building with Garfunkel—when they were still calling themselves Tom and Jerry. The song made it onto **Billboard**'s Hot 100 list. It even made it all the way to the playlist on KYNT in Yankton, South Dakota. That's where I heard it during my summer job as a nighttime disc jockey.

A rock-and-roll DJ needed a nickname in those days, so I was Terrible Tom. Sorry about that. My colleagues included Lively Leo and Perky Perry. Airtime in our minute market couldn't have helped "Hey, Schoolgirl" much, but the song made enough money for Simon to buy a red convertible and to appear with Garfunkel on **American Bandstand.** They were just sixteen and they seemed to be on their way.

But suddenly they hit a dry spell and decided to separate and do other things. Simon finished college and began performing solo on the folk circuit in England and Scandinavia. Garfunkel enrolled in architecture school.

In 1964 Simon came up with a haunting number that seemed to speak to every member of the new generation trying to find its way through a new world with an escalating war, exploding racial conflicts, the assassination of a president, and the leap into a sexual revolution fueled in part by Enovid, the newly available birth control pill. Released in 1965, it was called "The Sound of Silence."

> **Hello, darkness, my old friend**
> **I've come to talk with you again**
> **Because a vision softly creeping**
> **Left its seeds while I was sleeping**
> **And the vision that was planted in my brain**
> **Still remains**
> **Within the sound of silence**

Simon and Garfunkel were living at home with their parents when "The Sound of Silence" was released. They were sitting in Simon's red convertible one day when they heard a New York disc jockey announce, "Simon and Garfunkel's 'Sound of Silence' is number one!" Simon has said that he remarked to Garfunkel in jest, "That Simon and Garfunkel must be having a great time."

They were on their way to becoming one of the most successful and beloved musical acts in American history. Among those listening was Mike Nichols, the cerebral satirist who had emerged in the late Fifties from the University of Chicago with his performing partner, Elaine May, to rewrite the rules for social commentary in the Sixties with their hip, ironic comedy routines.

After directing plays on Broadway for several years, in 1966 Nichols took his genius to Hollywood and was nominated for the Academy Award for Best Director his first time out (with the movie version of Edward Albee's famous play **Who's Afraid of Virginia Woolf?**).

His next project was the screen adaptation of an obscure novel about coming of age. It was called **The Graduate**, and it starred an unknown newcomer, Dustin Hoffman, as Benjamin Braddock and the well-known actress Anne Bancroft as Elaine Robinson. Everyone involved—including the picture itself—won Oscars. Mike Nichols took home the Best Director statuette.

Benjamin, the directionless sexual innocent, and Mrs. Robinson, the glamorous, seductive, and decadent wife of his father's business partner, represented two different generations, one based in hope and confusion, the other grounded in self-indulgence and boredom. The characters were strong; the writing was witty and insightful; but Nichols knew the movie needed a hip, contemporary soundtrack, so he began laying in tracks from this hot new duo he admired, Simon and Garfunkel.

The producer, Lawrence Turman, signed the young men to produce three original songs for the film, but Simon was so busy with concerts and his frantic new life that he had trouble completing his end of the deal. Besides, he was spending too much time fiddling around with some lyrics that included references to Mrs. Roosevelt, as in Eleanor, the wife of Franklin Delano Roosevelt.

Mrs. Roosevelt was many things, but glamorous, seductive, and decadent weren't among them. Why, then, Eleanor Roosevelt? "I don't know," Simon told me, laughing. "When Artie told Mike I was working on this song and Mike heard I was using Mrs. Roosevelt, he said, 'No, it's Mrs. Robinson,' so I changed the name, and while the film was wrapping, I still wasn't finished with all the lyrics." He says he still doesn't know just where he got the idea for the final stanza of "Mrs. Robinson":

> **Where have you gone, Joe DiMaggio**
> **A nation turns its lonely eyes to you**
> **What's that you say, Mrs. Robinson**
> **Joltin' Joe has left and gone away**

"Mrs. Robinson" became one of the most popular songs ever produced for a film, and the rest of the soundtrack secured the place of the two schoolboy friends in the pantheon of American musicians, as well as in the hearts and minds of the young men and women of an entire generation.

However, Simon and Garfunkel did not live happily ever after. They broke up in 1970 after **Bridge over Troubled Water** became a phenomenally successful album. Garfunkel wanted to spend more time acting, and Simon, who wrote all their songs, wanted more artistic freedom. They reunited briefly in a benefit concert for George McGovern in 1972, and then not again until 1981, when they lit up New York's Central Park with a reunion concert that drew half a million fans.

They've been back together briefly since, notably in a concert at the Colosseum in Rome with a sellout crowd, a joint appearance at the Rock and Roll Hall of Fame in Cleveland in 1990, and Old Friends tours in 2003 and 2004. But mostly, they have led separate lives, with Simon constantly working to find new music and new rhythms to complement his lyrical appetite.

His album **Graceland** brought to Western audiences the throbbing, emotional music of Africa with the Zulu choir Ladysmith Black Mambazo. His 1990 album **The Rhythm of the Saints** provided a similar window on the dynamic music of Brazil. A peripatetic traveler, Simon says, "I find wherever I go, the musicians know the country best and can explain what's really going on."

What does the current reign of hip-hop say about music in America today? Simon pauses and then comments, "It's interesting rhythmically, but I don't think the depiction of what's going on in African-American neighborhoods is balanced. I spend a lot of time at 125th and Lenox in Harlem [a neighborhood undergoing a renaissance with new shops, restaurants, and apartments], and I see a lot of new hope up there. I don't hear that in hip-hop. The trouble is, artists get trapped in a style. If they start 'bad,' they gotta stay 'bad,' even if conditions are changing."

When I ask if he'd like to start over in the business now, he says, "Well, YouTube is a little like the old days. All I wanted to do when I was young was to record a song and hear it on the radio. Now you can get it on YouTube."

But the economics, he acknowledges, are a great deal different and not very user-friendly. You may get on YouTube, but you won't get paid for it. If you actually manage to make a hit record, getting paid for it is a problem now that many former customers seem to think that music belongs to anyone who can download it for free onto their computer or iPod.

As for his role in the glory days of Sixties music, Simon isn't sure what to believe. When I ask, "Are you flattered when you look out into a concert audience and see parents bringing their kids to hear you?" he answers, " 'Flattered' is not the right word, because it's not just about me. It's a whole feeling about the music and the time."

He is moved, however, when he breaks into one of his old standards and sees his fans weeping. He has said, "For people who were there, the songs are associated with a certain memory or person, and the power of that magnified over the years. The songs are our lives. If I tried to write something like 'The Sound of Silence' now, it would be wrong. That time frame doesn't exist anymore."

He dismisses the title often accorded him—"a legend"—explaining that he's spending most of his energy these days trying not to be "an old fool. When you're in your twenties, you make mistakes. When you're in your sixties, what's your excuse?"

He's concerned that so much of what is going wrong in the world now is no longer being made the subject of popular music. "The culture we're in now," he has said, "is controlled by popular polarizers. If that's the way the world is headed, we're in for a lot of pain.

"I have an exceptionally privileged life, and I am not entitled to any complaints. But then I go on and complain anyway."

As he walks me to the elevator in the Brill Building, after all these years still in the place where it all began for him over half a century ago, Simon talks about the Yankees' prospects, about possible destinations in Asia for a family vacation, about a dinner that night with his pals Lorne Michaels, the creator and producer of **Saturday Night Live,** and the actor Steve Martin. I like to think that when the elevator doors closed and he made his way back to his office, he picked up his guitar and played for himself a few bars of "Old Friends."

Jann Wenner

Jann Wenner became a very rich man by riding the long wave of rock and roll all the way from the San Francisco Bay Area to a publishing empire centered on **Rolling Stone** magazine in midtown Manhattan. When he was a Berkeley student in the Sixties, he tells me, "I became convinced the music and this generation would be transformative. It would be political by culture and conduct. It would be led by music . . . as the place where the real poets of my generation were talking and writing. I had this thought that music would be . . . the glue that held this generation together."

He remembers as a teenager rock music speaking to his generation about subjects that were not getting attention elsewhere. "The Beatles came along and said, 'Freedom!' you know, 'A Hard Day's Night.' They're being rude and cheeky and they're having so much fucking fun and they're my age. What's not to like about that?

"The Stones, the Byrds, the Dead were really expressing a point of view you couldn't find elsewhere. I was raised on **Father Knows Best,** and that was still going on in the Sixties."

He also sees a compression of the generations in the popular culture. "I couldn't share cultural things with my parents . . . the symphony or **South Pacific.** But now you can talk about music or movies with your kids. I go to concerts and movies with my kids. There's no generation gap."

As for the current generation of young people, Wenner understands the conflicts they're facing, but he's not sure they're more socially conservative. "The drug culture—wide open. The sex culture—wide open. What makes them more conservative is that they're more sober about the way the world works, about a career, about the need to have a job."

Nonetheless, Wenner believes the fundamental values of the Sixties are still intact and embraced by the current generation of American college students.

Wenner devotes a lot of personal energy and his magazines' pages to the environment, publishing long articles by Al Gore and Robert F. Kennedy Jr. on the subject.

Global warming is a pet cause, yet when I ask him about the hypocrisy of flying around in a private jet, emitting CO_2 at stupendous rates, he is uncharacteristically sheepish and mumbles something about how hard it is to get airline connections to Sun Valley.

As for music, Wenner is a big fan of the new downloading technology because it makes rock and roll, hip-hop, and all the other forms more widely available and therefore reinforces the interest in what his magazine publishes.

Wenner gets excited as he describes how the place of music has expanded through the new technology. "Now it's instantly available on your computer, on your desk—anytime, night and day, and that progression is just so damn powerful.

"The people who were fighting it, they may want to go back to something that was safe or easy. It just doesn't exist anymore. The population has changed and the type of music has changed. It's no longer gonna be a society of small towns run by white guys."

He's also reassured by another aspect of downloading: It makes it so much easier for this generation to be exposed to the music that shaped Wenner's generation. "You know the Beatles are still the most popular thing with kids; they're listening to songs such as 'All You Need Is Love,' 'Give Peace a Chance,' 'Rocky Racoon,' and all the rest of this funny, mad, cynical, imaginative, playful, uplifting shit. It's part of what's making this generation the natural heirs to the baby boom."

It's also very good business for Wenner Media.

Warren Beatty

Rock and roll in all of its variations was the lingua franca of the Sixties, but films gave those days an artistic visual texture that went well beyond the nightly offerings on the network news. Again, the transformation was led by young filmmakers such as Martin Scorsese, Francis Ford Coppola, Bob Rafelson, Steven Spielberg, Mike Nichols, and their contemporaries behind the cameras; and by Robert Redford, Warren Beatty, Jack Nicholson, Diane Keaton, Faye Dunaway, Dustin Hoffman, Dennis Hopper and Peter Fonda, Jane Fonda, Robert De Niro, Liv Ullmann, Julie Christie, Al Pacino, Candice Bergen, Woody Allen, and their contemporaries in front of the camera.

Warren Beatty, in a way, was a charter member of both groups. He was a star at the box office and a canny producer in the executive suite.

Beatty was not just a big box-office star, he was also an entrepreneur, a star who could develop his own projects. Inside Hollywood, his business acumen and financial savvy were the traits most likely to generate admiring comments.

The films **Shampoo, Heaven Can Wait,** and **Reds** were all star turns for Beatty the actor, but the Oscar came to him for best director on **Reds** (his acting and screenplay also earned Oscar nominations). Then came Elaine May's **Ishtar,** a film that seemed like a great idea but turned out to be a colossal embarrassment of legendary proportions for Beatty and Dustin Hoffman and everyone else involved.

Warren Beatty with
Robert F. Kennedy
during the 1968
presidential
campaign

Warren Beatty with his wife, Annette Bening,
and their children at the Kennedy Center
Honors in 2004

Beatty remains a keen student of the economics of Hollywood, if not an admirer of the current trends. They began, he says, way back in 1975 with the producers of a Charles Bronson film called **Breakout**. The producers realized they didn't have much of a film, but they had a "helluva sixty seconds," and on the principle of waste not, want not, they decided to release it.

"So they put a tremendous amount of money into two thirty-second spots and opened the movie in an unprecedented number of theaters. The movie made a lot of money; everyone was thrilled. **Bonnie and Clyde** opened in two theaters, so the public could catch up with the content, the word-of-mouth factor.

"It took time. Now you can make your money back in a few weeks, and that's impossible for the corporate appetite to resist. But," he adds, "I think it depends on a certain level of untruth in advertising."

Beatty sees the Internet as a mixed blessing. It makes the word-of-mouth factor possible again, at warp speed. As a result, he is encouraged that more personal, unconventional films are making their way back onto the screens. But with the huge amounts of money needed for marketing and the constant threat of piracy, he worries the studios will gravitate more and more to the **Batman** or **Spider-Man** type of epics, pouring their big marketing budgets into those films to rush them to the theaters.

Beatty is married to his **Bugsy** costar, actress Annette Bening, with whom he has three daughters and a son, all under sixteen; his old-school charm is undiminished and his passion for politics untempered. He's still a Democrat, but he's also a friend of John

McCain and an occasional luncheon companion of Nancy Reagan.

We meet in the library of his secluded, elegantly furnished English Tudor–style home on the ridge between Beverly Hills and the San Fernando Valley. The most prominently displayed photos are of Beatty and his son on a Hawaiian fishing trip and a candid shot of Eleanor and Franklin Roosevelt in the president's open touring car.

He is eager to talk, but, as he always has been when it comes to on-the-record statements, he is agonizingly careful with the words he chooses. With one exception: He talks freely about the place of stars in Hollywood. "It's all small screen now," he says. "No mystique. No privacy. I've even heard of some people you'd know caught in compromising positions by cell-phone cameras. I feel sorry for the young ones coming up."

When I ask about the effect of the Internet and sites such as YouTube on all of this, he says, "Well, I had an interesting experience recently. I don't go out much, but some of my pals invited me to one of those hot new L.A. clubs, and they promised I could get in unnoticed through the back door, which I did. I sat around for a while, feeling like Aristotle Onassis, and decided to leave.

"I went out the same back door to this small, darkened parking lot, and when I got to my car, maybe twenty flashes went off. Paparazzi. I had nothing to hide, so I smiled and wondered how long before this gets out. My picture was on the Internet before I got home. There are no secrets anymore."

Beatty knows his way around the World Wide

Web. "I always go to the right-wing sites to see what they're up to," he says. "I do worry about all the misinformation out there. I know they say 'the truth will come out eventually,' but in this climate, I am not so sure.

"My kids are on the Internet all the time, although we do have parental controls on their computers. But they make movies, write books, talk to each other. They think the technology exists just for their benefit. I can't keep up with them, hard as I try."

Beatty, who keeps promising to make a new film but never quite gets around to it, was said to be interested in the role of Richard Nixon in the screen adaptation of **Frost/Nixon,** the hit stage play based on the interviews that the British talk-show host David Frost did with Nixon after he left the presidency. But the role went to Frank Langella, the celebrated character actor who played the part to rave reviews on the London stage and also on Broadway. Beatty, true to form, apparently took too long to make up his mind.

Langella deserves the role, but it would have been intriguing to see Warren Beatty play Nixon—the Antichrist of his younger years as a campaign activist for George McGovern and Gary Hart. That would have taken the Sixties through more than one pane of the looking glass.

Lawrence Kasdan

One of the few successful Hollywood figures to rise up out of the protest milieu of the Sixties and make it big in Hollywood is Lawrence Kasdan, the writer and director of **The Big Chill**, an ensemble film about what happens to a group of Sixties friends who meet ten years after they've left college. It is arguably the best film made about what happened next to the ideals, loyalties, and choices of a certain Sixties set.

I say "certain" because in the conceit of many who went through the Sixties, the far left side of the campus was the only universe that counted. When you speak to those who hold that view and remind them that far more people their age were either nearer the center or even uncommitted, not to mention that most of their contemporaries were in military uniform, in work clothes, or in trade schools, rather than alongside them on the barricades, it is a little jarring to their sense of time and place—not to mention their egos.

Indisputably, however, the college activists did symbolize the time, and that was the world that Kasdan so perfectly captured. He wrote **The Big Chill** after spending four years at the University of Michigan, 1966 to 1970. After growing up mostly in rural West Virginia, it was a liberating experience to be around people who shared his more radical political beliefs.

He had chosen Michigan because it had a generous endowment for undergraduate writing contests, and his decision paid off. He won four prizes there, and that helped finance his education.

Michigan was the alma mater of Tom Hayden, the controversial and seminal figure in social activism on campuses, especially the antiwar movement. By the time Kasdan arrived at Michigan, Hayden had left the campus for a larger playing field, but his radical spirit remained.

Of his own participation, Kasdan says, "I took part in a lot of the protests, but I never considered myself a terribly committed activist. From my sophomore year on, there was a lot of running around for no particular reason. I remember rioting, teargassing, cops chasing people."

When he went home to West Virginia, he was singled out for his long hair. "People called me a homosexual, things like that. I had a lot of friends there, but it just got harder and harder to go back." He was aware that while he and his Michigan classmates were able to avoid military service, the kids back home in West Virginia were volunteering for Vietnam. "At Michigan I was living in a bubble of privilege with a deferment and then, later, a high draft number. But I also thought the war was insane for everyone, so I didn't think, 'I deserve this and others don't.'"

When he graduated from Michigan in 1970, Kasdan headed for Los Angeles and a brief but unsuccessful stab at pursuing his dream of writing screenplays. Before long he returned to Michigan to be with his soon-to-be wife, Meg. Despite his happy marriage and the birth of a son, this was a very difficult period in his life. "I got a master's degree in English, thinking I might teach, but there was a glut of English teachers because everyone was trying to avoid the draft. It was almost as hard getting a teaching job as it was selling a screenplay."

He landed a job in advertising through a friend of

Director Lawrence Kasdan (front left) with the cast of The Big Chill, **on location in 1983**

Kasdan on the set of Dreamcatcher, 2003

Meg's, but he was truly unhappy in that line of work, and it would be seven years before he sold a screenplay.

It was during those years in advertising, he said, that he felt "a big chill" because his life was so much more difficult and uninspiring than during those heady undergraduate years. "My friends were experiencing the same thing," he says now. "College gave us a false sense of power and entitlement, and then we hit the real world.

"I think our generation felt the loss of innocence more profoundly than others. The Greatest Generation . . . went through real trauma, not innocence."

He continued to work on his screenplays, finally getting a bid for one called **The Bodyguard** (which was eventually made into a Kevin Costner film). "They offered me a little money," Kasdan said, "not enough to live on, so my wife made me ask for more." He did, and to his agent's surprise, he got the extra cash and was able to quit advertising.

Three months later, he struck real gold, selling his screenplay **Continental Divide** to Steven Spielberg for "a lot of money." He was asked to write the screenplays for **Raiders of the Lost Ark** and George Lucas's fifth and sixth **Star Wars** epics, **The Empire Strikes Back** and **Return of the Jedi**. Finally, at twenty-eight, he had achieved that best and most elusive of all conditions in Hollywood: He was hot. He wanted to direct, and he hit paydirt again his first time out with a stylish and sensuous film of his original script called **Body Heat**, starring Kathleen Turner and William Hurt. It had a modern film-noir quality—dangerous, smart, and very sexy—that the critics and the moviegoers loved.

He was fully aware of his good fortune to be doing something that he loved, while his old classmates were still trying to find a life. The idea for **The Big Chill** came to him during a reunion of Sixties friends. But it was a dialogue-heavy screenplay with no central role to attract a big box-office star.

Lawrence Kasdan, despite his run of successes, had hit the wall. The studios weren't interested. "I pitched it seventeen times, and this is when people wanted to be in business with me. They kept asking, 'Who's the hero? Who **are** these people?'"

Finally, a woman at Columbia Pictures, "Marcia Nasatir, an old lefty, read the script and went crazy for it. She pushed it through. Everyone fought her, but we got it made and previewed it in Seattle. Everyone there laughed in all the right places—because they could hear the language of the times and knew what the attitudes were."

Most of the film is set in the gracious ante bellum South Carolina home of Kevin Kline's character, a newly minted sports-shoe mogul. Jeff Goldblum's character, who intended to teach in Harlem but wound up as a celebrity profiler for **People** magazine, looks back on their college years and says, "That's when property was a crime."

The Big Chill opened on a modest eight hundred screens around the country and didn't do well on the first Friday it was shown. But the next night, there were lines around the block in Westwood, California, and it was a big hit. It played there for six months, a run now unheard of in the film business.

Not everyone loved it. Pauline Kael, the influential critic for **The New Yorker,** wrote, "Anyone who believes himself to have been a revolutionary . . . in the late Sixties is likely to find **The Big Chill** despicable." After all, the characters were a successful sports-shoe-store owner; his wife; a yuppie doctor; a writer for **People** magazine; a television actor; and a Vietnam veteran.

Kasdan says Kael later apologized for that review, but he wasn't troubled. He knew that most of the Sixties students weren't real radicals and that a few years later, they were scrambling for jobs or new meaning in their lives. They were his audience because he was telling their story.

As with **The Graduate,** the soundtrack was an integral part of the film's impact. It was, as Kasdan says, "magical. My wife picked it out from the stuff we loved in college." It is a soundtrack that continues to sell. "I Heard It Through the Grapevine," by Marvin Gaye; "My Girl," by the Temptations; "Joy to the World," by Three Dog Night; "(You Make Me Feel Like) A Natural Woman," by Aretha Franklin; "Wouldn't It Be Nice," by the Beach Boys; and Martha and the Vandellas' "Dancing in the Street" were just a few of the nostalgic hits providing an audio complement to the cast of Glenn Close, Kevin Kline, William Hurt, JoBeth Williams, Jeff Goldblum, Meg Tilly, Mary Kay Place, and Tom Berenger.

Kasdan, who is now fifty-eight and financially secure thanks to an ongoing string of successful films, is a fierce opponent of George W. Bush's administration and the decision to go to war in Iraq. He admits that when the subject comes up at dinner with his friends, everyone feels the same but at the end of the evening everyone just goes back to their comfortable homes.

"It is inconceivable this would have happened in the Sixties," he says. "I'm as guilty as anyone." The end of the draft, he thinks, made the difference. People of privilege are no longer threatened by having to interrupt their careers, much less having to fight. Besides, they're too busy thinking about how to make more money. "Now you have old Sixties radicals becoming billionaires."

Hollywood has always been much more about the money than the message, but never more so than now, with the competition from YouTube and the other Internet offerings, downloaded music videos, made-for-television movies, and the "I'll wait to watch the DVD on my home entertainment center" attitude.

Kasdan misses the competitive spirit of his early days in Hollywood, the Seventies and early Eighties, when, he says, "we were trying to make films about our time, **about** something. It was exciting. This town was filled with people who came out of the Sixties—writers, directors—and we wanted to make films about what was going on.

"I made **Grand Canyon** in 1991. I couldn't get something like that made now." **Grand Canyon** was another ensemble film, this one about midlife crises, the extended lives of **The Big Chill** generation. It received enthusiastic reviews but was only a modest success at the box office. It has been, however, a very popular DVD.

Looking back, Kasdan believes the most important thing his generation did was to challenge the culture—

to force a fissure, as he puts it, in the old world so that a new world could grow out of it.

Kasdan also acknowledges that his generation gave up at some point and succumbed to the impulses of getting rather than giving. "'I want the house, I want the car, I want the school.' No matter how strong your beliefs are, you'll be under constant pressure. It's like trying to hold back the ocean. You don't want the fear of having no money."

He is encouraged that there is now a new cause that his generation can rally around. "The environmental thing," he says, "is gratifying. It's driven by a sense of self-interest, which is vital for any movement. If it weren't for the self-interest—for the future of their kids—I don't know if they would be as interested."

Lorne Michaels

Comedy on television was also changing in the Sixties, and one young man from Canada who was present at the creation is still there and still making it happen.

Lorne Michaels arrived in Southern California from Canada as a gifted and ambitious young comedy writer shortly after Robert Kennedy was assassinated in the late spring of 1968. Michaels went to work on an unconventional new show scheduled for NBC's prime time. It was called **Rowan & Martin's Laugh-In,** and it featured a comedy team that had been working in Las Vegas and on the hard road of the nightclub circuit across the country.

Dan Rowan was the handsome, suave straight man

who seemed to have been born in a tuxedo. Dick Martin played the cheerful, slightly goofy younger brother type with a perpetually startled expression. Although Rowan didn't sing, the two men freely admitted that they had decided to team up after watching Dean Martin and Jerry Lewis, the reigning superstars of comedy duos through the Fifties and early Sixties. Rowan and Martin were Martin and Lewis Lite, but they were doing well, and a prime-time television show could lift them to a level beyond the one-night stands.

The show broke all the standard rules of network comedy. It had a large repertory company of gifted but little-known sketch artists who delivered jokes and performed sight gags at a rat-a-tat pace, making fun of politicians and news events while also mocking the emerging hippie culture. Goldie Hawn, until then a dancer in Las Vegas and New York, boogied across the screen in a bikini with jokes painted on her lithe body. Henry Gibson held a large flower while reading short offbeat poems. Arte Johnson was a Nazi soldier who leered into the camera while saying, "Verrrryyy interesting." Lily Tomlin was Ernestine, the Forties-style telephone operator who snorted impatiently at inquiries.

There were an obviously gay sportscaster and a regular parody of network news, a forerunner of the satirical "Weekend Update" newscast each week on **Saturday Night Live,** which itself begat **The Daily Show with Jon Stewart** and **The Colbert Report.**

Laugh-In was fiercely bipartisan in its targets, taking on Democrats as well as Republicans, and it was never dark or mean-spirited. Rowan and Martin held it all together with their witty repartee and a manner that seemed to say to the audience, "It's okay, folks; we're all in this together, and what else can you do but laugh?"

Laugh-In was a huge hit. It ran against **I Love Lucy** on CBS, the gold standard of television comedy, and tied **Lucy** in the ratings. It was so popular that presidential candidate Richard Nixon's advisers persuaded him to appear on a segment and repeat the line made popular by Judy Carne, then Burt Reynolds's wife. Nixon, desperately trying to be just one of the boys, looked into the camera and said, "Sock it to **me**?"

Laugh-In was also the godfather of **Saturday Night Live**, now television's longest-running comedy and sketch show, the breakthrough concept that was created by Lorne Michaels. When **Laugh-In** ended its run in 1973, just as the Watergate crisis was entering its final stages in the Nixon White House, Michaels moved to New York with **Saturday Night Live** already in mind. In producing specials with Richard Pryor and Lily Tomlin, he had learned that the expectations of network executives were merciless when it came to prime time. They wanted shows that commanded at least 40 percent of the available audience, and to do that required big, established stars who appealed to the masses.

Instead, Michaels proposed moving to the outer fringes of the television schedule, Saturday night at eleven-thirty, and producing a show with young unknowns for an audience of his generation, the burgeoning baby boomers. To underscore his strategy, he named his cast "The Not Ready for Prime Time Players." It was a daring concept, and it was so contrary to established practices that when Michaels asked a young

Lorne Michaels (left) with Chevy Chase,
Dan Aykroyd, and John Belushi at the
Washington Monument

member of Chicago's Second City troupe to consider joining, John Belushi said, "I don't do television."

Michaels persuaded Belushi, Chevy Chase, Dan Aykroyd, Gilda Radner, Jane Curtin, and the others who followed that he didn't intend to "do television" by the old rules. It would be broadcast live, late on a Saturday night, on a set that looked like a funky downtown club, with one of the best house bands in the business. A mix of cool mood lighting and hot rock and roll set the stage for a new generation to establish their own rules.

The first one was: Don't play it safe. From the beginning, **SNL** (as it soon became widely known) was always a little mad, bad, and dangerous to do. You didn't know what was coming next or even whether it would be funny—which it occasionally wasn't. But you did know that this wasn't your father's television show.

Michaels, who is now sixty-four, wealthy, and gray-haired, remains the show's presiding guru, overseeing each weekly edition from his office above Studio 8-H, the home of **SNL** since its inception.

A few times I joined the cast for the regular after-show party, but I quickly learned I could no longer keep up with the all-night, hard-drinking habits of the twentysomethings. Their drug use was more discreet, but it was hardly a secret. It was part of the gestalt of being the coolest new kids on the block, wickedly funny, as manic in their art form as in their private lives.

John Belushi, a former high school football star, combined the intangible quality of lovability with the sometimes less-than-lovable quality of being a nonstop primal physical and emotional force. On more than one occasion, Belushi and Chevy Chase barreled into the NBC studios as Jane Pauley and I were about to open the **Today** show at seven A.M. After being out all night partying, they would solicitously inquire if we needed any help that morning.

When Belushi died of an overdose, I wasn't surprised, but that didn't make it any easier to accept. He was a great talent, but he was a reckless soul who crashed through every barrier he came up against. He connected to his contemporaries, just as James Dean and Elvis Presley had prompted my generation to rethink the rules of life.

Around that time a workman at our house who was about Belushi's age approached me at the end of his shift and asked, "Did you know John Belushi?" I said I did. He said plaintively, "Was he a good guy?" I assured him he was, and he thanked me, walking away as if leaving the funeral of a close friend.

The description of Belushi's death—getting shot up with a cocktail of lethal drugs in a hotel room by a woman he knew only slightly—was so pitiful it rattled his friends and fans. Suddenly, drugs weren't so edgy or amusing anymore.

Belushi's death was also a marker for SNL, and the show's notorious backstage drug use got cleaned up.

By 1982, a show that had started as a satirical counterpoint to the institution of television had become something of an institution in its own right. The loss of Belushi and the outpouring of grief and attention it elicited were reminders that SNL was not just another seasonal distraction. It had become a meaningful landmark, as well as an agent of change, on the American entertainment generational landscape.

When Lorne Michaels and I talked about that transition in television entertainment, he had a neat summary. When he was a writer on **Laugh-In** at the age of twenty-four, all the other writers were fifty and older, and most of them were veterans of radio comedy shows. When Michaels started **SNL**, he was, at thirty, the oldest member of a staff that had grown up entirely in and on television. **SNL** was the first major show produced by a purely television generation.

About **SNL**, Michaels now says, "I don't think it would have worked without Watergate. That made everything fair game." The resignation of a president, the imprisonment of his closest aides, the vice president forced from office for accepting bribes, the lies about the conduct of the war in Vietnam, and the determination of a generation to write its own rules—all combined to create an environment in which there were fewer and fewer sacred cows.

"I remember," he says, "when Chevy was doing his famous 'Jerry Ford as president' stumbling bit. There was a nanosecond when he didn't get a laugh, so he blew his nose on his necktie. I thought, 'Oh, God, have we gone too far?' But there was almost no negative reaction." President Ford publicly laughed at the parody; at one big Washington dinner, he imitated Chase imitating him.

Music, the defining language of the generation, was also critical to the success of the show. Television productions had been notoriously deficient about getting the sound right when it came to music. As Michaels says, "They'd put up a boom mike, and that would be it. I brought in [the legendary rock producer] Phil Ramone to help us design a sound system that would attract the best groups."

Among those who answered the call: Paul Simon, a big star who gave **SNL** cachet with an appearance early in the first season. He was followed by Paul McCartney, Linda Ronstadt, James Taylor, Mick Jagger, Brian Wilson, Chuck Berry, Frank Zappa, Carly Simon, James Brown, the Grateful Dead, Van Morrison, Chicago, Joe Cocker, and Elton John, to name a few. **SNL** was the premier site for rock on television long before MTV.

Michaels knew that big-name music was important not just because it attracted viewers but because it allowed him to produce a whole show. He remembered that **That Was the Week That Was**, a British import that tried to do an hour every week satirizing the news, would run out of gas about a third of the way through.

Music gave him a chance to pace the sketches. If one died or just lingered, he could bring on the band and keep the rhythm going until the next bit. He also preferred the ninety-minute format on commercial television. "It's a discipline," he says, "a box that forces me to think about context in a way cable television doesn't require. I like where I am."

It does have its constraints, because it is carried on a network that uses the public airwaves. The language on **The Sopranos** is part of the patois of the young people who watch **SNL,** but they will not hear the F-word spoken on **Saturday Night Live.** If they did, the FCC would heavily penalize NBC and its owned stations. Michaels is amused that "fuck" has long been showing up in mass-circulation literary publications such as **The New Yorker** but not yet on network television, and he's doing just fine without resorting to it.

He watches the newer social-satire programs closely—**The Daily Show with Jon Stewart**, **The Colbert Report**, and the animated series **The Simpsons** and **South Park**. He particularly admires **South Park** because it is willing to take the greatest risks with its dialogue and plot lines. He's a little perplexed by all the press attention devoted to **The Daily Show** and **The Colbert Report**.

First, the audience for both broadcasts on Comedy Central is a fraction of what **Saturday Night Live** attracts even during reruns. It's about five million fewer viewers than what **SNL** draws at eleven-thirty on Saturday night. **The Daily Show** and **The Colbert Report** are smart and funny, a welcome commentary on the absurdities of conventional politics and the practices of the news media. They're helped immeasurably by the foibles of the Bush administration and the caricatures that figures such as Dick Cheney, Donald Rumsfeld, Condoleezza Rice, and Bill O'Reilly of FOX News represent to their young audience. That's their territory, and they stay within it.

One of the most telling commentaries on **Saturday Night Live** is that parents who were just entering college when the show began are now watching it with their college-age children. Michaels, the graying boy wonder who has been keeping succeeding generations near a television set at eleven-thirty on Saturday nights for thirty-five years, is quietly pleased that he's been able to entertain them all, parents and their children alike.

Dick Gregory

Saturday Night Live, The Daily Show, and **The Colbert Report** are direct descendants not just of **Laugh-In** but also of the likes of satirists Lenny Bruce and Mort Sahl; comedians such as Tommy Smothers, who had a popular show on CBS from 1967 to 1969 with his straight-man brother, Dick; and the black comic Dick Gregory, who broke the color barrier at white clubs.

Gregory, born in 1932, was a child during the worst days of segregation in St. Louis. The teachers at his segregated school were impressed by his quick wit and his outstanding athletic ability. They encouraged him and directed him to a scholarship at Southern Illinois University, where he ran track and set records for the mile and half mile.

But his first love was comedy, and his distinctive style was to deal with racism head on and find some kind of healing for his audiences of both races through laughter. "Segregation is not all bad," he'd say. "Have you ever heard of a collision where all the people in the back of the bus got hurt?" He was a leading part of a new generation of black comics, such as Bill Cosby and Godfrey Cambridge, who made it possible for the genius of Richard Pryor to blossom only a short while later.

When Dick Gregory broke the color line by being

booked at Chicago's Playboy Club in 1961, the manager was nervous because the club had been reserved for a private party that included a lot of white Southern men. Gregory insisted on going onstage, and almost immediately, one of the white patrons stood up and called him "nigger."

Gregory smiled and responded, "Hey, I get fifty dollars here every time someone says that, so would you all stand up and call me 'nigger'?" He was onstage for three hours, giving the Southern white guys more than their money's worth. "A Southern liberal? That's a guy who will hang you from a low tree." He dislikes what he considers the cheap use of the word "nigger" by rap groups today. To be sure, he used it onstage first. But that was done consciously to achieve the specific effect of turning it back on white audiences and letting them know that he could handle it while mocking their cowardice and bigotry.

Hugh Hefner gave Gregory a contract, and there were glowing articles in **Esquire** and **The New York Times**. He could name his ticket, but he had something else in mind.

Beginning in 1962, he went south to march with Dr. Martin Luther King Jr. to join his crusade for civil rights. Gregory wasn't just a celebrity tagalong. He was a full-blown committed activist, getting beaten up and jailed on a regular basis.

His biographer Robert Lipsyte of **The New York Times** has said, "He was blowing his career. Promoters were too frightened to hire him. But Greg knew that his presence at demonstrations could save lives." He was shot in the leg, apparently by rioters, when he tried to bring peace to the Watts riots in Los Angeles in 1965. He says, "I yelled out, 'All right, you shot me, goddammit; now go home!'"

Gregory became close to Malcolm X and Muhammad Ali. He also soon became the country's best-known man on a fast. He'd quit eating for a month at a time and then subsist on a limited vegetarian-and-juice diet. When I'd see him at public events, I worried that he was about to expire of starvation, but he would get off a witty line like "I go to a lot of funerals, and they're always for you eaters."

One of his best lines, I thought, did involve eating. He described sitting down at a Southern lunch counter, and "three big white brothers came up behind me. You know their names—Ku, Klux, and Klan. And they said, 'Boy, whatever you do to that chicken, we're gonna do to you!' So I picked up the chicken and kissed it!"

Gregory ran for president on the Freedom and Peace Party ticket in 1968 and constantly challenged the administration of Chicago mayor Richard J. Daley. He has long been a conspiracy theorist on the deaths of Dr. King, John and Robert Kennedy, John Lennon, Malcolm X, Lenny Bruce, and Ron Brown, President Clinton's commerce secretary.

Now in his seventies and still lecturing and writing on dieting and ethics, Dick Gregory looks back with pride on what was accomplished. "We marched. We were beaten. People died but we did not fail.

"Never in the history of the planet has any group made the progress in forty years that African-Americans have. It's the power of the movement. A black man is

Dick Gregory outside the
1968 Democratic National Convention

Dick Gregory today, near
the Washington Monument

now the head of the state troopers in Mississippi. Condoleezza Rice and Colin Powell. We didn't create those people. They've always been there, but we created the environment in which a president can pick them without everyone getting upset.

"I'll tell you who saw it coming. They did. The redneck sheriffs and the KKK. This was their nightmare."

Tommy Smothers

Tommy Smothers is now living in California, playing in celebrity golf tournaments and producing wine at his Remick Ridge vineyards in the Sonoma Valley. He's also a little angry and bewildered by what happened to the spirit of the Sixties.

Tommy and his brother, Dick, were popular performers on **The Tonight Show** with Johnny Carson and in clubs and college concerts when CBS decided to put them on in prime time against the NBC Western blockbuster **Bonanza**. Tommy remembers, "We had no agenda when the show started, but we wanted to be relevant. It was a very passionate time, and we were the only show reflecting that viewpoint on Vietnam and civil rights."

Tommy Smothers remembers one skit in which he was playing the part of a Southern minister at an interracial marriage: " 'Do you, Brother Jackson, take Sally Smith as your lawfully wedded wife until death do you part?' He said 'I do' and as the minister, I responded, 'The rope, please.' "

In the 1968–1969 season, after Richard Nixon

had been elected president, **The Smothers Brothers Comedy Hour** began to get more attention from the CBS censors. The show was a big hit, but it became a lightning rod for a great deal of hate mail after, for example, Joan Baez appeared and wanted to dedicate a song to her husband, who was going to jail for resisting the draft.

Tommy remembers, "We wanted to put up a sign, 'Another Mother for Peace,' a common sign in those days, but CBS said no. We had Harry Belafonte on singing calypso songs over footage of the '68 Democratic convention riots, and CBS yanked that."

In April 1969 CBS canceled the show, a decision that the Smothers Brothers challenged in court, where they were awarded $776,300 in damages. While the case was pending, the show won its first Emmy for writing. Tommy says, "In the end we won, but it didn't matter. I lost my sense of humor. Only in hindsight did we recognize that we made some sort of impact. I enjoyed the hell out of the show, and it's neat to have gotten some respect."

Tommy Smothers laments the fact that what little social satire survives is now mostly on cable, and he hates the trend toward what he calls "foaming at the mouth." He says, "We always attacked policies, not people. You can talk all you want about freedom of speech, but it is freedom of hearing that counts."

He's critical of the news media for not giving more emphasis to the protestors at the beginning of the Iraq War. But most of all, he's puzzled by what happened to the Sixties generation. "What a waste of energy. Now they just all sit around and let this happen."

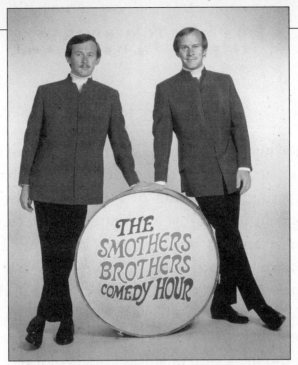

The Smothers Brothers Comedy Hour
became an unexpected hit on CBS
during the 1968–69 season.

Tommy Smothers today

Leonard Riggio

It was not just in music and films that the Sixties took a historic turn in content, style, and merchandising; the marketing and selling of books went through no less a revolutionary cycle. Again, the reviews were mixed as American business took a beating from the counterculture crowd.

It may seem a contradiction that some of America's most successful and creative entrepreneurs of the twenty-first century emerged from the Sixties culture. Many of the successful business leaders of today used the counterculture as a petri dish to grow new models for a new generation of conspicuous consumers markedly different from the generation of thrift that had emerged from the Thirties and Forties. The boomers' tastes quickly expanded along with their bank accounts.

Leonard Riggio is at once a seminal figure in, and a conspicuous beneficiary of, that evolution in the American economy. He transformed the business of selling books in America by mass-marketing a full range of titles in settings that adopted the coffeehouse culture of the Sixties. As a result, local consumers in, say, Billings, Montana, or Cape Girardeau, Missouri, as well as in New York City, Los Angeles, Chicago, or any other big city, can get a book of their choice, a hot latte, and a wireless hookup for their laptop in the kind of cozy setting that belies the Fortune 500 reality that prevails at the home office of Barnes & Noble.

Riggio didn't set out to be a billionaire business visionary. He was a bright and ambitious kid, but in his

Brooklyn, New York, working-class neighborhood, success had more modest dimensions. "I came into the Sixties very naive," he says. "The world I knew was a world of great families, food on the table, Mom at home, Dad working, maybe driving a cab or a truck, and yet still owning their own home. I had a pocketful of allowance money and good times with my friends. Life was good."

Riggio was called Joe College by his pals because of his drive and intelligence, but now he's astonished by what he **didn't** know. He was born in 1940 and educated in public schools at a time when history books put a particular gloss on the world, especially when it came to the place and benefits of living in America. "I didn't know about the Holocaust," he says, "or poverty, or oppression of women and minorities, because I didn't see or experience any of that in our Italian-American neighborhoods."

In 1958, Riggio, studying for an engineering degree at New York University, found himself encountering an exotic new world: Manhattan and the campus of NYU, with its vibrant, cosmopolitan environment of urban intellectuals. He was hired as a clerk at the campus bookstore, and his world suddenly took on much wider dimensions. A colleague was charged with buying a new form of books called paperbacks—reduced-size editions of serious, classic titles, not just the pulp variety, that were bound with soft paper covers instead of cloth hard covers.

"He'd hand me books such as **The History of the Peloponnesian War** and say, 'Here, read this.' I'm taking whole books and just devouring them, thinking,

'Oh my God—what I don't know.' The world is opening for me. It's because paperbacks were available."

It was for Riggio a moment not unlike the one Dustin Hoffman's character in **The Graduate** experienced when a family friend counseling him on a path to success whispered the magic word: "Plastics." Riggio's inner voice told him, "Paperbacks." Working at the campus bookstore, he was aware of the tyranny of that marketplace. Students who needed a title in a hurry were often told it wasn't in stock and that they should come back in two weeks.

Riggio decided that with the paperback revolution he could rewrite the rules of supply and demand for student books, so he opened the SBX—the Student Book Exchange—in 1965, just down the street from his old employer. Riggio was filling a market need, but he says he was also staying true to his roots.

His father was a cabdriver, a very successful local prizefighter, and a social radical. He opposed America's participation in World War II not because it involved his homeland but because he thought it was the rich sending the sons of the poor off to die.

"My dad taught me to serve the aspirations of everyone. The idea is that if you make books available to people on a major scale, they can improve their lot and become participating members of society—so they can compete with the snobs and the already arrived." Riggio also helped his own cause by making the basement of his store available to student activists as a kind of protest-sign factory. He gave them space and materials to make posters and banners for rallies against the Vietnam War.

Riggio had an unexpected ally in the early days of the SBX. "Remember Conor Cruise O'Brien?" he asks. "He was a radical professor and he taught a course called Revolution and Literature—and the reading list was sixty-five books. He was such a cult figure they had to put the class in a lecture hall that held two hundred and fifty students. I swear to you, these kids read all sixty-five books cover to cover. Of course, the NYU bookstore always ran out. The kids were frantic—they had to have the books.

"So they would go to other bookstores—Brentano's, whatever—and they wouldn't have the books because they were cheaper, and the elite bookstores wouldn't carry them. So we found them for them. You didn't sell what you wanted to carry, you sold what they wanted. You were intuitive about what they wanted, and you carried what they asked you to carry. And the kids went along with us. No one in those days wanted to be told they had to buy from the university bookstore."

Riggio began to expand his college bookstore empire, and he still gets excited by what he witnessed on campuses such as Columbia in the Sixties. "It was a debate that was waged, fought furiously, and resolved. We grew intellectually. Books were a part of it. I liberated those when I took over the Columbia University bookstore, then the Harvard Coop, the epitome of the establishment."

His pricing and mass-inventory concepts weren't limited to Ivy League campuses. "When I moved out of New York with the superstores, people said it couldn't be done. The publishers and the newspapers scoffed. I said, 'Hell, watch me.' I had always known, because I had traveled so much, [that] there was a touch of genius across the country; America was full of very smart people who wanted to grow, to study and read. I thought it was a joke that New Yorkers believed they were intellectually superior to people from Lincoln, Nebraska."

Riggio created the superstores after he bought out two of the biggest names in the American book business, B. Dalton and Barnes & Noble. He applied the same formula to them that he did to the campus book business. He believed the big, prestigious stores were elitist; that they concentrated too much on the best sellers and the big names; and that they weren't keeping pace with a new generation of readers who had a wider appetite for all kinds of material.

He made the stores into community centers–cum–bookstores, complete with large, well-marked public restrooms. Typically blunt, he says of the customers and the restrooms, "Hey, once I got them in the store, I didn't want them leaving."

He was also a big believer in location, location, location, which, in the Eighties and Nineties, meant the big, new shopping malls in the rapidly expanding suburban neighborhoods that were becoming the modern equivalent of the old town square.

Visibility, he says, is the key. "People don't wake up and say, 'Let me go to a bookstore.' But if they walk by a bookstore, they say, 'Oh, I think I'll stop in.' "

As a result, the Barnes & Noble store is now almost as familiar to modern shoppers as the Sears, Roebuck store was when I was growing up in the small towns of the Midwest. Riggio cites Cape Girardeau,

Missouri, a town of some thirty-five thousand, as a template for his formula. "We were in a B-plus location, doing about three million a year, and the lease ran out. We found an A-plus location, and now we're doing six million a year—in Cape Girardeau."

Riggio bristles a bit at the familiar criticism that he's hurt the small, independent bookseller—what he calls the "John and Jane business." He has studied the buying habits of their typical patrons and concluded, "Their audience was largely customers predisposed to read, and their locations were in neighborhoods where that was likely to happen. We were in general commercial areas a long way from those neighborhoods. Places with high visibility, highway intersections.

"They sell mostly best sellers and our critics think that's all we sell: Pile 'em high and let 'em fly. But only two percent of our sales are best sellers; ten to fifteen percent of their sales are best sellers because they don't have the depth of inventory. They actually lose more business to price clubs than they do to us.

"I was trying to create a place where those on the way up were just as welcome as those who have already arrived." He takes great pride in his inventory of religious books that previously were found primarily in religious bookstores or in gift shops attached to churches. Again, it is a case of the good businessman meeting the Good Samaritan.

While most Americans spent approximately the same amount annually for books in 2004 as they did in 1968 (around seventy dollars, in 2004 dollars), the sale of religious books soared heavenward in the same time period, a reflection of the rise of the evangelical movement and the literary ambitions of the most prominent televangelists. Rick Warren, a Colorado-based minister, became a one-man publishing phenomenon with his guide to a happier spiritual life. No one promoting the benefits of the turmoil of the Sixties saw that coming.

Riggio's competitors and suppliers may be amused by his emphasis on the social value of his vision. When they speak of Riggio, it is his hard-driving business brilliance and his take-no-prisoners style that they emphasize.

Riggio, who's now in his midsixties, misses the social ferment of the early days, when students were lined up to buy the books on the reading list for courses such as the Literature of Revolution. He can track the country's mood by book sales, and these days he sees a lot of "self-indulgence . . . how can I be healthier, live longer, be more beautiful, make more money? How can I be hipper? What's the latest fad? They think they can go off to business school and automatically become millionaires."

Riggio repeats these talks to student audiences around the country. When he was invited to Texas A&M to be honored for his retailing successes, he told an auditorium full of business majors, "Seek the dollar before the million. Seek the principle before the solution."

He's waiting for the next Sixties-style movement, when people once again start participating in debates, "intellectually and spiritually—even when they're on the outskirts. We're not participants anymore," Riggio worries. "We're witnesses."

Riggio, who is famously combative as a business competitor, is also a realist. As we sit in his roomy Park Avenue apartment, surrounded by important works of modern art, fresh-cut flowers, and stylish furnishings, he's cool and definitive when I ask if there's a young Leonard Riggio somewhere out there, determined to do to his business what he did to the old-fashioned bookstores.

"Absolutely," he says. "It should happen at some point—and it will be digital. You can go into a Barnes & Noble, and the place is packed, but the sales are off two percent because people who love books are now able to get them in a different way. You keep that up, year to year, and the business proposition collapses."

Riggio, who managed to survive a direct assault from Amazon.com by getting Barnes & Noble online and building in new efficiencies and appeal, says bluntly, "You're gonna have fewer and fewer books in stores over time. It's almost impossible for us to convert our culture to digital, because why would anyone want to download from us when they can get it from Google or Yahoo!?"

A few years ago he told a reporter that at his age— he was in his early sixties—his goal was to get his golf handicap down to single digits, but he's showing no signs of slowing down in business. He says he doesn't "need to make any more money," and that becomes a bit of a challenge, because it removes the incentive to do something creative in the marketplace, where he's always thrived.

"I need a big idea," he says. "The nonprofit world— the boards are a pain in the neck." But the kid from the old Italian-American neighborhood in Brooklyn who grew up to change the book business and become a billionaire in the process is not about to retire.

The legacy of his socially conscious working-class mother and father, the excitement he felt when he made more books available to more people, the great lessons he came to learn while reading the classics as a clerk in the university bookstore, the art he can now afford—far more than his golf handicap, these are what matter in Len Riggio's life.

It is impossible to make a single big, sweeping judgment about the changes in the pop culture brought on by the Sixties—from music to films to comedy to books. It is still a matter of individual taste and tolerance.

It is generally those on the right, vigorous defenders of the free market in the economy, who are the most judgmental and censorious when it comes to what is available on television and radio, on the big screen, and on iTunes.

Equally ironic, it is those on the left who embrace human rights and dignity who are the most timid about criticizing misogynist or racist lyrics or violent videos. The children of peace and love rarely rally against the mindless, violent overtones of some rap songs or video games.

In a new century, after the play-it-safe content conventions of the Fifties were replaced in the Sixties on television, in movie theaters, in music and books and magazines, the popular culture has taken another dramatic turn.

Now the debate is not so much about content as it is about the delivery systems. The iPod, YouTube, DVDs played on home theater systems, home movies edited on laptop computers, downloading, uploading, and electronic books have given new meaning to the concept of "mass appeal."

Who could have guessed in the heady days of the Sixties that pocket electronics would become the realization of that popular but amorphous slogan "Power to the people!"?

PART THREE

Reflections

Seeing What Connects

The View from
the Moon

Stay hungry. Stay foolish.

—Final issue of
the Whole Earth Catalog

When you see Earth from the moon,
you realize how fragile it is and
just how limited the resources are.
We're all astronauts on this spaceship Earth—
about six or seven billion of us—
and we have to work and live together.

—Captain James Lovell

W HEN DID WE KNOW the Sixties were over?

A comedian on one of the late-night talk shows said, "You know the Sixties are over when someone flashes the old two-fingered 'Peace' sign but now it means, 'Two Coronas with limes, please.' " Moving symbolically from peace to a beer order makes a memorable one-liner, but the reality is obviously much more complex.

As I worked on **Boom!** and listened to others at this virtual reunion, reviewing together the cosmic developments that the book covers, I also had the opportunity to think in new ways about those times and how my life was affected by them, and it has been an instructive and introspective experience. I also thought about my travels as a citizen and as a journalist across this country in the years since the Sixties and how often I encounter a wide and deep impatience with the hardened ideological and partisan positions that have emerged in post-Sixties America.

There is a longing among us to take the best from across the spectrum of the Sixties and find common ways to deal with the lingering problems of that time, as well as with the new challenges arising every day. It is my hope that this virtual reunion of some of those who experienced the Sixties from so many different perspectives will be a catalyst for our moving on together, with fresh ideas and lessons learned.

For all the cosmic changes from the Sixties to now, there is this: As in the Sixties, America is again at war in place where we don't speak the language, where the enemy mingles easily with the people we're supposed to be defending, and where the definition of victory is elusive and deeply controversial.

Time and again in the preparation of this book, Sixties antiwar activists said about the Iraq War, "I can't believe I'm not out there doing more against this war." One of the things that is different now, and in the Iraq War, is the absence of a constant drumbeat of opposition in the streets and, even more, the absence of a large-scale generational debate in America about whether to serve, whether to undergo the personal risk connected with military duty, or whether to help in some other way.

The war in Iraq has reminded us of another historic change that came out of the Sixties: the move to an all-volunteer military force as a result of the protests against the draft during Vietnam.

Once the United States became involved in Iraq, a serious, long-term war, it became clear that the all-volunteer force has created a bifurcated society, with one part in uniform and in harm's way and the other, larger part disconnected from the war as a personal reality and disconnected from the sacrifices—the long separations, the lasting physical and psychological wounds, the dangers and deaths faced by military families. And the most terrible wound of all, the flag-draped coffin.

The war in Iraq, whatever you think of its origins, execution, and lasting effects, has exposed a great schism in American life and in the construct of our national security requirements. Anyone can freely choose not to participate in the armed services, and they are not required or even expected to have any kind of relationship with those in uniform or their families.

That disconnect is most striking between the working class, where voluntary participation in the military is high, and the privileged class, where it is not.

It is true that men and women in uniform are now treated with the kind of personal respect denied them during Vietnam. But that is not enough. If President Bush inexplicably hasn't asked for some meaningful sacrifices on the home front, why didn't the survivors of the antiwar movement of the Sixties summon up some of the old moral outrage to show solidarity with the military families in a meaningful way?

Garry Trudeau

One who has done just that is Garry Trudeau, as anyone who has followed his **Doonesbury** comic strip over the years knows. Trudeau, who was two years behind President George W. Bush at Yale, is no fan of the president or of his war in Iraq.

However, what many do not know is that Garry

makes regular visits to Walter Reed hospital in Washington, D.C., to visit with wounded veterans. He has active e-mail relationships with men and women on active duty in Iraq. As a result, **Doonesbury** has become a window on their frustrations, their dark humor, and the unique, existential culture that grows up in any combat zone.

Trudeau's long-running character B.D. lost a leg in Iraq, and the daily comic strip documented the physical pain and psychological torment, using the language and knowledge Trudeau picked up during his Walter Reed visits. He has also brought the family relationships—the angst, bewilderment, and pride in military families—into his work.

When I visited the hospital, one of the surgeons said to me, "Trudeau is our archangel."

When I told Garry that, he said, "Yeah, can you believe it? Forty years ago I was participating in antiwar demonstrations, and now I'm being asked to speak at reunions of Vietnam veterans."

As a longtime friend of Garry and a close student of **Doonesbury**, I think he's doing his finest work now, because, in his way, he is reminding us that for the soldiers and the veterans and their families, the war in Iraq is not just a political issue. It is a personal issue.

The deeply divisive effect of the Sixties on American politics is much remarked upon. It is felt in large ways and small. One evening in 2007 I attended a reception in the Capitol building in Washington, D.C., and two engaging young men approached me. They asked what it had been like living back in what they called "the good old days in Washington."

They explained that they were friends; one worked for a Republican congressman and the other for a Democrat. It was highly unusual now, they said, for people like them to have any personal connection, since their bosses had different party affiliations. "If you're a Republican up here," one said about the present, "you don't hang out with a Democrat, and vice versa."

They were eager to hear stories of an earlier time when, for example, a conservative congressman could engage in heated battles all day long on the House floor with a liberal adversary and then go have a drink with him at night.

I explained that all that largely changed after the Sixties when politics became more of a blood sport, financed by big-money campaign budgets and increasingly dominated by ideological zealots or interest groups that were single-minded in pursuit of their goals.

Any number of prominent Republican and Democratic politicians who retired early or were defeated at the height of their careers have told me that, beginning in the Seventies, the comity of the House and Senate gave way to the polarization that had grown out of the deep divisions created during the Sixties.

How many times recently have I heard a longtime officeholder, a journalist, or a student wise in the ways of Washington say he or she hopes the election of 2008 will mark an end to this polarization. The failure of goodwill, and of a willingness to find common ground in a country that in election after election is so evenly divided, is a disgrace. It is a condition that discourages many of our best and brightest from volunteering to go to Washington to serve in appointive offices. When I appear before audiences of business leaders, academicians, or civic-minded citizens active in their local communities, I often ask, "How many here would like to go to Washington to serve in some capacity?" In a crowded room, maybe one or two hands will go up. Maybe.

More people are inclined to be active in public service in their local communities or states, rather than at the national level, because the results are more obvious and because the rewards of serving in Washington today don't seem commensurate with the sacrifices.

The press, especially the electronic press, has a major role to play if we are going to change this tone.

With the advent of all-news radio and 24/7/365 cable channels, political coverage too often is reduced to "gotcha" moments, or conflict for the sake of conflict. Anyone interested in a public career is almost immediately under suspicion, in an extension of the guerrilla tactics of the Sixties, on the right as well as on the left.

Modern talk radio is dominated by conservatives who specialize in the old tactic of the left in the Sixties: attack, attack, attack. In the Sixties, in much of the public discourse, the description "conservative" was said with a sneer. In recent years it is the "liberal" who is a pariah.

Other Voices

On the right, Kevin Phillips, the scholarly philosopher of modern Republican party politics, irritated Karl Rove and other contemporary architects of GOP successes in recent election years by warning that the party, in effect, had sold its soul to big oil, the South, and Southern Baptists.

In his critically acclaimed book **American Theocracy**, Phillips warns starkly, "We can begin by describing the role of religion in American politics and war with two words: 'widely underestimated.' " This from the man who wrote in 1969 one of the most important books of that era, **The Emerging Republican Majority**, in which he presciently described the opportunities for the GOP as a result of the fractures within the Sixties Democratic Party.

In his densely argued new book Phillips describes the accelerated decline of mainstream religion during the Sixties and the concurrent rise in popularity of the evangelical movement, especially the Southern Baptist Convention, and also the Mormon Church. Between them, the Mormons and the Baptists added more than nine million members in the last third of the twentieth century while the Methodists, Presbyterians, Episcopalians, and United Church of Christ lost between half a million and two million members each.

As a result, Phillips declares, "The world's leading economic and military power is also—no one can mistake the data—the world's leading Bible-reading crusader state, immersed in an Old Testament of stern prophets and bloody Middle Eastern battlefields."

He acknowledges that there is a large and growing secular culture in the United States, especially among Northern university graduates and elites. In that crowd, he says, "it is stronger by far than the biblical and salvationist contingent." However, Phillips warns, it is no match for the Republican coalition that grew out of the Sixties and is now headed by a born-again Christian, George W. Bush.

Phillips figures that George W. Bush, by representing the 30 to 40 percent of the electorate "caught up in Scripture and the prospect of suddenly being transported to God's side," not only won two presidential elections but also developed a foreign policy to reflect the Armageddon prophecies of those constituents.

The Republican Party that Phillips enthusiastically foresaw taking shape back in 1969 is now a party that he believes is hostage to what he calls "scriptural fidelity and religious nationalism," especially in the South. As a result, he writes, "From presidential election dominance to military adventurism and Southern Baptist expansion . . . more Dixie ambitions have been fulfilled than any Confederate War Veterans convention could have contemplated."

To his critics, Phillips has his own Armageddon hang-ups when it comes to writing about a party he no longer influences as he once did. He's accused of assigning motives and projecting outcomes that are much too personal and dark.

Nonetheless, it is true that no one anticipated in 1968, when the Republican Party began to put together a presidential majority out of the wreckage of FDR's New Deal Democratic coalition, that within a dozen years a fundamentalist Christian view of the world would be such an important criterion for GOP worthiness.

This did not happen in a vacuum. The attacks on what were thought to be traditional values of family and faith in the Sixties opened the way for shrewd, ambitious, and energetic promoters of fundamental Christianity such as the late Reverend Jerry Falwell and Pat Robertson. They used the tools of the left in the Sixties—television and political activism—to advance the agenda of the right from the Eighties right up until today.

Todd Gitlin, a former president of the radical SDS, has remained a student of those times and a prolific writer on the subject as a professor of sociology and journalism at UC Berkeley and Columbia University. He has written, "The interesting, genuinely divisive question is which Sixties to embrace and which to criticize. . . . The Sixties that were the seedbeds of fanaticism were the Sixties of George Wallace as well as Jerry Rubin, police goons as well as the Black Panthers, napalm as well as flag burning."

"The Sixties continue to perplex," he says, "partly because whatever the sound biters may think, the currents and the movements did not line up neatly with one another. The antibureaucratic, libertarian, and communal strands of the Sixties did not want to be folded, stapled, or mutilated. They too wanted to live free or die."

Gitlin calls conservative critics of the Sixties "terrible simplifiers" because, he says, the hard-core left has softened—not least because the absolute passions of the Sixties were forced to give way to the practical consequences, which included the political success of the right in exploiting the excesses of the Sixties.

Roger Rosenblatt, a liberal who liked President Reagan and is a long-recovered junior faculty member at Harvard in the Sixties, sums it up nicely: "For liberals in the Sixties, we were riding a tide where everything was win or lose, black or white. And now we resent it when it's win or lose, black or white."

This formulation came up during a conversation Roger and I had about the paucity of conservative voices during the Sixties and Seventies on issues such as abortion. "When **Roe v. Wade** occurred, all the liberals had total suasion over every social matter in America," Roger says. "Instead of taking half a second and saying . . . 'This is a very personal, painful issue, this is not just a political issue,' the liberals said, 'This is great!' " As a result, women and their families who were genuinely personally conflicted about abortion felt distant from those political reactions.

Roger has mixed feelings about the youth culture that came out of the Sixties, saying, "I think in general the coddling of children—the perpetuation of childhood and childish ideas—is a bad thing. If you carry childhood through life, thinking freedom is limitless, you're gonna be in a lot of trouble."

But he is a big fan of his children and their friends, who are now all in their thirties and early forties. "If the Sixties were so destructive, I might not have that opinion," he says. "The kids who had the most to lose or gain from their boomer parents seem to be just fine, decent and hardworking."

But Roger doesn't envy them the world the Sixties—we—have handed them. He believes that the assault on institutions—academic, governmental, financial, and religious—led to a climate in which time-tested standards, loyalty, and worthy traditions were swept aside. Now, he says, "it is every man for himself."

Alan Brinkley was also at Harvard in the Sixties, and he shares many of Rosenblatt's views. His inventory of the Sixties is mixed. "Vietnam drove people away from the establishment, but living in a world without an establishment is a lot worse."

Establishment is another word for structure, and what form of human activity doesn't require structure? Biology, faith, politics, the economy, literature, music—they all depend on structure to survive.

Brinkley says, "The World War II generation put a lot of effort into trying to determine how to move the country forward. That's not there today. Where are the people committed to trying to move us forward in the world today?"

He agrees that some campuses have become too politically correct but hastens to add that universities and the intellectual world have always been left wing. "I don't think there's a tyranny of political correctness," he says about universities, "but I think there's not enough ideological diversity," referring to the long-standing tradition of liberal influences at universities.

Alan agrees with the criticisms of what passes for public discourse these days. "It's often very angry; coarseness is more important than content. There is a lack of seriousness."

The Sixties did give us a new way to look at big-time sports. I am personally grateful for the stripping away of the contrivances of mythmaking. So much of the credit for that goes to Muhammad Ali in the Sixties, but there were others.

In 1968 American sprinters Tommie Smith and John Carlos, first and third in the two-hundred-meter dash at the Mexico City Olympics, mounted the medal stand and raised their gloved fists in a black power salute.

I had many reservations about the black power movement because of its reliance on alienation and violence, but at that moment I knew Smith and Carlos were telling us something else: We're not just your sprinters-for-hire to carry the American flag in the Olympic Games. We have other issues, and it's time someone paid attention to them.

The pitcher Jim Bouton gave us a funny and unblinkingly honest look inside major league baseball with **Ball Four,** his breakthrough book about his 1969 season with the Seattle Pilots. Bouton, a free spirit and former Yankee star, rewrote the rules for sports reporting by describing honestly what happens in the locker room when the press is not around or on the road in professional sports.

When I asked an old-line professional football coach about Bouton's book when it first came out, the coach snarled, "He's a traitor." When I told Bouton about the remark, he said, "I'm not surprised; those guys think what happens in a locker room is a matter of national security."

The Sixties also changed the appearance of America. Forty years ago, I went everywhere in a jacket and tie; now I am much more likely to wear that uniform only when absolutely necessary. My friend Tom Wolfe, who wrote so many scathingly hilarious essays on the indulgences of the Sixties, does not approve of this emphasis on staying young.

Tom, who sports white suits, a fedora, and even spats, says we now have a generation of executives going around in jeans, motorcycle jackets, and T-shirts emblazoned MOM WAS WRONG. Too many people, he says, try to look twenty-seven by dressing like they're thirteen, which leads to a new aging disease: juvenility to go with senility.

Personal style is just a piece of the determination to look and stay young in the post-Sixties world. For ten years after my days as a high school athlete, from 1958 to 1968, my idea of physical activity was lighting up a cigarette or pulling up a bar stool. I know I'm not unusual when I say that at age sixty-seven, I now work out regularly, take long bike rides and hikes, swim laps, ride horses, and never take an escalator when there are stairs.

Neither my father, Red, nor Meredith's father, Merritt, nor their friends and contemporaries in the World War II generation did any of that. Red died of a massive coronary at the age of sixty-nine, and Merritt died of other health complications at the age of sixty-seven. Health and fitness are often overlooked as beneficial consequences of the emphasis on youth and staying young that emerged during the Sixties and has continued afterward.

The boomers who uncritically ingested whatever was passed to them in whatever form at a rock concert or a human be-in can now be found heading to the organic foods section of the supermarket and reading the fine print on the labels of canned goods.

The marketplace also changed to include more inexpensive but high-calorie fast foods and snacks to feed the younger, on-the-go population that all but abandoned the Fifties ritual of family dinners or supper, as we called it in the Midwest. Obesity became the odd counterpoint to the fitness fad.

Paradoxically, of course, the Sixties was also the time that gave us what is now a large and permanent drug culture. The criminal production and sale of drugs, drug use and abuse (and there is a difference), the devastating impact of drugs on the quality of life in the lower socioeconomic strata of society, and the attendant violence that comes with drug distribution are not just a sorry hangover from the Sixties.

They are also a consequence of the current one-size-fits-all war on drugs that has failed to alter the basic rules of the marketplace: supply and demand. The United States has declared war on cocaine growers in Colombia, marijuana cartels in Mexico, and drug dealers in the United States but it is the **appetite** for drugs among otherwise law-abiding Americans that drives the market.

There is also the generation gap when it comes to the public consequences of addictive and abused drugs. Most members of my generation have lost more friends to tobacco- or alcohol-related diseases than they have to any kind of drug abuse.

No question, serious drug taking—heroin, cocaine, speed—is dangerous to the individual and costly to society. If we're really concerned about drug abuse and the criminal class it supports, then we will have to develop a new model that is as tough on the user as it is on the seller. An inner-city kid selling bags of pot or heroin is much more likely to go to jail than his white suburban customer.

As for marijuana, William F. Buckley, the intellectual patron of the modern conservative movement, makes a persuasive case for the reform of marijuana laws, especially for medical relief. He points out that the United States spends ten to fifteen billion dollars a year making marijuana arrests, mostly for small amounts in possession. He estimates that one hundred million Americans have smoked marijuana, adding, in his droll Buckley way, "It requires less effort for a college student to find marijuana than it does for a sailor to find a brothel."

In Buckley's view, it all adds up to an increased cynicism about the law. Buckley hopes there will be a national groundswell of support for the regulation and control of marijuana that will follow the model for alcohol.

It is change that must come from the ground up,

he says, because "we're not going to find someone running for president who advocates these reforms."

Another of the subtexts of the Sixties was parenting. Hippies—real and virtual—rejected the strict parental-control pattern of the Fifties. Some of them stuck with what could be called the "free-range" method of raising children: Give them lots of room and let them find their way. But others from that time are now raising what may be the most overmanaged generation of children in the history of the planet. Professional tutors to improve a young person's SAT scores, therapists, regimented sports leagues to replace casual afterschool playtime, summer retreats for the arts, computer camps, nutritionists to balance the diet—so much for the Sixties idea of celebrating being young and "doing your own thing."

As young parents in the Sixties and early Seventies—our kids were born in 1966, 1968, and 1970—Meredith and I relied for the most part on the model our parents had applied to us in the Fifties.

Our children spent summers with their grandparents in South Dakota so they could experience many of the rhythms of life that were so important to us. Now in their late thirties and early forties, they still recall the leveling influence of those summers.

Our extended family member and fellow Midwesterner Calvin Trillin, the writer, put it best when he told his daughters in their Greenwich Village home, "All evidence to the contrary, you're being raised in Kansas City."

As they aged, baby boomers also demanded more regulation in everyday life, despite their unregulated youth. Arlo Guthrie, a platinum member of the "do your own thing" generation, misses the days when kids could still pile into the back of a pickup truck for a short ride to the beach without their parents getting a ticket for violating child safety laws.

One area that brought generations together in the Sixties was the environment. The demands for clean air, clean water, and better control of pesticides reversed a troubling Fifties trend of economic expansion at whatever the cost to the environment.

The environment, the steady gains for African Americans and other minorities as a result of the civil rights movement, the ever-expanding opportunities for women in the economy, the entrepreneurial spirit of the young, the freedom to step out of the closet, the chance to escape a world of button-down collars and panty girdles—all of that came from the Sixties.

While great progress has been made on important issues, the work ahead on race and poverty, women's issues, the changing climate, is in many ways more difficult than it was forty years ago.

The residual issues—motherhood versus career, the growing poverty gap, developing realistic alternative energy sources—cannot be solved with the passage of a few laws or a march on Washington.

Add to that list the arrival of the baby boomer generation at the age of entitlements—Social Security, Medicare, and the expectation of senior citizen discounts. If this is the richest, most compassionate generation in history, why isn't it leading the way to reform the government entitlements that were designed for another time? These entitlements are about to become an onerous burden for succeeding generations. Baby boomers should be the first to say, "If I can afford to pay more for Medicare, I'm willing. If you want to delay my Social Security eligibility a few years, fine."

That's just one example of how aging activists could demonstrate that they were not simply summer-stock players in the great issues of their day.

Any reunion of the Sixties will bring out not just the issues but the personalities who made, in one form or another, a lasting imprint on that time.

Joan Baez and Don McLean

The music of the Sixties produced not only songs that stirred a generation but artists who endured and prospered for their busi-ness savvy as well as their creative contributions. Bob Dylan, Paul McCartney and John Lennon of the Beatles, Mick Jagger and the Rolling Stones, Barbra Streisand, these were much more than musicians onstage. They were conglomerates with multimillion-dollar record deals and labels, elaborate and theatrical concert tours. Only Frank Sinatra and Bing Crosby before them had managed to become such a business force in their culture.

They were also closely aligned with the issues of war and peace, race and culture.

If any one artist personified the Sixties—and it would be hard to settle on just one—Joan Baez would be a finalist. From 1959, when she first appeared at the Newport Folk Festival, to 2007, when Pentagon officials denied her permission to appear at a concert at Walter Reed Army Medical Center for wounded veterans of the Iraq War, Joan Baez has been both an admired and a mocked figure.

Through it all, she has lived her personal philosophy of non-violence, which she first embraced as a teenager after hearing Dr. Martin Luther King Jr. speak on the subject. By then she already had a worldly view as a result of living in France, Switzerland, Italy, and even Baghdad. Her father, a Mexican-born physicist, worked for the United Nations on educational and social issues.

Through the Sixties and Seventies, Baez was a ubiquitous figure at folk concerts, peace demonstrations, and civil rights rallies. She often appeared with Dr. King during the early days of his campaign for racial equality, including his historic March on Washington in 1963. Everyone remembers Dr. King's "I Have a Dream" speech at that rally. What they may not know is that Baez had earlier sung the movement's anthem, "We Shall Overcome," at the mass gathering. In 1968, after an earlier, well-publicized affair with Bob Dylan, Baez met and married David Harris, a Stanford student who had organized a draft resistance commune. Fellow folkie Judy Collins sang at their wedding, and they quickly became the new left's version of king and queen of the prom, a handsome, committed couple of great intelligence and talent.

When Harris was jailed in Texas for evading the draft, Baez, pregnant with their son, Gabriel, continued to make public appearances, including an early-morning one at Woodstock. She wrote songs about her imprisoned husband, and when she sang them in that haunting, crystalline soprano voice, her fans were almost religiously reverential.

But the marriage didn't survive. A couple of years after Harris was released from prison, Baez announced she preferred to live alone, a status she has maintained ever since.

Baez continued her resistance to the Vietnam War, and in 1972 she made a controversial trip to Hanoi to deliver Christmas presents to American prisoners of war. While in the North Vietnamese capital, she was caught in the massive bombing ordered by Richard Nixon, an attempt to get the Hanoi regime back to the bargaining table.

By then Baez was increasingly interested in the cause of universal human rights and in advancing her personal commitment to nonviolence. She helped establish a U.S. branch of Amnesty International and she founded the Institute for the Study of Nonviolence in Northern California, where she lives with her mother and her son.

She continues to sing, although she admits those sweet, high notes are a little tougher to reach now that she's in her sixties. She has performed with Bruce Springsteen; at a concert for former Czechoslovakian president Vaclav Havel; at the funeral of singer Lou Rawls; with John Cougar Mellencamp, the Indiana rocker who wanted her at his side for the Walter

Reed concert; and at various antiwar demonstrations, anti–capital punishment protests, and humanitarian benefits across the United States and in South America.

When we talked, she looked back on the Sixties with a mixture of puzzlement, amusement, and frustration. "I'm not sure why it all happened," she says. "It was kind of mysterious. It probably was just the pendulum swinging from the rigidity of the Fifties to something new and liberating.

"In music there was a real rebellion against the bubblegum sounds of the Fifties, and it was surprising to me that so much of the Sixties music became mainstream. But the music was one thing; social change was another. Music happened faster. It takes longer for social movements to take root."

When I asked Baez why the spirit of the antiwar movement in the Sixties wasn't rekindled by musicians as a protest against the war in Iraq, she answered, "I don't know if concerts would mean much; they're mostly for us, the performers. The only real social change comes when you're willing to risk something."

She recalled the worldwide phenomenon of the Live Aid concerts, which were organized to draw attention to and raise money for the victims of the terrible African droughts in the Eighties. "The only risk involved in Live Aid is that you might not get invited to perform," she said.

Baez also reminded me that during the Sixties many artists stood on the sidelines. She mentioned a friend, a very popular artist she wouldn't cite by name. "He'd come to me and say, 'I so admire what you're doing; I'm getting ready to make a stand myself.' But then he'd back away. The next time I'd see him he'd say, 'I'm ready to get committed, but I don't want to alienate my audience.' There was a lot of that."

When the United States withdrew from Vietnam, Baez confesses, "all of us had a problem with our identity. When your life is defined by something that big, it's clear what you're fighting for. When it ends, it's a difficult adjustment."

For Baez, however, her commitment didn't end when the United States left. As a testimony to her core philosophy of nonviolence and human rights, she stunned and angered many of her old friends on the left when she spoke out against the Khmer Rouge atrocities in Cambodia and the oppressive policies of the North Vietnamese against the South Vietnamese after Saigon fell and the United States was gone.

She helped sponsor a full-page ad in major American newspapers in the spring of 1979 critical of what she called "the nightmare of North Vietnamese rule." In a speech at the San Francisco Commonwealth Club two years later, she described meeting two of the South Vietnamese boat people, refugees from the takeover by the North. One was a writer and the other a defrocked monk. Both had been opposed to the U.S. role in Vietnam. Yet when the North took over they were so appalled by the gulags, prisons, and forced labor that they decided to risk their lives to flee to America. That made a deep impression on her, and she thought it was important to let people know about it.

She told the Commonwealth Club audience, a distinguished roster of San Franciscans accustomed to hearing from presidents and prime ministers, secretaries of state, and ambassadors, that the refugees forced her to ask a fundamental question: "Was I still concerned about the people of Vietnam?"

Other questions followed for her and her friends in the anti-war movement: "Could we face up to the fact that though we had tried for ten years to liberate that tiny country . . . to bring self-determination and democracy to Vietnam . . . perhaps we had failed. I realized that five years after the withdrawal of American troops Vietnam was being run by seventeen aging Stalinists who were making life hell for the majority of the population."

She made it clear that she didn't regret for a moment any of her earlier efforts to end the war. Moreover, she said the outrage among her old friends on the left over her criticism of the totalitarian practices of North Vietnam led her to diagnose them as having what she called "an eye disease," in which people see only what they prefer.

Baez discovered the extent of the eye disease when she reached out to antiwar activists to sign a letter protesting human rights violations by the Communist government in Vietnam. Only eighty-one agreed to sign, leading her to remark, "What we risk by seeing fairly and justly through both eyes is our attachment to ideology. I discovered," she went on, "how blessed I am never to have been burdened with an ideology. I believe I am capable of seeing through both eyes." In that eye disease she sees a fundamental truth of the Sixties: "There was no staying power."

Joan Baez finds her staying power in her Institute

for the Study of Nonviolence, in her commitment to human rights, and in therapy, which she says she avoided for most of her adult life. She thinks large-scale, civil, nonviolent demonstrations against the war in Iraq, involving ordinary citizens, would be hard for even the Bush White House to ignore.

"I'm not out on the front lines anymore, carrying a banner. I'm getting to know my family after all these years. I'm meditating and spending more time on environmental issues, such as climate change. And thinking about finally getting rid of George Bush."

There is one other matter. When asked by a newspaper reporter about her long-ago three-month romance with Bob Dylan in 1965, she had a mixed review. After all, he once said of their fling, "She brought me up. I rode on her but I don't owe her anything." The Baez version: "His songs were brilliant . . . he always had a rainbow pen; the stuff just pours out of him. But Bob doesn't have much awareness of other people. You can take some artistic liberties, and all of us do to a certain extent—but he takes them all."

Then, remembering how their brief relationship always comes up, Baez comments, "When people say to me, 'You're going to be linked with him in history forever,' I think that's a pretty fucking honorable place to be."

With both eyes wide open.

One of the lesser stars but big success stories of the Sixties musical scene was Don McLean, a rebellious New York teenager who was influenced by Woody

Guthrie, the Weavers, and other old lefty groups from the Forties and Fifties who fought back in their music against the Communist witchhunts and blacklists of Senator Joe McCarthy of Wisconsin.

McLean's teenage years were scarred by his father's death and by the assassination of President Kennedy. As he says, "I became an instant nonbeliever in the Warren Commission investigating the murder—and that made me a cynic about government."

He decided to follow his heroes, like Guthrie and Pete Seeger, and become a troubadour of social action. He was already a popular performer and songwriter in the Hudson River Valley of New York when in 1971 he wrote an enigmatic and soulful song called "American Pie."

We were singing,
bye-bye miss american pie.
Drove my chevy to the levee,
But the levee was dry.
Them good old boys were drinkin' whiskey and rye,
And singin' "this'll be the day that I die.
"this'll be the day that I die."

In twenty-six stanzas, including a maddeningly catchy chorus, the lyrics included poetically intriguing references to slow dancing; a widowed bride; a lonely teenage broncin' buck; moss growing on a rolling stone; John Lennon; Helter Skelter (the Beatles' song title that became the crazed mantra of the Manson family); the Father, Son, and Holy Ghost; the Bible and church bells. Students who would have been bored after ten minutes of analyzing the images and references in T. S. Eliot's

Don McLean, whose 1971 hit "American Pie" became an anthem of the times, seen here at an antiwar event in Croton-on-Hudson, New York

Don McLean in 2006

"The Waste Land" spent hours arguing about the meaning of McLean's words.

Flattering the pop cultural insider knowledge of its audience, it quickly became an anthem of sorts. It was also, as they say in the record business, a bullet, shooting to the top of the charts.

Jann Wenner, the publisher of **Rolling Stone**, hates the song. I love it. I was living in California when it was recorded in 1971, and it seemed to speak to all of the conflicting currents of life we'd been going through on the West Coast.

As I read the lyrics almost forty years later, having heard them sung countless times, I have to confess that I still have no idea what McLean was really trying to say.

When asked what the lyrics of "American Pie" mean, he often says, "They mean I don't have to work anymore." On his website, however, he explains it is his epic poem, tracing what he saw as the lightness of the Fifties to the darkness of the Sixties, beginning with the death of singer Buddy Holly in an Iowa plane crash in 1959.

McLean has had other pop hits, and he continues to tour with his songs of social protest but nothing will ever compare with his success with "American Pie," the song that got him into the Grammy Hall of Fame and the National Academy of Popular Music Songwriters Hall of Fame.

Yvon Chouinard and Doug Tompkins

A combination of youthful creativity, independence, and personal passion is always evident when I spend time with Yvon Chouinard, the founder and owner of Patagonia, the outdoor clothing company, and Doug Tompkins, the founder of North Face, an outdoor equipment and clothing company, and later, with his ex-wife, Susie, of Esprit, the popular women's apparel company.

In the Sixties, Chouinard and Tompkins were hippies who were world-class rock climbers, skiers, surfers, and kayakers. Neither had gone to college, and they were proud of their "dirt bag" status as outdoorsmen. They were much more interested in the next big wall to climb or wave to surf or river to run than they were in conventional lives. They were intensely interested in the environment because their passions depended on the preservation of wild places, not because of some movement organized on a college campus or in Washington, D.C.

In 1968 they were stuck in an ice cave on an approach to Cerro Fitzroy, a granite spire that shoots skyward out of the glaciers of the Andes mountain range in southern Patagonia. They were waiting for the weather to clear so they could attempt a first ascent on a heretofore unclimbed route of the forbidding monolith.

As they huddled in their sleeping bags, they began to talk about what they wanted to do when they returned to the United States. Tompkins had just sold North Face, but he was intrigued by the possibilities of some simple dress patterns his then wife, Susie, was cutting out on their kitchen table back home in San Francisco.

Yvon Chouinard, already a legend in the rock-climbing and alpine world for his innovative retooling and manufacturing of ice axes and pitons, was so unhappy with the quality of the available expedition clothing that he decided to expand his company to include apparel.

Eventually the weather on Cerro Fitzroy cleared enough for them to make a successful climb to the summit. They went back to California with one mission accomplished and two others about to begin: Esprit and Patagonia, Inc.

The companies developed a cult following in the post-Sixties world, celebrated for their hip yet functional styles, their quality and cachet, and their marketing.

The two former hippies brought to their businesses the same discipline and exacting standards that had made them so successful in their high-risk sports, but their affluence didn't diminish their appetite for hard-core adventure in wild places, including life-threatening storms in Antarctica, avalanches in the Himalayas, and kayaking expeditions to remote rivers, including in the Russian far east. To the relief of their friends, they also remained contrarian, railing against politics as usual, especially where environmental matters were concerned.

Tompkins became immersed in what he called "deep ecology"—a no-compromise approach to the preservation of land in its natural state and a return to a lifestyle of conservation instead of consumption. In 1990 he sold his share of Esprit and headed to South America to bring his vision to life.

Chouinard shared those sensibilities, and he brought about breakthroughs in the use of organic cotton and recycled materials for the manufacture of new fabrics that were efficient, light, warm, and effective in the worst kinds of weather. He wanted to produce clothing that would endure, so customers wouldn't have to discard a jacket or a sweater at the end of a season.

He also formed 1% for the Planet, in which he gives 1 percent of Patagonia's annual sales to local environmental organizations that are making an impact. He also successfully marketed that concept to more than two hundred other companies around the American West.

Tompkins and Chouinard knew by instinct and personal choice that the generation coming up right behind them was not satisfied with simply mocking the wardrobes or activities of their parents. With Esprit and Patagonia they helped form the new tastes of a younger generation, which in turn allowed them to invest in their environmental interests.

In 2005 Tompkins was completing a masterful but controversial project in Chile: Pumalin, an eight-hundred-thousand-acre wilderness area he had personally purchased along the western front of the Andean range to make into a new national park. It encompassed soaring peaks, deep, glaciated valleys, rain forests, and rivers running to the sea. All but a tiny fraction of the land would be left in its natural state.

At first the Chilean government and local residents worried that the project was some kind of sinister conspiracy to divide the country at its narrowest point and control any north-south commerce. There was even a rumor that the Israelis were somehow behind the acquisition of all that land. Tompkins, who is neither political nor gregarious, stubbornly kept to his plan. He had similar projects under way in Argentina. With Yvon and Malinda Chouinard he was converting another Chilean **estancia,** or ranch, from an agricultural operation to a wilderness preserve.

When Pumalin was finished in 2006, complete with lodges, cabanas, arts and crafts stores, a nursery, and a state-of-the-art honey-making operation, it was transferred to a foundation controlled by Tompkins and his wife, Kris, a former professional skier and Patagonia, Inc. CEO. They opened it to the public, and the president of Chile attended the dedication ceremonies.

It was a magnificent gift to the people of Chile and, in its own way, a tribute to the freethinking and ethos of conservation that emerged from the Sixties. That was reinforced for me as I sat in a woodsy Pumalin structure made primarily from recycled timber and listened to Tompkins and Chouinard talk to students from the Wharton School of Business at the University of Pennsylvania.

The students had come to this remote, wild corner of southern Chile on a kind of Outward Bound consciousness-raising session organized by the school. They had camped out in the rain, and by the time we saw them they were a wet, raggedy group. I thought,

"I'll bet they're wondering if this is what you have to go through to become a hedge-fund manager."

They would get no advice on hedge funds at Pumalin. Instead, Tompkins and Chouinard, still lithe and athletic in their sixth decade, talked to the students about the choices they could make in life.

They told them to carry the values of ecology, the environment, and conservation into whatever endeavor they started or joined. Tompkins described how he had decided to sell Esprit when he realized that the success of the company depended on his ability to market more clothing to an individual than he or she really needed. "I just decided," he said, "I no longer wanted to be part of the excess game, filling up closets with more shirts and dresses."

Chouinard shared with the students his decisions to use only organic cotton and radically downsize the packaging for his products in the store. He used the example of Patagonia boxer shorts, which had been displayed in fancy plastic and cardboard containers. "When I said, 'Let's just put a rubber band around the shorts,' everyone told me I was nuts. They wouldn't sell. Guess what? With the simple rubber-band packaging our underwear sales went way up."

He then gave the budding business executives a line to live by: "Whenever we were told we were doing the wrong thing, it turned out to be the right thing, and we made more money."

They reminded the students of a memorable lesson from David Brower, a founding father of the Sierra Club in the Sixties: "There's no business to be done on a dead planet." They concluded by saying that they had not been perfect in their lives or in their businesses. Chouinard said, "We're probably going to hell, but you have a chance to do better."

When it was my turn, I reminded the students that Tompkins and Chouinard were not just environmental missionaries, they were also fine businessmen who showed it was possible to combine business profit and the common value of the public good.

Chouinard incorporated his unorthodox but successful business lessons into a book called **Let My People Go Surfing,** in which he described the payoff for recycling materials, reducing packaging, and providing day care for his employees. He was astonished by its reception by conventional enterprises, including Wal-Mart. The retailing giant sent a team to Patagonia's California headquarters to learn more about new forms of packaging and recycling plastic wrapping and shipping materials.

In the choices that Doug and Kris Tompkins and Yvon Chouinard and his wife and business partner, Malinda, make, they try to help nudge their friends in the same direction. They've combined the idealism of the Sixties with their own iconoclastic instincts and independent entrepreneurial skills to make money and make the world a better place. They've done that because they so passionately believe in the essential idea of stewardship and preservation of all that is natural and wild.

Jack Weinberg

The environment became the mission for another of the seminal figures of the Sixties whom I first encountered when he was a shy young man in Berkeley. He now devotes his life to international environmental matters after many years as an activist for racial equality, free speech on campus, and social justice for union workers.

When I mention Jack Weinberg to people familiar with the Sixties, the name generally draws a blank or puzzled expression. I tease, "Hey, c'mon, he gave your generation one of its indelible lines," when he told a San Francisco newspaper reporter in 1964, "We have a saying in the movement that we don't trust anyone over thirty"—a succinct summary of the attitude of the generation that thought it had nothing to learn from their parents or other older authority figures.

At the time, Weinberg was a graduate student in mathematics at Berkeley. He was a familiar figure on campus for having spent more than thirty hours in a police car after he was arrested for violating the university rules on speech.

Weinberg had set up an information booth in front of Sather Gate, the main campus intersection, to lobby students on behalf of CORE, the Congress on Racial Equality, an aggressive civil rights organization. University administrators had ruled that the campus could not be used as a site to promote off-campus activities, and so Weinberg was arrested by campus police and placed in a squad car.

Mario Savio protesting the arrest of fellow student Jack Weinberg during the Free Speech Movement at the University of California, Berkeley, in 1964

Jack Weinberg was detained in a police car for thirty hours after violating the university's ban on political advocacy.

Jack Weinberg, in front of a wall mural of the "police car incident" of 1964, taken at the Free Speech Movement Café on the UC Berkeley campus in 2007

Hundreds of students quickly surrounded the car and kept it from moving. The standoff went on through the day, into the night, and well into the next day. It was a festive affair, with the police allowing sympathizers to pass food and water to Weinberg while other activists climbed atop the car to rail against the prohibition on free speech on behalf of outside causes. One of the speakers was Mario Savio, a close friend of Weinberg.

Although they were friends, Weinberg had a different style from Savio. He kept a low profile, and his celebrated remark about not trusting anyone over thirty was not calculated to bring him fame. He made it in response to a newspaper reporter who had suggested that the movement was being directed by Communists. "I was just trying to tell him to back off; no one was pulling our strings."

Weinberg was a committed activist, first for civil rights and free speech, then against the war in Vietnam. He became disillusioned with the turns taken by many parts of the movement. His early involvement with the Black Panthers soured when they became more and more violent and criminal. He also thought that the campus antiwar movement had become pointless: "Berkeley wasn't the whole country. . . . I had a hard time relating to the fact we could make a revolution in one college town. Besides, the movement had become very self-absorbed. It was time for me to move on."

Thus began the pilgrimage of a truly committed social activist. From 1970 to 1977 he worked in auto plants in Los Angeles and Detroit, as a member of the

UAW, the United Auto Workers union, trying to bring more power to the shop floor and more democracy to the union movement.

From 1977 to 1984 he worked in Gary, Indiana, in the U.S. Steel plant as a member of the United Steelworkers union. He organized the plant rank and file to join him in successfully stopping the construction of a nuclear power plant on the shores of Lake Michigan, just a few miles from where many of the workers lived.

When Weinberg and I talked about those now long-ago days, he was candid about his failure to bring about what he called "a socialist revolution" within blue-collar America. He was very aware of the deep divisions between the radical students running the antiwar movement and the working class of the country, so he had wanted to try a new tack to build a new socialist-progressive movement.

He had calculated that by the 1960s the era of economic prosperity in the industrial Midwest was coming to an end and that the workers would be ripe for revolution. "The theory was right," he says, but the reality was something different. "When the economic situation changed downward, the reaction of the workers was not to become more radical and demand more leadership, it was the opposite." The workers took buyouts from the companies, retrained for other occupations, and moved on, still in pursuit of their working-class American Dream.

Weinberg counts his years in the plants as a great learning experience, however. He says his original notion was "too romantic" but he got a real grounding in how many Americans really live and what they believe in. He also learned some painful truths about getting along in a workplace that was not only ethnically but also culturally diverse. He had to spend time with racists, misogynists, and bigots of all kinds, and he feels that experience better prepared him to get along anywhere in the world. "When I was in Berkeley, I was a radical student and I could only relate to people like me. A lot of the activists in the Sixties would have benefited from the same experience because they were elites and they could maintain their ideology because they had power. But in a steel mill a worker has no power or much control over his life."

During his auto plant and steel mill days, Weinberg became increasingly aware of the pervasiveness of pollution and its harmful effect on life and Earth. He worried a lot about nuclear power and what he considered to be the nuclear industry's arrogance in dismissing its dangers.

When he realized that his plans for reorganizing industrial unions weren't really going anywhere, he moved on. He resettled in Chicago and took a job as a computer tech in a small start-up typographic and design company.

His friends thought his days as a radical organizer were over, that he finally had burned out at the age of forty-nine. They were wrong. He had at least one more big move in him, one that continues to define his life.

He went to work for Greenpeace International, the organization that plans aggressive political and physical confrontations to advance its agenda of alerting the world to pressing environmental issues. Weinberg was hired to work on a Great Lakes project designed to eliminate from those large bodies of fresh water the toxic substances that were polluting them.

Weinberg organized a boat and took the message of what he called the Zero Discharge Alliance to U.S. and Canadian communities surrounding the Great Lakes. He managed to persuade the conservative members of a commission organized by the U.S. and Canadian governments to adopt the Zero Discharge Alliance's very stringent recommendations for reform of the chemical industry and control of the toxic discharges.

The industry fought back, he says, with "tens of millions of dollars" to defeat the proposals. Weinberg kept pushing, getting the affected communities to write letters and going into the plants to organize the unions against the industry position.

He realized that all of his personal political passions, and all that he had learned during his working years, had now come together in the international environmental movement. He worked with the Canadian government to form a global, legally binding treaty to protect human health from toxic contaminants. And he organized the International Persistent Organic Pollutants Elimination Network, to raise awareness of and develop policies for dealing with pollution.

Weinberg came to understand there was no realistic substitute for capitalism or the corporations in the modern world. If he couldn't defeat them, he could work around them. "You need," he says, "to try to figure things out that work and what doesn't and go with what works."

He harkens back to the early days of the civil rights movement, when many of the younger activists were disdainful of Martin Luther King Jr.'s nonviolent, community-building philosophy. Weinberg, after a lifetime of activism, is now impressed that Dr. King "always had his eye on public policy." The goal of activism, Weinberg has concluded, is not just to win by whatever means it takes but to have the victories institutionalized "into new public policy and a new public culture."

He now uses what he calls "the toolkit" he's accumulated in many years of activism to help other countries develop campaigns and treaties to protect human health against chemical pollution. He's often called on by UN agencies to participate in conferences and to devise programs for developing countries.

While he remains worried about the many and great problems of the day, he is encouraged by the increasing degree of international cooperation on the environment. "When I look at the world today, I see more positive things, more hope in multilateral meeting after multilateral meeting. I have hope even though the United States is almost always out of sync with the rest of the world on these matters. Everybody gets together, and then the first order of business is how to get America to stop acting like a cult figure" with all the answers, and answerable to no one.

Jack Weinberg is in his mid-sixties now and he has a fantasy that he could retire from his activist life before he's seventy. He doesn't really think that will happen because he still has too much work to do. He expects to keep flying around the world, spreading the message about global cooperation on the environment and particularly the harmful effects of toxic chemicals on health, and building institutions to deal with it.

As he left my office, I asked him what was the most money he had ever earned in a year.

He paused, cocked his head, and thought for a moment. "Oh, I guess sixty thousand dollars," he said with an expression that seemed to say, "Who cares?"

Stewart Brand

Stewart Brand is another member of the Sixties generation who, like Jack Weinberg, does not seem to care about material wealth. Unlike Weinberg, Brand has never been very big on activism. He prefers to deal in the currency of ideas. A 1960 Stanford graduate in biology and early experimenter with LSD, Brand founded the **Whole Earth Catalog.** He's an Internet pioneer, a prolific writer on architecture and the dynamics of buildings, and a contrarian inside the environmental movement because of his promotion of nuclear power and genetically modified food.

A tall, gentle man with a fringe of gray hairs showing beneath his leather bush hat, a carryover from the standard Sixties wardrobe, Brand was dressed in Levi's and a work shirt when we met, ever faithful more to function than to fashion. He contemplated my questions with a quicksilver smile, often closing his eyes for a moment before answering.

He is not a man of the facile response.

True to his roots, Brand lives on a meticulously restored tug-boat in the houseboat community of Sausalito, the old hippie enclave just across the Golden Gate Bridge from San Francisco. When hippies first moved into Sausalito they were mostly squatters on the water, but now the floating residences are connected to the local sewer system and have television satellite dishes and, in some cases, more than a thousand square feet of living space.

He's always been someone who could live in two worlds, dating to his privileged childhood in Illinois, his attendance at prep school at Exeter, a Stanford degree, and an ROTC commission that led to two years as a lieutenant in the U.S. Army when, as he says proudly, "John F. Kennedy was my commander in chief."

In the military, Brand took up photography, and when he was discharged he began a dizzying pilgrimage that led him to Indian reservations in Oregon, where he says he was "blown away by what I saw—a complex, grounded culture and interesting people doing amazing things. Indians were off everyone's map at that point. They weren't even being romanticized about very much."

At the same time he was reading a cult favorite novel, **One Flew over the Cuckoo's Nest** by Ken Kesey, also a Stanford graduate and the founder of an early counterculture group called the Merry Pranksters, postgraduate bohemians based in San Francisco who delighted in taking hallucinogenic drugs and doing pretty much anything that would challenge the conventions of the Fifties.

The narrator of **Cuckoo's Nest** was Chief Bromden, an Indian resident of a ward at a mental institution. Brand was impressed that Kesey would give an Indian such an important role in his novel, and he arranged a meeting with the author. When he was met at the door by Kesey proffering a joint, he decided to sign on.

In his book on the Merry Pranksters, **The Electric Kool-Aid Acid Test,** Tom Wolfe described Brand as a member of the "restrained, reflective wing of the . . . Pranksters," even though when he met Wolfe he was wearing a disk on his forehead, an Indian bead necktie, and a white butcher's coat adorned with medals from the king of Sweden on it.

Despite his quirky costuming, Brand was seen as a pragmatic Prankster; he was along for the ride, but he didn't take all the side trips. He did take a few, however.

Having tried LSD a couple of times, at the beginning of 1966 he conceived and organized the Trips Festival. This "happening" was held in the Longshoremen's Hall in San Francisco. The idea was to combine the creative efforts of the Grateful Dead and Big Brother and the Holding Company with artists and a light show to simulate the experience of tripping on LSD. For those who required more than imagination, or more empirical research, quantities of the drug were also available.

Shortly after the Trips Festival, Brand had his last—and most meaningful—LSD experience. He ingested the drug while he was on a roof in San Francisco. Suddenly he was on a mind trip, floating about three stories above the roof, with an aerial view of the city. That led him to wonder, "Why haven't we seen the whole earth yet?"

As a student of the philosopher and engineer Buckminster Fuller, Brand thought a photograph of the earth would advance Fuller's mission of getting people to understand where they fit into the scheme of things and how they should respect the essential place of nature and the planet in their lives. So Brand produced a button that asked simply, WHY HAVEN'T WE SEEN A PHOTOGRAPH OF THE WHOLE EARTH YET?

When NASA did produce a memorable photograph of Earth from space, it was even more powerful than Brand could have imagined. It was, in fact, stunningly beautiful, and in the deep blackness of space, with the filigree of clouds, oceans, and land covering the planet, Earth somehow looked fragile and vulnerable. The photograph seemed to say, "Here I am, a precious place. Take care of me."

Brand had anticipated that effect before anyone else had. He also understood society was ready in 1968 for the tools to begin taking care of that precious place, the earth. When Brand's father died, he had a modest inheritance, and he used the money to start what became a publishing phenomenon and one of the enduring symbols of the Sixties: the **Whole Earth Catalog**.

It was a large, thick publication with both front and back covers showing the photograph of the earth from space. The opening line of Brand's introduction remains a classic: "We are as gods and might as well get good at it." To get good at it, to become stewards of the earth, and to fulfill our place in the scheme of things would require what he called "tools," and the catalog would provide "access to tools."

The **Whole Earth Catalog** was a potpourri of facts and ideas, purportedly describing what tools were necessary to be stewards of the earth, what they could do, why they were important. The book had everything: welding equipment and chain saws; plows and hoes; shoe repair tips; yoga and solar power; essays on organic gardening and the history of science in China; tractors and wheelbarrows and windmills. It was an instant hit. We had one in our California home, but I was mostly amused by the writing and the very idea of it. After all, I'd grown up with a dad who was a Mr. Fix-It. Red Brokaw had made me a power lawn mower from spare parts in the garage. Because I'd grown up with that do-it-yourself ethos, I was more interested in escaping it than embracing it.

In the end, the **Whole Earth Catalog** was essentially a fantasy for most of its middle-class and student readers. They could **imagine** plowing the ground, developing orchards, and raising pigs, but there was no way they would actually do it.

The **Catalog** had a natural audience among those romantic souls living in communes, mostly in rural New England or the Pacific Northwest, but they were short-lived experiments, brought down, as Brand says, because "the ideals would run into the real problems of sex, money, and power. Sharing sex, money, and power just didn't work out."

There were also the practical problems of having to do the very hard work of farming. "Living off the land" is a phrase that flows easily off the tongue, but the reality is hard to do.

Brand was not surprised by the commune collapse. "They didn't work in China," he says, "they didn't work in Russia, they didn't work in Israel." There was also the underlying commune culture. Having tried one commune in Mexico, he gave up. "I could not bear one more all-day meeting about nothing," he says.

Yet to this day Brand encounters people who say, "I read the **Whole Earth Catalog** when I was young." When he asks, "Why?" he says he rarely gets a satisfactory answer.

"I'm delighted they've kept [the book]," he says, "but I guess it's mostly for emotional reasons."

One of the early devotees of the **Whole Earth Catalog** was Steve Jobs, one of the founders of Apple, the most imaginative of the personal computer companies.

In a commencement speech at Stanford in 2005, Jobs told the students that when he was young the **Catalog** was "sort of like Google in paperback form, thirty-five years before Google came along; it was idealistic and overflowing with neat tools and great notions."

Jobs referred to the final edition of the catalog, which had a picture of a country road on the back cover with the line "Stay hungry. Stay foolish." That was Jobs's final wish for the Stanford graduates as well: Stay hungry, stay foolish.

Jobs's Google analogy for Brand's vision was not just coincidental. Brand had also been into the idea and the power of personal computers at an early stage. When I sat with him on the edge of Sausalito Bay in

2007 and we talked about the momentous events of 1968, he said that one event is always overlooked. It was a demonstration in the fall of 1968: Douglas Engelbart showing off a new device he had invented and how it would help move information through a personal computer. The device was called a mouse.

Brand remembers that only about a thousand people were in attendance, most of them computer geeks, but they were about to change the future of the world in a way no flower child in nearby Golden Gate Park could even begin to imagine. After all, so much of the culture of protest in the Sixties was directed at the IBM computer card—the admonition "do not staple, tear, or bend" was transferred to T-shirts and used to mock the soulless impersonality of corporate technology.

Brand quickly became a guru of the dawning computer age. In 1972 he wrote a visionary article for **Rolling Stone** on the work under way to link up personal computers so they and their users could communicate with one another. He expanded that article into a book called **Two Cybernetic Frontiers**. He considers this to be one of his most important works because "these were long-haired counterculture types not doing drugs. They were doing computers, and they were quietly and intentionally changing the world."

By 1984 Brand was one of the founders of the WELL—the Whole Earth 'Lectronic Lab—one of the Internet's first virtual communities, linking the San Francisco Bay Area's counterculture community. It was a prototype of the World Wide Web. Two years later he was a visiting scientist at the MIT Media Laboratory, where the most advanced work was being done on the impact of the new age of information technology. He turned that experience into the best seller **The Media Lab: Inventing the Future at MIT.**

In that book he wrote, "Information wants to be free. Information also wants to be expensive. Information wants to be free because it has become so cheap to distribute, copy and recombine—too cheap to meter."

Hello, Google?

In the early days of the Internet the social and nonprofit sectors were dominant—the dot-orgs and the dot-edus—but then the commercial interests came in and, as Brand tells me, "Everyone thought, 'There goes the neighborhood.' But even with all the money and all the smarts on the commercial side, the dot-orgs and dot-edus remained. I think you can credit the culture of the Sixties for that.

"Every time we embraced technology, it rewarded us. It led us in directions that were fruitful for the world. That happened in the Sixties, and we happened to be the guys who were around."

Stewart Brand is described by friends and admirers as the best they know at creating intellectual cross-pollination. He excels at putting disparate people and ideas together so they can learn from one another. He is essentially a teacher who is very curious, an explorer of ideas that ultimately will benefit people and Earth.

During a visit to Venice, Italy, he marveled at the permanence and adaptation of the ancient structures, which in turn led him to write a critically acclaimed small book called **How Buildings Learn,** a treatise on the dynamics of architecture to adapt to society's constantly changing requirements.

Stewart Brand, one of
the "Merry Pranksters," in 1966

Stewart Brand in 2004

His latest project is what he calls The Clock of the Long Now (www.longnow.org/projects/clock/), a timing device set up in the California desert that will tick once a day and chime once every hundred years and run for a hundred thousand years. He calls it "an icon of optimism" designed to give people some perspective so "they can feel at home in a longer time frame."

As for one of his own time frames, the Sixties, Brand has very mixed feelings. "I'm much more of a pragmatist now than a romantic. We got a lot wrong. It wasn't a revolution, but it was a lot of fun and instructive trying to find where the edge was. We were trying everything. That was the deal.

"We weren't looking for work, and work wasn't working for us. But some of the new left stuff was terrible. Kids waving those little red books of Mao Tsetung—one of the three great monsters of the century. We could have looked into that and discovered how bad he was.

"We were rude to our parents. We prevented more people like me from going into the military by chasing ROTC off campus. I didn't like the Vietnam War, but I thought most of the protestors had the wrong perspective on military people.

"When a generation talks just to itself, it becomes more filled with folly than it might have otherwise."

One of the rallying cries to emerge from the Sixties was "The personal is political." It arose from the feminist movement, as women organized politically around personal issues such as reproductive rights.

The "personal is political" thesis went beyond feminism, however. It was also applicable to the civil rights movement, in which black citizens demanded that their individual rights receive political protection. In the antiwar movement, young men eligible for the draft but opposed to the war argued that their personal beliefs were powerful political arguments.

Citizens have always voted their personal interests, and there will always be conflicting agendas. But the codification of "politics is personal" in the Sixties, it seems to me, encouraged a stronger strain of selfishness in the public arena. The country was divided into many more parts, highly organized and politically aggressive.

The financially rich and politically influential pro-choice and antiabortion organizations competing against each other with their large, loyal memberships are powerful examples, but there are others. Teachers' unions and trial lawyers, for example, have become muscular forces in the Democratic Party, just as evangelical Christians and gun owners have a strong hold on the Republican Party.

I find in my travels and reporting a longing for common cause, a call to citizenship that goes beyond "What can you do for **me?**" We need to be mindful that this is a smaller planet with many more people than forty years ago, and that the future will depend a great deal more on cooperation, large and small, than confrontation.

Astronaut
James Lovell
and his family

Captain James Lovell, crew member of the Apollo 8 mission to the moon in December 1968. After the mission, the crew was inundated with messages from people around the world saying "Thank you for saving 1968."

768 | TOM BROKAW

Captain Jim Lovell

There was at the end of 1968 an event that remains an inspirational symbol for the challenges ahead. For the Sixties were also the glory years of the American space program, and of astronauts such as Captain Jim Lovell.

Lovell, who will be eighty in 2008, retains the boyish enthusiasm of an Eagle Scout, an award he earned growing up in Milwaukee, Wisconsin, during the Depression, the son of a single mother. His father had died, and times were not easy for the Lovells. "We had a one-room apartment with a Murphy bed that came out of the wall," he remembers.

The young Lovell was fascinated with rocket science. He'd read Jules Verne's **From the Earth to the Moon** at thirteen and he began building and launching some primitive backyard rockets a few hundred feet into the air.

When he realized his family couldn't afford to send him to the big-time science institutions such as Cal Tech or MIT, he applied to the U.S. Naval Academy. He was rejected on the first pass but got in after two years at the University of Wisconsin.

When he graduated from Annapolis in 1952, he became a Navy fighter pilot and then a test pilot. The American space program was still in its planning stages, and Jim Lovell was still dreaming about a trip to the moon.

By 1959 NASA—the National Aeronautics and Space Administration—was looking for seven pilots with the Right Stuff, in Tom Wolfe's enduring phrase about the first astronauts. Lovell was among the thirty-four military pilots considered, but he was rejected because he had a rare blood-pigmentation condition; it wasn't life-threatening, but it took him out of the running.

He was disappointed but not discouraged. He wrote in his diary, "There will be other space projects and who knows, I might be part of them. . . . We learn through failure."

Three years later he was selected for the second group of astronauts. In 1965 and again in 1966 he went into space aboard a Gemini module, spending almost three weeks orbiting the earth.

The big goal was leaving Earth's atmosphere and landing on the moon, to keep the pledge President Kennedy had made in a speech at Rice University on September 12, 1962. JFK inspired many all around the world with his words that day: "We choose to go to the moon in this decade, and do . . . other things, not because they are easy but because they are hard, because that goal will serve to organize and measure the best of our energies and skills, because that challenge is one that we are willing to accept, one we are unwilling to postpone, and one which we intend to win."

By 1968 Lovell, Anders, and Borman were training for Apollo 8, a dress-rehearsal flight for a lunar landing. Originally they were not scheduled to leave Earth's atmosphere. They were only going to test the slingshot effect—a high-velocity orbit of the earth that would launch the capsule on a flight to the moon. But there were rumors that the Russians were trying to get there first, so NASA changed Apollo 8's flight plan.

Now Apollo 8 would fly to the moon, orbit around the dark side, and return to Earth in the last week of December. If it all went well, the spacecraft would be orbiting the moon on Christmas Eve, 1968. The training for the momentous flight went on feverishly all during 1968. When I met Lovell at the Adler Planetarium in Chicago—where he helped organize an elaborate exhibit commemorating the flight—I asked if the astronauts had been aware of all that was going on outside of NASA that year—the riots, the assassinations, the antiwar protests.

"We were all senior military people," he said, "and we were so intent on our project we put all of that aside. We did talk about the Tet Offensive in Vietnam, and we worried the cost of the war would eat into the space program."

Lovell says that even though he wasn't paying too much attention, he thought the culture was disintegrating. "My background," he says, "was more patriotic. Listening to your elders, taking direction, trying to be a leader. The hippie movement sort of soured me."

On December 21, 1968, in the predawn darkness, Lovell was getting ready to enter the spacecraft atop the giant Saturn V rocket at Cape Canaveral, Florida. Borman and Anders were already inside the vehicle. Lovell tells me, laughing, "I was left alone. I looked down, and I could see the lights of the press cars coming in for the launch. I thought, 'These people are serious. We're going to the moon!' "

At 10:41:37 A.M. Eastern Standard Time, less than

three hours after the successful launch from Florida
and an orbit of the earth, Apollo 8 went into what was
called "the trans-lunar injection." They were headed
for the moon, 240,000 miles and three days away.

"We got the proper course and velocity . . . and
we looked back at Earth. You could see it getting
smaller and smaller because our velocity was so high.
It reminded me of driving through a tunnel and looking out the back window and seeing the entrance
shrink in size."

Early in the morning on December 24, Apollo 8
was within reach of the moon's gravitational pull but
the astronauts couldn't see the lunar surface. The
spacecraft's blunt end blocked their view. The crew
fired an engine and manipulated the spacecraft to get
into position for a lunar orbit. Lovell's voice still rises
slightly with excitement forty years later as he recalls
the moment. "All of a sudden . . . just sixty-nine miles
below, the ancient craters of the far side of the moon
were slowly slipping by. We forgot the flight plan. We
were like three kids in a candy store window."

The best was yet to come. "As we kept going,
suddenly on the lunar horizon, coming up, was
Earth." He remembers the vivid contrast between the
lifeless moon and the vibrant earth. "The moon is
nothing but shades of gray and darkness. But the
earth—you could see the deep blues of the seas, the
whites of the clouds, the salmon pink and brown of
the land masses."

He says, "At one point I sighted the earth with my
thumb—and my thumb from that distance fit over the

entire planet. I realized how insignificant we all are if everything I'd ever known is behind my thumb. But at that moment I don't think the three of us understood the lasting significance of what we were looking at."

Borman, Anders, and Lovell had another gift to the world on that Christmas Eve. Before launching they had wrestled with what they might say with so many people listening in—the worldwide audience was estimated at a billion—and so a NASA executive contacted a friend in Washington, who in turn got in touch with Joe Layton.

Layton was a newspaperman famous for his later career as a government public information officer in several administrations. He was known as a smart, witty source who always seemed to know what was going on in whatever department regardless of which party was in charge.

Layton was struggling with what the astronauts could say, so the story goes, when his wife suggested the opening verse of the Bible, from Genesis in the Old Testament.

And so it came to pass that on Christmas Eve, 1968, Frank Borman, Jim Lovell, and Bill Anders divided up the scripture and began to read.

"In the beginning, God created the heavens and the earth. And the earth was without form, and void; and darkness was upon the face of the deep. And the Spirit of God moved upon the face of the waters. And God said, 'Let there be light'; and there was light. And God saw the light, that it was good; and God divided the light from the darkness.

"And God called the light Day, and the darkness he called Night."

When the mission commander, Frank Borman, read the final passage—book of Genesis, chapter one, verse ten—the long, deeply painful, and disorienting year of 1968 and all those who went through it had an opportunity to stop and contemplate their place in the vast universe of history.

"And God called the dry land Earth; and the gathering of the waters he called Seas; and God saw that it was good."

Lovell says when Apollo 8 returned safely to Earth three days later, the crew was inundated with messages from people around the world saying, one way or another, "Thank you for saving 1968."

Two years later Jim Lovell became famous again and assured himself a place forever in the dictionary of memorable quotations. As mission commander of the crew of Apollo 13, he expected to achieve his childhood dream and finally set foot on the lunar surface.

They were almost 200,000 miles from Cape Canaveral when a small explosion on board wrecked their chances of landing on the moon and possibly of even getting back to Earth.

Lovell's laconic test-pilot Right Stuff notification to NASA headquarters of trouble on board remains a classic:

"Houston, we have a problem."

There followed four harrowing days of seat-of-the-pants flying with NASA engineers radioing instructions and suggestions.

As we all know, Lovell and his crew of Fred Haise Jr. and John L. Swigert Jr. made it back.

Lovell says that very close call changed him. "I live my life one day at a time now. Nothing rattles me."

He's been married for almost sixty years to his college sweetheart, Marilyn, and they have four grown children, two daughters and two sons. He is a partner with one of his sons in a restaurant in Lake Forest, Illinois. Always an enthusiastic and affable man, Lovell likes to visit with patrons and answer questions about the space memorabilia on display.

He is eternally grateful for the chance to have traveled more than seven million miles in space during his astronaut career. He believes one of the overlooked benefits of the Sixties is the technology that came out of the space program. He still listens to the popular music of that time, including the score from **Hair,** the first counterculture musical, even though he walked out of the performance on Broadway at intermission. As a career military man, a stage full of hippies, many of them naked, was not his idea of an entertaining evening.

When he's at the family cabin on a lake north of Chicago on a summer night, Jim Lovell will look up at a full moon and remember Christmas Eve 1968. "When you see Earth from the moon," he says, "you realize how fragile it is and just how limited the resources are. We're all astronauts on this spaceship Earth—about six or seven billion of us—and we have to work and live together."

Stewart Brand placed that shot of Earth on the front and back cover of the **Whole Earth Catalog** with the inscription, "We can't put it together. It is together."

Forty years after one of the most divisive years in American history, I asked Brand what that means.

He replied, "I suppose it is seeing what connects rather than what divides."

December 1968: Earth as seen from space
during the Apollo 8 mission

ACKNOWLEDGMENTS

When I decided to write about the causes and the effects of the Sixties on a disparate group of Americans who had experienced the triumphs and the failures of that time, I realized I was stepping back through a looking glass in which images and memories are shaped by very personal perceptions on matters large and small. It was not going to be an easy assignment and I would need help.

Gratefully, I had at the ready the best team any author could want. The team had been with me before, and we added new members who fit in seamlessly and brought to the common effort exceptional contributions.

Beginning with **The Greatest Generation**, I have been privileged to have at my side Liz Bowyer, the captain of the team. Quite simply, this book would not have been possible without her indefatigable dedication. Liz, a lawyer and an organizational genius, was a tireless and persuasive interviewer as well as an enthusiastic and perceptive student of the subject, and—get this—she became a first-time mother in the middle of the project. She managed it all with grace and great good humor, and I am forever indebted.

Frank Gannon, a friend and a peerless editor, made smart, witty, and occasionally insistent suggestions, observations, and contributions. Frank generously shared his encyclopedic knowledge about the Sixties, much of it gained while he was in the cockpit for some of the greatest turbulence of the time.

Other members of what in my office they call Team Brokaw included the eagle-eyed Michael Hill, fact checker extraordinaire; Meaghan Rady, a Random House alum who's put up with me since **The Greatest Generation** and is now part of the NBC News family; and John Balz, who tracked down players, facts, trends, and heretofore underreported consequences of the Sixties.

As she has been from the start of my book-writing career, Kate Medina, executive vice president and associate publisher at Random House, was cheerful, patient and persuasive as friend and editor. Her constant encouragement and polite but pointed suggestions got me through difficult days, especially when I knew I was careening toward our deadline. We made it, Kate, once again. Thank you.

Thanks also to Gina Centrello, the boss at Random House, who signed off on this book and was unfailingly supportive from the beginning.

Robin Rolewicz worked diligently to corral the people I interviewed in this book into sending us their personal photographs, and was helped in the research effort by Carol Poticny. Abby Plesser seemed never to go home as she worked her magic through e-mail, FedEx—everything but the Pony Express—to get messages, direction, and questions from midtown Manhattan to me in the remote reaches of Montana. Production editor Evan Camfield worked very hard to make this book happen, and Barbara Fillon worried about publicity for the book so I could concentrate on finishing it.

Others on the Random House staff who stayed up late and worked hard: Avideh Bashirrad, Rachel Bernstein, Sanyu Dillion, Benjamin Dreyer, Richard Elman, Lisa Feuer, Frankie Jones, London King, Sally Marvin, Dana Maxson, Allyson Pearl, Thomas Perry, Jack Perry, Kelle Ruden, and Carol Schneider.

Carole Lowenstein, as she has in the past, came up with a fine interior design.

Gene Mydlowski created a book jacket that, in my judgment, strikes just the right chord, and designer Beck Stvan did a great job in helping to make it a reality.

Laura Goldin, the Random House lawyer, asked the right questions and steered me away from potential legal difficulties.

Not to be overlooked is Ken Starr, my business manager (not the special prosecutor), who represented my interests so well. Thanks, Ken.

I am deeply grateful to the computer wizards at NBC News who gave up holidays and weekends to help me through several vexing problems with lost files, stubborn firewalls, and balky downloads.

My assistant at NBC, Mary Casalino, came on the job just in time to juggle a crazy-quilt pattern of travel, appointments, and inquiries across two time zones.

Erika Beck always had time to help out on a moment's notice. So did Andy Franklin.

I was helped immeasurably by the recollections and suggestions of friends and acquaintances who had their own take on the Sixties.

In the end, of course, what you read here is what I wanted to convey. The Sixties gave me many choices and if **Boom!** fails to satisfy the expectations of those who want to revisit the time, it is entirely my fault.

Most of all, I have been blessed with the forbearance of my family: Meredith; Jennifer, her husband, Allen, and their daughters, the darling Claire and Meredith; Andrea and her husband, Charles, and their daughter, the giggling Vivian Aranka; and Sarah, our youngest. They pulled me away from **Boom!** in mid-August so as a family we could celebrate the forty-fifth anniversary of our marriage. That was on August 17, 1962.

Forty-five years later, we have been through so much together—Boom!—but we have survived and thrived. We are richer in every way for the experience.

Tom Brokaw
McLeod, Montana

TIMELINE

1963

AUGUST 28: More than 200,000 people congregate at the Lincoln Memorial for the March on Washington, where Dr. Martin Luther King Jr. delivers his "I Have a Dream" speech.

NOVEMBER 22: President John F. Kennedy, forty-six, is assassinated during a midday motorcade in Dallas, Texas. Vice President Lyndon B. Johnson is sworn in as president.

1964

SUMMER: Thousands of civil rights activists descend on Mississippi for "Freedom Summer," a sweeping effort to register disenfranchised black voters.

JULY 2: President Lyndon Johnson signs the Civil Rights Act of 1964, the most comprehensive civil rights legislation since Reconstruction.

AUGUST 7: Following two purported attacks by North Vietnamese torpedo boats on U.S. destroyers in the Gulf of Tonkin, Congress passes the Gulf of Tonkin

Resolution, giving President Johnson the power to take whatever action he deems necessary in Southeast Asia.

NOVEMBER 3: Lyndon Johnson defeats Republican Barry Goldwater in a landslide, taking 61 percent of the popular vote.

DECEMBER 3: The Free Speech Movement sweeps the University of California, Berkeley, after the university bans the distribution of political materials on campus.

1965

FEBRUARY 13: President Johnson orders bombing offensive Operation Rolling Thunder against North Vietnam.

FEBRUARY 21: Malcolm X, thirty-nine, is assassinated in Detroit.

MARCH 7: Alabama state troopers brutally attack civil rights demonstrators attempting a peaceful protest march from Selma to Montgomery, Alabama, on "Bloody Sunday."

MARCH 8–9: The first American combat troops arrive in Vietnam.

AUGUST 6: President Johnson signs the Voting Rights Act of 1965, making poll taxes and literacy tests illegal.

AUGUST 11–17: Race riots erupt in Watts, California. Thirty-four people are killed.

1966

JUNE 30: The National Organization for Women (NOW) is founded with twenty-eight members.

Betty Friedan, author of **The Feminine Mystique,** becomes its first president.

AUGUST 5: Chinese leader Mao Tse-tung launches the Cultural Revolution to purge and reorganize China's Communist Party.

OCTOBER: Bobby Seale and Huey Newton found the Black Panther Party in Oakland, California.

1967

JANUARY 14: Former Harvard psychology professor and leader of the League of Spiritual Discovery Timothy Leary speaks at a hippie gathering of thirty thousand in San Francisco, coining the phrase "Turn on, tune in, drop out."

APRIL 4: Martin Luther King Jr. denounces the Vietnam War during a service at the Riverside Church in New York City.

JUNE 5–10: Six-Day War. Israel defeats Egypt, Syria, and Jordan and widens its territories to include the West Bank, the Gaza Strip, the Sinai Peninsula, and the Golan Heights.

JULY 12–17: Race riots explode in Newark, New Jersey, setting off the "Long Hot Summer" of urban riots in major cities across the country, including Detroit and Washington, D.C. Sixty-nine people are killed in the riots, while thousands are injured and arrested.

SUMMER: In San Francisco's Haight-Ashbury neighborhood, 100,000 join in the "Summer of Love."

OCTOBER 21: More than 100,000 antiwar demonstrators gather at the Lincoln Memorial and march on the Pentagon.

NOVEMBER 9: The first issue of **Rolling Stone** magazine hits newsstands with John Lennon on the cover.

DECEMBER 4: Martin Luther King Jr. and the Southern Christian Leadership Conference (SCLC) launch the Poor People's Campaign to address economic inequalities through nonviolent direct action.

DECEMBER 8: The Graduate, starring Dustin Hoffman and Anne Bancroft, premieres in Los Angeles.

1968

JANUARY 30–31: Seventy thousand Vietcong and North Vietnamese troops launch the Tet Offensive, surprise attacks that kill more than one thousand U.S. troops and South Vietnamese in two weeks.

FEBRUARY 29: In its report on the 1967 race riots, the Kerner Commission finds that "our nation is moving toward two societies, one black, one white—separate and unequal," pointing to problems including chronic poverty, high unemployment, and lack of access to good schools and health care.

MARCH 12: Senator Eugene McCarthy comes within seven percentage points of beating President Lyndon Johnson in the Democratic primary in New Hampshire.

MARCH 16: Senator Robert F. Kennedy announces his candidacy for president of the United States.

MARCH 16: American GIs kill more than four hundred Vietnamese civilians in the small Vietnamese village of My Lai. When the incident is revealed more than a year later it marks a turning point in American public opinion of the war.

MARCH 31: President Johnson announces on national television that he will not run for reelection.

APRIL 4: Martin Luther King Jr. thirty-nine, is shot to death while standing on his motel balcony in Memphis. Race riots follow in 125 cities. Forty-six people are killed, three thousand injured.

APRIL 6: Stanley Kubrick's **2001: A Space Odyssey** premieres.

APRIL 23–30: Protesting the Vietnam War and other issues, students at Columbia University occupy administration buildings and shut down the university.

MAY 13: Paris peace talks begin with delegates from the United States and North Vietnam in attendance. The talks later expand to include South Vietnam and the Vietcong.

JUNE 5: Robert F. Kennedy, forty-two, is assassinated at the Los Angeles Ambassador Hotel minutes after his victory speech following the California Democratic primary.

JULY 1: Sixty-one countries, including the United States and USSR, sign the Nuclear Non-proliferation Treaty.

AUGUST 5–8: Republican National Convention in Miami. Richard Nixon receives his party's nomination for president.

AUGUST 20–21: Soviet tanks roll into Prague, ending the Czechoslovakian experiment with liberalized Communism known as the "Prague Spring."

AUGUST 26–29: Democratic National Convention in Chicago. Violent clashes ensue between protestors and National Guard and Chicago police officers. After a tumultuous convention, Vice President

Hubert H. Humphrey is nominated as the Democratic candidate for president.

OCTOBER 2: Mexican military and police crush a massive student demonstration in Mexico City, just ten days before the Summer Olympics begin, killing an estimated two hundred to three hundred people.

NOVEMBER 5: Richard Nixon wins the presidency in one of the closest general elections in history, winning over Democratic challenger Hubert Humphrey by just .7 percent of the popular vote.

NOVEMBER 22: The Beatles release their top-selling record, the "White Album."

DECEMBER 21–27: NASA launches the successful Apollo 8 mission, the first manned orbit of the moon.

1969

JANUARY 20: President Nixon takes office, promising "peace with honor" in Vietnam.

JUNE 8: Nixon announces first troop withdrawals from Vietnam.

JULY 14: Easy Rider, starring Peter Fonda and Dennis Hopper, premieres in the United States.

JULY 20: Astronauts Edwin "Buzz" Aldrin and Neil Armstrong take "one small step for man, one giant leap for mankind" with the world's first lunar landing.

AUGUST 15–18: Woodstock Music and Arts Fair. Nearly half a million people gather in the nation's largest celebration of hippie music and culture in upstate New York.

SEPTEMBER 24: The Chicago Seven—including "Yippies" Abbie Hoffman and Jerry Rubin—stand trial for conspiracy to incite a riot at the 1968 Chicago Democratic Convention.

1970

APRIL 21: First Earth Day.

MAY 4: Ohio National Guardsmen open fire on a Vietnam War protest at Kent State University, killing four and wounding nine.

1971

JUNE 13: The New York Times begins publishing the Pentagon Papers, the Defense Department's secret history of the Vietnam War.

1972

JANUARY: Only 133,000 American servicemen remain in South Vietnam.

FEBRUARY 21–28: President Nixon visits China, marking the first step toward normalization of relations between the United States and the Communist Peoples's Republic.

MARCH 22: The Equal Rights Amendment (ERA) is passed by Congress and sent to the states for ratification.

JUNE 17: Five burglars are arrested trying to bug the offices of the Democratic National Committee at the Watergate office complex.

JUNE 23: Title IX of the Education Amendment to the Civil Rights Act bans sexual discrimination in schools.

JULY: First issue of **Ms.** magazine is published.

SEPTEMBER 5: The PLO group Black September seeks revenge for the 1970 defeat of Palestinian guerrillas, breaking into the Olympic Village at Munich and killing one coach and one athlete and taking nine Israeli athletes hostage. A standoff with international authorities ends in the death of the hostages and commandos.

NOVEMBER 7: President Nixon wins a landslide election against Democratic senator George McGovern, garnering over 60 percent of the popular vote.

1973

JANUARY 22: In **Roe v. Wade,** the Supreme Court rules that women have a constitutional right to abortion.

JANUARY 27: All warring parties in Vietnam sign a cease-fire agreement known as the Paris Peace Accords.

MARCH 29: The last American combat troops leave South Vietnam.

MAY 17: Televised Senate hearings on the Watergate scandal begin in the United States.

SEPTEMBER 20: Billie Jean King defeats Bobby Riggs in the "Battle of the Sexes" at the Houston Astrodome.

OCTOBER 6: Yom Kippur War. Egyptian and Syrian forces attack Israel on Yom Kippur.

OCTOBER 17: Oil crisis begins when, in response to the ongoing Yom Kippur War, OPEC determines that it will not export oil to Israeli allies, including the United States, Western Europe, and Japan.

1974

MARCH 17: Oil crisis ends when most OPEC nations end their five-month embargo.

JULY 27–30: Congress adopts three articles of impeachment, charging President Nixon with obstruction of the Watergate investigation, violation of his oath of office, and failure to comply with congressional subpoenas.

AUGUST 9: President Nixon resigns. Gerald Ford becomes the thirty-eighth president.

PERMISSIONS AND CREDITS

ministered by EMI Blackwood Music Inc. All rights reserved; international copyright secured. Used by permission.

PAUL SIMON MUSIC, INC.: Excerpts from "The Sound of Silence," copyright © 1964 Paul Simon (BMI); excerpts from "Mrs. Robinson," copyright © 1968 Paul Simon (BMI). Used by permission of Paul Simon Music, Inc.

UNIVERSAL MUSIC PUBLISHING: Excerpts from "American Pie" by Don McLean, copyright © 1971 and copyright renewed 1999 by Music Corporation of America, Inc., and Benny Bird Co., Inc. All rights administered by Songs of Universal, Inc./BMI. All rights reserved. Used by permission.

VIKING PENGUIN, A DIVISION OF PENGUIN GROUP (USA) INC.: "Preface: The Longest Revolution," from **The World Split Open** by Ruth Rosen, copyright © 2000 by Ruth Rosen. Used by permission of Viking Penguin, a division of Penguin Group (USA) Inc.

PHOTOGRAPH CREDITS

Page 6: (top) NBCU Photo Bank; (bottom) NBCU Photo Bank, TV Guide, Inc., June 24, 1967

Page 7: Courtesy the Brokaw family

Page 24: (top and bottom) NBCU Photo Bank

Page 37: (top) © Frederic Ohringer; (bottom) © Mathieu Bourgois

Page 59: (top) ©1965 Spider Martin/The Spider Martin Civil Rights Collection. All rights reserved. Used with permission. (bottom) © Peter DaSilva/Corbis/Sygma.

Page 68: (top) © Bettmann/Corbis; (bottom) NBCU Photo Bank

Page 80: (top and bottom) Courtesy Tom Turnipseed

Page 89: (top) Courtesy Thomas Gilmore; (bottom) © Flip Schulke/Corbis

Page 108: (top) © Condé Nast Archive/Corbis; (bottom) Evan Agostini/Getty Images

Page 113: (top) ©Bettmann/Corbis; (bottom) ©Alison Teal

Page 139: (top) Courtesy Pat Buchanan; (middle) © Corbis; (bottom) © Blake Madden, **The Augusta Chronicle**

Page 173: Courtesy Leslie H. Gelb

Page 179: (top) Courtesy Nellie Coakley; (middle) Courtesy Tom Coakley; (bottom) Courtesy Tom and Nellie Coakley

Page 197: (top and bottom) Courtesy Jeffry House

Page 211: (top) Courtesy James Webb; (bottom) Courtesy Senator Webb's office

Page 252: Courtesy Nora Ephron

Page 267: (top and bottom) Courtesy Joan Growe

Page 271: Courtesy Muriel Krazewski

Page 277: (top and bottom) Courtesy Judith Rodin

Page 286: (top) © Ted Streshinsky/Corbis; (bottom) © Christopher Felver/Corbis

Page 289: Courtesy Carla Hills

Page 296: (top) Courtesy Lissa Muscatine; (bottom) White House photograph

Page 301: (top) AP Images; (bottom) © Krista Kennell/Zuma/Corbis

Page 311: (top) © Ted Streshinsky/Corbis; (bottom) Jeff Chiu/AP Images

Page 318: (top) Courtesy Judy Collins; (bottom) © Suzanne Szasz, Figaro, 1965

Page 321: (top) Michael Ochs Archives/Getty Images; (bottom) © Joe Traver/Reuters/Corbis

Page 329: (top) © Annie Leibovitz/Contact Press Images; (bottom) Courtesy the Jann S. Wenner Archives

Page 335: (top) Courtesy Kris Kristofferson; (bottom) Photo by Mary Ellen Mark. Courtesy New West Records. © 2006 New West Records.

Page 339: (top) Steve Kagan/Time & Life Pictures/Getty Images; (bottom) © Vaughn Youtz/Zuma/Corbis

Page 351: (top and bottom) Courtesy Woody Miller

Page 379: (top and bottom) Courtesy Charlene Stimley Priester

Page 385: (top) Courtesy Ouida Barnett Atkins; (middle) AP Images; (bottom) © Greg Campbell Photography

Page 393: (top and bottom) Courtesy Stan Sanders

Page 418: (top) © Ernest C. Withers for **Jet** magazine; (middle and bottom) Courtesy Rita Steele

Page 450: (top) Courtesy Bill Clinton; (middle) Dick Swanson/Time & Life Pictures/Getty Images; (bottom) Callista Gingrich, Gingrich Productions

Page 456: (top and middle) Senator George McGovern Collection, McGovern Library and Archives, Dakota Wesleyan University, Mitchell, South Dakota; (bottom) Dakota Wesleyan University, Mitchell, South Dakota

Page 461: Courtesy Gary Hart

Page 478: Ron Edmonds/AP Images

Page 479: (top) University of Wyoming/AP Images; (middle) White House photo by David Bohrer; (bottom) Courtesy the Cheney family

Page 506: (top) Courtesy Hillary Clinton; (middle) © Brooks Kraft/Corbis; (bottom) © Rick Wilking/Reuters/Corbis

Page 523: Courtesy Carl Pope

Page 531: (top and bottom) Courtesy Ed Crane

Page 538: (top) Arthur Schatz/Time & Life Pictures/Getty Images; (bottom) Paul Sakuma/AP Images

Page 548: (top and middle) Courtesy David Cadwell; (bottom) Gertrude O'Sullivan

Page 553: (top) Courtesy Colin Powell; (bottom) Alessandra Petlin/CPi

Page 561: (top, middle, and bottom) Courtesy Wayne Downing

Page 568: (top) Courtesy Senator McCain; (middle) © Corbis/Sygma; (bottom) Eli Reed/Magnum Photos

Page 574: (top) Courtesy Richard Nixon Library and Birthplace; (bottom) Courtesy Bob Kerrey

Page 583: (top and bottom) Courtesy Chuck Hagel

Page 590: (top, middle, and bottom) Courtesy Charles Desmond

Page 596: (top and bottom) Courtesy Ron Armella

Page 619: (top) © American Legion Auxiliary Hoosier Girls State, Inc.; (bottom) Courtesy Jane Pauley

Page 626: (top) Courtesy Karl Fleming; (bottom) © John Sharaf

Page 641: (top) Courtesy Dorothy Rabinowitz; (middle and bottom) Courtesy Ruth Simmons

Page 647: Courtesy Susan Miller

Page 658: (top) © Henry Diltz; (bottom) © Stan Grossfeld/**Boston Globe**/Landov

Page 664: (top) Courtesy Paul Simon; (bottom) © Robert Clark/2006 Warner Brothers Records Inc.

Page 675: (top) Burton Berinsky/Landov; (bottom) © Margot Schulman

Page 681: (top) Hulton Archive/Getty Images; (bottom) Dreamcatcher © WV Films II LLC. All rights reserved.

Page 689: © 1976 **The Washington Post**, photo by Gerald Martineau. Reprinted with permission.

Page 698: (top) Burt Glinn/Magnum Photos; (bottom) Michael J N Bowles

Page 701: (top) Courtesy Tommy Smothers; (bottom) © Jonathan Exley

Page 741: (top) Courtesy Don McLean; (bottom) Patrisha McLean

Page 750: (top and middle) Steven Marcus Free Speech Movement Photographs (BANC PIC 2000.002—

NEG Strip 6:8 and BANC PIC 2000.002—NEG Strip 2:10), The Bancroft Library, University of California, Berkeley; (bottom) Ravi Agarwal

Page 764: (top) © Bill Young/**San Francisco Chronicle**/Corbis; (bottom) Ryan Phelan

Page 767: (top) Courtesy Captain James A. Lovell Jr.; (bottom) NASA

Page 776: NASA/Time & Life Pictures/Getty Images

INDEX

Page numbers in bold refer to photographs.

JFK refers to John F. Kennedy. LBJ refers to Lyndon B. Johnson. RFK refers to Robert F. Kennedy.

ABOUT THE AUTHOR

Tom Brokaw is the author of four best sellers: **The Greatest Generation, The Greatest Generation Speaks, An Album of Memories,** and **A Long Way from Home.** A native of South Dakota, he graduated from the University of South Dakota with a degree in political science. He began his journalism career in Omaha and Atlanta before joining NBC News in 1966. Brokaw was the White House correspondent for NBC News during Watergate, and from 1976 to 1981 he anchored **Today** on NBC. He was the sole anchor and managing editor of **NBC Nightly News with Tom Brokaw** from 1983 to 2005. He continues to report for NBC News, producing long-form documentaries and providing expertise during breaking news events. Brokaw has won every major award in broadcast journalism, including two DuPonts, a Peabody Award, and several Emmys. He lives in New York and Montana.

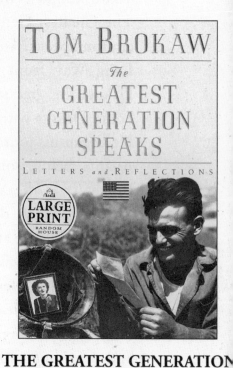